I0140200

Perils of the Victorian Stage

Alan & Brenda Stockwell

VESPER HAWK

ISBN 978-0-9565013-8-7

Published by VESPER HAWK PUBLISHING
WWW.VESPERHAWK.COM

INTRODUCTION TO THE HAZARDOUS WORLD OF VICTORIAN ENTERTAINMENT

In the 21st century we do not consider a night at the theatre to be a hazardous occupation. The only fear we are likely to have is the possibility we might not catch the last bus or train home, or that the leading actor may be indisposed and we are fobbed off with an understudy. We do not expect somebody to fall from the balcony and land on top of us, neither do we expect the actors to maim or kill each other, and the likelihood of the entire audience rioting or panicking is such a remote possibility we do not even think of it.

However, prior to the 20th century, theatre-going was not only hazardous but downright dangerous, and the experiences given above were by no means rare. It astonishes how many people suffered injuries during a night at the theatre, how often disputes arose, and how commonplace seems to have been falling down stairs and getting trampled on. Theatre buildings themselves were particularly susceptible to fire, and partial collapse seemed to happen unexpectedly at any time.

All these aspects of Victorian theatregoing are revealed in a companion volume *Jeopardy within the Victorian Theatre*.

The performers were no safer as accidents onstage and backstage were rife, many an eye or a limb being lost in the process, with fatalities far from unusual. There were some compensations in dealing with the disasters of those days. Today, when policemen no longer patrol beats at night, rarely investigate burglaries, and ignore shop lifting, it is salutary to see how often policemen were on the spot in the 19th century. While patrolling their beat in the night time they were often the first to see a fire, and they were present nightly inside theatres to quell trouble makers. They were there to prevent crime, and catch miscreants. If a constable was in trouble in the street, the sound of his whistle or rattle would bring companions running to his rescue, and most honest citizens would assist. They were supported by magistrates who took a very dim view of a person interfering with a policeman carrying out his duties. To strike a policeman or resist arrest was particularly heinous.

Magistrates were active daily, most arrests were dealt with the following day resulting in immediate fines or prison sentences. More serious offences were carried forward to the next assizes. I have often been surprised and sometimes perturbed at the variance in sentences meted out to malefactors – men sent to jail for selling a fake free pass, and a performer who discharged a cannon in a music hall killing a boy in the gallery not receiving any punishment at all!

In the matter of fatal accidents, inquests were also customarily held the following day after death, certainly within the week. A far cry from today when an inquest is often years after the tragic event. Again it is disturbing how rarely blame is attributed or compensation sought, juries concluding the affair was "a simple accident".

Another great difference between the Victorian era and today is that there always seemed to be a doctor and a chemist to hand in an emergency. Of course, there was no free health service, but if somebody was injured in the audience or on the stage, there was often a doctor in the very audience watching the show. So much so, one suspects they may have been there not for pleasure, but for the chance of possible business. Should no medical man be present, there was always one round the corner who appeared on request at the drop of a hat, and chemists seemed to be open at all hours. You will find examples where an actor was injured during the play, taken to hospital, attended to and returned to continue his role in the play! Remember that next time you are in A & E for over four hours before getting attention.

This book is devoted to accidents that actually happened in performance or rehearsals but a few entries – including a murder – are outside that strict definition.

The individual entries are mainly taken from contemporary newspaper reports, in most cases amplified by research from elsewhere. Words in ". . ." commas are quotations from news items and a small number of entries are entirely brief verbatim paragraphs. The date of each entry is the actual date of the accident or incident and is as accurate as I have been able to ascertain. Where I cannot be positive, the date is followed by a small 'c' for circa.

I have used the term 'onstage' but in Victorian times that included in the circus ring, music hall and concert platforms, pleasure gardens and open-air galas, even swimming pools – in fact anywhere that performances took place. The unfortunate artistes included herein comprise trapeze artistes, wire-walkers, acrobats, divers, as well as singers, dancers, musicians, comedians, fire-eaters, magicians etc, and, of course, a plethora of actors and actresses. The accident situations are various – falling scenery, open trapdoors, collapsing rostrums, falling bodies, shootings and stabbings. Fatalities are highlighted with the date in **BOLD.** There is one major digression from the consecutive sequence – costumes catching fire. This occurrence was so commonplace that I have given those accidents a section to themselves.

So turn the pages to find the Victorian stages that harbour a *pot-pourri* of disaster, destruction and death . . . .

Perils of the Victorian Stage

MONEY - HISTORICAL NOTE

The currency in use during the period was based on pounds, shillings and pence (£ s d).
£1 = 20 shillings   1 shilling = 12 pence   1 penny divided into ½d (ha'penny) and ¼d (farthing)

These denominations were rendered variously as, for example:

£209 or 209*l*	(Two hundred and nine pounds)
£37.10s	(Thirty seven pounds and ten shillings)
£203.14.6 or	(Two hundred and three pounds, fourteen shillings and sixpence)
7/- or 7s	(7 shillings)
4/6 or 4/6d	(four shillings and sixpence – colloquially called "four and six")
6½d	Sixpence-ha'penny
1¼d	Penny-farthing

1837_01_13 LONDON (Covent Garden).   ACCIDENT TO TIGHTROPE WALKER

This theatre, once the pride of the legitimate stage, had lowered its sights in view of competition from the many new London theatres that had arisen which, presenting melodrama, pantomime and burletta, were more to the common taste. Both the patent theatres of Covent Garden and Drury Lane, repositories of the classic drama, were now showing circus acts, including horses and lions.

During her act as a rope walker, Madame Louise Irvine walked an inclined rope from the stage up to the gallery, and then turning, descended again. The rope being rather slack caused her to miss her footing, and she fell on to the stage, balance pole and all. Fortunately, she had passed over the orchestra pit at this point otherwise several people may have been injured. As it was, the audience arose with a cry of horror, the curtain was lowered, Madame was scooped up by colleagues and taken to her dressing room, and a surgeon was summoned.

1. Covent Garden

As Madame had not fallen far, the damage was limited to a broken arm. Not too good for a gymnast but far from life threatening. However, some sections of the press used the event to beat their drum against the major theatres: "It is to be hoped that this horrifying exhibition, which has so long disgraced a national theatre, will henceforth be discontinued."

1837_03_29 MANCHESTER (Queen's).   FATAL GUN ACCIDENT

The afterpiece was *Lillian the Show Girl* which includes a scene where Everard has to fire at some robbers. Mr Egerton, playing this character, duly fired his gun but it misfired. In the theatre it is always best to have cover in case of a pistol not working on cue, and in this instance a property man called Finlayson stood in the wings with another gun which he could fire, so preserving the verisimilitude of the scene. Rightly, Finlayson elevated the barrel so there was no danger of anybody being hit. Unfortunately, the standby weapon was a holster pistol as used by cavalry men, and totally unsuitable for use in a theatre. An actor called Campbell was offstage behind a flat elevated some eight or nine feet, ready to make his entrance by descending steps as if coming from an upper apartment. Receiving the gun load in his left side, he fell to the stage with a groan. It was the last sound he was to make, as by the time the surgeon arrived he was dead.

Finlayson was arrested and kept in custody until a post mortem with a jury. The police surgeon who inspected the body said every indication was that the deceased had bled to death, there being two quarts of blood in his chest. In the left lung there was a five inch shattered part of a wood ramrod with a brass tip. Finlayson said he only used wet paper for the wadding, as he loaded the gun in a hurry, and everybody involved agreed he could not possibly have been aware of Campbell's position at that time. It seems as though the ramrod had been replaced in the barrel rather than its holder underneath though this was not stated at the inquest. The jury's verdict was 'accidental death' and Finlayson was discharged from custody.

Mr and Mrs Campbell had only joined the company of Henry Beverley a week previously. Mr Campbell was a healthy and vigorous man of about 35 years of age. He now left a widow and three children of which the eldest was 14. "The deceased was a young man of remarkably mild gentlemanly manners; and he and the wretched man who deprived him of his life were intimate friends." Mr Beverley said he would not only pay all the funeral expenses but continue the salary of the deceased for the benefit of his widow, who remained as part of the company. This was considered exceedingly bountiful.

1837_11_10 LEEDS (Theatre).   DANCE ACCIDENT TO ACTOR-MANAGER

Mr Downe, the manager of the York circuit which included Leeds and Hull, sustained an injury on the last night of his season at Leeds. When partaking of a dance onstage he was somehow thrown to the ground, suffering injuries which included a broken Achilles tendon. The piece was abandoned to be replaced by a substitute item. The company went on to Hull as planned, but Mr Downe was not sufficiently fit to travel with them.

1838_09_03 WINDSOR (Theatre Royal).   GUN ACCIDENT

At the morning rehearsal, as required by the script, Mr Williams held a gun to Henry Howe's face. Unfortunately, the gun went off accidentally and, the muzzle being close to Mr Howe's face, he received the wadding very near to his eye. On inspection, the fear that he might lose his sight was allayed but he was very likely to be disfigured which is a blow to any young actor. He would not be able to appear again during the season, but the manager "has in a very handsome manner allowed him to take a benefit" and the young new queen sent 10/-. Howe framed the banknote and went on to have a very long and successful career in the London theatres without gaining stardom.

1838_11_22 LONDON (Drury Lane).   ACCIDENT TO STAR PANTOMIMIST

Probably the finest pantomimist of his time, George Wieland, who had suffered three previous accidents, suffered yet another in a new ballet called *The Spirit of the Air* in which he played the North Wind. As usual Wieland's "jumpings, caperings, and curvetings were exceedingly grotesque and truly comic."

On this night, between 11pm and midnight, Messrs Gilbert and Wieland, enacting aerial spirits, were suspended by wires high above the stage when the wires snapped and they hurtled 20ft to the stage below. Both were immediately carried off into the greenroom, apparently insensible, with blood gushing from nose and mouth. Gilbert, who had hit the ground first, suffered internal bruising but remarkably no broken bones. Wieland, who landed on top of him, received a broken finger, two dislocated ribs, and severe bruising to arm and shoulder. Gilbert was soon able to walk about, recovering via copious hot baths and the application of leeches, whereas Wieland's ribs overlapped each other and, once restored to their correct alignment, he had to lie in a recumbent and quiescent position to give them time to heal. It was considered extremely fortunate that both men had been bled before leaving the theatre on the night of the accident. In those days bloodletting was considered an essential panacea for every disease and injury.

2. *George Wieland*

Amazingly, the indomitable pair was considered well enough to return to work within a fortnight, appearing in the same play on 4 December. On the night the ballet resumed, the typically eclectic programme comprised Rossini's Grand Opera *William Tell*, followed by the American lion tamer Van Amburgh, ending with the ballet *Spirit of the Air*. Both the injured men were warmly greeted on their re-appearances, and the ballet went off with great *éclat* with the conclusion of the first act – where the accident had happened – omitted.

1839_05_08 MARKET DRAYTON (Theatre).   FATAL GUN ACCIDENT

3. *Henry Betty*

The star guest at this country theatre was Henry Betty, the son of the once famous prodigy Master Betty (fl. 1802–1808). On the second night of his visit he was playing Norval in *Douglas*, his father's most famous role. Following the interval he also performed in the afterpiece *The Pilot*. During this play while Betty was leaning over a boy called John Merrill, one of the other actors dropped a percussion gun with the muzzle only a few inches from the boy's chest. It exploded and he was shot to the heart by the wadding and instantly expired, the wadding lodged in his left ventricle. "The shrieks of the mother, on learning the fact, were heartrending. The occurrence was purely accidental."

1840_07_05 LONDON (Her Majesty's).   ACCIDENT TO MDLLE TAGLIONI

[Marie Taglioni, 1804 – 1884 born in Sweden and mainly trained by her father was one of the star ballet dancers of the era. She spent most of her career in France and Austria though she had some short seasons in London. Mdlle Taglioni is recognised as the first star of the Romantic ballet era, being the first to introduce the long flowing white tutu. She is also thought to be the first ballerina to dance *en pointe*. She retired at the age of 43 but for some years thereafter remained a force in the world of ballet.]

4. *Marie Taglioni*

During a season in London at Her Majesty's Theatre, which at that time was known as the Italian Opera House, Mdlle Taglioni had an accident. Whilst performing in *L'Ombre* she descended within an iron hoop which was rent asunder causing her to fall, first striking a table, and then the stage itself. She received many bruises, but was able to rise and cross the stage unaided, although not speaking, to reassure the audience she was unhurt.

1840_08_12 LONDON (Astley's). ACCIDENT TO PANTOMIMIST

Mr Elliott a well established and popular pantomimist was performing in a spectacle *The Tournament*. For his part in this he wore a heavy suit of armour with a steel helmet on his head. It sounds as though it was much akin to a genuine suit of armour. Whilst crossing the stage, a part of the machinery above the stage gave way and fell exactly atop Elliott's head. The helmet broke and a piece of the helmet entered the unfortunate man's skull. Mr Ducrow the manager had the injured man taken to his home and bled by a surgeon, who gave no hope of recovery.

1841_06_23 LONDON (Adelphi). MAGICIAN'S GUN ACCIDENT

[John Henry Anderson (1814–1874) was a famous Scottish magician. Orphaned at the age of ten, in 1830 he started his career appearing on the stage with a travelling dramatic company. At 17, he began performing magic and in 1837, at the age of 23, put together a show which toured for three years.]

The popular Professor Anderson, known as The Wizard of the North, was particularly celebrated for the gun trick in which an examined bullet, fired by a man from the audience, is caught by the magician, sometimes on a plate, sometimes, even more incredibly, in his teeth. Several magicians throughout history have failed to pull off the trick efficiently and died as a result. On this night Anderson, struck in the face by the wadding of the gun, lost a tooth and received lacerations to nose and upper lip. Anderson was able to gasp that no blame should be attached to the man who had loaded and fired the gun, before collapsing to be hauled off to his dressing room. Two physicians were speedily in attendance and accompanied Anderson home in a coach. He was later pronounced out of danger.

5. *J H Anderson*

1841_11_15 LONDON (Olympic). ACTOR FALLS THROUGH STAGE

In Victorian times there were lots of entertainments called by unfamiliar names such as 'burletta', 'extravaganza', 'melodrama' and it is difficult to see what differentiated each from the other. The main thing was they all contained a musical element. The play on this night was described as a *farcetta* called *Angels and Lucifers*, in which Mr George Wild and Miss Lebatt were dancing and singing a duet. Partway through the dance, Mr Wild suddenly disappeared as a section of the stage flooring collapsed leaving him supported by his elbows, only head and shoulders visible. Assistance was immediate, which was very fortunate because under the stage was a 30ft drop to the concrete base of the building. After being hauled out, the indomitable George carried on with his dance, concluding to tumultuous applause and shouts of 'Bravo!'

The curtain was then lowered while the manager Mr Baker came forward and said there would be a slight delay while the stage was repaired. He attributed the weakened stage to the horse appearing in the first piece, whose unusual weight had caused the planks to spring from their position. The show then continued.

6. *George Wild*

1841_11_17 LONDON (Olympic). ACTOR FALLS THROUGH STAGE

Two days after the incident mentioned above, at the very same Olympic Theatre, Mr Leman Rede was starring in his own play *Jack Rann the Reever*. Rede, a successful and popular playwright specialising in 'blood and thunder epics' but acknowledged to be a poor actor, was often advised not to play in his own works as he did not do them justice. In the exciting chase scene where the Reever, to elude the police, jumps from a window dropping to the stage, Mr Rede went through it in an identical manner to George Wild (*see* above). He was stuck with head, shoulders and arms spread out to support himself. The curtain fell,

7. *Leman Rede*

and Mr Baker strode on to address the audience. He assured them that Mr Rede was not hurt in any way and within a few minutes the play would continue. After a few minutes the show carried on, Mr Rede reappearing "and although evidently suffering from the accident, maintained the personation of the character throughout." It is to be hoped after these two accidents that Mr Baker did something permanent about his stage.

11

1842_01_21 LONDON (Garrick). GUN ACCIDENT

In the middle of a melodrama, Mr C Alworthy was hit in the face by a discharge from a pistol. The powder and wadding severely burned his face, but a positive forecast was given for his recovery.

1842_10_10 DUMFRIES (Theatre). GUN ACCIDENT

For the play of *Rob Roy*, loaded guns were in the wings for firing later. Halfway through the play, "One of them went off by chance" just as the manager Mr Pritchard – playing Rob Roy – was nearby. The powder was driven into his face, and the wadding hit and cut his lip. He was floored by the violence of the shock, the curtain was lowered and the show halted. A surgeon, promptly in attendance, found that there was no damage to the actor's eyes and serious injury had been avoided. Pritchard was all for continuing, but his medic would not permit it, so the show continued with Mr Holmes in the role. Pritchard, though unable to appear the following night, was soon back at work.

1843_04_19 READING (Theatre). GUN ACCIDENT

The play was *The Pilot*, a well-known drama in which the lead role of Long Tom Coffin was played by Mr Harrington, an American actor guesting with the resident company. In the second act, Harrington was withdrawing a pistol from his belt when it exploded, and the contents were lodged in his abdomen causing a gaping wound through which his intestines protruded. The curtain was instantly lowered, help summoned, and Harrington stretchered off to hospital. He was critically ill for some days with his life despaired of but, after a long haul with a wife and large family anxious for his recovery, Harrington was eventually discharged from hospital at the end of June.

1843_06_16 BIRMINGHAM (Theatre Royal).   ACCIDENT TO PANTOMIME CLOWN

[The harlequinade had been the main feature of pantomimes throughout the 18th century, but after Grimaldi's time it went into a long decline, although still a regular part of the show in the Victorian era. The main characters were Harlequin, Clown, Pantaloon and Columbine who, ideally, were played by special pantomimists. The harlequinade relied on trick scenery and acrobatic chases with the performers diving through flaps in the scenery to be caught in canvas slings held by stagehands at the back. It was physically exhausting and downright dangerous. A Harlequin called Paul Redigé known as the Little Devil leapt through a scene flap and, because of the absence of the stagehands with their sling, hit an iron staple on the stage floor and was killed instantly. The artistes relied on these same men to propel them with pulleys up through trapdoors in the stage, shooting them high in the air.

The three Ridgway brothers were leading star pantomimists who played Harlequin, Pantaloon and Clown together. However, George died at the early age of 22 from tuberculosis leaving Tom as one of the top clowns of the period, and Jack who married a dancer, performing with his wife in the roles of Harlequin and Columbine.]

8. *Tom Ridgway*

These three were engaged for a short series of appearances in various pantomimes, and pantomimic sketches. As yet, pantomimes were not confined to the Christmas season. In *The Man in the Moon*, Tom was seated on top of a coach about eight feet high, which revolved. On this night it started so rapidly that Tom was thrown off and dashed down to the stage with great violence. He lay insensible with injuries to his kneecap, head, arm and side.

The pantomime thus finished without the clown. However, pantomimists had to be made of stern stuff and be physically fit, and Tom, soon recovering, took part in the benefit performance for the Ridgway trio before leaving the town.

1843_07_22 EDINBURGH (Adelphi).   GUN ACCIDENT TO THE AMERICAN GIANT

[Charles Freeman known as the American Giant was a pugilist who claimed to be 7ft 3in, though when measured in 1842 he was 6ft 11½in. He weighed in at 333lbs. As well as boxing, he also appeared on stage in 'monster' roles.] He was appearing on this night as the Monster in a play called *Presumption*. During the show he was hit in the mouth by the wadding from a gun which knocked out a tooth and caused other injuries, but not of a dangerous or serious nature. When firing a pistol on stage it was usual to fire upwards to avoid injury. In this case, no account was taken of the man's unusual height, thus he received the discharge at his mouth, whereas it would have sailed over the head of the average actor. Freeman died two years later at the early age of 26. His skeleton which still exists measures 6ft 9ins.

9. *Charles Freeman*

1843_08_07 WINDSOR (Theatre Royal).   ACCIDENT TO ACTOR IN STAGE FIGHT

Professor Abel was appearing in a piece called *My Poor Dog Trey* the climax of which is a terrific death struggle with another actor – on this occasion Mr Osborne. In the realism of the fight, Abel fell on his left hand causing dislocation of the two bones in his forearm. This obviously prevented him from continuing the show with his celebrated Grecian Statues.

The Statue routine is believed to have originated with Andrew Ducrow the equestrian Wearing white 'fleshings' he posed on horseback as various characters from Ancient Greece. For actors with the necessary physique the act was a godsend as it offered them the opportunity to display a one-man speciality, and also offered 'cultural' titillation to their lady admirers.

Professor Abel obtained the services of surgeon George Chapman who, with his aptly named assistant Mr Gildersleeves, succeeded in replacing the dislocated bones, though the Prof had to be patient as it would be a minimum of two weeks before he could resume normal duties.

1843_09_27 LONDON (Marylebone).   CANNON EXPLODES IN ACTOR'S FACE

The play being presented was *The Heroine of Spain; or Napoleon's Mandate*. In the scene where Spanish troops march over a drawbridge in front of six cannons charged with powder, one of the cannons exploded as a young man called Nice was passing before it. The contents lodged in his face and blood streamed as the poor chap staggered backwards.

Nice was immediately taken to his father who was a surgeon in nearby Duke Street. It was found that both eyes had been perforated, the sight in the right one entirely gone. The young fellow was in excruciating agony, and the assistance of Dr Guthrie was sought who was able to alleviate the pain to some extent. It was thought that the sight of the left eye would be restored.

1843_10_30 LONDON (Drury Lane).   BALLET STAR FAILS TO CATCH GRISI.

10. *Carlotta Grisi*

11. *Marius Petipa*

[Carlotta Grisi was the star of the moment with her performance at Drury Lane as the enchanting Peri in the ballet of the same name. This ethereal creature of Persian and Turkish folklore was an ideal role for the dancer, and her big moment came when she leapt over a waterfall into the arms of her human lover, danced by another great star Marius Petipa who astonished with his almost acrobatic but graceful lifts.] On this night, Petipa failed to catch Grisi and both ended up sprawled on the floor. The audience was appalled, fearing that one or both may have been injured, but that was not the case, and Mlle Grisi went back to take position to try the leap again.

At this the audience cried as one: "No, no, don't do it!" but Grisi would not be daunted. Petipa stood waiting, shaking like an aspen, as she soared into her leap again, which Petipa caught in great style. It is said the roar of applause was the loudest ever heard in Drury Lane.

13

1843_11_17 MANCHESTER (Theatre Royal).   ACTRESS FALLS FROM WIRE

Miss Gardner was playing Ariel in *The Tempest*, swinging on a wire some height above the stage. The wire broke causing Miss Gardner to drop to the stage with a sudden crash. Fortunately, apart from a cut chin and some bruises she escaped any injury.

1843_11_26 LONDON (Surrey).   ACTRESS INJURED IN HIGH JUMP

During the first performance of the play *The Bohemians of Paris*, Mrs R Honner had to jump from a bridge to the stage, a height of some 15ft. In doing so she missed the mattress placed to break her fall and was so severely injured it was impossible to know when, or if, she would work again. Her part was taken over by Mrs H Vining. Mrs Honner, the wife of the manager, shared leads with Mrs Vining. The newspapers then, as now, liked to exaggerate calamities as the fully recovered Mrs Honner was able to play in the next production launched in December.

1844_01_10 WINDSOR (Theatre Royal).   ACCIDENT IN STAGE FIGHT

Mr Otway had been guesting all week with the Windsor company and for his benefit night he chose to play Hamlet. In the last scene of the play there is a struggle over a poisoned chalice between Hamlet and Laertes, played by Henry Reeves the lessee of the theatre. During this, Otway was struck forcibly on the forehead with the prop, cutting his head in the region of the temporal artery. Blood torrented down the actor's face and the play had to be abandoned whilst help was sought. Mr Andrews, a local surgeon, was soon at hand but it took a good time before he was able to staunch the flow of blood. The house waited in considerable anxiety to find out the result. Otway was called for after the play and appeared with his head bandaged, and walked with considerable difficulty.

1844_02_05 EDINBURGH (Theatre Royal).   GUN ACCIDENT

"Towards the close of this Mr Sullivan met with a rather serious accident caused by the wadding of a gun hitting him on the cheek which caused considerable swelling and bleeding, but we are glad to learn that there are no fears of more serious consequences." *Caledonian Mercury* 1844_02_08.

1844_02_06 HULL (Theatre Royal).   ACTOR-MANAGER INJURED IN FALL

Mr Pritchard the manager of the York circuit – which included the Hull theatre – was demonstrating to an actor how he wanted him to swing from point A to point B on a rope in the play *Zembuca*. Unfortunately, the scenery had not been properly secured and Mr Pritchard fell to the stage, his chest landing on a piece of wood. As a result he was confined to his bed for some days. He returned on 22 February for a benefit in aid of Hull Infirmary.

1844_02_12c RICHMOND (Theatre).   ACTOR-MANAGER FALLS ON SPIKES

Mr Henry Reeves (*see* 1844_01_10) slipping off the stage, fell with his back against the spikes of the orchestra. I have not been able to ascertain how badly he was hurt, as to fall with force on the row of spikes would have been similar to having two or three daggers simultaneously striking one in the back. As no more seems to have been said about the incident, he probably got off lightly.

1845_01_20 LONDON (Astley's).   FATAL ACCIDENT TO SUPER

This unusual accident happened in the pantomime *Johnny Gilpin* and the victim was not a pantomimist, whose profession instils a permanent apprehension of accidents, but a mere 'super' going in to earn a modest 1/- a night. The term 'super' is short for supernumerary and equates with the modern 'extra' of the film industry.

The super was William Blake (38) and amongst other crowd appearances during the evening he was required to be one of several customers bustling about in an old clothes shop. The Clown (Mr Barry) and the Pantaloon (Mr Bradbury) had a rope which they held across the door. The joke was to raise this as each separate customer emerged making him trip up. Blake was clearly not practised in making comic falls (a technique essential to all pantomimists) and went violently over, falling flat with great force on the stage. Unfortunately, Mr Blake was wearing a metallic truss which was forced into the lower part of his abdomen causing severe internal injury. He died two days later leaving a widow and seven young children unprovided for. At the inquest before a jury, a verdict of accidental death was given, and the jury asked that the Coroner inform Mr Barry that he was not to be blamed in any way.

1845_02_01 LONDON (Astley's).   ACCIDENT TO HARLEQUIN

As explained above (*see* 1843_06_16) stagehands were often absent when it was their duty to catch pantomimists, sometimes deliberately so if they had not been tipped sufficiently. Not long after the fatality above, Mr Lewis, the Harlequin in the pantomime *Johnny Gilpin* took his usual leap from the front of the stage through a trap in the scenery, but with nobody there to catch him, he crashed to the floor suffering many bruises though fortunately not breaking anything. His wounds were dressed but he was unable to continue further that evening.

1845_04_22c LIVERPOOL (Amphitheatre).   GUN ACCIDENT

Mr Somerville, performing in *The Fox Hunt*, was pulling a loaded gun from his belt when the trigger caught on a button and the entire charge entered his abdomen. Dr Jeffreys was summoned to the scene and gave favourable hopes for the victim's recovery.

1845_09_15 LONDON (Victoria).   GUN ACCIDENT

While Mr Harris was waiting in the wings for his cue, a musket in the hands of a super nearby went off. Harris, struck in the eye by the wadding, was immediately taken to a nearby surgeon and thence to Charing Cross Hospital where it was feared that the sight in that eye was entirely gone.

1846_01_19 LONDON (Garrick).   CLOWN FALLS FROM WIRE

One of the gags in the pantomime was for Henry Earles as Clown to put up an umbrella, Harlequin then waved his wand and Clown floated up to the flies. The trick had been performed many nights but on this occasion the wire supporting the clown broke and he crashed down on to the stage, shattering his umbrella. This got a huge laugh from the audience who supposed it was part of the show. However, when Earles did not rise, and colleagues came onstage to bear him off, the laughter turned to deepest sympathy. He had severe contusions on head, shoulders, and other parts of the body making it likely to be some time before he could return to the stage.

1846_02_03 LONDON (City of London).　　　　　　STAGEHAND FALLS THROUGH TRAP

Mr Canfield a "professor of athletic exercises" presented what came to be known as a 'strong man act'. He concluded his presentation by supporting a cannon weighing around 5cwt on his breast while it was fired with a full charge of powder. After this feat, six men lifted the cannon off Canfield who then made his exit.

One of the six men assisting was Thomas Brittain (56). The men manhandling the cannon were in three pairs. In the wings watching the proceedings was a labourer William Willshire, engaged by the theatre. As the men carried the cannon upstage, Willshire, noticing that a trapdoor looked insecure, called out to warn the men. The first pair avoided the trapdoot but the middle pair stood on it, and it gave way pitching them to a depth of 12ft. The rear pair of bearers unable to support the cannon, let it drop on to the stage, where it paused and then followed the men through the trapdoor.

Willshire and others rushed down to the understage cellar to find the cannon lying across the head and face of Brittain, and across the chest of Jones the other man. When the cannon was raised, the two men were rushed to hospital but Brittain was dead on arrival, Jones too had fearful injuries and was not expected to survive. There could only be one verdict at the inquest on Brittain which was "Accidental Death".

1846_03_10c BIRMINGHAM (Circus).　　　　　　ACCIDENT TO SLACK ROPE WALKER

"Last week, in Bedford Street Circus, Birmingham, Mr Chapman was performing on the slack rope, when he missed his hold, and fell to the ground with a tremendous crash, suffering a fracture of the thigh bone." *Bath Chronicle and Weekly Gazette* 1846_03_19.

1846_03_20c MADRID, Spain.　　　　　　　　　　ACCIDENT TO MADAME SAQUI

[Madame Saqui, a noted French tight-rope walker or 'rope dancer' was born as Marguerite-Antoinette Lalanne in 1786. In April 1816, her performance descending a tightrope stretched at an incline over the auditorium at Covent Garden Theatre made her name in England. The proprietors of Vauxhall Pleasure Gardens subsequently engaged her for four years. Her hugely popular act included her descent at a run, on an inclined tightrope stretched from a mast, to one of the main walkways, in a storm of fireworks. She was a 'character' known all over Europe, of whom there are several anecdotes. She made and lost a fortune and was still performing on the rope at the age of 75 when it was "a wondrous but sorry sight to see her". She died in poverty in Paris at the age of 80. At the time of the accident described below she was 60 years of age.]

"The *Heraldo of Madrid* of the 23rd mentions an accident in that city to the celebrated Madame Saqui, the rope-dancer. As she was making an ascension amidst a display of fireworks she lost her balance, and would have fallen to the ground if she had not fortunately caught the rope with her hand. Her dress took fire, but the flames were extinguished before she could sustain any injury." *London Daily News* 1846_04_02

13. *Madame Saqui*

1847_08_13c MONTREAL, Canada.   WALLACK IN PLATFORM COLLAPSE

[James William Wallack (1794c–1864) was an Anglo-American actor born in London. At 18 he joined Drury Lane playing Laertes in Hamlet, and similar secondary roles. He also acted throughout the provinces, gradually winning popularity. In 1824, he became stage manager at Drury Lane. He first visited America in 1818 and, in spite of suffering an accident which nagged him all his life, made his career there, playing as a leading tragedian in Shakespeare and lesser works, making occasional forays back to Britain. From 1837 he was boss of New York National Theatre. In this report he is acting in Canada in one of his most famous roles.]   James Wallack in the play *Don César de Bazan* was clambering over a balcony in one of the scenes when a platform gave way and he was thrown down on to the stage.   After a slight delay he

14. *James Wallack*

carried on performing though in evident pain. "The next evening he did not appear."

1847_12_06 NEW YORK, USA (Chetham).   AMUSING BALLET ACCIDENT

"An amusing scene took place at the Chetham Theatre, one evening last week, Madame De Bar was dancing in the ballet of *La Giselle*, when her robe was torn in one of her pirouettes, the audience fell into loud laughter at the accident, which they encored at every bound of the unlucky danseuse. Finally she stopped short, came forward to the footlights, and addressed the laughers: 'Ladies and gentlemen, if you continue to laugh at me this way, either to my face or behind my back, I give you warning that I shall leave the stage, and then you will get nothing for your money.' This was conclusive; the audience regained its gravity, and the dancing went on without further interruption." *New York Harbinger* 1847_12_06.

1847_12_11 HULL (Theatre Royal).   ACTOR-MANAGER FALLS THROUGH TRAP

Mr J L Pritchard, the lessee and manager of the Theatre Royal, was playing the role of the Vampire in the play of the same name. The framework of the trap gave way and the actor was plunged into the understage cellar, landing on the floor some 11ft below. He sustained injuries to both legs. These kept him off the stage until 29 February 1848. In the meantime, while carrying out all his other duties, he became embroiled in an unfortunate affair whereby a tragedian called George Jones was claiming benefit performances for the purpose of raising funds to buy Shakespeare's birthplace. Thinking it was going to the official fund-raising committee, Pritchard handed over the takings plus a private contribution of £10. Alas, it seems to have been a scam.

1848_01_03 EDINBURGH (Theatre Royal).   SWORD ACCIDENT

The fact that many plays, including Shakespeare's, require sword bouts meant that an ability to fence was a necessary accomplishment. Mr Glover was acting the part of Richard III "with his usual spirit and effect" in the final scene of the Battle of Bosworth. His opponent in the sword fight was Mr Wyndham playing the Earl of Richmond. During the bout, Wyndham accidentally stabbed Glover in the arm-pit, but nobody was aware of this as Glover completed the scene – which probably wasn't difficult as Richard dies anyway. After the play it was discovered that although Glover had had "a narrow escape from serious injury" he was unable to perform for the next few nights.

1848_01_22 GLASGOW (Theatre Royal).   GUN ACCIDENT

The play was *Rob Roy*, and the scene where Helen McGregor – played by Mrs Wallis – holds a gun to Francis Osbaldistone – played by Mr Cathcart. During the course of the action, the gun suddenly went off within a yard of Cathcart's head. He immediately put his hands to his face and wheeled round, his back to the audience. Mrs Wallis stood petrified holding the gun, and the manager who was playing one of the other parts stepped forward, relieved her of the gun and gave a brief homily of the awkwardness of stage weapons. Cathcart was completely unscathed and the play continued, only to be interrupted again by Mrs Wallis bursting into tears and grasping Cathcart's hand. The manager stepped forward again and said a few more words about the unsettling nature of stage accidents. When composure had returned the play proceeded as it should to the end, the tremendous applause for Mrs Wallis showing how much the audience felt for her. That there was negligence there is no doubt.

1848_05_31 LONDON (Princess's).   ACCIDENT TO CHORUS SINGER

Mr Seymour was booked as a backing singer in the opera *The Crown Diamonds*. He was also engaged in a similar role in *The Castle of Otranto* at the Haymarket Theatre which went on at a later hour. On this night the first opera did not end until later than usual, so Seymour and three more singers in the same position hurried from the stage down an unlit unfamiliar passage to get to their dressing room. The singer, falling through a trapdoor which had been left open, dropped 14ft into the under stage cellar. His screams brought assistance and he was taken to Middlesex Hospital where he underwent a serious and painful operation to his ankle.

He was confined to the hospital until November when he was discharged. Because of further problems he had to be readmitted at the end of January 1849, getting his final release on 27 March. During all this lengthy period, a subscription had been set up under Mr Wallack but the total raised was only £8 or £9 – not sufficient to maintain the patient in hospital, even on a weekly allowance of 12/-. Mr Maddox the Princess's manager did not contribute anything to this fund, and also refused compensation on the grounds that Seymour had brought the misfortune on himself by going on a passage along which he was not entitled to pass. A court action for recovery of compensation was held on 14 June 1850. The plaintiff brought witnesses to back his case, the defendant offered no evidence. The jury was out for 2½ hours and on their return the plaintiff was awarded £30 in damages.

1848_06_19 LEEDS (Theatre).   SWORD ACCIDENT

Mr Pritchard (*see* 1847_12_11), engaged leading tragedian William Macready – well known for his violent acting – to give his most famous role of Macbeth. Pritchard was the Macduff on this occasion and received a gash on his right cheek, cutting the cartilage of his nose, and upper lip, penetrating to the bone. He was unable to speak his part because of the blood filling his mouth. Mr S Smith the surgeon attended promptly and, because the weapons were blunted, the wound was much lacerated and had to be closed with sutures. Said the press: "We are happy, however, to learn that, although the gash was extensive, no more serious result is likely to emanate from the accident than the inconvenience of a few days confinement."

15. *J L Pritchard*

18

1849_06_19 LONDON (Royal Italian Opera).   SWORD ACCIDENT

Covent Garden Theatre was now restyled as the Royal Italian Opera House. Signor Mario, one of the major opera stars, performing in *The Huguenots*, accidentally wounded one of the dancers Mr Bologna in the hand. At the end of the opera he enquired of the gentleman he had unintentionally injured, to be told he had departed to see a surgeon. At the theatre the next morning Mario asked for Bologna, to be told he had not reported in. He hailed a fellow dancer of Bologna and gave him a £10 note saying: "Do me the favour to give Mr Bologna this; and express my regrets for the accident. Say I will pay his doctor's bill also; and desire him not to come to the theatre until his hand is quite well, as I will pay his salary myself."

16. *Signor Mario*

The hugely inflated salaries and *prima donna* behaviour of most foreign opera stars was a regular bone of discord with the English audiences much as they fawned and swooned over them. So *The Era* was gratified to say: "This circumstance affords a grateful contrast to the indifference shown generally to the humbler theatrical brethren by the foreign artistes at our lyrical theatres."

1849_09_29 MACCLESFIELD (Theatre).   STABBING ACCIDENT

It was the last night of the season and the play in progress was *Forest Foundling*. Mr Acraman, raising his dagger, accidentally stabbed Mr Calhearn through the cheek, the depth of the wound only being prevented by contact with his teeth, one of which was broken. The play was abandoned at that point, but some extra songs and dances, plus the farce of *Eton Boy* were substituted.

1849_10_22 NORDKOEPING, Sweden.   EQUESTRIAN ACCIDENT

Mdlle Tournaire the noted equestrian, who made an impression with her grace and ability when performing at Drury Lane, was on an engagement in Sweden when her horse took fright, becoming unmanageable. Mdlle Tournaire, thrown with great force against the ring fence, suffered two serious wounds to the head and a severe contusion on the right shoulder. At that point her life was considered to be in danger. I have not been able to find how long she was indisposed but an advertisement of 16 February 1850 shows she was riding at Astley's on that night.

1849_11_09 SHEFFIELD (Theatre)   SWORD ACCIDENT

[Cross dressing is not a modern phenomenon, many a Victorian actress passed themselves off as Hamlet or Romeo. Not many have ventured parts that were not young men though Julia Glover played Falstaff and Charlotte Cushman played Cardinal Wolsey. In recent times we have seen mature actresses play roles like Malvolio, Timon of Athens and even King Lear and Richard III.]

Mrs J F Saville was playing Romeo, Mr Rolfe was Tybalt. When it came to the fight Mrs Saville was so carried away with "stage excitement" that she stabbed Tybalt in the side for real. A surgeon was immediately called in but the wound was not as serious as had been first thought and Rolfe was fast on the road to recovery. "Mr and Mrs J F Saville have been unremitting in their attention to Mr Rolfe since the accident". I bet they had!

19

1850_01_11 CHATHAM (Wombwell's).

DEATH OF LION QUEEN

Ellen Bright (17) was a niece of George Wombwell of travelling menagerie fame, and had been employed for a year as a 'Lion Queen'. Her duty was to enter a cage housing a lion and a tiger several times a day to put them through a short routine of simple tricks. On this night, while presenting the lion, she was attacked by the tiger seizing her by the throat and dragging her to the ground. A groom entered with an iron bar and succeeded in forcing the tiger to drop its victim. Miss Bright, copiously bleeding, was pulled free of the cage by two further grooms and attended by two doctors who happened to be present. Alas all medical ministrations failed and her heart stopped within a few minutes.

17. *Death of Ellen Bright*

20

1850_05_01 GLASGOW (Queen's).

ACTOR KILLED IN STAGE ACCIDENT

[James Calvert already operated one of the popular "low theatre" booths on Glasgow Green – the very large wooden Royal Hibernian. In July 1849, he got permission to erect a brick theatre, complete with gallery, in Greendyke Street next to the Episcopal Chapel. He called it the Queen's Theatre, in honour of Queen Victoria's visit that year to the city.]

William Langley, a popular actor at the new Queen's Theatre, sliding instead of leaping on the stage, broke one of his legs. Death followed within a few days. Mr Calvert organised a benefit performance for the widow and children. Mr Powrie, the manager of the Dundee theatre, took advantage of a recess in the Edinburgh theatre's season to engage the actors from there to go to Dundee for a benefit show in aid of Langley's widow and family, as the actor had long been a local favourite there. The Directors of the Edinburgh, Perth & Dundee Railway also contributed, allowing all the actors and staff from Edinburgh to travel to Dundee and back at a nominal charge.

1850_10_10 LONDON (Adelphi).

SCENERY FLAT FALLS ON ACTORS

A flat is a scenic wing piece comprising a wooden frame covered with stretched canvas painted to match whatever backcloth is in place. Tall and unwieldy to move, it is not unknown for one to fall over as there is a matter of keeping the balance vertical when moved by a man only a third or even a quarter of its height. On this night during *Rory O'More* such a flat fell on to Mr Hudon and Miss Chaplin who were in the wings waiting for their entrance. The lady received a blow which cut her forehead, but was able to resume her performance, whereas Hudson received a blow to his knee which was so injured medical help was immediately summoned. The play continued with Mr Gallot taking over the part. Both the injured thespians were able to resume their duties after several days rest.

1850_10_29c LONDON (Lyceum).   SWORD ACCIDENT

[Charles James Mathews (1803–1878) was the son of the actor Charles Mathews. He was apprenticed to Pugin and thereafter spent some years as an architect. In 1835, he made his stage debut in his own play at the Olympic. In 1838, he married widow Madame Vestris the lessee of the theatre, and thereafter the couple managed in turn the Olympic, Covent Garden and the Lyceum, none with much financial success. As an actor in light comedy Mathews was outstandingly successful – excelling his own father in a similar line – and after Vestris died, ventured to America where he acquired a widow as his second wife. Returning in 1861, over the following decade he emulated his father's At Home one-man shows, appeared in Paris, and played many roles in London and the provinces. In 1869, he embarked on a world tour including a further visit to America, returning home in 1872 where he continued his career until death.]

18. *Charles Mathews*

In Planché's comedy *My Heart's Idol* in 1850, Charles Mathews and Mr Vining had a sham dual. On this night the point of Vining's sword passed completely through the fleshy part of Mathews's hand between thumb and first finger. Mathews silently left the stage, the audience unaware of the accident. Mr Roxby the stage manager entered and begged the indulgence of the audience, explaining Mathews had suffered a serious wound and medical attention had been summoned. The curtain then fell and the orchestra played a selection of melodies. Mathews had fainted on reaching the greenroom. Fortunately his own doctor was in the audience and he, together with another surgeon, did the necessary. The wound was causing the most acute pain, but was not considered of a serious long term nature. However, Mathews was totally unable to continue that evening. Fright and natural anxiety precluded Madame Vestris (Mathews's wife) from continuing the play with an understudy. The theatre, closed during Mathews's incapacity, re-opened on 9 November.

1851_03_09c PARIS, France (Italian Opera).   ACCIDENT TO MDLLE ROSATI

Stage traps were an ever present source of accidents. Even when in order and used properly many a careless performer has forgotten they should avoid it. But all too often the mechanics of the thing fails or a stagehand neglects to bolt the trapdoor closed after it has been used. In the premiere of the production of *La Tempesta*, Caroline Rosati playing Ariel, stepped on to a trap that had been left unfastened and was thrown on to the stage. As she was helped offstage it was feared that a serious injury may have occurred. The audience was fearful as the stage remained empty and all proceedings halted. Star ballerinas were highly regarded and it was known that some in the past had ceased their careers because of accidents.

19. *Mdlle Rosati*

After a wait while the stage remained empty, the stage manager appeared to announce that Mdlle Rosati would endeavour to continue the performance. Appearing shortly afterwards to great applause and, though obviously suffering pain with a large blood stain on her leg, she danced with a great deal of grace and elegance. Having managed to get through the opening night she was too indisposed for the second performance which had to be postponed.

1851_04_12 NORWICH (Theatre Royal).   ACTOR IN SERIOUS ACCIDENT

Mr F Phillips was playing in the opera *Rob Roy*, in the course of which he had a scenic bridge to cross. This collapsed as he was passing over and he was hurled to the stage breaking his ankle in two places. He was taken to hospital in a precarious state and it was deemed necessary to amputate the lower extremity of the bone. In September, it was reported that the surgeon Peter Nicholls had "outvied his former almost miraculous efforts" and the patient was well on the way to a return to the stage. However, this took a little longer than anticipated as he did not return until 31 January 1853 appearing to a tremendous ovation in the character of Shylock – the Jewish gabardine concealing his lameness. Mrs Phillips, who had continued acting throughout her husband's indisposition, played Portia.

1851_08_16 ST LOUIS, USA (Theatre).   FATAL ACCIDENT TO ENGLISH ACTRESS

"Mrs Shea, an English actress, has been killed on the stage of the St. Louis Theatre, by a mass of iron from which a lamp was suspended having fallen upon her." *Norfolk Chronicle* 1851_08_16.

1851_09_13 LONDON (Her Majesty's).   DAGGER ACCIDENT IN *OTELLO*

Signor Pardini as Otello, and Madame Sontag as Desdemona were performing when Pardini, getting a bit carried away with his dagger, struck Madame Sontag on her arm causing the blood to flow copiously. The dagger was apparently a sharper and more dangerous instrument than is normally used on the stage. However Dr Gluck, at hand to staunch the blood and the consternation, stated there was nothing to prevent her from resuming work the following evening.

20. *Madame Sontag*

1851_10_17 PARIS, France (Hippodrome).   ACCIDENT DURING CHARIOT RACE

From time to time circuses in several countries have had the urge to emulate Roman chariot races but only Paris could have come up with the idea of female charioteers!

Mdlle Joséphine was driving four horses pulling her in a chariot when they took fright and galloped in a frenzy round and round the circus ring. A colleague attempted to halt the mad gallop by seizing one of the horses' heads, but was dragged along and just managed to throw himself sideways to avoid the wheels. Another artiste who had great strength grasped the leading two horses and managed to halt them after they had circled the ring over 20 times. Throughout Mdlle Joséphine had clung on to the reins greatly shocked and with severely cut hands, but otherwise, unharmed.

21. *Chariot racing at the Hippodrome, Paris*

22

1852_01_09 LONDON (Colosseum).   FATAL ACCIDENT AT REGENT'S PARK

This venue was not an actual theatre but an auditorium for the display of panoramas, though theatre scenic devices were used. Thomas Foreman (32) who for many years had been engineer at the venue, was oiling the engine when he fell into the machinery in the presence of his fellow workmen. "Although the engines were immediately stopped, his body was taken out lifeless, horribly mutilated."

1852_04_26 BOLTON (Star Inn).   FATAL ACCIDENT TO BOY ACROBAT

Richard Dewhurst the well-known equestrian clown, and son Richard Jr (17) were engaged for performances at the Star Inn, Bolton. The acrobatic troupe comprised three people – Richard Jr being the star of the trio. The youth was very keen to master throwing a double somersault but his father was against his attempting this feat because of the inherent danger. However, around mid-day on Monday morning, his father being absent on business in the town, Richard attempted to practice the manoeuvre on the stage. In his attempt to perform a double somersault, the youth failed not only miserably but fatally. Instead of two revolutions of the body, he made one and a half turns, landing not on his feet but with tremendous force on his head.

Mr Muir, a fellow artiste, immediately sent for medical aid and kept the boy company until it arrived. Richard was well able to speak rationally but the limbs of the talented youth were dead, and his spine was broken. He died at 6.30am on Tuesday morning and was buried on Friday. The same evening a benefit performance was held for his father whose future engagements had disappeared with the sudden and irreparable loss.

23

1852_07_12 LONDON (Adelphi).   ACCIDENT TO MRS KEELEY

22. *Mary Keeley*

[Mary Anne Keeley (1805–1899) made her London debut in 1825. She married Robert Keeley in 1829 and they appeared in many plays together. She was a petite vivacious performer who specialised in playing lissom youths – in 1839, the role of Jack Sheppard being her biggest success. Some critics deplored her continuing playing the role as "it thoroughly vulgarises all her other clever personations" and the play was considered by the Lord Chamberlain as so dangerous he banned all plays on the subject.]

Rehearsing *Jack Sheppard* at the Adelphi Theatre, Mrs Keeley was to descend a ladder and, fearing its stability, she queried it with Jacob the stage carpenter who said "Madam, it will bear your weight." She started her descent when it slipped, causing her to fall and "one of her ancles was violently sprained." By far the most common result of any type of accident was a damaged ankle. I do not know whether stage folk were particularly vulnerable in the talocrural region, or whether the Victorians as a whole were lacking in calcium and vitamin D. This may be so in the smog bound cities of the period – a good PhD subject for somebody to pursue. Apparently she was a bit of a ham as she exclaimed "Oh, my prophetic soul!" when asked if she was hurt. Indisposed for a month, she returned to the role on 5th, 6th and 7th August. On the 9th August she moved with the Adelphi company for a summer season at the Haymarket Theatre.

1852_12_08 BRIGHTON (Royal Pavilion).　　　　ACCIDENT AT COOKE'S CIRCUS

Performing at the Royal Pavilion Circus at Brighton, Miss Emily Cooke had an accident on the opening night which kept her off until nearly the end of the Brighton stay, then on the Wednesday of the final week the large chandelier hanging over the circus ring fell with a tremendous crash. Fortunately nobody was in the ring at the time otherwise there would have been severe injuries if not fatalities.

1853_01_10 LONDON (Olympic).　　　　ACCIDENT TO PANTOMIME SPRITE

During the pantomime of *Queen Mab*, one of the characters, a sprite, slipped from a rope falling heavily on to the stage. With his right arm broken in two places he was whisked off to the surgery of Mr Walker where he received every attention.

1853_01_30 MANCHESTER (Theatre Royal).　　　　TRAP ACCIDENT TO MRS J WOOD

[Mrs J Wood (1831?–1915) born Matilda Charlotte Vining made her first appearance in Brighton at the age of ten. In 1848, she married actor John William Wood and was known thereafter as Mrs J Wood. In 1849, the couple were the comedy leads at Manchester Theatre Royal where they had a huge and appreciative following for several seasons.

The Woods went to America in 1854 where Mrs J Wood was hailed with immediate acclaim. She separated from her husband, became a major player and also went into management. She did not return to the UK until 1866 acting leading roles in London. Apart from two short returns to the USA, the rest of her career was centred on periods of managing various London theatres and playing a range of comedy and singing roles with an essence of French chic.]

23. *Mrs J Wood*

It was the second night of *Uncle Tom's Cabin* in which Mrs J Wood was playing Eliza Harris. Unbeknownst to her a trapdoor in the stage had been left open but with a canvas covering it. Mrs Wood stepped on to the canvas which promptly gave way, one leg going down through the stage, the other remaining on the stage "inflicting injuries which it is impossible to describe." She was not absent long with the indescribable injuries as she had returned by 19 February to appear in *Gil Blas*.

1853_02_10 LONDON (Olympic).　　　　ACCIDENT TO CHILD ACROBATS

A man made his entrance onstage bearing a high pole at the top of which was a small crossbar. Whilst balancing it, two small children entered and climbed up to the top of the pole. They performed several evolutions on the crossbar, then to the horror of the audience both fell to the stage. One was unhurt but the other fell head first. The stage was cleared and the audience waited in suspense after calling for the manager. With deep emotion he told them that the child's arm was broken, and furthermore there "should be no more performances of that kind at the Olympic."

This is the first report I have located regarding child acrobats. There will be many more as the public had a penchant for juvenile gymnastics, and many children gained employment onstage and in the ring. However, the reader will find a gathering storm ahead and much discussion regarding banning and regulation which becomes in the nature of a theme.

1853_10_17 LIMERICK (Penny gaff).   MYSTERIOUS DEATH OF A CLOWN

Henry Rowan the clown of a penny theatre temporarily pitched on the Parade at Limerick was found dead in bed on Monday morning. The man had performed as usual the previous night, but for some three weeks had been complaining of headaches and other after effects from a blow received in a fight in a public house. The blow was from the belt of a soldier named Reilly of the 2nd Regiment, and it was presumed that Rowan's skull had been fractured thereby.

1853_11_02 LONDON (Astley's).   CERTAIN DEATH FROM FOOLISH ACCIDENT

George Palmer, a super at Astley's, was particularly stupid. In one scene his job was to fire a gun offstage; he had been doing this for some time when he found a little trick of his own which went like this: He put the muzzle of the gun in his mouth and by placing the nipple near to a gas light extinguished the gas by suddenly blowing the finer parts of the loose charge through the touch-hole. He had been warned that this stunt was rather dangerous but having mastered it he was proud to show off his prowess. Came the night when he was again demonstrating his skill, but placing the touch-hole against the light he inadvertently breathed in. This drew the flame down to the priming which immediately exploded while he had the muzzle in his mouth. The explosion was such that he was thrown several yards, falling bleeding and insensible, the roof of his mouth completely shattered, his whole face totally lacerated and a segment of the back of his neck blown away. "There was not the slightest hope of his recovery". It is conjectured that another super might have increased the size of the charge as they often played tricks on one another, a favourite being to put more than one bullet in a gun. What a hilarious prank!

1853_11_30 BIRMINGHAM (Theatre Royal).   BENEFIT ACTOR FALLS OFF LADDER

It was the benefit of Mr J Davis, the play was *Night and Morning*. Davis was acting an escape scene which depicted the roofs of houses with a rope slung between two. Davis and fellow actor Barton had to cross the rope. In the normal course of action, Davis got across but Barton was shot and fell to earth where a mattress was conveniently waiting to receive him. On this night Davis losing his grip on the rope fell some 14ft, fortuitously on to the mattress. Unfortunately, he still broke his leg, and in the stunned silence his *sotto voce* stage whisper of "I have shattered my leg" was heard by all. Removed from the stage with much confusion, he was taken to hospital where his leg was re-set in plaster. It is to be hoped that the benefit had brought in sufficient takings to tide over the poor chap for several workless weeks.

1853_12_01c HEREFORD (Theatre).   ACCIDENT WITH BLUNDERBUSS

This is not really a stage accident but as it involves Mr Chadwick of the Hereford Theatre who possessed a quaint old blunderbuss which was no doubt used many times as a stage prop it only seemed right to include it. Chadwick "offered the gun to a gentleman of the town". I do not know if he was trying to sell it, loan it, or simply to boast about it. In order to show its capabilities and to ensure all was in working order, he loaded it with a large charge of powder well rammed with paper on the top. He then fired the gun with the unfortunate result that the barrel burst, shattering his left hand so extensively that it had to be amputated at the wrist.

25

1853_12_29c PARIS, France (Gaieté).   TRAPDOOR GIVES WAY UNDER ACTORS

The play was *Cosaques*. In the middle of a fight scene a large trapdoor in the stage gave way precipitating half-a-dozen actors below the stage. In some confusion they assisted each other to scramble out of the void to take up their original position. This gave satisfaction to the audience who, fearful of unpleasant results, was pleased to have any fears allayed.

1854_01_25c CARDIFF (Theatre).   FENCING ACCIDENT

Mr Melville, a leading tragedian from the Bristol and Bath theatres, was playing Macbeth at Cardiff. In the final desperate sword fight with Macduff, played by Mr Howard, the latter managed to slice a bit off Melville's nose. I don't suppose that fits in with my theory that all stories about noses are funny!

1854_03_06 BIRMINGHAM (Theatre Royal).   SERIOUS ACCIDENT TO A HARLEQUIN

Mr Gilmer, playing Harlequin in the current pantomime at the theatre, suffered a very serious accident during the course of the performance. The business of the harlequinade required him to leap through a glass globe in a druggist's window – a feat commonplace in harlequinades and not in itself particularly dangerous, but requiring care in positioning and timing. In the leap his left leg came into contact with the bar or sill of the opening in the scenic flat and his knee-cap was completely split.

He was carried insensible into the greenroom and Mr Taylor the surgeon sent for immediately. The limb was dressed as well as possible and Mr Gilmer sent home in a cab. The likelihood of Gilmer being able to resume his position as ballet master in the near future was considered remote. A benefit ball at Mr Walker's Rooms was announced for Gilmer and the hope expressed that it would provide a "substantial benefit to one who publicly and privately deserves liberal support."

1854_03_31 LONDON (Victoria).   OUTCRY AT SUBSTITUTE ACTOR

24. *Mr Hicks as Mazeppa*

The play was *Mazeppa* and the crux of this drama is that the hero is tied to a wild horse and driven into the wilderness. To give verisimilitude to the piece a number of horses were hired and the role of Mazeppa was given to Mr N T Hicks. All went well until the moment when the wild horse of Tartary pursued by wolves rushes over the mountains, at which point the horse lost its footing and Hicks, pitched off, crashed down head first against some of the machinery. Severely injured, he was carried away. Medical attention was sought and he was transferred to his home.

Mr J T Johnson stepped into the breach taking the role of Mazeppa for the rest of the performance. How it was possible I do not know, but certain members of the audience were unaware of the accident and seeing that Hicks had been replaced by another actor setforth a hooting and a hissing. Mr Johnson came forward to explain the reason for the substitution and the nature of the accident, and, once explained, the excuse was then accepted and the rest of the show passed off with éclat.

1854_12_23 SUNDERLAND (Lyceum)   **DEATH OF A PANTALOON**

Mr Grammar, professionally known as Grammani, playing Pantaloon suffered an injury which, added to a former injury, caused a rupture from which he died the following day. He left 12 children and a widow shortly to be confined. This family was now in a state of complete destitution and *The Era* newspaper taking it upon itself to invoke contributions from "the charitable and good-hearted", started a fund for contributions no matter how small. On 21 January it announced that contributions ranging from £2 to 1/- totalled £4.3.6d. Independently, Mr Davis the manager of the Sunderland and Newcastle theatres announced that the companies of both theatres had made contributions, and these plus the profits of a benefit, plus several private individual contributions altogether totalled £26.17.6d

It is quite terrifying today to realise how easily – and regrettably often – complete destitution could descend, and how short a time such a sum could be eked out by a mother with 12 children.

1855_01_03 GLASGOW (Theatre Royal).   **GUN ACCIDENT**

On this day, during the performance of the pantomime, an actor had two of his fingers shot off in the discharge of a pistol. "The accident was not known to the audience, and the performance passed off with its usual success."

1855_01_04 LONDON (Drury Lane).   **ACCIDENT TO GYMNAST**

During the performance of the pantomime, one of the Italian Brothers gymnasts on the trapeze, suffered a fall through the breaking of a rope on their apparatus. He fell a distance of some 20ft incurring a "severe shake and a trifling sprain of his left arm." The lessee announced he would not engage any more such acts during the period of his lease.

It was noted above (*see* 1853_02_10) that a manager at another theatre where a gymnastic act suffered a fall made a similar pronouncement. It was a strange situation because at that time gymnastics of all kinds – including weight lifting and static trapeze work – were becoming more and more popular with young men in all walks of life. Schools encouraged team games and supervised athletics. Public schools and universities championed the theory of balanced moral, intellectual and physical development. Rowing, cricket and boxing were manly sports that suited the theory of "muscular Christianity" while games like tennis, hockey and croquet were approved for women. Walking, running, swimming and bicycling became just as favoured by young women as with men. Therefore, one would not be surprised that acts featuring acrobatics in all its guises had become popular. The problem was that the public, especially women, did not like to see artistes injure themselves, and therefore agitated to have such performances banned. As will be seen in forthcoming entries this whole thing gathered momentum, especially after Léotard introduced the flying trapeze in 1859.

Then two years later Blondin the high wire walker made his London debut after causing a worldwide sensation by crossing the Niagara falls on a tightrope. The combination of these two superstars had a profound affect on showbusiness as hosts of gymnasts jumped on the bandwagon by copying, or rather trying to emulate these new attractions. Tightrope walkers or 'rope dancers' as they had been formerly known were now accused of "doing a Blondin" no matter how untalented they proved to be.

1855_03_05 NORWICH (Theatre Royal).   ACCIDENT TO PANTOMIME PERFORMERS

A scene in a burlesque version of *St George and the Dragon* involved two female performers – one of whom was leading lady Mrs Sidney – ascending in a balloon. Balloons were all the rage at the time, with many accidents causing injuries and often death being reported on an almost a daily basis. These are not included in this work as balloon ascents are not within my remit. This, however, was a scenic prop affair and not a proper balloon ascent.

The balloon had risen about ten feet above the stage when some malfunction in the machinery tilted it on one side leaving the two actresses in danger of toppling out. In an attempt at rescue, one of the stagehands climbed on to the ceiling and managed to put his foot through the proscenium arch showering laths and plaster on to the orchestra and pit. The audience, thoroughly alarmed, thought something much worse was about to happen as members of the stage crew, attempting to help the actresses, now rushed offstage out of the way.

Mr Sidney, the leading man, came forward to assure the audience that no danger was present. The ladies were gradually rescued, and the performance, after this brief interruption, continued with much success.

1855_07_25 LONDON (Adelphi).   ACTOR ARRESTED IN MIDDLE OF PLAY

This is not an accident but included as a light diversion – though not for the actor involved! William Waldron was an actor who specialised in 'heavy business', a term used to describe the villain parts. He was playing the role of Blueskin in *Jack Shepherd*. On this night, unknown to him, while he was onstage in Act I, two policemen and another man waited in the wings and arrested him when he made his exit. He was refused permission to continue in the play and was led away.

As the play had stopped, the audience started clamouring for Blueskin until the manager walked on to say that Mr Waldron was suddenly and unexpectedly unable to continue, and the part would now be played by Mr Pearson, then the play continued.

The reason for Waldron's arrest was very simple. At a past time when performing in Derby he had employed a labourer called Jonathan Styles then left town without paying his full wages. Some time passed and Styles, now in London, seeing that Waldron had been engaged at the Adelphi, got a magistrate's summons against him for the missing wages. Waldron ignored the summons and a further demand was served which he also ignored. Judgment was made against him and the magistrates issued a warrant for his arrest. This was carried out in the manner described above.

Brought before the magistrates and warned that he stood committed to jail, the matter was subsequently resolved and he was set at liberty. Phew!

1855_10_20 PRESTON (Theatre).   GUN ACCIDENT

The play *Three Fingered Jack* is based on the true story of a slave uprising in Jamaica. Three Fingered Jack was the name given to Jack Mansong the leader of a band of runaway slaves in the Colony of Jamaica in the eighteenth century. In the play, Jane Howarth, playing a boy, in the scene where the youth escapes out of a window after stealing a gun, was holding it by the muzzle. The trigger of the gun unfortunately catching on the spindle of the chair she was standing on, the weapon went off. Her hand was damaged and surgical assistance immediate, but it was feared that she would never be able to fully recover its use. Fortunately, not Three Fingered Jack in reality then.

1855_12_27 LONDON (Adelphi).   PANTALOON INJURED
     Mr C J Smith the Pantaloon jumped through a trap in the scenery where the men who were
employed to catch him in a canvas sling were absent. He was severely injured but managed to walk
through the performance in great pain. These easily avoided accidents would not happen if the catchers
did their job. It is impossible to believe the callousness of absent stagehands.

1855_12_28 LONDON (Covent Garden).   HARLEQUIN INJURED
     Mr C Brown the Harlequin hastening to the stage after being called, struck his head on a
protruding piece of wood, fell heavily on his shoulder which was dislocated, and for a short time was
insensible. Prompt medical attendance advised that he should be taken home which, in a state of great
suffering, he was. The panto, of course, had to carry on without him.

1856_03_01c NEW YORK, USA (Broadway).   HORSE AND RIDER FALL OFF STAGE
     At the Broadway Theatre a new hippodrama called *Herne the Hunter* was being performed
when Mr Sylvester reined in his horse so tightly that both horse and rider fell off the stage on to the
partition dividing the orchestra from the stage. This, as in many theatres of the time, had a row of iron
spikes along the top to deter invasion of the stage. Both horse and rider were severely injured by the
piercing of spikes, but the orchestra played on unharmed.

1856_09_20 MOSCOW, Russia (Opera House).   DOUBLE ACCIDENT TO MDLLE CERRITO
     Mdlle Cerrito was appearing on the second night of the ballet *Alma; or
La Fille Du Fue*. Mounting a pedestal designed to sink her into the lower
regions, the machinery fell about her person inflicting several small wounds.
Simultaneously, her dress caught fire, but prompt action from those around her
saved her life. Truly *The Girl of Fire*, she was expected to be back at work
within a few days. For one's dress to catch fire was commonplace, and as such I
have grouped all the examples – over 100 – in a special section at the end.

25. *Mdlle Cerrito*

1856_12_17 MANCHESTER (Theatre Royal).   ACCIDENT TO MR MATHEWS
     We met Charles Mathews in an earlier accident (*see* 1850_10_29c). On this evening, the
popular comedian, performing in *Cool as a Cucumber*, slipped on the stage, injuring himself so
severely that the theatre had to be closed immediately. He was unable to appear at subsequent booked
venues Birmingham and Leamington Spa.
     On his return to London he was still indisposed with erysipelas of the arm – a relatively
common bacterial infection of a layer of the skin characterized by a raised, well-defined, tender, bright
red rash. Drury Lane where he was acting manager, had to alter its programme. He was sufficiently
recovered to take part in a slight piece on 19 January 1857.

1856_12_19 NEW YORK, USA (Brougham's).   ACCIDENT TO MR DAVENPORT
     "The Davenports are still playing at this establishment. Mr Davenport, while playing Richard
the Third, on the 19th ult, met with an accident, narrowly escaping losing the sight of an eye. He had
not since played." *The Era* 1857_01_04.

1857_02_02 NEW YORK, USA.   SWORD ACCIDENT IN *KING LEAR*
While there was a crowded house for Edwin Forrest as Lear, the lesser actors had their own problems. In the combat scene between Edgar (Mr Daly) and Edmund (Mr Elmore), a misdirected thrust shattered one of Daly's fingers and it was thought amputation would be necessary.

1857_04_13 STAMFORD (Theatre).   ACCIDENT TO CLOWN
Mr Guyton was the clown in the pantomime of *The Forty Thieves*. Several tricks and stunts had passed off efficiently prior to the part where the clown runs off with an umbrella. The idea was that he should then descend from the flies using the umbrella parachute fashion. However, jerked from his hold of the apparatus he fell to the stage with great force. He rolled himself over to the wings where hands dragged him off. Five minutes later he reappeared badly limping to continue with the pantomime, even carrying out other daring feats. At the end of the show, a doctor examined Guyton's foot and found he had broken a bone in his ankle. He was completely disabled and off work for several weeks.

1857_05_02 HUDDERSFIELD (Theatre Royal).   ACTOR ACCIDENTLY SHOT IN EYE
The season was coming to an end and the week's business had been very bad. In a performance of the play *Dred*, Mr T Cornforth, playing a minor part, was accidently shot when parts of the pistol load lodged in one of his eyes. Hopes surfaced of a favourable outcome though the actor was seriously injured. Alas, the outcome was far less than favourable as Cornforth lost his sight in that eye. He had recovered by 27 June when a benefit was held for him. As the local amateurs gave of their services, it was expected a bumper turnout would result. Alas again, the poor injured chap had a disappointment as the receipts amounted to little more than the expenses.

1857_06_01 LONDON (Cremorne).   HIGH TIGHT ROPE WALKER FALLS
[London's pleasure gardens had been popular and numerous from the middle of the previous century when the upper classes had strolled to the music of Handel and Arne. The gardens were spaced all round London the chief ones being Ranelagh in Chelsea, and Vauxhall. But by the middle of the 19th century several of the gardens had either closed or were in a state of imminent abandonment. The surviving gardens were thronged with the masses wanting more popular fare than classical music, preferring balloon ascents, daredevil stunts and brass bands. In the Victorian period Cremorne was the most popular place to rendezvous.]
Mdlle Adams, from the Cirque Imperatrice in Paris, was performing outdoors at a considerable height. An "artiste of the highest reputation", her feats were daring and astonishing. Unhappily, she fell dislocating her shoulder on landing. She was announced to be recovering rapidly and would reappear in a few days.

1857_06_02 NOTTINGHAM (Polytechnic).   ACCIDENT TO COMIC VOCALIST
During a ballet called *The Barber and the Beadle*, comic vocalist Henry Miller threw a somersault from a cottage window about nine feet above the stage, overbalanced, landing on his head on the stage. He was taken to the General Hospital "where he now lies in a very precarious state". It is necessary when throwing a somersault to have sufficient power to complete the turn to land feet first.

1857_08_17 LONDON (Astley's).   EMBARRASSING EQUESTRIAN ACCIDENT

Mr Palmer was galloping round the ring dancing a hornpipe on horseback in the guise of a British tar, when his foot slipped, he tumbled to the ground and the horse passed over him. Fortunately, he was not hurt and leapt on to his feet to be cheered by the spectators. Unfortunately, he did not realise that his head was now displayed completely bald as his flowing locks were left on the ground. He snatched up his wig and "rushed out somewhat disconcerted."

1858_01_28c NANTES, France.   ACCIDENT TO OPERA SINGER

The opera was Rossini's *Othello* and the Moor was played by M Duprat. Unfortunately, he got so carried away with his part that he forgot he had a real dagger in his hand and when he stabbed Desdemona it went through her dress, her stays and entered her side. The wound bled profusely but was not considered to be too drastic. Phew!

1858_01_28 BOSTON, USA (Theatre).   ACCIDENT TO JEROME RAVEL

[The Ravel Troupe was a famed family of French acrobats who were immensely popular in the USA. The star of the troupe was Gabriel who was also a notable man-monkey and natural successor to Mazurier. Gabriel later broke away from his family to star in his own troupe with the Martinetti family of pantomimists. He caused friction and confusion by retaining the name of Ravel Troupe, as two different troupes were then operating throughout the USA under the same name. The celebrated high wire-walker Charles Blondin started his career with the Ravel family.]

A play called *Bianco* was presented for the first time. On the second night acrobat Jerome Ravel of the Ravel Family troupe fell from a wire landing on his back, breaking two ribs. A benefit performance for Jerome was held on 9 March at which his brother Gabriel was a huge success as an overgrown schoolboy in a pantomime called *The Schoolmaster*.

26. *The Four Ravel Brothers*

1858_01_30 LONDON (Royal Standard).   DEATH OF HENRY BIRD THE PANTALOON

This does not seem to have been an accident although Bird's brother said at the inquest that on Boxing Day, when the pantaloon jumped through a trap, the men designated to catch him were not there. This was strenuously denied by all the stage crew who said that this had never happened, and the manager Mr Douglass claimed it was a slur on his staff who had never deserted their posts at any performance. But it was definitely a death, though totally unexpected.

Henry Bird had been playing Pantaloon in pantomime at the Royal Standard, Shoreditch until 26 January when on returning home he complained of a severe abdominal pain. He relinquished his engagement, and on Friday the 29th he was seized with a fit, dying the following day. The point was raised that he had been a pantomimist for seven years and he always painted his face with a white paint which from time to time made him ill. Every year he was warned about using this paint, but the inquest did not seem to attach much importance to the fact. A post mortem revealed "the vessels of the brain were congested, and the brain itself was very large and flattened on the surface. Long continued anxiety and very active bodily excitement, combined with insufficient sleep would produce this condition of the brain."

Douglass said in print that he always had to engage another artiste ready to play Pantaloon "as he has never been able to finish out the run of the pantomime." One wonders why he booked Bird year after year if such was the case. Most pantomimists were lowly paid and could not afford to accumulate any savings. Bird, who was only 37, had not contributed to any fund so his widow and family were immediately destitute. Mr Douglass the manager of the Standard agreed to hold a benefit at which several eminent pantomimists would appear, including Flexmore and Boleno. *The Era* showbusiness newspaper said Mr Albert Smith had sent them a guinea to launch a fund for the family, and the paper announced it would accept further contributions.

1858_06_10 LONDON (Astley's).   ACCIDENT TO MR COOKE JR
In the hippodrama *The White Palfrey*, at this performance, Mr Cooke's steed, trained to fall down as if wounded when a shot rang out, instead leapt high prior to falling, thus trapping Mr Cooke's leg under it and injuring his ankle. Cooke managed to limp through the remainder of the play but was not able to leave his room afterwards.

32

1858_06_20 YORK (Gala).   ACCIDENT TO ETHARDO THE ASCENSIONIST
[Signor Ethardo (1825–1911) English-born Stephen John Etheridge known as 'The Spiral Ascensionist' was a fake Italian who walked up a spiral route on a large ball. "The globe on which this extraordinary performer works his way up and down is 30 inches in diameter, and 90 inches in circumference. The width of the winding platform is 12 inches, and flat, with no groove or protection of any sort to assist the ascent or descent, and the height of the spiral column is 50 feet. The incline winding from the base to the capital of the column is upward of 180 feet in length. The globe is constructed of wood and iron, without any India rubber, gutta-percha or other adhesive material to assist the Signor in his difficult task."]

Ethardo had been performing for three days at a gala in York without any trouble. After the gala, Ethardo was dismantling his apparatus with the "assistance of his coloured servant, Jacob Simmons." They had stripped the structure down to its basic pole which was held up by guy ropes. The pole was

27.

in two sections, the upper dropping into a socket at the top of the lower section. It was while manoeuvring the parting of the two that the whole remaining apparatus collapsed throwing the two men to the ground. Ethardo, from his experience, managed to save himself from harm, but Simmons was insensible and ministered to by a surgeon. He came round later in the day but barely able to walk.

1858_11_23 DUBLIN (Circus). FATAL ACCIDENT TO GYMNAST

Macarte and Clarke's Circus was ending its season with a series of benefits. James Cooke produced the astonishing feat of throwing a triple somersault in the air as a special treat for the benefit of the popular Alfred Moffatt. On the following night, Edward Platt a clever acrobat thought he would try the same feat to liven up his own benefit. To achieve this he stood at the front of the gallery while 12 men held a large quilt stationed over a thick mattress in the centre of the ring. The distance was around 22 feet. He failed to perform a triple, executing what was only 2½ somersaults, landing head first, dislocating his neck and fracturing his spine. He was rushed to hospital but predicted unlikely to survive more than three or four days. He was completely paralysed and although in full possession of his mental faculties and able to speak, nevertheless died on 3 December. He was 28 years of age.

When Cooke's turn came for his benefit, he advertised he would throw a quadruple somersault, but in view of the horror provided by Platt's failure, it was judged prudent to ban Cooke from essaying the feat.

1858_11_30 LONDON (Astley's). ACCIDENT TO MR COOKE JR

William Cooke Jr, the leading equestrian of the day, suffered another accident when rehearsing a new hippodrama. Again he was trapped under his horse (*see 1858_06_10*), and this time Cooke had his leg broken. The press statement that his leg had been amputated was refuted by his father who, playing down the accident, said his son was progressing as well as could be expected. Cooke Snr also saw fit to write to the papers that the Queen and Prince Albert had sent a messenger to enquire after his son, and "In heartfelt gratitude for such condescending honour, I should wish the public to know that our Majesty's feeling heart is ever open to the poor player and equestrian under affliction. Long may our country be blessed with this bright example of greatness is the fervent prayer of her humble and grateful subject." Which nowadays reads absurdly unctuous. Cooke returned on 26 March.

1859_06_14 LEEDS (Gala). TIGHTROPE WALKER FALLS FROM ON HIGH

There were almost 20,000 people in the gardens when Madame Rossini appeared on a tightrope some 30ft in the air, stretched over the Great Lake. Having completed most of her act, she had returned to her starting place amid fireworks when a stay rope burned through causing her to fall on to the lake bank and then roll into the lake itself. Mr Bishop the surgeon was sent for and on examining her after her ducking, found she had dislocated her hip. The fireworks were to blame.

1859_10_13c BALLAARAT, Australia (Theatre). ACCIDENT TO JULIA HARLAND

[Julia Harland, (c1825–1872) born Julia Susannah Wallack in the USA, sister of James William Wallack, was married to English actor William Hoskins – who claimed to have taught elocution to Henry Irving – in 1850. In 1856, the couple emigrated to Australia, touring extensively until 1858 when Hoskins became lessee of the theatre at Ballaarat where the accident below occurred.]

Miss Harland slipped and fell, breaking a small bone in her arm. She played in excruciating agony with her arm in a sling, which was brave but the audience would have preferred her to have retired because they thought it cruel for her to perform in such a state. The game girl was prepared to tackle the afterpiece too, but the manager Mr Brown forbade it and substituted another play.

1859_11_05 MANCHESTER (Bell's).   ACCIDENT TO ONE OF THE BROTHERS HANLON

[Founded in the early 1840s, the troupe consisted of the six Hanlon brothers – George, William, Alfred, Thomas, Edward and Frederick. Though all born in Manchester or Liverpool, they were vastly popular in America and throughout Europe. The older members were trained by Professor John Lees, and when he died they added his name in tribute to become the Hanlon-Lees. They were versatile jugglers, acrobats and aerialists, and performed in knockabout sketches that were self-devised.

In 1866, the six split into two separate units and took on other gymnasts and apprentices so that over the years the name Hanlon covered many different actual performers. The Hanlons thus continued in various forms until the early 1900s.]

While performing at Bell's Hippodrome, William fell, dislocating his elbow, but "with perfect sang froid" said he would be back within a week. In fact it was six months before he was fit enough to resume work. During his time off all the brothers moved to America where they became a major attraction for many years and after the invention of the flying trapeze (*see next entry*) William soon became highly adept, starring as one of the leading gymnasts in the USA.

1859_11_12 PARIS, France (Cirque Napoleon)   THE FIRST EVER FLYING TRAPEZE ACT

[By no means an accident, this was a historical landmark – but did lead to a great many accidents thereafter! Jules Léotard was born in Toulouse, France on 1 March 1838, the son of a gymnastics instructor who ran a swimming pool. At the age of 18 he began to experiment with trapeze bars, ropes and rings, and is said to have practiced his routines over the pool which would be a safety measure when he fell. Suspended trapezes and Roman rings had been long known but Léotard invented the first 'flying trapeze' routine utilising three swinging trapeze bars in a row progressing from one to another, making a public debut on 12 November 1859 at Cirque Napoleon. Although the dancer's ubiquitous costume is named after him, his own costume was

28.

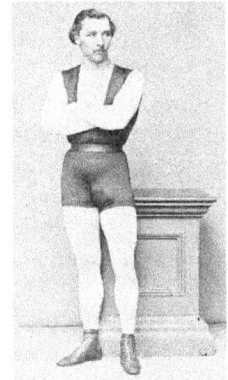

29. *Léotard*

known as a *maillot* or swimsuit, presumably developed from his outfit while practising over his dad's pool. Léotard died from a contagious illness, possibly smallpox, at the age of 32 on 17 August 1870.]

1859_11_29 HALIFAX (Theatre).   ARROW ACCIDENT TO ACTOR

[The story of William Tell wherein a father has to shoot an apple off his son's head was very popular in Victorian times and many versions were produced. The story was so well known that trick sharpshooters could reference it in their act. (*see 1877_09_20c and 1882_11_30*)]

Mr Watson was acting in the play *William Tell* and in the scene where Tell instructs his son in the art of archery by practising at a target, Watson was holding a sheepskin near the target to shield other actors who might be passing by. He had just warned a lady to take care of flying arrows when one struck him in his own eye. The sight was immediately destroyed.

34

1860_01_10c FRANCE (Circus).   FATAL ACCIDENT TO LADDER ACT

[This must have been a particularly awkward accident as the act in progress would not have been a particularly dangerous one. Usually known as 'an unsupported ladder act', this routine is based on a specially built metal ladder with wide rungs normally about 6ft to 8ft high, sometimes higher. The performer stands on the next to the top rung with the top rung between his legs. In this basic position he keeps his balance by gently rocking the ladder, and 'walking' it in small steps. Performers once in place atop the apparatus normally carry out juggling, do handstands etc or as in the case here play a musical instrument. The performance often takes place on a raised dais, otherwise on a flat board on the ground.]

We know nothing of Mr Price, our subject, except he was performing in a circus in France, playing the violin whilst at the top of his ladder. *The Journal du Havre* said: " Mr. Price, who at the Cirque, it may be remembered, played the violin so well, while standing on a ladder placed perpendicularly on a platform, and which he at the same time made to move about, has just met with a fatal accident in one of the cities in the centre of France. By a false movement he fell from the ladder and was killed on the spot."

1860_02_06 BATH (Cooke's Circus).   EQUESTRIAN ACCIDENT

Mr Cooke and his circus often seem to have suffered from a varied collection of accidents to buildings and personnel, some of which are included in the companion volume. On this occasion it was Mr Adams the equestrian clown falling from his horse while in the sketch *The Grandmother*. He bashed himself against the ring fence breaking his arm in two places. He was patched up in hospital and progressed favourably thereafter.

1860_02_15c NEW YORK, USA (Cooke's).   EQUESTRIAN ACCIDENT

Mr Cooke again, this time at his newly created American establishment at Niblo's Garden. In a spectacle called *The Sports of Old England* Mr Armstrong, a very active and daring equestrian, was thrown violently to the ground when his horse jibbed at jumping a hedge. For all his skill and agility, he was unable to break his fall and fractured his arm in two places. He was taken off to be attended to by a surgeon while the show continued. Then another, unnamed, equestrian took a tumble while attempting to leap a fence on a bareback horse. In his case after "a little repose" he mounted the unruly steed and continued to the enthusiastic applause of the audience. Armstrong was able to return to the ring in mid-July.

1860_03_15c MEMPHIS, USA (Theatre).   SULLIVAN ALMOST KILLS HIS CORDELIA

Barry Sullivan was on an 18-month tour of America. On this night he was acting King Lear, his Cordelia being Jenny Stanley. In the final scene the dead Cordelia is carried on in the arms of Lear with a rope round her neck, as she has been hanged. As the actor laid the corpse gently on to the stage floor, unnoticed by all, the rope had become entangled around her neck and when the final curtain fell she was truly insensible. It must have been a worrisome time for Sullivan as "it was several minutes before she could be restored to consciousness." Sullivan himself had several accidents (*see* 1868_10_23).

30. *Barry Sullivan*

1860_06_18c MELBOURNE, Australia   CHILD THROWN FROM ON HIGH

[Gustavus Brooke (1818–1866) toured the English provincial theatres for some years, as a leading tragedian. In 1848, he made a successful debut in London as Othello and other roles. In December 1851, he went to America for a triumphant 18 months. In 1854, Brooke went to Australia to give two hundred performances in the major towns there which proved so fruitful he stayed in Australia for more than six years.

On his return to England about the middle of 1861, he played a season at Drury Lane with so little success that he found himself in financial difficulties having lost large sums in unsuccessful business ventures. He was also drinking heavily. Eventually, he decided to return to Australia where he had had such acclaim, leaving Plymouth on 1 January 1866 in a ship which went down in a storm ten days later. He was 47 years old. The accident below happened during his last year in Australia before returning to England.]

31. *G V Brooke*

Acting the role of Gambia in *The Slave*, Brooke had to throw a child across a chasm to its parents. The child, played by a six-year-old called Master Willie Brooke – apparently no relation – had a harness clipped to a wire so that he could actually swing across when he was 'thrown'. At this performance somebody neglected to clip the wire, so Brooke, not realising anything untoward, went ahead and flung the child who, instead of gracefully gliding across, fell with a wallop on to the stage. The curtain was lowered and manager Mr Jackson came forward and said the boy was not hurt and would shortly reappear, which he did to thunderous applause.

1860_07_31 NEW YORK, USA (Niblo's).   THOMAS HANLON FALLS

The six Hanlon Brothers were back in America performing at Niblo's Garden when Thomas fell to the stage, a distance of some 40 ft. While still in the air he was able to turn his body so that he landed on his feet which caused considerable jarring to the tendons of his foot. He said the cause of the fall was the fact he had not worked for some days and his hand was soft and unable to hold his grip. He returned to the stage to acknowledge the plaudits of the audience and to show he was not seriously hurt, then limped away. Thomas had had a previous fall on 30 January and it will be recalled that William Hanlon had an accident when performing in Manchester (*see* 1859_11_05); that occasion and now this were claimed to be the only two accidents suffered by the original troupe.

1860_08_23 DUBLIN (Gala).   FATAL ACCIDENT AT "BLONDIN'S IRISH DEBUT"

[Charles Blondin (1824–1897) was a Frenchman born Jean-François Gravelet. At the age of five, he was sent to the École de Gymnase at Lyon and, after six months of training as an acrobat, made his first public appearance as The Boy Wonder. He developed into a man wonder and joined the famous Ravel family troupe of gymnasts who went to the USA in 1855. Certainly an excellent circus performer, in 1859 he achieved world-wide fame by crossing the Niagara Falls on a tightrope.]

"Blondin" was appearing at an outdoor gala at the Portobello Gardens. He was in the middle of the rope when his apparatus collapsed killing two men who had been employed to erect it. The dead men, James Cunningham and Patrick Neal, were employees at the Gardens who had been chosen to carry out the construction of the rope set-up as instructed by Daniel Morel, employed by Blondin to supervise his equipment. Morel was arrested.

There was much discussion about the rope that had apparently broken allowing the poles of wooden support towers to fall on the two men. It was of 5" circumference, around 2" in diameter; it had been used many times, and last used two weeks previously at Bath, but was examined to see any flaws that would account for its breaking. As Blondin pointed out – of course he thought it was perfectly safe, otherwise he would not have ventured on it. He had had a narrow escape and could easily have lost his own life. What is more, he said he would trust his life to the remaining portion of the rope.

Eventually, it was decided to blame the unknown manufacturer of the rope, but Blondin and Daniel Morel were arrested and kept in custody. The following day they were released on their own bail of £50 each, to appear when called upon to answer a charge of manslaughter. In October, it was decided that there was no charge against Blondin but one stood in the case of Morel and a warrant for his arrest was issued. Neither man was in court but thought to be back in Niagara where Blondin's latest feats included crossing many times with variations such as blindfold, pushing a man in a wheelbarrow, his feet in baskets, on short stilts and with his manager on his back. It is said he offered to take the Prince of Wales across on his back, an offer politely declined.

In Dublin a fund had been set up for the widows and families of the two deceased men and in March 1861 Widow Cunningham thanked all the contributors and announced she had been able to open a shop for "the sale of cakes, fruit, toys and trimmings."

In January 1861, Blondin wrote to *The Era* newspaper from the USA announcing his intention of coming to the UK at the suggestion of the Prince of Wales. He had heard that a number of "Blondins" were about and he wished to show the nation's inhabitants the genuine article. *He had never previously been to the British Isles.* The item above concerns an imposter! I think I am the first writer to reveal this, previous references assuming the Portbello incident was the UK debut of the genuine Blondin.

When the real Hero of Niagara arrived to appear at London's Crystal Palace, an English tightrope walker called d'Alberte claimed to be able to duplicate all Blondin's feats and became well known himself for performing similar stunts at high altitude over English rivers and gorges. As he was often referred to as "Blondin's double" I suspect this was the man in the Portobello accident, especially as he gave his name in court as Albert Blondin.

After a sensational season at the Crystal Palace in London where he was paid £100 a night, on 14 and 15 August 1861, the genuine Blondin appeared at the Portobello Gardens before the Dublin public and they idolised him just as London had done. Nowhere was there a whisper about the previous year's imposter and the tragic

32. *The one and only Blondin*

consequences. d'Alberte (Albert Daniel Morton), whose performance seldom lived up to the promises of his advertising, had reasonable success for a few years before marrying and with his dancer wife becoming a music hall song-and-dance act.

1860_09_06 LONDON (Princess's). ACCIDENT TO FLYING WITCHES

During a performance of *Macbeth* – in those days more like a musical with a bevy of singing witches – a section of the machinery used in the ascent of the witches gave way, falling upon the stage beneath, seriously harming Mr H Saker who was playing Second Witch and "bruising some of his brother actors who were very near him at the time." The mishap having been observed in full view of the audience, led to wild rumours of greater misfortune being erroneously spread. Nevertheless Saker, though out of danger, was unable to work for several weeks.

1860_09_06 CAMBRIDGE (Theatre) ACCIDENT TO MISS AMY SEDGWICK

[Amy Sedgwick (1835–1897), born in Bristol as Sarah Gardiner, made her debut in 1853 then appeared throughout the provinces including a three year booking in Manchester. Her London debut was in 1857. She excelled in light comedy roles and was always available to give her comic version of Serjeant Buzzfuzz at charity events. Another speciality was her dramatic recitation of *The Charge of the Light Brigade* accompanied on the trumpet by a survivor of the Battle of Balaclava. She had three marriages due to short-lived husbands, retiring after each but always coming back.]

33. *Amy Sedgwick*

This popular actress had arrived at Cambridge to make a guest appearance as Pauline in *The Lady of Lyons* a part in which she had made her name and was expected to excel. Arriving at the theatre at the usual time she slipped on a step as she made her way along an "ill-contrived, dark, and narrow descent". She fell with some violence to the ground, twisting her ankle so painfully she could not bear her foot on the ground. The part was played by a substitute. On the following night, still unable to perform, to appease her fans she sat in a chair and read a scene from *The School for Scandal,* and several poems including *The Charge of the Light Brigade*. She was obliged to delay her return to her role at the Haymarket

1860_10_11 PARIS, France (Hippodrome) ACCIDENT TO TRIO OF TIGHTROPE WALKERS

At the Paris Hippodrome, an "aerian trio" would make a "pyramidical ascension at a height of 100 feet above the ground". In publicity, the trio were named as Mdlle Louise, M Hippolyte and M Francais, but after the accident were described as a father and two sons.

Whatever the combination of the personnel, the fact of the accident was that while arranging themselves into a daring combined pose on parallel wires, one of the ropes broke, precipitating them 75ft downwards, turning over as they fell. The audience shrieked and several women fainted. The artistes were carried out and medical attention summoned. The director of the venue entered and said that the performance must of course terminate, asking the audience to leave in an orderly fashion.

One of the trio was killed instantly in front of the audience, one died in hospital and the third was lingering in great danger. It was probably from this moment that a swell of public opinion arose against high tightrope walkers. Blondin, who was so expert that he died an old man in his bed, was blamed for other people taking up 'Blondism', so fomenting the idea that the practice should be banned.

1860_11_05 HULL (Queen's).   ACTOR FALLS DOWN OPEN TRAP DOOR

Frank Calhaem was taking part in a new play called *Cartouche* in which, during the last act, he had to make his exit via a trap door in the stage. Lifting the trap he prepared to descend but lost his balance, falling heavily through to the floor of the cellar under the stage. The distance was only eight feet, but he sustained a serious injury to his spine.

1860_11_20c TROY, USA.   ACCIDENT TO BLONDIN

"Blondin at Troy, a few days ago, fell off the rope while turning a somersault on stilts, the cause of the calamity being the breaking of a crotch which held the rope. He was considerably though not badly hurt. Except the firework burning, this is his first accident of any importance." *The Era* 1860_12_16.

1860_12_28 GT YARMOUTH (Theatre).   SUDDEN DEATH OF PANTOMIME CLOWN

Not strictly an accident. "The pantomime at the Theatre had a melancholy fInale on Friday evening last. After the harlequinade was over the Clown named Algar went to the dressing-room, but before he had changed his clothes, he was seized with sickness, and laid down and died almost immediately. It seemed that the poor fellow was suffering from disease of the lungs whilst he was endeavouring to set his audience in a roar with his jokes and drolleries." *Taunton Courier and Western Advertiser* 1861_11_09.

1861_01_07 LONDON (Astley's).   MAN MAULED TO DEATH BY LION

At 8am James Crockett, the 'lion tamer' of the lions at Astley's received a message to say the lions had got loose. Hastening there he seized a two pronged hayfork and found a lioness out of its cage sitting – like a dog over a bone – over a man lying on the ground. He drove the lion away, picked up the man and carried him up to the hall. The man, a circus worker named Smith also known as Jarvey, was covered in blood and dead from hideous wounds.

34. *James Crockett*

Crockett went back to the cage which housed three lions. The cage was of iron bars surrounded with sections of wooden shutters; there were two down and the barred door – opening inwards – was open. At the inquest it was stated by Crockett that he had lowered one of the shutters previously, but could not account for the other one being lowered. He said that particular beast wagon had travelled for three years over roads of all kinds, including stony and bumpy surfaces, and he had never known a panel to fall accidentally. The lions and cage belonged to Mr Sanger of Sanger's Circus and were appearing on an option contract having been there on that basis for nine weeks. When he was asked if he was sure he had locked the door after lowering the panel, Crockett said he was perfectly sure. When asked if the lions had been fed, Crockett replied he never fed them on Sundays, and that they would sometimes go four or five days without food.

A doctor described the wounds – totalling 80 in number from deep to superficial – minutely and suggested from the positions that the man had been attacked from behind. The jury returned a verdict of 'accidental death' with a recommendation that a stronger cage should be made to contain animals such as lions. The coroner said Crockett was absolved from any blame, but warned that any recurrence of such a case would result in a trial for manslaughter.

A letter under the pseudonym Vox was published in *The Era* suggesting a testimonial in the shape of a belt with lions thereon should be awarded to Crockett for his bravery in rounding up the escaped lions. The suggestion was made by Mr Batty the lessee of Astley's, and contributions came promptly from the Sanger Brothers (£10), Batty (£5) and a whip round of Sanger's Company brought in two dozen contributions ranging from 1/- to 10/-. Sanger made himself responsible for all expenses of the accident including the funeral, paid for the dead man's father to travel from a distant town, and added "a handsome *douceur*" (ie a 'sweetener').

1861_01_16 SHEFFIELD (Theatre Royal).   ACTOR IN TRAP ACCIDENT

40
Mr Williams was acting in the play *The Will and the Way* in which he had to disappear into "a mysterious passage". This was accomplished by his lifting up a stage trap and descending six or seven feet to a kind of mezzanine floor at that level. Below this floor there was a deep cellar into which scenery was lowered. Mr Williams on reaching the mezzanine was on a platform with railings round three sides. He should have stepped forward, but instead he stepped backwards thus falling into the scenery pit. In falling he struck a projecting beam leaving him with four broken ribs.

1861_03_28 LONDON (Alhambra Palace).   FALL OF FLYING TRAPEZE ARTISTE

Since Léotard's invention, (*see* 1859_11_12) he and many others had developed the basic principal of the flying trapeze. At this venue a troupe called the Rocky Mountain Wonders were attracting great applause for their feats. At the very end of the act, the star of the troupe, a man named Maggelton, known as 'The Spider' fell head first. Underneath the trapeze a wooden platform had been erected with a mattress designed to prevent injury should there be a fall. This precaution proved useless as he was severely injured in the spine. *As I write this, many present circuses have an aerialist dressed as Spiderman from the cinema franchise.*

1861_04_08 LONDON (Alhambra Palace).   ON WITH THE SHOW WITH REPEATED FALLS

After Maggelton's accident (*see above*), the trapeze act had been on hold, although billed for Easter Monday minus The Spider. The two fliers J B Rochette, and J E Fisher were presumably the other Rocky Mountain Wonders, with Rochette taking over Maggelton's role. At the very first effort, one of the ropes came loose and Fisher was thrown on to the stage below. He fell heavily, but appearing uninjured, mounted to try again. Many in the audience protested at the continuance, but the ropes were re-adjusted and the performance continued. Both men repeatedly fell but persisted until they had accomplished all they attempted, retiring amid loud applause. The absent Maggelton was progressing favourably in hospital having partially regained the use of his limbs.

1861_05_04 PARIS, France (Cirque Napoleon). BOYS ON THE FLYING TRAPEZE

35. *Cirque Napoleon*

This is not a tale of woe, far from it. I have included this as a counter to the people mentioned in the above entry, and because of much anti-child gymnast propaganda that crops up later. At the Cirque Napoleon in Paris, the venue where Léotard first showed the new act, three "slim, healthy-looking, bright-eyed boys of 15, 14 and 13 as well as could be judged" performed on three trapezes as if it were the "finest piece of fun in the world". Henri, Steckel and Joseph Pfau executed all their tricks with perfection to thunderous applause. In 1868, Joseph joined the Hanlons who since 1866 had recruited young boys to train and present their own act as "Hanlon Midgets". The idea of developing new talent to take over from the original Hanlons as they aged seemed a good idea at the time. However, these recruits adopted the Hanlon name as their own causing William Hanlon later in life much time and trouble.

1861_09_06 CAMBRIDGE (Theatre). TRAP ACCIDENT TO MRS HOOPER

Mrs Hooper slipped at a trapdoor at the theatre, greatly damaging her ankle. It is a curious coincidence that this accident happened in the same theatre on exactly the same date that the previous year Amy Sedgwick had her misfortune which also damaged the ankle.(*see* 1860_09_06).

1861_10_30 LONDON (Crystal Palace). ACCIDENT TO BLONDIN

[Blondin made his London debut in 1861 (*see* 1860_08_23) and he earned prodigious amounts of money. His influence was great and many new performers appeared 'doing a Blondin'. Alas, many of these attempted feats beyond their powers and accidents were manifold. The rumours of the fees that Blondin commanded were a spur for mundane performers who were lucky to get £5 a week. Thus appeared an American Blondin, a Swedish Blondin, an African Blondin, Young Blondin, Le Petit Blondin etc and a host of Female Blondins, and one's mind boggles at the thought of a Baby Blondin! The incident below was during Blondin's first season in England.]

This day was the final day of Blondin's season and he was making his 33rd ascent on the rope. In the afternoon, he had crossed a lower rope slung across the indoor transept and during this his pole, breaking in two parts, had fallen into the organ. Even the newspaper report was suspicious that this was but a ploy to increase the excitement, as Blondin coolly picked up another pole. The long balancing poles used by tightrope walkers at a height are heavily weighted at the ends to hold down the man in the centre of gravity. So watch out if such a pole is ever dropping your way!

36. *Blondin in trouble?*

The evening show, on a higher rope outdoors, concluded with fireworks. Blondin's final feat was to push along a wheelbarrow full of exploding fireworks. When he got to the platform at the end of the rope, the man who was to take the barrow must have it done it clumsily, as it threw Blondin off balance and, dropping his pole, he ended head downwards clinging on to the rope by his legs. Swinging himself upright he regained his platform and bowed to the thundering plaudits of the crowd of 12,077 people. Perhaps another ploy to generate excitement? There is a phrase 'throwing a trick' which gymnasts use. This means deliberately failing to achieve what they are trying to do. Of course they have to repeat it which they then do successfully, thus gaining extra applause. Nowadays, first-class performers do not stoop to such tricks, but third-raters still do. There are suspicions that both Blondin and Léotard were not above such antics.

1861_11_11 EDINBURGH (Queen's).   LEADING MAN STRUCK ON THE NOSE

The opera was *Norma* with top stars Mdlle Tietjens and Signor Giuglini. In the scene where Norma goes to strike a sacred gong, in error Tietjens struck Giuglini on the nose with the drumstick, immediately drawing blood. The error would have passed unnoticed, but a minute or two later Giuglini fled the stage leaving his colleague stranded, and the curtain suddenly dropped. Manager Wyndham appeared, explained the slight accident, and within a few minutes the Signor presented himself again, and, with the blushing priestess, brought the Opera to a brilliant close. A funny nose story?   37. *Mdlle Tietjens*

1861_11_18 STAMFORD (Theatre).   ACCIDENT TO TRAPEZE ARTISTE

George Balfour was attempting to leap from the *cord elastique* to a trapeze above. Either the trapeze was set too high or he misjudged the power of his leap because, failing to reach it, he fell 30ft on to his head. There were two medical men in the boxes who immediately attended to him. After their ministrations Balfour reappeared to "appease the anxiety" then was taken to his lodgings.

1861_12_23c LONDON (Standard).   ACCIDENT TO PANTO COLUMBINE

In the Standard Theatre pantomime Kate Maudelbert was to have played the Princess in *The Sleeping Beauty in the Wood* and afterwards Columbine, but on the final day of rehearsals she broke her leg and was confined to bed. Her doctor said it would be several weeks before she could resume her professional duties which was on 25 February 1862 when she played Ophelia in *Hamlet*.

1862_01_10 ABERDEEN (Bon Accord).   ACCIDENT TO TIGHTROPE WALKER

Mrs Davies, described as a rope-dancer – now an outmoded description – fell while "doing some of Blondin's feats". One of the guy ropes gave way causing her to fall 25ft and break her arm.

1862_02_01c BOURGES, France (Theatre).   TRAPDOOR ACCIDENT TO ACTRESS

Madame Coste was appearing in a tableau in the fairy play *Amours du Diable* in which she had to sink through the stage. Her foot slipped and she fell nearly 30ft, striking her head on the edge of the opening in the stage as she dropped. Remarkably, apart from a wound to the head, her other injuries were slight. It was the second accident she had suffered within a year at Bourges.

1862_02_20 BRUSSELS, Belgium (Theatre Royal).   FELLED BY COLLAPSING SCENERY

The play was *Jerusalem* and actors representing a group of crusaders were passing over a scenery mountain. This gave way at one end and the actors were thrown violently on to the stage. It was particularly alarming as they were carrying lances and other weapons which, in the confusion, could have caused serious injury, but only two actors were slightly hurt, the rest getting off scot-free.

1862_02_28 BELFAST (Bell's Hippodrome).   ACCIDENT TO THE LEAPING M CLEVORI

It was the final week of the season at Bell's Circus and the benefits were taking place. M Clevori performed on a fixed trapeze placed 50ft above the ring. His final trick was "a leap for life" to a second bar which he only managed to reach with one hand and, losing his grasp, fell. He landed on his back and shoulder and was taken to the General Hospital where he was found to have "sustained a serious concussion of the spine". The local press opined that such performances were "not conducive to the amusement of a respectable audience. Indeed, rather are they repulsive, it being evident that such feats cannot be accomplished without great risk to life."

Clevori cannot have been too badly injured as he was advertised as appearing at the next stand on 12 April and resumed his "leap for life" for the rest of the tour.

1862_03_10 LIVERPOOL (Theatre Royal).   ANOTHER ACCIDENT TO BLONDIN

At Blondin's opening performance at this venue the attendance was very poor which was remarkable for a man who had just had a season in London at £100 a night and was the talk of world. Presumably, the toff element thought such a performer was misplaced at the ex-patent theatre, and the lower orders were not used to attending such a venue. Blondin, of course, presented his usual routine regardless, and all went well until his final feat which was to traverse a rope from the stage up to the front of the gallery with a man on his back. The gallery end of the rope passed over an iron bar before being tied off. When Blondin reached the top the bar gave way, allowing the rope to suddenly jerk and drop 12 inches throwing Blondin on to his back. However, nothing daunted he continued, gaining his feet, and still carrying the man, returned down the rope to the stage.

He reappeared on Tuesday, but it was announced on Wednesday that he had presented a medical certificate stating his inability to appear for some time to come. So either he was more injured than supposed, or business was still poor and he was not going to risk his life and reputation for a mere handful of provincial snobs.

1862_04_10 SHEFFIELD (Surrey).   ACCIDENT TO FEMALE BLONDIN

In December 1860, Madame Salvi fell while walking above a big top. In falling, she managed to catch the wire with one of her arms, and was eventually rescued by men with a ladder. At Scarborough in March 1861, Madame Salvi, had a "narrow escape for her life, at least her limbs", due to strong gusts of winds which caused her to fall. At the Surrey Music Hall in Sheffield she was performing – as many tightrope walkers did in theatres – over the pit audience on a sloping rope anchored at the ends on stage and the gallery. She went up and down in various ways, including blindfold. She did her act successfully for three days, but on the fourth night the wire broke, precipitating her some 25ft into the sparsely occupied pit below falling amongst the seating. Medical aid was summoned and it was found she had broken some ribs and was taken to have them bound up.

43

1862_06_22 ST ETIENNE, France.   M LAURENÇON LOSES HAND IN ACCIDENT

Étienne-Hugues Laurençon was a comic dancer, considered by many to be the natural successor to the great Mazurier. He was performing with the actors of the Grand Theatre of Lyons in the ballet of *St Job*. He had a comic scene where he attempted to commit suicide with a wild-goose gun, the long barrel reaching over his shoulder. On this occasion the gun burst, and Laurençon's left hand was almost blown off. Amputation was immediately performed, and the patient was expected to recover.

1862_08_08 LONDON (Canterbury).   ACCIDENT TO TRAPEZE ARTISTE

Max Argonaud was presenting his act shortly before 11pm when he attempted to fly from one trapeze to another, misjudged the distance and fell with a resounding crash on to one of the large chandeliers illuminating the hall. He suffered severe but not fatal injuries.

1862_08_14 LONDON (Highbury Barn).   ACCIDENT TO A FEMALE BLONDIN

This was another accident that made a big public impression. Selina Young, known as The Female Blondin – there were several of these – was performing at Highbury Barn Gardens. She had, the previous season, gained much publicity from crossing the Thames on a tightrope. On this occasion she started her act on a rope some 70ft off the ground. She did several crossings including blindfold, with a wheelbarrow etc with great success. At her final stunt, however, things went amiss. She was crossing with a long balancing pole with fireworks on both ends designed to explode in turn, in pairs. Maintaining an equilibrium until Miss Young was three quarters across, the firecrackers got out of sync disturbing the performer who, dropping the pole, staggered, then fell, catching the rope with her leg, and hanging there for a moment until she dropped head first into the trees beneath. Medical assistance was prompt, but it was feared that the lady would be crippled for life.

The proprietors said they had apprehensions because of the wet conditions, the rope would be slippery and thus too dangerous for her to attempt the act that night, and had tried to persuade her not to perform. Is it too cynical to assume that they were trying to shuffle out of any responsibility?

Selina Young became something of a cause célèbre when it was revealed she had an invalid sister and aged parent to support. A fund for contributions was set up, and a benefit performance where both Blondin and Léotard appeared with other gymnasts. Mr Giovanelli the manager of Highbury Barn Gardens held a benefit which raised £78.18.0d but with expenses deducted made only £41.4.1d for the damaged gymnast.

The above two accidents in quick succession were widely disseminated with dozens of newspapers repeating the original reports. Some newspapers took the opportunity to register disapproval of such entertainments with attacks on several fronts presented in summary thus:

Unlike the Spaniard with his bull fighting, we no longer tolerate cruelty to animals – the RSPCA was founded in 1824, the first Cruelty to Animals Act was passed in 1835 – so why do we tolerate cruelty to human beings? Prize fighting where men deliberately attack each other has long been controlled by formulated rules. Why are there no rules to prevent men and women risking their lives? This argument seemed to imply that gymnasts risked their lives to avoid poverty.

The huge fees paid to Blondin and Léotard encouraged untrained people to attempt to emulate them to earn similar amounts. Many people still live with this fantasy attitude today – they think if a top footballer earns £200,000 a week then somebody who is a tenth as good earns £20,000 a week (he doesn't). In fact, traditionally pantomime performers (the main occupation of gymnastic performers prior to music halls) were notoriously poorly paid compared to actors, who in turn were poorly paid compared to opera singers. Even the most famous pre-Victorian clown Grimaldi at the height of his fame (1810–20) only earned £12 a week (£900 in today's money).

Aerial performers are pandering to the basest tastes and morbid appetites of man, who simply go to see if they will fall and kill themselves. If Blondin performed on a rope a mere eight feet from the ground he would be just as skilful and the public would watch him with pleasure and not in fear and trepidation.

Even if the audience is absolved of being so degraded as to actually desire accident and death, it is deluded into a supposition of peril for the purpose of excitement, a tendency which transgresses natural boundaries and a more wholesome public taste is desirable.

The performances are dangerous to the public as the trapeze artists and wirewalkers often have their apparatus slung above the pit.

1862_08_17c LEEDS (Amphitheatre).   TWO ACCIDENTS AT THE AMPHITHEATRE

Detard was appearing at the Amphitheatre in an act based on that of Léotard, swinging from one trapeze to another. He misjudged a leap, missed the second bar and fell to the stage. He landed on his feet, smashing both kneecaps and suffering other injuries. He was taken to Leeds Infirmary.

Later, M Stevetti a gymnast whose speciality was leaping over chairs was turning a somersault over six chairs lined up with legs in the air, and hit a projecting leg on the sixth chair which punctured his lung. He was called before the curtain and took his bow with hand over chest, oozing blood. On his exit he promptly fainted and he too ended up in Leeds Infirmary breathing through a tube. Following closely on the previous two accidents the same paragraph was widely disseminated through the national press.

1862_08_20c LE HAVRE, France.   ACCIDENT TO TRAPEZE ARTISTE

The acrobatic troupe of Maze and Leyznoie was appearing in a large tent in the town. An English youth aged about 16 whose name was given as Lionney, was performing the trapeze stunts of Léotard, and missing the second bar fell to the ground breaking his arm in two places. Presumably Leyznoie and Lionney are two different versions of the same name.

1862_09_13 SOUTH SHIELDS (Theatre).   TRAP ACCIDENT TO TRAGEDIAN

Mr and Mrs George Owen, were particularly popular in the area as George had formerly been the lessee of the theatre. They were engaged for three weeks and on the last night of their stay while performing in *The Corsican Brothers*, the tragedian fell down an open trap and broke his leg. The couple were due to open at Whitby on Monday, now "Mr Owen will be unable to appear on the boards of any theatre for some time to come." On 20 October, Owen, "now able to leave his bed", took the theatre again for four nights under the direction of Mrs Owen.

1862_12_31 NORTHFLEET. ACCIDENT TO TIGHTROPE WALKERS

Handbills touted a pair of wirewalkers on a vacant plot next to the road and near the church. A rope was stretched between two sets of poles at a height of 20ft from the ground. The female Blondin, about 18 years of age, climbed a ladder, and mounting the rope, crossed it there and back. Then donning a blindfold she started to repeat her walk while one of the party of gymnasts "a man of colour" climbed the poles to receive her. He had no sooner reached the top when he called for her to go back and at that moment the supporting pole broke in two and the two performers were thrown into the road. The female Blondin was bruised and shaken by the fall, but otherwise uninjured, whereas her companion had one arm broken in three places and was taken to Gravesend Infirmary.

In these entries I use 'wirewalker' and 'tightrope walker' indiscriminately.

1863_01_20c LONDON (Lyceum). SWORD ACCIDENT

[George Vining (1824–1875) was a member of the vast sprawling Vining theatrical family. He created a host of parts in new plays including Count Fosco in the first dramatization of *The Woman in White*. He was one of the many solid reliable actors always in work but never to achieve stardom.]

38. *George Vining*

The play was *The Duke's Motto*, the actors in a duel were Mr Fechter and George Vining. Fechter's foil was not buttoned and a thrust at Vining was not parried, causing the point to enter the actor's thigh. Vining was not aware of it at the time and the actors, ending the scene, made their exit. Fechter was in the wings waiting to make his re-entrance and realising his companion was not there hastily sent a message for Vining. (Today the stage manager would call through the Tannoy "Mr Vining, you're off!")

Vining was in his dressing room without his breeches, trying to stop a copious flow of blood. There was a short interval while Vining bandaged himself up, found another pair of breeches, and returned to the stage to carry on as though nothing had happened.

The show must go on!

1863_02_10c ST PETERSBURG, Russia. GUN ACCIDENT

In the play *Courier de Lyon* given for the benefit of M Haase, Act I ended with a scene featuring brigands firing guns. The pistol of Haase went off at half-cock and the charge struck the face of M Gerstel who was "taken away in a dreadful state". Fortunately the injuries proved not to be serious.

1863_02_14 BRIGHTON (Canterbury). ACCIDENT TO SLACK-WIRE PERFORMER

Don Jose Manoel, a Brazilian slack-wire performer, missed his balance and fell, landing on his feet. Unfortunately he landed on one of the gas burner footlights which pierced his foot. On examination by a doctor it was pronounced as merely a flesh wound between the big toe and second toe, but would keep the man from working for a short time. I do not know how short the time was but he was appearing at Chatham on 26 April.

46

1863_04_08 LIVERPOOL (Adelphi).   ACTRESS IN FALL ON STAGE

This was a burlesque of the popular play *The Peep O'Day* with Miss Elton in the role of Ann Kavanagh. In jumping down in the quarry scene she fell from the raised height on to the stage and broke a leg. However, she was confident that she would be able to resume her professional duties in two or three weeks.

1863_05_26 GREAT YARMOUTH.   ACROBAT'S FATAL FALL FROM MONUMENT

Not an onstage, but this was an accident to a professional acrobat caused by hubris triumphing over commonsense. Charles Marsh (36) and a colleague named Wharton, who were appearing in the town, ascended the tall Nelson monument on the South Denes. When they reached the viewing platform at the top, Marsh got outside and clambered up the caryatids, thence on to the statue of Britannia where he performed a handstand on her helmet. He lost his grip and fell to the ground, a distance of 140ft. Wharton, who had remained inside, did not realise his chum had clambered outside and, seeing he was no longer there, assumed he had descended the stairs again. Hastening down he arrived to find his friend sprawled out dead on the footpath. Marsh left a widow and family to mourn his foolish antics.

39. *Nelson Monument, Gt Yarmouth*

47

1863_06_25 LONDON (Cremorne).   FATAL FALL BY TIGHTROPE WALKER

At Cremorne Gardens for some two months, Carlos Valerio (25) an Italian attired in a golden costume, had walked a wire the whole length of the gardens – a distance of some 600ft – backwards and forwards, sometimes with his feet encased in baskets, at others with his head covered by a sack. On this night, when a shackle on his apparatus broke, Valerio fell 60ft to land on his head. When he fell, crowds gathered in distress, women cried and fainted, and three doctors who happened to be in the gardens that evening hastened to the rescue. Valerio was taken off to hospital, and half-an-hour later, the incident was forgotten, the crowds continuing with their dancing, eating and drinking. Valerio died within hours of having fallen.

As this tragic event followed less than a year after Selina Young was left a mangled cripple, (*see* 1862_08_14) along with other reported accidents, there was a righteous clamour taken up nationwide that such entertainments should be banned by law. Said a commentator in the *Oxford Times*: "The public are now at the point of disgust at ropewalking and all other man-monkey exhibitions. The death of poor Valerio, who fell from his 'wire rope' at Cremorne has rendered this kind of 'entertainment' peculiarly unpopular, and I trust the salutary reaction will be felt elsewhere." The newspaper was way off beam – aerial acts of all kinds were growing in popularity. A man-monkey was a form of gymnastic act where the performer dressed as an ape and Valerio, clad in a splendid gold costume, was not a man-monkey.

At the present time, I am the author of the first and only book devoted to man-monkeys. The subject is a fascinating one as it was not just a circus act but dramatic plays had an ape as a character.

1863_07_20 BIRMINGHAM (Gala).   **FATAL ACCIDENT TO FEMALE WIREWALKER**

Madame Geneive, a well-formed woman of around 35 years, was a high tightrope walker in the manner of Blondin, and the main attraction at a fête on Monday night in Aston Park. When the rope was produced for fitting up the equipment, it was seen to be 1½ in diameter but frayed and ragged in many places, causing an official to state he would not let a dog go on that. However, the apparatus was set up ready for the huge crowd that gathered in the spacious park.

DEATH ON THE ROPE.

40. *Madame Geneive*

There was a big cheer as Madame arrived and mounted to the platform where she was handed the balancing pole by her husband who also chalked the soles of her boots. Madame walked to the middle, knelt on her knees, stood on one leg, then walked back. Next her husband linked her arms with a chain, and her ankles with another. Thus encumbered she walked again across to the other platform where an assistant took off the chains and blindfolded the artiste. He then placed a cloth bag over her head and once again she moved forward. She had taken three steps only when the rope snapped, the man and platform collapsed backwards into the trees and Madame hurtled to the ground. Porter and Oates, two surgeons who happened to be in the grounds rushed to assist but it was fruitless, Madame Geneive was dead. "Another victim to the morbid and not too much to be reprehended taste for strong sensations, which disgraces English people in this nineteenth century."

The rope had broken at or near where Madame's husband had spliced it the previous day. It was disclosed that Madame was a local woman by the name of Powell, the daughter of a fairground clown known as Funny Joe, had six young children and was seven months pregnant with another. She only performed around a dozen times in the year clearing a profit of £8 or £9 each time.

In Parliament the Earl of Malmesbury drew attention to the accident and called upon the government to ban dangerous exhibitions. Earl Granville, acknowledging the disgraceful character of such exhibitions, said they were intended to gratify a morbid curiosity on the part of a portion of the public. However, he believed that an expression of censure on the part of Parliament and the force of the public press against such exhibitions would have "a far more beneficial effect than any legislative act". So the proposal for an act of Parliament was shelved. The Queen wrote to deplore that the park she and Albert had opened for healthy exercise and rational recreation should have been used for an exhibition that sacrificed a female subject to the gratification of the demoralising taste of shows that held great danger to the performers. A fund was set up for Madame's invalid husband and his children with a benefit at Vauxhall Gardens. However, these were early days in the battle to legislate against acrobats and there is much more conflict ahead.

48

1863_08_16c SEVILLE, Spain.   BLONDIN IN ACCIDENT
Blondin, who wrote from Spain to *The Era* to comment about the uproar against ladies falling off tightropes and killing or maiming themselves, claimed that in 30 years of performing he had never had an accident that caused him to leave the rope. Accidents happened to people who were untrained and worked cheaply, as opposed to well-practised artistes who not only have the talent to perform on the rope but also the skill and experience to hang on to it when something happens to go amiss.

He had probably only just posted this when, at a performance in Seville, he was walking the rope with a wheel of fireworks on his head pushing a barrow as was his wont. He used to have his daughter in the barrow but he was now forbidden to do that after the entire anti-rope furore started. Halfway across he set light to the fireworks on his head and the rotary motion was so violent that he let go of barrow and pole, and tried to unfasten the cord which held the firework contraption on his head. He suspended himself by one leg while he succeeded in ridding himself of the still exploding headgear, then came down in safety to wild cheering from his audience.

The cynical press said he had tried this trick before, it was 'an accident done on purpose', and he may perform it once too often. (*see* 1861_10_30).

1863_08_27 VALENCIA, Spain.   MADAME SAQUI REFUSED A LICENCE
This is not an accident but information about the famous Madame Saqui. The veteran tightrope dancer had been forbidden a licence to perform in France because of her age. She was thought to be 92! In fact, I think more truthfully she was about 77 – but still? Madame had moved to Valencia where she hoped to have better luck. (*see* 1846_03_22c).

1863_10_30 LEEDS (Amphitheatre).   TRAPEZE BOY INJURED IN FALL
The young French brothers James (13) and Thomas (12) were trapeze artistes working at a height of 20ft. James lost his hold and fell to the stage breaking both forearms, as well as incurring lesser injuries. "The proprietor of the Amphitheatre has announced that in future he will not allow any performances of a dangerous character." This was another accident to provide ammunition for the anti-gymnastics brigade.

1864_01_22c LONDON (Drury Lane).   FAMOUS PANTOMIMIST INJURED

Tom Matthews (1805–1889) was known as "the Clown with a mouth like Piccadilly Circus". He joined the company at Sadler's Wells Theatre in the early 1820s and was a pupil of Grimaldi, proud to own a wig and pair of shoes from his old master. Matthews appeared in pantomime at Covent Garden and Drury Lane as its principal clown for over forty years. At the time of this accident he was in his penultimate season.

Tom Matthews playing the part of Ali the Merchant in the annual pantomime, stumbled and rolled down an incline in the scenery of the Dwarf Kingdom. As a result he damaged his knee and was confined to bed with it considerably inflamed. He was off work for several days.

41. Tom Matthews

1864_03_12 LONDON (Lyceum). ACCIDENT TO MR FECHTER

[Charles Albert Fechter (1824–1879) was an Anglo-French actor who also trained as a sculptor. He had success in the French theatre for ten years including two years as actor-manager of the Odéon Theatre in Paris. He was lured to England with a tempting offer, arriving in 1860 after studying the English language. In 1863 he became actor-manager of the Lyceum Theatre. His later career after 1870 was spent in the USA.]

On this night, Fechter, playing Angelo in *Bel Demonio*, had an accident in a scene where he escapes through a window. His clothing caught on part of the scenery and he was momentarily turned and suspended upside down, his costume immediately either coming adrift or tearing caused him to drop to the stage head first. He suffered contusions over face, head and body and also a hand penetrated by his sword. He was off work, other plays being substituted, and expected to be back on stage on Easter Monday which was 28 March. In the event he returned on 2 April to play in a benefit for the sufferers of the Sheffield Inundation. (On 12 March a new dam serving Sheffield with its water had burst its retaining wall.) Fechter then went absent again as he still suffered from the sword wound, his part taken over by George Jordan. Also at this time Fechter had promised to play Hamlet for the Shakespeare Tercentenary Committee, which had put Samuel

42. *Charles Fechter*

Phelps's nose out of joint as he was expecting to play it. Fechter then withdrew, and chaos was caused. In the event the Committee had to settle for the less starry George Vining.

1864_03_28 LONDON (New Royalty). NEW ACTOR SUDDENLY DROPS DOWN DEAD

Mr H Seymour was playing the part of a miller in a burlesque, and having appeared in an early scene made his exit to backstage where he had a fit and died. The play carried on without the miller, and the audience was none the wiser about his subsequent absence it being the first night of a new work, so only informed of the death at the end of the evening.

Seymour was the *nom de theatre* of Richard Smith (38) formerly a time-keeper with the London General Omnibus Company and it was his first appearance on the stage. He had appeared very agitated throughout the evening. A post mortem showed the heart was enlarged, the lungs diseased, and half a pint of serum was on the brain. The man had been patently unfit to attempt such a nerve-wracking role as excitement was the immediate cause of death. "Verdict: Death from apoplexy".

1864_07_16 ST HELENS (Theatre Royal). FATAL ACCIDENT OF ACTOR-MANAGER

This is a case of a slight accident happening to be brushed off in order to follow the maxim that the show must go on.

Robert Stoddart, his brother and father were joint lessees of the theatre. On this Saturday night, Robert was due to act in a play, and at around 7pm, going from the stage to the orchestra to open a side door, his foot slipped and his chest was thrust heavily against a wooden beam. Nothing daunted he went on and acted two acts of the play but then fell down and had to be carried home. Dr Twyford discerned a ruptured blood vessel. Robert lingered until Monday morning then died.

1864_08_08 NIAGARA FALLS, USA.   ROPE WALKER FALLS CROSSING NIAGARA

[William Leonard Hunt, (1838–1929) known as Farini, was a rival to Blondin in Niagara-crossing stunts. Later he moved to London where he became a noted performer until 1869 when he gave up performing as he feared that one day he might fall. He then started producing aerial acts employing other performers, the most famous being a boy named Samuel Wasgatt (or Wasgate) whom he adopted at the age of ten. This youth went by the stage name El Niño Farini, and became known for an act where he hung from a trapeze supported only by his neck while playing a drum. Later he appeared in drag as Lulu the Male-Female Acrobat (see 1876_08_07). Farini also invented the 'Shot from a Cannon act' now known as the 'Human Cannonball' in 1876, the first flyer being the 14-year-old Rossa Richter known as Zazel. Hunt had a long, varied and adventurous life, but here he seems to have come unstuck.]

43. *William L Hunt*

The tightrope walker Farini, a rival to Blondin some years previously, was to attempt a crossing of Niagara on iron stilts on 15 August. On this day, he carried out a rehearsal, got halfway across when a stilt broke or gave way and Farini fell into the rapids. Fortunately, he was above Robinson's Island which stands on the very brink of the Falls, and he was able with a struggle to haul himself on to it. He had a leg injury and seated himself on a log with placidity. The man was stranded only 800ft from the bank, but surrounded by swirling rapids and only 200ft from the tremendous lip. Some forty-eight hours later it proved possible to get some food to him, but a method of rescue seemed as far off as ever.

It seems this escapade was milked like mad for publicity value. No doubt the fall was an actual accident, especially as this was a rehearsal and not the advertised performance. However, it was 'revealed' that Farini's brother threw a rope to him and contrived to remove him when spectators had left and he spent the night at the local inn. Who ever knows the truth in Victorian showbusiness, especially in the USA, home of showman supreme P T Barnum?

1864_09_19 HANLEY (Myers's Circus).   TRAPEZE FALL BY NOVICE ARTISTE

Mr Myers had arranged to give a special performance for local school children. It was oversubscribed and many disappointed youngsters turned away. One of the acts was a trapeze artiste* known as Young Julien, a youth who had once been a performer but for the last three years worked as the property keeper. As the former trapeze group had recently left the show, this youth volunteered to take up his dormant career again. He was performing at a height of 53ft when he fell to the ground landing on his hands and knees, his heading striking the ground with sickening violence. He was carried out insensible but with good fortune on his side had avoided serious injury and it was expected he would soon be able to resume his work.

*A point of interest occurs here – the press at large seemed not to have known the difference between a trapeze and a tightrope. In the report of this accident is the phrase "he had not been on the rope long", which would indicate a tightrope walker especially as the height was stated precisely. Probably because of the incidence of Blondin and the new invention of the flying trapeze by Léotard being contemporaneous, and accidents from performers working at a great height becoming common, they were all lumped together indiscriminately.

1864_09_25 MAGDEBURG, Germany.   FATAL ACCIDENT IN SCENERY COLLAPSE

"During the performance of *Robert and Bertram*, the scene of a part of the first act passes in a tower raised at a considerable height above the stage, and while the play was in progress the tower suddenly fell to the ground with two actors who were in it at the moment. Those men were both killed on the spot, an actress had her arm separated from her body, and a number of other persons received injuries from the fall of the beams and planks of which the tower was constructed." *Lloyd's Weekly Newspaper* 1864_09_25.

1864_09_28 KLAUZENBURG, Transylvania.   ARROW ACCIDENT TO INSPECTOR

The play was the old favourite *William Tell*. The lead actor being short-sighted mistook a signal and fired off his arrow prematurely. Unfortunately the theatre inspector was in the wings that night and he received the arrow in his eye. He fell to the ground unconscious and was stretchered off to hospital where "inflammation of the brain having soon after supervened, little hope is entertained of his recovery."

1864_11_07 HEREFORD (Theatre).   DAGGER ACCIDENT

John Archibald Young, appearing in a play called *The Warlock of the Glen*, had got to the last scene when, during the business of the action, a dagger point entered under Mr Young's right breast to a depth of 1½". The actor-manager was pronounced out of danger by Dr Smith who gave the accident his immediate attention.

52

1864_11_26c BURGOS, Spain.   ACCIDENT TO MADAME SALVI

Madame Salvi was the stage name of Mrs Potter, an English tightrope walker who had embarked on a major tour in Spain billed as "the Star of England and rival of the illustrious Blondin". In Burgos, walking the rope 30ft above ground with a cannon ball attached to each leg – the efforts to outdo each other knew no bounds – she lost her balance when turning to walk back across the rope. Madame fell with "great violence" into the orchestra bashing her head on a music stand, but suffered only bruising and was soon back on the rope "solely prompted by her intense *amour de l'art*".

1864_12_08 DUNDEE (Theatre Royal).   SWORD ACCIDENT

The play was *Rob Roy* – always popular in Scotland – with an exciting broadsword fight between manager Mr E D Lyons as Captain Thornton and Mr Pillans as Dougal. Unfortunately, Lyons received a heavy blow on his right hand almost severing his thumb, so both play and evening had to end. Some days later it was announced the manager was "progressing favourably". Lyons was back at work on the 9 January 1865.

1864_12_20c GHENT, Belgium.   GUN ACCIDENT

The play was *Les Huguenots* and for the battle scenes a group of young soldiers had been hired as supers. Whether they thought they were in a real battle, or had never been in one and their zeal got out of hand is hard to say, but they fired a volley – point blank – at an actor who was only three paces away. The actor left the stage with his head in his hands, and the play came to a halt. Though seriously wounded close to the eye, it was not certain that the eye would, in fact, be lost.

1865_06_22 LONDON (Knightsbridge).   ONE-LEGGED DANCER FALLS INTO PIT

Signor Tescano was a one-legged dancer who performed with a cloak. At the Knightsbridge Music Hall the footlights were unguarded and Tescano, noticing this, knew to avoid his cloak getting anywhere near. However, in avoiding such a danger, he scored an own goal by over-balancing into the orchestra pit. Quickly recovering, he leapt back on to the stage and concluded his act.

1865_10_11 LONDON (Astley's).   ACCIDENT TO MISS MENKEN

[Adah Isaacs Menken, (1835–1868) born in arguable circumstances, was an American actress, and would-be painter and poet, well known as the 'Naked Mazeppa' for her notorious performances in the popular melodrama *Mazeppa* that featured her, apparently nude, strapped to a horse on stage. Of course the Victorians' idea of nudity was very different from today! After several years of great success with the play in the USA, she brought her talents both to the UK – appearing at Astley's – and to Paris. She went through four husbands in seven years and many lovers – including an affair with Blondin – and died in Paris at the age of 33. In the accident below she was neither on a real horse nor 'nude'.]

44. *Ada Isaacs Menken*

Miss Menken was appearing at Astley's in a play *Child of the Sun* wherein she rode on a dummy horse across a stage of stormy seas and rocky shore. On this night, as she was halfway across, she and dummy horse fell through an open trap to a depth of 10ft landing on a stagehand who happened to be standing underneath. The man broke her fall, and Miss Menken, suffering nothing worse than bruised side and shoulder, was able to resume after a short break. The condition of the stagehand and dummy horse was not reported.

1865_12_16 JARROW (Theatre).   FEMALE HAMLET FALLS THROUGH STAGE TRAP

The current fad for so-called 'cross-gender casting' is not new. Julia Seaman, starring at the Jarrow Theatre, was due to conclude her engagement on Saturday night as Hamlet. In one scene she retreated to the back of the stage forgetting there was an open trap and fell down through it. Severely shaken and bruised, she was unable to continue. Neither was she fit enough to travel to her next engagement at Bradford until a few days later than anticipated. Dr Kelly, her medical attendant, foresaw nothing to hinder her from pursuing her career.

45. *Julia Seaman*

1866_01_01c LYONS, France (Tivoli-Lyonnais).   SWORD ACCIDENT

The play had a duel in the final act. The actor playing the hero Lagardère did not have the customary button on the point of his sword and he stabbed the abdomen of his opponent who fell to the stage with a cry. The audience applauded the excellent acting, until blood flowing copiously appeared, and the curtain was lowered. Hopes were entertained that the wound would not prove fatal.

1866_01_20c PARIS, France (Cirque Napoléon).   LION TAMER PUTS HEAD IN LION'S MOUTH

[Isaac A. Van Amburgh (1808–1865) self-styled as the "Brute Tamer of Pompeii" dressed in a quasi-Roman costume, and claimed to be a tamer of wild beasts – his technique being to batter them into submission using iron bars if necessary. He is credited with being the first man to put his head in a lion's mouth. Why the animal did not take the opportunity to bite it off is hard to say because no man is more powerful than a lion. The claim is tenuous as Winney is thought to have been the first to perform the feat in a touring menagerie in 1825. Winney went on to perform at Astley's in 1832 under the name of Zoomkantorah. During Van Amburgh's season at Drury Lane in 1839 the young Queen Victoria went to see him six times, probably smitten by the tamer rather than the beasts. Van Amburgh was the earliest and most famous star lion tamer and died in his bed at the age of 54 having made a fortune while gaining few wounds.]

46.

Thomas Batty was appearing with five lions at the French circus. One of his stunts was to place his head in the mouth of a lioness. Most performers do this by wrenching the mouth open, holding it wide with their hands, thrusting their face into the gaping stretch. Batty, however, took the more risky ploy of then putting his hands behind his back, trusting to the lion to keep its mouth agape until he withdrew his head. On this occasion the animal moved its jaws, causing its teeth to inflict deep scratches on each side of Batty's forehead "from which the blood flowed profusely". This caused a cry of horror to arise from the audience, and many made a rush from the building – which seems a bit illogical since the animals were in a cage. Batty calmly asked for a pocket handkerchief which he accepted through the bars, wiped the blood from his face, fired blanks from his revolver to drive the animals away from the door of the cage, then calmly left the ring to have his wounds dressed. Mr Cool, eh?

It was subsequently announced that the wounds were slight, but the Director had decreed that the head-in-mouth stunt would be dropped forthwith. Mr Batty was to have a further contretemps with his charges (*see* 1867_07_10).

1866_03_24 AT SEA.   FINAL MESSAGE IN A BOTTLE FROM G V BROOKE

[We met G V Brooke in 1860 (*see* 1860_06_18c). After losing a lot of money in business failures during recent years in England, he decided to return to Australia where he had had such acclaim. He left Plymouth on 1 January 1866 in a ship called *The London* which went down in a storm ten days later. He was 47 years old. Some crew members were rescued and appeared at the Britannia Music Hall for fees escalating up to £30, their normal salary onboard being £2.15.0 a month.]

On this day, his widow published his last words written in pencil on a torn envelope found in a bottle washed up on Brighton Beach. They read as follows: "11th of January, on board the London. We are just going down. No chance of safety. Please give this to Avonia Jones, Surrey Theatre — Gustavus Vaughan Brooke."

54

1866_04_13 LEEDS (Princess's).   TIGHTROPE WALKER ATTEMPTS TO HANG HIMSELF

This was an unusual accident. Panchette a performer on the slack rope had a peculiar act wherein he "simulated the struggle of a person dying by hanging". At this performance, while carrying out this oddity he suddenly went limp, all movement ceasing. The manager and assistants rushed to his aid and found Panchette insensible. The rope was cut and he fell as a dead weight into the arms of people in the pit. After a couple of minutes he revived and was taken backstage. He soon re-appeared, pretending that it was a stunt to fool them, but the explanation was not credited and the belief persisted that he had almost lost his life. As a matter of interest, the man-monkey Monsieur Gouffe suffered a similar fate on three occasions and this is scientifically discussed in my book *Man-Monkeys*.

1866_08_09 LONDON (Olympic).   JUMPING ACCIDENT

George French was appearing in *Six Years After* in which he was required to jump from a balcony down to the stage. The height was around 8ft. He managed to fracture two bones in his left leg and dislocate his ankle. He was taken to King's College Hospital.

1866_08_21 LONDON (Crystal Palace).   ACCIDENT TO ASCENSIONIST

We previously met this gymnast in an accident to his assistant (*see* 1858_06_20). Now an outstanding attraction in London, Ethardo was ascending to a great height walking on a ball via a spiral track. On this occasion, he achieved the task, but returning downwards – when the skill is preventing the ball from running away – the ball slipped from under his feet and fell into the net spread below. Ethardo leaping on to the track as the ball fell was considered more wonderful than his normal performance! Rescuing his ball he repeated his descent with élan.

1866_10_02c PARIS, France (Porte de Saint-Martin).   FALL OF CRYSTAL CURTAIN

The show was *Parisiens a Londres*. At 11.30pm the curtain rose on the fifteenth tableau which was constructed entirely of glass to resemble crystal. This was then raised slowly to display an inner scene illuminated by electric light, a great new novelty. The stage was crowded with players when a crack was heard and the entire crystal curtain crashed down. Women screamed – Victorian women always seemed to either swoon or scream in adversity – men jumped out of the boxes and splintered glass shattered everywhere. The stage lighting was turned off and the curtain lowered.

1866_10_20c PARIS, France (Cirque Napoleon).   FLYING TRAPEZE ARTISTES FALL

The two Segundo Brothers were performing at a height of 40ft above the ring. Making a miscalculation in the timing of their swing, both fell into the net suspended below in case of accident. Unfortunately, one of the corners gave way and they hit the ground, but less heavily than if the net had not greatly broken their fall. One had to be carried out while the other brother could walk away. Later in the evening they returned to show they were not injured although one still had to be supported. In fact, one – or both – was badly injured, as they were not fit enough to resume work until the middle of January 1867.

[Interestingly, the brothers were using a net. Léotard, the originator of the flying trapeze, worked at a low level over a row of mattresses. Subsequent flyers copied the idea as can be seen in some contemporary illustrations. The Hanlon Brothers claim to have patented the net in 1870.]

55

1866_11_29 DUBLIN (Theatre Royal).   ACCIDENT TO MRS CHARLES KEAN

While coming down a set of steps as Portia in the last scene of *The Merchant of Venice*, Mrs Kean fell and sprained her ankle. "Prompt and skilful measures were adopted" by Surgeon Rawdon Macnamara and it was hoped that she would be able to reappear later in the week.

1867_01_08c PARIS, France (Gaiété).   ACCIDENT TO MISS MENKEN

The play was *Pirates de la Savane* in which Miss Menken, bound to the back of a horse, is carried over the mountains – yes, it was just like *Mazeppa* but probably with clothes on. The horse lost its footing and slipped with her on to the stage. "An exclamation of terror burst forth" and the curtain lowered. Miss Menken, however, was unhurt and came before the curtain to prove it. The performance then resumed.

1867_01_20c PARIS, France (Gaiété).   ANOTHER ACCIDENT TO MISS MENKEN

Same place, same play *Pirates de la Savane,* same situation – Miss Menken bound to the back of a horse which lost its footing (*see* above). This time, however, she did not escape as lightly receiving a cut ear, and severely bruised arm and leg, and was unable to continue the performance.

1867_01_25c NEWCASTLE (Theatre Royal).   ACCIDENT TO HARLEQUIN

The pantomime *Papillonetta* was a very successful and popular one but, unfortunately, Mr Pugh the Harlequin met with an accident while leaping through the scenery. The reason was not given so we might be forgiven if we assume it was because the men were not there to catch him. "Mr White has filled his place for the last fortnight" and it was unlikely that Pugh would be able to return to the stage for some time.

1867_01_28 LONDON (Sadler's Wells).   DEATH OF SADLER'S WELLS CLOWN

Alfred Tolkien, known under the professional name of Boleno Marsh was the clown in the pantomime *The Golden Cask*. On the first night of the run, he had a dive through a window in the scenery which, because the men were not there to catch him, ended in him hitting the floor. He had not seemed to suffer any injury from this though complained of a stoppage of the bowels, thereafter playing as normal for many performances. He had continued working until Wednesday night. A doctor, called to him on Thursday night, sent his brother who prescribed for him, the doctor himself visiting on Friday when he found the clown insane. He was resting hands on knees and appeared insensible. He died in a comatose state on Monday morning. The post mortem found nothing untoward externally or internally and, though the clown's white make-up was considered as a possible cause, gave the reason for death as coma and epilepsy brought on by the exertions of his profession.

1867_04_30 NEW YORK, USA (Metropolitan).   ACROBATIC TROUPE STRUCK BLIND

"During the performance of the Arabs three of the members of the troupe met with an accident which, at the time, commanded but little attention, but afterwards proved to be not a little painful. In the act of breaking up or dissolving one of their complicated pyramids, these men fell backward from their elevated positions, and struck with great violence on their heads. The shock to the nervous system was so great in each that they were rendered totally blind." *The Era 1867_05_26.*

1867_06_12 NEW YORK, USA (Academy).   ACCIDENT TO TIGHTROPE WALKER

At the Academy of Music one of the members of the Japanese gymnast troupe – a boy nicknamed 'All Right' – was making a descent down a rope from the dome of the building to the dress circle when one of guys gave way, and losing his balance he fell into the aisle in the parquet. He was carried insensible to the dressing room and a doctor sent for who soon restored him to consciousness. Fortunately, little 'All Right' was soon all right again and returned to the troupe on 1 July with a special poster.

1867_07_10 PARIS, France (Porte de Saint-Martin).   LION TAMER ATTACKED

Batty the lion tamer was in the news again (*see* 1866_01_20c) when appearing in a show called *Biche au Bois*. One of the lionesses had produced four cubs, three of them being promptly eaten by lions in the same cage. The mother hid the fourth behind her but was "dull and melancholy all day" – well, anybody would be considering the circs – although at night she did her usual stuff in the act. As Batty was leaving the cage, he noticed the cub and stooped to scoop it up thinking to rescue it from the fate of its siblings, but the mother, assuming she was going to lose her final child, sprang

47. *Thomas Batty*

at him, bit him on the thigh and tore a piece of flesh from his back. He managed to escape from the cage, and the curtain was lowered. Many women had fainted, and a great many left the building. After a while Batty appeared at the footlights and was wildly applauded. His wounds were judged "serious but not dangerous."

1867_08_26 BRIGHTON (Theatre Royal).   GUN ACCIDENT

A benefit night was intended to be a boost to an actor's usual income. If he was granted a benefit he took all the takings for that night. The catch is he had also to pay all the expenses. These could often outstrip the income. Mr Haywell a popular local actor was taking part on his benefit night when, in the course of the action, a pistol was fired in his face. "With heroic fortitude" he carried on through the remaining few minutes to the curtain. Then he was taken to the dressing room where it was feared his sight was destroyed. However, under the skilful treatment of Dr Taaffe that was averted and he was able to return to the stage only one week later, though "the pain he is suffering is great". The local paper suggested his friends might like to arrange an extra benefit for him as "rest and release from study might thoroughly restore his sight, but overstraining it just now might be productive of serious consequences hereafter." The poor chap had no savings so must keep on working.

1867_09_12 BALTIMORE, USA (Holliday Street)   DAGGER ACCIDENT TO MR BOOTH

Edwin Booth (1833–1893) son of the eminent Junius Brutus Booth, followed his father by becoming a tragedian. Even today he is regarded by many as America's greatest actor of any period .

His career included the managing of several theatres, and his achievements included being the first actor to play Hamlet for 100 consecutive nights. His personal merits were often overshadowed by being the brother of actor John Wilkes Booth who assassinated President Abraham Lincoln.

The play was the tragedy *The Apostate*. Towards the close of the play, Hemaya rushes at Pescera (the Booth role) with a dagger and slays him. On this night, the actor playing Hemaya was somewhat overzealous and inflicted two cuts on Booth's right hand. The following night, Booth played Benedict with his arm in a sling. The night after he was Richard III, fighting the final combat with his left hand. They don't make them like that any more! However, his exertions inflamed his wound, and his physician decreed he must stop playing and take immediate rest.

48. *Edwin Booth*

58 1868_01_27 LONDON (Agricultural Hall).   ACCIDENT TO STUNT 'MAN-FLY'

Professor Palmer did an act walking upside down at a great height, in the manner of a fly. He had a piece of plate glass about 50ft long and 2ft wide in a wooden frame fixed at a height of some 80ft over the ring at Sanger's Circus in the Agricultural Hall. Around 30ft below was a net in case of accidents. The Prof intended doing his act without a net but Sanger insisted and provided one.

The Prof, his feet bound up in rubber, carefully commenced his walk at one end of the glass. As he lifted his foot the mark of some glutinous substance was left on the surface. It is very likely he had suction pads on his feet. Thus he traversed head downwards, almost to the end of his walk when, in error, he put his foot on the wooden frame, rather than the glass. His ruddy face blanched as he supported his entire weight on one foot, then he fell. He landed just on the border of the netting – which could have been wider to advantage – his body wrapped in a tight ball. Then he descended with the aid of a rope ladder. A great cheer went up when the audience knew he was safe, and all the ladies who had averted their gaze looked up, and anyone who had fainted was restored to sensibility. Some gentlemen from the front seats went into the arena to shake the Prof's hand, and instead of a failure he was lauded as a hero. He must have been grateful for the net as he fell three times in the first week!

1868_02_27 DUNDEE (Music Hall).   TRAPEZE ACCIDENT TO BROTHERS BELLENA

The two brothers were executing clever and daring feats on the trapeze "which many of the audience especially females could not behold except with fear". The older and stronger of the two hung from a trapeze by his legs, catching the flyer who crossed carrying out various feats. It is not clear if they were above the stage, above the audience or half-and-half, but were stated to be about 20ft up. The trick they were next attempting was catching the flyer by his left ankle. This was obviously mistimed, as with hands and ankle some inches apart, the flyer fell head foremost into the orchestra pit. Screams and sobs rent the air and some men in the front seats rushed forward to see if the intrepid gymnast had been killed.

Having broken the neck off a violin, the flyer lay unconscious at the bottom of the pit, but more frighteningly, having hit his head on the sharp edge of the conductor's rostrum. He had a large scalp wound 3" long on the crown of his head, and slight bruises on his forehead but "he did not appear to have suffered any serious injury"!

1868_04_06 LONDON (Holborn).   ACCIDENT TO TRAPEZE ARTISTE

Mdlle Azella was appearing at the Holborn Circus presenting an "unrivalled performance on the flying trapeze, which includes a flight across the arena of 100ft terminating in a somersault at an elevation of 30ft from the platform." Azella, working without a catcher in the style of Léotard, relied on a trapeze being swung out to her to coincide with the swing she was making. On this night the timing was off and Azella missed her hold, falling to the platform flat on her face, stood up, fainted and was carried off insensible. She later made an appearance looking weak and pale, and was loudly cheered by the spectators. Her absence brought to the fore Madame Senyah (Mrs Haynes) who was working at three different halls a night at 9pm, 10pm and 11pm. Mdlle Azella returned to work at her former venue on 1 June.

49. *Madame Senyah (see also* 1879_08_18 for Mdlle Azella)

1868_07_25 WARREN, USA.   ACCIDENT TO TIGHTROPE WALKER

Warren, Rhode Island, was the open air venue for Professor Sweet's performance on the tightrope. Having successfully gone through most of his act he was at that moment balancing on one foot intending to spring up and return – in other words a hopping movement. Unfortunately, some person tugged at the arm of one of the men holding the guy lines causing the rope to sway. When the prof came down it was to the side of the rope, and he fell to the ground 30ft below. He shattered the bones of his left foot just below the ankle, and his left arm was broken above the elbow, with internal injuries also suspected. He was taken immediately into the nearby hotel where three physicians arrived to tend his wounds.

1868_08_28 EXETER (Theatre Royal).   ACCIDENT TO MISS RIGNOLDS

Miss Rignolds was playing the leading role in *Stolen; or the Sweet Ballad-Singer*. In the play there was a scene where she crossed a bridge which at this performance collapsed under her and she fell to the stage – a drop of around eight feet – with several pieces of scenery on top of her. The curtain was instantly dropped and the severely injured leading lady taken to her lodgings.

1868_09_11c SWANSEA (Theatre Royal).   GUN ACCIDENT

Morgan Smith was engaged to play the lead in tragedies and sensational dramas. In one of the latter, he was called upon to fire a pistol at the heroine. It had been overcharged and the wadding flew out, hitting the actress on the arm and causing a severe laceration which necessitated an immediate visit to hospital where she was expected to remain for some time.

1868_09_14 PRESTON (Theatre Royal).   ACCIDENT TO AERIAL GYMNAST

Mr Lyon's company of performers had been working for several nights, the leading light of the troupe being 'Mons Clevoyn the Monarch of the Air'. He had a single trapeze fixed to the roof of the theatre above the front of the stage. On Monday night, to start his act he performed 'the Leap for Life' which entailed him swinging on a rope from the upper gallery, across the pit, and landing on his trapeze. He then went through a series of gymnastic evolutions before reaching his climax – that of descending head first down the rope. It was at this point that he somehow lost his grip, fell on to the stage and lay stunned with his head out of joint. A man called Lewis cried out for Henry Aspden, a manufacturer of ginger beer, who was in the audience. He went forward as requested and wrenched the Monarch's head back in place. The gymnast had also sprained a wrist and suffered a bit of damage round his face. He was taken to his lodgings and medical aid arrived.

On Friday night, Mr Lyon put on a special programme as a benefit for Clevoyn. The response was very disappointing with only a thin attendance, the likelihood being the venture would be a loss rather than a benefit. Clevoyn appeared to thank the audience for coming, clearly very weak, his arm in a sling, cuts around the left eye and forehead. He was thought to be progressing favourably but was unable to resume his work for some weeks to come.

1868_09_20c WEST BROMWICH.   FALL FROM SLACK ROPE

An acrobat called Finch had been performing on the slack rope for 20 years without an accident (said he), and for the previous week had been appearing in front of a show on some waste ground in the town. On Tuesday night, before a crowd of 2000, he went through his repertoire of stunts, culminating in what was supposed to be an apparent fall saved by his catching the rope with his leg. The fall part went all right, but not the leg catch bit – he fell head first into the crowd. Consternation all round, but no need to fear as Finch popped up on the platform as perky as ever, re-ascended to his rope and, with a boy on his back, went through another lot of stunts.

We have no further report on the fact that "his fall was broken by the heads of those he fell upon, some of whom were more or less injured."

1868_10_23 LIVERPOOL (Amphitheatre).   ACCIDENT TO BARRY SULLIVAN

[Barry Sullivan (1821–1891) of Irish parentage, entered the profession in 1837 by joining a strolling company. At Cork he was given an engagement at 15/- a week as a regular member of a stock company. He then progressed to Murray's stock company at Edinburgh, at a salary of 30/- a week. Sullivan soon began to play leading roles, supporting Helena Faucit and G V Brooke among others. He made his London debut in1852 as Hamlet, and once established as a leading actor he played principal parts during the next eight years in many of the plays of the period. He toured America and Australia, and in both nations was highly popular, becoming a public favourite. Probably the leading provincial tragedian in the UK, he also had many opportunities of playing in London.

Sullivan was the lessee of the Holborn theatre for three years. Then for the next 20 years he was constantly touring, including a return to the USA. Sullivan was never really accepted as a top-flight actor in London, but was a true star in the provinces and overseas where his robust style was much appreciated. G B Shaw preferred Sullivan to Irving, and in 1879 it was Sullivan who was the first leading man to play at the newly opened Memorial Theatre in Stratford.]

In 1868, in the grand final scene of *Don Caesar de Bazan*, Sullivan, as the eponymous hero, strode on to confound the king – who thought him dead – with the stirring words "Not yet, sire!" and promptly put his foot into a 'sloat' that had been left open. A sloat is a long narrow trap used for raising flats from understage – think of it as a hinged floor board.

Some incompetent fool had left the flap open and the star suffered. Sullivan, a tough nut, carried on regardless. After the show, several medical men who had been watching the play offered their assistance, Mr Bickersteth being the chosen one. As soon as he saw the foot "swollen to a great size" he forbade the star from appearing for the rest of the week, with a foreboding that it may be impossible for several weeks. "Nonsense!" cried Sullivan, and after a wasted week he travelled to Bristol where he opened on Monday 9 November. (*See* 1844_02_05 & 1860_03_15 *for previous accidents*)

50. *Barry Sullivan*

1868_12_03 LIVERPOOL (Colosseum).   ACCIDENT TO TRAPEZE ARTISTE

Hugh Kelly, of the Brothers Culleen, was appearing on a trapeze set-up comprising Roman rings and a bar trapeze set some yards apart with a safety net suspended above the audience. The flight from rings to bar was misjudged and Kelly leapt short, missing the bar and falling to the net. He only reached the edge of it, bouncing off and falling with violence on his head on the floor below. He was insensible when picked up and taken to the Infirmary. In addition to internal injuries, he suffered a broken arm, and concussion of the brain.

1869_01_08 LONDON (East London).   MAN DRESSED AS A WOMAN INJURED

One of the scenes in the harlequinade had a super – dressed as a woman – tossed in a blanket. As Ross, the poor 'female', was thrown higher and higher, the audience roared with laughter. At the greatest height he flew over the heads of the tossers to land heavily on the stage very near the footlights. On being picked up, he was found insensible and rushed to the London Hospital where his injuries were discovered to be a dislocated shoulder and a fractured bone. He was probably paid 1/- a night for that.

1869_01_13 KIDDERMINSTER (Powell's Circus).   ACCIDENT TO NEW TRAPEZE ARTISTE

Appearing on this night was "Jeffes, the African vaulter and trapezist". It seems the vaulter had only recently added the trapeze to his repertoire, but was progressing with his daring and skill. In the middle of his trapeze act, he was seized with cramp in his hand, and though he held on as long as he could, he fell to the ground. He was unconscious when picked up and taken for medical help where it was decided no bones were broken, but other injuries would preclude a swift return to work.

1869_01_22 GLASGOW (Royal MH).   FALL OF FEMALE TRAPEZE ARTISTE

Madame Leopold was presenting daring evolutions on the trapeze when, missing her hold, she fell heavily on to the stage from a height of 15ft and rendered unconscious, but recovered within hours.

1869_02_16c BRIGHTON (Theatre Royal).   ACCIDENT TO TRAPEZE ARTISTE

One of the attractions of the successful pantomime which was in the last week of a seven week run was the trapeze act of the Martinette Brothers. During their benefit, one of the brothers fell, hitting the stage with a thump. He broke a small bone in his wrist, not very jolly for a trapeze artiste.

1869_03_16 HULL (Queen's).   ACCIDENT TO TRAPEZE ARTISTES

The theatre had been occupied for two weeks by Pablo Fanque's Circus. On this night the performance was under the patronage of Capt Forsyth and officers of HMS Dauntless. The star turn was Les Freres Trevanion in their "thrilling and exciting act – the double fall for life". The set-up was as described for the Culleen Brothers' act – Roman rings and a trapeze with bar set some distance apart. One Trevanion hung as a catcher from the trapeze as his brother launched himself from the Roman rings. The flight was well timed and their hands met but did not clasp, with the flyer falling to the floor. Clearly there was no safety net in use, as the man lay on his side and was borne off by colleagues in an insensible state.

The surgeon from the Dauntless hurried round to give assistance. He decided no bones were broken, neither was there any internal injury. How they could tell without X-rays I do not know. It was announced from the ring that he only required "rest and freedom from excitement". The fall was of 35–40ft but the ring surface of cartloads of fresh mould mixed with sawdust may have provided something of a cushion. One wonders if it was bravado, or poverty that caused these acts to work without a net. On the same evening, a youth named Pablo, one of the stars of the circus company, fell from his horse during an equestrian feat and dislocated his right arm. This was probably Pablo Fanque Jr who worked under the name of Ted Pablo, and became a noted boxer.

1869_04_06 BIRMINGHAM (Theatre Royal).   MIGHTY SCENIC COLLAPSE

[Dion Boucicault (1820-1890) was an important writer, actor and theatre manager in the world of the Victorian theatre. He had his first play produced in 1838 and three years later his first huge success with *London Assurance*. He had many more successful plays becoming producer, manager and actor in both the UK and the USA where he became a naturalised citizen.]

The play was *After Dark*, the two actors on stage were Edward Price and Mr F Gould, the scene was an underground railway. Old Tom (Price) had just dragged Chumley (Gould) clear of the track where he had been tied, when on whooshed the train, a realistic sensational effect. Unfortunately, on this occasion the train, propelled by a massive counterweight, hit the edge of the

51. *Dion Boucicault*

scenery representing the railway arch and was thrown on its side, dragging with it half the set and landing close to where the two actors were lying. The engine, although a scenic prop, weighed several cwt and the funnel actually hit Gould's head, taking off his wig. Both actors escaped unhurt.

This example shows how up-to-date melodramas were getting with more elaborate scenic effects that would only really come off properly when silent films were invented. Looking back we tend to think that pretty ladies tied to the railway track were a cliché of early films, whereas they were really filmed versions of successful existing stage plays. *After Dark* had a long shelf life being performed in London for the last time in 1896 and two film versions (in UK and USA) were made in 1915.

1869_04_10 LONDON (Olympic).   ACCIDENT TO HORACE WIGAN
[Horace Wigan (1815-1885) was an actor, dramatist and theatre manager. He made his theatrical debut in 1853 at Dublin, and his London debut the following year. For ten years his career was entirely at the Olympic Theatre, becoming the manager in 1864. His biggest success was as the creator of Hawkshaw the detective in *The Ticket-of-Leave Man*. In 1875, he became manager of the Theatre Royal, Holborn, renamed it The Mirror, and departed a year later.]
Horace Wigan was performing the role of Jules de Valois in the melodrama *The Thirst for Gold*. In Act II his ship sinks through the ice by means of lowering it through a trap in the stage. On this night Wigan caught his arm in the machinery working the trap and was severely injured. At subsequent performances his role was played by Mr Vaughan.

1869_04_20 BIRMINGHAM (Day's).   ACCIDENT TO TRAPEZE ARTISTE
Tom Alvantee, a solo trapeze artiste, performed on a single trapeze over a safety net. However, he also had a rope suspended from the roof that was not over the net. In a stunt where he leapt from his trapeze on to the rope he failed to catch it and fell 30ft on to the conductor's music stand. "Mr Yates the surgeon was at hand and rendered every assistance." No specific injuries were stated, and I do not know his recovery

1869_04_20 CHELTENHAM (Wellington).   ACCIDENT TO THE BROTHERS TREVANION
Now performing at the Wellington Circus and Music Hall, the Brothers Trevanion once again flopped in the stunt they liked to call 'The Leap for Life' (*see* 1869_03_16). The flyer and the catcher failed to lock wrists and the flyer fell to earth in the arena. He must have been getting used to it as he sprang up and "was able to make a show of continuing the performance."

1869_05_04 PARIS, USA.   FATAL EQUESTRIAN ACCIDENT
Not Paris, France, but Paris, Kentucky. The famed equestrian James Madigan, attempting to throw a double somersault, fell and broke his neck.

1869_05_15c MELBOURNE, Australia (D of Edinburgh).   ACCIDENT TO TRAPEZE ARTISTE
The performer was Edward Magilton. This could well be Maggelton known as the Spider who had an accident previously (*see* 1861_03_28). His apparatus was a single trapeze set high in the roof some 40ft above ground. To get to this he climbed a perpendicular rope, hand over hand. He was within grasping distance of the trapeze bar when the rope parted above him and he dropped like a stone into the orchestra below. He was carried out insensible, but within a short time had recovered sufficiently to be led back onstage to show he was no worse for his fall, and was soon working again.

1869_05_20 LONDON (Astley's).   HORSE ACCIDENT AT ASTLEY'S TRASHES BAND
The drama was an equestrian version of *The Battle of Waterloo*, the scene on stage was the entrance of Napoleon and his entourage. Unfortunately, one horse went backwards on to the footlights, demolished the metal bar that ran along the front and crashed into the orchestra pit, smashing instruments in all directions as it thrashed about with the rider underneath. Most of the musicians escaped without injury except the clarinettist who had his collar bone broken.

1869_06_02 WINDSOR (Wellington).   FATAL ACCIDENT TO THE BROTHERS BECONA

The trapeze act of Frederick Thurrell and Henry Julian went by the name of the Brothers Becona. On this night in their act they both fell together a distance of 17ft on to the floor of the hall. Julian was unharmed but Thurrell was severely injured and immediately taken to the Royal Windsor Hospital. Inspection showed injuries to the spine had caused paralysis to his limbs. Mortification and exhaustion took its toll, and the daring gymnast expired on 26 June. For goodness sake use *nets!*

1869_06_13 PHILADELPHIA, USA (American).   ACCIDENT TO CHILD TRAPEZE ARTISTES

The DeLave Sisters, Zoe and Lila were juvenile performers on the trapeze. On this night, the younger one flew from a trapeze, turned a somersault and was caught by her sister. Then she was lowered down to the stage, but the man deputed to catch her bungled his task and she fell on to the stage, striking her head. Although momentarily stunned, the man who failed to catch her – probably her father – insisted she repeat the trick. This proposal was greeted with cries of dissent from the audience, and the child left the stage. However, she returned and was announced as repeating the stunt causing more dissention, with applause and cheers from some, hissing and booing from others. She started swinging on her trapeze but, having neither the strength nor will to fly, hung there swaying back and forth while people cried "Shame! Shame!" Several men then took it upon themselves to assist the child down to safety "from her perilous position, and the exhibition ended."

64 **1869_06_15c** BERLIN, Germany.   FATAL FALL OF TWO TIGHTROPE PERFORMERS

The gymnast Biermann and his pupil Kolbe (16) were performing on a high tightrope when the rope suddenly broke and they fell to the ground. Kolbe was killed on the spot, Biermann so badly injured he died the following day.

1869_08_18 PARIS, France (Hippodrome).   FATAL ATTACK ON LION TAMER

52. *Mendez trying to save Lucas*

Lucas the lion tamer, entered the cage to confront two lions and two lionesses with only a whip in hand instead of the heavy cudgel he normally carried. A lioness immediately attacked him, seizing him by the nape of the neck. The other animals, attracted by blood, joined in the attack. A cry of horror arose from the spectators, many fleeing the building, and a goodly number of women fainting. Mendez, Lucas's beast-man who had never before entered the cage, did so with an iron bar and drove the animals back while he dragged Lucas out of the cage. It was reported that Lucas said to him "Go away, leave me to die alone." Not a very nice thing to say when a fellow has risked his own neck for you. In the event, Mendez's bravery counted for naught as Lucas died from his injuries within the week.

1869_09_13 SHEERNESS (Oxford).   ACCIDENT TO PANTOMIMIST

This type of accident was fortunately becoming rarer as the harlequinade was diminishing in attraction, and fewer specialist pantomimists were trying to make a living. Since the advent of Blondin and Léotard, acrobatic performers found more employment in gymnastic work rather than pantomime. At the Oxford, the attraction was a comic ballet called *Quicksilver Dick* with Jem Etherington. It is not clear if he was a dancer, a pantomimist, or an actor, but whatever his status he had to take a high leap, expecting to be caught by at least two men. The men were not in position and Etherington, a big man, crashed to the ground with great violence, seriously injuring his hip and spine.

1869_12_02 LEEDS (Thornton's).   ACCIDENT TO 'AFRICAN BLONDIN'

[Thornton's Music Hall built in 1865, measured 72ft x 36ft x 30ft high, and still does as it remains in use today under the name of the City Varieties]

The tightrope walker Carl Trowers was billed as the African Blondin. His rope stretched from the stage up to the gallery, and while walking along with his hands shackled to his ankles the rope gave way. He fell into the pit a distance of 25ft or so, and so did his balance pole which broke a man's nose and frightened a woman with a child. Trowers, none the worse for his fall, put the accident down to the chafing of the end of the rope at the stage end. There is a website devoted to this performer.

53. *Carl Trowers*

65

1869_12_14 LEEDS (Theatre Royal).   ACCIDENT TO CLOWN IN REHEARSAL

The pantomime was *Robinson Crusoe* and rehearsals were well under way. Clown was to be played by an acrobat called Gabriel Devani (31) and during rehearsal he threw a double somersault but on landing suffered a fracture of the patella (kneecap). He was taken to the Infirmary where he was expected to remain some time. The poor chap had a wife and six children dependent on him who were put in a parlous state as he would be unable to resume work for several months. E Clinton Hall of the theatre, started a relief fund for the family and, as was the custom of the time, wrote to *The Era* newspaper to solicit alms. The paper, always willing to attend to these matters, listed an appeal for several weeks with contributions from 2/- upwards regularly reported. A Devani benefit held on 22 January 1870 brought in £70.16.0.

1870_01_31 LONDON (Gaiety).   ACCIDENT TO ADELAIDE NEILSON

[Adelaide Neilson (1848–1880), after an impoverished upbringing and a minor debut in Margate, became a major star in both the UK and America. She played many Shakespearean roles and testing parts in other dramas. Her career was short as after some fifteen years she suddenly died in Paris at the age of 32.]

When crossing the stage after her performance, Adelaide Neilson was careless and did not look up as all performers should when crossing the stage between scenes. Thus she was hit on the head by the bar at the bottom of a backcloth being lowered in. After medical attention it was decreed she should have a few days off and her part in *Uncle Dick's Darling* was taken by Miss J Rignold. Miss Neilson was back the following week receiving a warm reception.

54. *Miss Neilson*

1870_02_05c MELBOURNE, Australia.   ACCIDENT CAUSES UNPLEASANT DISPUTE

[Daniel E. Bandmann (1837–1905) was an internationally known German-American Shakespearean actor. In 1863, he made his debut in New York as Shylock, following this with a widely acclaimed Hamlet. He made his London debut at the Lyceum in 1868. During his career he made extensive tours of Tasmania, New Zealand, Australia, the Malay Peninsula, China, India and Hawaii.]

55. *Daniel E Bandmann*

The play was *Othello*, the Iago was Herr Bandmann, Emilia was Mrs Steele. During the course of the play Bandmann wounded Mrs Steele in her lower back. The doctors said the wound was a trifle that would heal in a couple of days but Bandmann, in a state about it, made all kinds of redress via his wife and Dr Nield her medical attendant. Mrs Steele refused any redress on the grounds that neither she nor her husband would like to profit from a mere accident.

Bandmann made preparations to hold a benefit for Mrs Steele, and it was announced that Mrs Steele would re-appear, her wound being thoroughly healed. However, the day before she was due to resume she sent a doctor's note to say she would not be fit enough to return as yet. A few days later she gave out her intention to sue Bandmann for £500. On finding she would get nothing by law, she accepted Bandmann's benefit for which he had to fork out £123. Showbusiness is one big happy family!

1870_02_15 NORWICH (Theatre Royal).   ACCIDENT TO HARLEQUIN

Mr C Strange, playing Harlequin in the pantomime, was taking one of the usual leaps through a window in the scenery, to be caught at the back by two stagehands with a sling. On this night the men allowed him to fall with a heavy thud on the ground, and it was feared his back was injured. Fortunately it turned out that, apart from the dreadful shock to the system, no bones were broken. It seems incredible that this primitive method of catching diving pantomimists was still going on, and even more so that stagehands were still willing to risk serious injury to others by neglecting their duties in such a cavalier fashion.

1870_05_29 MILAN, Italy (Myer's Circus)   GUN ACCIDENT

Richard Orlando was a gymnast in Myers's Grand Cirque Americain which was touring Italy. Also in the cast was John Cooper and his lions. For reasons that are by no means clear, Orlando was holding a loaded gun that Cooper used in his performance, perhaps he stood ready in case Cooper was attacked by his animals, who knows? Anyway, the thing went off, shattering his hand to such an extent that amputation was the only option to save his life.

Orlando's career was over, Myers had a whip round of his troupe and wrote to *The Era* asking them to insert his letter starting a fund. Circo Ciniselli in Milan had a collection amongst its personnel, and Pinder's Circus troupe gathered £10.10.0d to launch *The Era's* fund. On 5 July, Myers was able to write again sending a cheque for £154.17.8d which represented £100 from Mr and Mrs Myers, the rest from the Myers circus troupe. Also sent was an Italian bank note for 25francs. On 14 July Myers sent banknotes for 300francs which were exchanged in London for £10.18.2p. Myers was certainly doing his best for his employee – guilty conscience or natural kindness?

1870_02_26 LONDON (Surrey).   EXPLODING HEADGEAR

The Surrey Theatre was presenting the pantomime *St George and the Dragon*. The part of the dragon was played by Mr R Sweetman who had a false head to his costume. This head was cleverly contrived to hold some squib-like containers with gunpowder. When ignited, the powder was blown forward through holes that were painted as the nostrils of the face, emerging as a shower of sparks.

On this night, the gunpowder exploded inside the mask, blowing it off Sweetman's head, scorching his hair and face and causing severe injury to his eyes. Three doctors arrived, did all they could to relieve the man's suffering and sent him home. Sometime later when improvements had taken place, Sweetman's left eye was still in danger of loss. The actor who took over the part of the dragon was not required to attempt fire from the nostrils

1870_05_31 WASHINGTON, USA.   ACCIDENT TO TIGHTROPE WALKER

Harry Leslie, a tightrope walker who crossed Niagara in 1865, gave a picnic and festival assisted by Maggie Nichols. The day was pleasant, the event well advertised, so a large crowd had gathered. The afternoon passed merrily with dancing, riding, cycling and so on, until the highlight when Leslie climbed up to his rope. This was set about 30ft from the ground and as Leslie reached the centre on his first crossing, he lost his balance and fell to the ground. He was taken to the adjacent hotel and medical help summoned. Three of his ribs were broken, also the bones of one arm and a wrist. It was feared he was also injured internally as on the following morning he remained speechless.

In 1884, Leslie was reported to be insane after the death of his wife and an inability to get work. He tried to stab a man, and attempted to buy major properties with worthless cheques. On one occasion he announced he would cross the street on his tightrope. After tying it to his window but not fastening it at the other end, when he emerged he could only climb down his dangling rope. A very sad end for a man who less than twenty years previously had crossed Niagara Falls on a tightrope.

1870_06_07 LONDON (Alhambra).   ENTIRE CHORUS IN PLATFORM COLLAPSE

56. *Les Fleurs du Jardin*

The Alhambra was a superior variety theatre in London's Leicester Square. With popular acts like E D Davies "the great ventriloquist" and the Hanlons on the trapeze, on the bill were three separate ballets *The Nations* where Russians, Spaniards and Tyrolese were brought on in turn with a grand finale of cascades of real water; a comic one called *The Terror of the Forest*; and the spectacular ballet *Les Fleurs du Jardin*. On this night, during the latter ballet in a scene where almost all the *corps de ballet* entered on an elevated platform, it collapsed and all the dancers were precipitated on to the stage below, the crashing of timber and the screams of women drowning out the orchestra which valiantly kept playing until the curtain was dropped and the performance suspended. Medical men and police swiftly arrived and the tangled mess sorted out. It was found that 11 dancers were injured, of these three or four were seriously hurt and taken to Charing Cross Hospital, the others taken to their respective homes.

67

1870_06_28 DUNDEE.   ACCIDENT TO TIGHTROPE WALKER

Fraulein Laura was performing in a garden in Dundee and had just ascended to her rope when the supporting apparatus gave way at one end. Fortunately falling between the collapsing poles she escaped serious injury. She was taken into a nearby cottage but soon made her reappearance, reassuring the crowd that she was not injured, and announcing she would perform the following day.

1870_07_15c NEW YORK, USA (Bowery).   LION QUEEN ATTACKED BY HER ANIMALS

57. *Minnie Wells*

Minnie Wells was the "The Lion Queen" who, dressed in a dashing "well-fitting suit of red", entered the cages of lions and tigers. The animals were only two years old and had been bought and trained by her father especially for her to show them. They were normally as docile as pets, but on this occasion one lioness was recalcitrant so Miss Wells attempted to chastise the beast. The animal did not care for this and promptly attacked, throwing her to the floor mauling her with teeth and claws. Her screams brought aid from her attendants who succeeded in beating the beasts off. Minnie came off lightly, her injuries keeping her off work for only a handful of weeks.

1870_08_14 BRADFORD.   ACCIDENT AT BRADFORD

The Whitsuntide galas of Bradford became renowned for the aerial artistes engaged every year. This particular year saw Henri and Le Vent (trapeze), feats of strength by Signor Napoli, Carl Trowers known as the African Blondin, Mons Adair with his mid-air flights, and the Eurali family of acrobats. Napoli's act included having a loaded cannon fired from his shoulder. All would have been well but for Mr Atherton – he had been presenting his performing dogs – lending his assistance, theoretically steadying the cannon by holding the muzzle. By mistake the cannon was fired too early and three right hand fingers went winging through the air.

1870_09_13 SCARBOROUGH (Adam's Circus).   FATAL EQUESTRIAN ACCIDENT

John Storey (21) a newly married skilful equestrian in Charles Adam's Circus was rapidly riding round the ring on Tuesday when he fell off his mount. The horse did not step clear, a blow from a back hoof striking the fallen man's head. This proved to be a death blow as Storey lingered in the accident ward until Saturday when life ebbed away.

68

1870_11_04 STOCKTON-ON-TEES (Theatre).

ACCIDENT IN PANTOMIME

[In earlier times pantomimes had ludicrous titles like *Harlequin the Children in the Wood, Old Father Aesop, Cock Robin and Jenny Wren*. When harlequinades went out of fashion, we had titles without him but still on the long side, eg *Queen Lucidora, the Fair One with the Golden Locks*, until in the 1860s it became popular to have one name titles like *Sindbad, Aladdin* and *Cinderella*.]

Mr Sidney Jr was Buttoni the Page, and Julia Leicester, Prince Poppetti in *Cinderella*. Together they were performing "the swing dance", clasping hands and revolving at great speed. Sidney – without warning – released his grip, and mid-spin Miss Leicester shot backwards and fell into the orchestra where she was picked up insensible. No bones were broken but the actress was so severely shocked and bruised she was thought likely to be confined to her bed for some time. The following evening Mr Sidney Jr was "greeted with disfavour". I bet he was!

image© The British Library Board

1870_11_12 BIRMINGHAM (Crystal Palace)　　　　FATAL GYMNASTIC ACCIDENT

Alfred Smith (18) was one of the Fritz Brothers acrobatic act performing on Saturday evening. Smith was standing on the fourth rung (only about 5ft from the floor) in the "double ladder feat" and about to throw a somersault when his foot slipped and, falling heavily, he appeared seriously injured. He was taken to Queen's Hospital where his spine was found to be so severely damaged that recovery was impossible. He lingered until Monday morning then expired.

1870_12_10 LIVERPOOL.　　　ACCIDENTS TO TWO SEPARATE GYMNASTS

"We regret to record that two more trapeze accidents have occurred at Liverpool. Mdlle Leon, while making a sensational leap at the Gaiety Music Hall, missed her hold and fell, sustaining a severe shock. At the Star Music Hall one of the Brothers Leoni, while attempting a daring performance on the high trapeze, slipped from his brother's arms, and fell heavily. He was removed in an insensible condition. The occurrence created great consternation." *London and Provincial Entr'acte* 1870_12_10.

1871_01_27 OLDHAM (Adelphi).　　　ACCIDENT TO TRAPEZE ARTISTE

This night was a benefit for the Brothers Banvard, a trio described as "American gymnasts". They were performing on trapezes when one of them fell head first into the orchestra from a height of 20ft. In the audience "men yelled and women screamed". Medical aid being summoned, the injuries to the gymnast were a broken arm, three fingers of left hand smashed, and a sprained ankle. "The same young man had his arm broken a short time ago through a similar accident."

Ironically, the Brothers Banvard were, on this very evening, due to be presented with two silver crosses for their daring feats. As there were three brothers in the troupe, perhaps the one who kept falling and breaking his arms did not deserve one?

SAFETY NET FOR TRAPEZE ARTISTES

Prior to trapeze artistes it would appear that builders in France used a type of net to catch falling bodies. In May 1866 a patent was granted for a new improved version and it is almost certain from this use that the idea spread to trapeze artistes who realised the row of mattresses as used by Léotard was inadequate. As mentioned earlier (*see* 1866_10_20c) a safety net for flying trapeze acts had been adopted by some aerialists. However, lesser performers were still performing without such a thing, and crashing to the ground when they lost their hold. The Hanlon-Lees claimed to have patented the aerial safety net in 1870. The Hanlon-Lees were the top trapeze act of the day and with their net not only gained safety should they fall, but commendation for not frightening the audience lest they did so! Their set-up was two trapezes on the same level set a distance apart with a catcher on each hanging head downwards. "Setting themselves in pendulum motion, the third brother, a smart wiry little fellow of nine years is caught hand by hand by the trapezist at one end, who at the next swing transfers him to his colleague at the other, which is repeated several times, the young gymnast throwing single and double somersaults in his passage through the air backwards and forwards."

At this time the act comprised William and Frederick Hanlon and an apprentice Little Bob. Of course, today, almost everybody knows how trapeze acts work but all these tricks were new in mid-Victorian times, and newspaper reporters had to summon up descriptions for the many readers who had never seen a flying trapeze act. But the main interest in this particular report is the safety net. The report goes on to say "All the feats are performed with surprising neatness, grace and skill, and although the element of sensationalism is strongly developed, yet danger is reduced to the minimum – almost to an impossibility – by an extensive net contrivance with side protections which is stretched the width of the hall. The net is made of cotton which has a certain degree of elasticity, so the force of a fall is not realised until the elasticity is spent."

The net was demonstrated privately to a group of gentlemen by the Hanlons deliberately falling into it, showing conclusively that there was no fear of injury should a performer miss his intention. This report appeared in the Birmingham press when the Hanlons were to perform there, but was copied elsewhere especially in *The Era* so there should, from this point on, be no more trapeze artistes performing without a safety net.

59. *The Hanlons and Little Bob*

1871_04_09 PORTSMOUTH (South of England).   ACCIDENT TO TRAPEZE ARTISTE

The act was the Brothers Hambro. In the 'Leap for Life' stunt the brothers missed each other's wrists and the flyer fell into the net below. His weight causing one of the ropes to give way pitched him into the stalls among the audience. The net having broken his fall, nobody was injured.

1871_04_17 DEWSBURY (Theatre Royal).   ACCIDENT TO ORIENTAL GYMNAST
This accident happened to the oriental gymnasts known as the Royal Tycoon Japanese Troupe. A youth called Foo Gee Chikee was presenting acrobatic feats on a vertical bamboo pole. At the top was a loop into which he placed a foot, enabling him to adopt a horizontal position as if he were standing laterally on the pole. He was no sooner in place when the loop broke and crashing on to the footlights he ended in the orchestra pit. "A thrill of horror ran through the assembled people, who feared the young man was killed."
Foo was handed back up on to the stage where, giving his usual salaam, he walked away to vociferous cheers. As the rest of the troupe carried on, Foo was taken to a nearby surgery and examined by a doctor who found one of the small iron pipes from gas jet footlights lodged in his left side between two ribs. Another pipe had entered the back of his right thigh making an ugly wound. Poor Foo was out of action for some time.
There were several rival troupes of Japanese gymnasts incorporating the word 'Tycoon' in their titles, making accurate identification difficult. Australian historians and genealogists seem to be particularly exercised with untangling them.

1871_05_12 YORK (Victoria MH).   ACCIDENT TO TRAPEZE ARTISTES
The Brothers Bonner were performing on the trapeze about 20ft above the pit. One brother was holding the trapeze bar with the other hanging below him when the uppermost one lost his grip and the pair plummeted into the pit, colliding with the chairman who escaped with a few bruises. The brothers also seem to have escaped with nothing more serious than a cut arm. It would appear there was no net.

1871_05_20 MANCHESTER (Theatre Royal).   MIRTHFUL COLLAPSE OF SCENERY
[J L Toole met Henry Irving in 1857 while they were both touring the country in the summer. They became the closest of friends and their careers blossomed in tandem, Irving becoming the leading tragedian and Toole the top comic actor.]
On this night, the play was based on *The Pickwick Papers* and the scene was a court room. The star of the show was J L Toole. The curtain rose to show the jury all sitting in the box. As Toole stood to address the court, the entire jury disappeared when the box gave way. At first the audience was stunned, but as the jury men swiftly reappeared unhurt, though looking very foolish, they were greeted with a veritable "hurricane of laughter which lasted several minutes".
The curtain was lowered while the scene was reset, and then restarted with Toole's speech in which he said of the jury: "that worthy body of steadfast and immovable men" which brought

60. *J L Toole*

another gale of laughter. An amusing feature of all this, unknown to the audience the jurymen were actually stagehands, whose job was to build up the court scene, so in this case they suffered by their own carelessness. You may laugh. Ho! Ho! Ho!

1871_06_08 NOTTINGHAM (Alhambra).   ACCIDENT TO PREGNANT TRAPEZE ARTISTE

This was a particularly tragic accident. We met the Brothers Trevanion earlier (*see* 1869_03_16) now Trevanion was performing with his wife Mdlle Cerissa who, mid-act, fell upon the stage. It was said at the time that she was not seriously hurt, but Mr Roche the owner of the music hall would not allow her to resume performing as she was great with child. She left Nottingham on Sunday 11 June to travel to Middlesbrough to stay with her husband's parents. There, premature labour came on and she died on Monday 19 June. She was no more than 21 years of age and had also contracted smallpox before she died.

1871_08_07c DUBLIN (Queen's).   ACCIDENT TO 'LITTLE FIREFLY'

Edith Sandford was an actress and equestrienne who, with her horse Etna, appeared as a *vivandière* (camp follower) called Firefly in a drama *The Ride for Life* a sensation piece which Miss Sandford had adapted from Ouida's novel *Under Two Flags*. Whenever the hero of the piece is in a tight spot Firefly and Etna come galloping to his rescue, including through blazing fire. "A sensational effect, without parallel in the annals of the stage; a feat of daring on the part of Miss Sandford, and an exhibition of reliance upon her beautiful horse."

On this night Miss Sandford slipped while going down some stone steps and fell, dislocating her ankle in two places and severely straining ligaments in her foot. As inflammation had set in after Dr Wade had reset the limb, it was likely to be some time before Little Firefly could be back onstage. During her convalescence she received a letter and handsome present from the Princess of Wales, and a letter from the Lord Lieutenant of Ireland. After a five week absence she returned to the stage on 18 September at Cork.

1871_08_07 CADIZ, Spain.   FATAL ACCIDENT TO SIGNOR EURARDO

This performer was not the well-known Ethardo (*see* 1866_08_21), but a copy-cat performer Eurardo also known as a Spiral Ascensionist. He was actually Joseph Rowley (26), a native of Sheffield. His apparatus was a tall pole round which a spiral track rose higher and higher. Rather than a large ball like Ethardo, the Signor walked on a large barrel up this track to the top. Unlike Ethardo he did not do a return descent via the spiral but once reaching the top he paused for the next part of his act which entailed him leaping to the bar of a static trapeze. On this occasion, he failed to reach it due to a rope breaking, and fell to the ground. Insensible when picked up, he expired within a few hours. He was buried in the English church next day, leaving a young wife and child.

1871_08_21 BOULOGNE (France).   FATAL ACCIDENT TO STRONG MAN

Vigneron (45) was a strong man well-known throughout Europe for his colossal strength and performing stunts utilising it. On this day, he was on the beach at Boulogne before hundreds of spectators and holiday makers who had gathered to witness his most famous feat. He lifted a loaded cannon weighing 600lbs on to his shoulders and fired a full charge of gunpowder. The stunt went with his usual success, but while lowering the cannon he slipped and fell. "The whole weight of the cannon fell on the face of the unfortunate man, splitting his skull completely in two. Death, of course, was instantaneous."

1871_08_31 COLUMBUS, USA (Opera House).   ACCIDENT TO HIGH TIGHTROPE WALKER

This tightrope walker, rejoicing in the name of Professor Dehum, announced he would walk on a rope attached from the roof of the Opera House to a building of similar height opposite, across the street. Over a thousand people gathered to watch the free show. The Prof got to the middle of his rope, sat down upon it and addressed the crowd for 10 minutes – on what topic I do not know – but having said his piece, while standing up to walk again the rope broke asunder, and the Prof, whirling over and over, fell to the ground with a heavy thud. On being taken up and into a drug store he was found to have cuts to his head, bruises on his body, and a broken leg.

1871_09_12c CAMBRIDGE (Theatre Royal).   SCENERY FIRE IN MIDDLE OF *MACBETH*

Just at the moment in the play when Macbeth hears of the death of Lady Macbeth, a part of the stage in full view of the audience burst into flames. As is to be expected, a shriek ran round the theatre and some of the audience rose and fled to the exits, but most remained to watch and cheer the efforts of the stage crew as they dealt with the unexpected fire. They ultimately triumphed, but Reginald Moore the stage manager, and Mr Raffell the second low comedian received some bad burns, and, of course, some new and valuable scenery was destroyed.

1871_10_07 DUBLIN (Exhibition Palace).   ACCIDENT TO PROFESSOR HERRMANN

[Alexander Herrmann (1844-1896) was born in Paris of German parents. His father was a medical man but a skilled amateur magician. His wife was a bit magical too as she produced sixteen children. Two of their many sons became professional magicians. Though Compars had a head start being almost three decades older, the younger boy soon became the more successful. One of the most famous names in magic history, self-styled as 'Herrmann the Great', he made his initial impact in the USA where he became a naturalised citizen. He went on three grand world tours, made and lost a lot of money with various theatrical ventures, and from 1870 spent three years in the UK. During that period he played a thousand nights at London's Egyptian Hall.]

61. *Alexander Herrmann*

On this, the last night in Dublin during a triumphal tour of the Provinces, Herrmann suffered an accident with the famous 'bullet catching trick'. His hands were seriously injured, which is a bit of a blow for a magician, and put an abrupt halt to his tour. He was later reported to be on the way to recovery and hoping soon to be back at the Egyptian Hall known as the 'Home of Mystery' because of all the magicians and spiritualists who appeared there.

1871_10_22 CHATTERIS (Foottit's Circus).   FATAL GUN ACCIDENT

[George Foottit formed a circus with two noted equestrians but, as George was too fond of the bottle, in the first season they parted company and he soldiered on with his own show dying in 1874 of liver cirrhosis (what else?!). The clown in the famous French act Foottit and Chocolat was George's son.] "During the performances at Foottit's Grand Allied Circus at Chatteris, one of the performers, named Hines, met with a fatal accident. His gun exploded and killed him." *The Era* 1871_10_22.

1871_11_02c ROCHESTER.   DAGGER ACCIDENT

62

The play was a melodrama called *Wrecked in Port,* the scene a typical one where the villain drags the heroine away in an attempt to run off with her. To her rescue comes the hero who stabs the villain with a dagger and takes the heroine in his arms as the curtain falls. So pretty much as the melodrama of cliché. The difference being that the villain had been really stabbed, fortunately not to a fatal extent. This incident was sufficient for one newspaper to hold forth about such accidents being too commonplace and, instead of real weapons, a trick dagger should be used where the blade is on a spring enabling it to disappear up into the handle when it appears the actor has been stabbed. No self-respecting modern actor would condone such a gadget as it has been known for the spring not to compress and the simple mechanism to jam, thus turning the prop into a genuine lethal weapon. (*see also* 1896_08_10)

1871_12_10 HARTLEPOOL (Theatre Royal).   ACCIDENT TO ACTRESS

Harriet Crossman, playing Betsy Trotwood in *Lost Emily,* accidentally fell down a staircase at the side of the stage leading to the cellars, and broke her leg. A bit more drastic than the familiar sprained ankle, and laying the lady up for some weeks. On 7 February, her manager wrote to *The Era* to point out that his actors had given up their pay for the day of the accident, he himself had paid her for four weeks but welcomed the setting up of a fund to assist her. She had only been with his company for 10 days and there must have been lots of past colleagues of Miss Crossman from companies in which she had spent much longer engagements.

1871_12_23c BRUSSELS, Belgium.   ACCIDENT TO THE BROTHERS DE COLMARS

The three brothers were a high wire act where one brother rode across the wire on a bicycle from which two trapezes hung on which the other two brothers performed. They had no sooner pushed off from the platform when the hook holding the wire broke in two, and the trio plummeted to the ground. The trapeze artistes were unhurt, but the insensible cyclist was taken to hospital where he remained for two weeks, fortunately suffering no lasting damage. The hook was not their own, having been manufactured on the order of the director of the venue. The De Colmars threatened to sue the blacksmith.

1871_12_29c CHELTENHAM (Theatre Royal).   ACCIDENT TO PANTOMIME CLOWN

Mr Laurence the Clown at the pantomime executed one of his customary leaps through the scenery to find out too late that the men deputed to catch him were absent. He crashed heavily to the floor gaining several bruises but managing to complete the scene. Although under medical treatment, he continued to appear. For pantomimists the problem of absent stagehands had gone on for over a hundred years without a sensible solution. It beggars belief that pantomimists went on for several generations without solving the worry of relying on indolent stagehands. It would seem to me that once that has happened you will lose all confidence in the staff for the rest of the season, thus being unable to dive and leap with your customary panache.

1871_12_30 NEW ORLEANS, USA (Opera House).   GUN ACCIDENT DURING OPERA

M Delabranche was singing in *Les Huguenots*. During the final massacre scene, a musket was fired early while in front of the tenor. His left eye was injured, and it was feared he might lose his sight. The right one was completely safe.

1872_01_08 LONDON (Standard).   SUDDEN DEATH OF YOUNG CLOWN

John Thorogood (21) working under the stage name of Johnny Johns, was engaged at the Standard Theatre, Shoreditch as Clown in the Christmas pantomime. During the matinee, struck with an unexpected and sudden fit, he was taken to the London Hospital and "placed under the influence of a galvanic battery". He returned to the theatre, but unable to work was taken home, where he died four days later. At the post mortem it was said variously that he had been injured coming through a trap in the harlequinade, or he had been mistreated at the hospital. The stage manager denied the trap argument, claiming the construction of it made this impossible (!), and the man was an experienced working clown. Dr Curling of the hospital said when the man was brought in he still had his clown make-up on, possibly obscuring some tell-tale discovery about his condition. However, there was no sign of epilepsy or paralysis, and an absence of apoplexy. After the battery treatment, he recovered, spoke and, asking to go home, walked away with friends. The absence of apoplexy gave no indication that the case was an urgent one. In Victorian times apoplexy referred to any sudden death that began with an abrupt loss of consciousness, symptoms being what today we call a stroke. Thorogood died from a rupture of a blood vessel in the brain, the jury's verdict being "Death from natural causes" and refuting any blame attached to the hospital.

63

75

1872_01_27 PARIS, France (Folies Dauphine).   ACCIDENT TO TRAPEZE ARTISTES

The venue was a minor music hall or *café conc*, the artistes were two trapezists known as Hemont and Rolland who had been performing there for some time. They informed M Aubin the owner that on this night they wanted to try out some new tricks in their act. He suggested that a net should be placed under their apparatus, a suggestion scorned by the duo who said there was positively no danger. Rolland had injured his leg some three months previously but had worked consistently since.

All went as planned up to a feat where Rolland, suspended downwards from the bar of the trapeze, held his partner by the wrists while he performed various gymnastic evolutions. Suddenly Rolland's recently cured leg gave way, and the duo fell in a heap among the spectators. Hemont escaped with nothing but a few bruises, but Rolland injured his head and right wrist and was taken to hospital.

Why did these aerialists think they were super-human that they should scorn nets? And did the customers feel happy sitting underneath aerial performers without a net above them? As we see from time to time when there is a net it fails in some way. There were two main reasons why a net was scorned. Firstly, expense. Secondly as most performers were changing venues weekly they only had Monday after band call to set the thing up in a manner that did not incommode the audience.

1872_03_01 NOTTINGHAM (Alhambra).   FATAL ACCIDENT TO APPRENTICE GYMNAST

We have met the Culeen Brothers before (*see* 1868_12_03). Thomas Culeen, formerly of the Culeen Brothers gymnastic troupe, had presumably retired from performing himself, as he had taken on an apprentice by the name of William Swann (15) who with another lad was performing as the Culeen Brothers. This was their first engagement after 5 months of training on the trapeze.

On Friday, the fourth night of the engagement, Swann came to the feat of turning a double somersault from the swinging trapeze, to land on a mattress on the stage. The trapeze at rest was only five feet from the ground. On this night, as he turned his somersault he caught his foot on the bar, causing him to release his hold on his thighs, leaving him with insufficient thrust to complete the somersault and he fell on his neck on the mattress. Culeen carried him off the stage and he was taken to the General Hospital. There it was found that his arms and legs were completely powerless because his spinal cord was damaged. Swann died on the following Wednesday.

The jury could only bring in a verdict of 'Accidental death', but added "such performances were useless, dangerous, and objectionable" and the Coroner said "it was a pity that the law could not interfere to prevent such exhibitions." Keep reading and you will find the law did try to interfere.

1872_03_20c EMMERICH (Germany).   FATAL FALL OF TRAPEZE ARTISTE

"One of the Brothers Palmer, whilst performing the flying feats at the Emmerich Circus, missed the ankles of his partner on the opposite trapeze, carried away the subtending net, and was killed on the spot. The deceased acrobat was only twenty-two." *Londonderry Sentinel* 1872_04_02.

1872_04_08 PLYMOUTH (Albert Hall).   ACCIDENT TO BOY GYMNAST

[The Silbon Troupe was – like the Hanlons – an English family of aerialists who became major performers in the USA and "one of the outstanding flying acts of all time."]

The venue was the Albert Hall, and the Silbon Troupe was nightly giving a series of shows on both trapeze and high wire. On this night one of the troupe, a little fellow aged eight, twice missing the trapeze, fell to the boarded floor. Nothing daunted, he climbed up again and tried for the third time. On this attempt, grabbing the bar with one hand and twisting round, he fell again breaking his collarbone "but fortunately his injuries are not of a dangerous description." I find it surprising that an act of this calibre was performing without a net.

1872_04_22 WEST HARTLEPOOL (New Gaiety).   ACCIDENT TO TIGHTROPE WALKER

The Great Dragon Troupe was comprised of Japanese gymnasts and jugglers. The lady performer on the high wire and slack rope created quite a *furore* with her feats. On this night she was ascending the sloping rope from the stage to the top of the gallery when within a few steps of the end she lost her balance. She fell 30ft on to the heads of people in the pit, on the way smashing some of the glass lamps at the front of the boxes. "The horror-stricken audience shrieked with alarm" but apart from a few bruises and the bodily shaking the dainty artiste was unharmed. More remarkably none of the seated people she fell upon suffered in any way. Within 15 minutes, the performer returned and the audience applauded her safe escape, but when she made to attempt her walk again, the audience vociferously pleaded with her not to do so. Ignoring the pleas, she walked to the top of the rope and back again without any difficulty whatsoever, receiving an ovation on her safe descent.

1872_05_25 CHICAGO, USA (Globe).   ACCIDENT TO ACTRESS WITH SULPHURIC ACID

The Wyndham Comedy Company was appearing in a repertoire of plays. On this night the production was *Mephisto's Mission* and during the play Annie Goodall drank a glass of sulphuric acid instead of wine. The game girl, though suffering agonies, went through her part but was not able to appear on subsequent nights. I have not been able to find out how this mistake occurred. Fortunately, she must not have suffered any permanent damage as she was able to rejoin her colleagues within a couple of weeks.

1872_07_04 LONDON.   SECOND READING OF THE ACROBATS BILL

Not an accident but the start of a movement to prevent accidents to children in acrobatic troupes. In the House of Lords, Lord Buckhurst moved the second reading of the Acrobats Bill which was basically intended to stop all acrobatic performances by people under the age of 16. Lord Shaftesbury supported it, but then he would, wouldn't he? However, Lord Morley opposed the bill on grounds of over regulation.

The profession immediately put pen to paper with George Sanger being foremost, pointing out that 16 is too late for training gymnasts, as it is for dancers. If the law was passed then there would be no British acrobats, they would all be from abroad. Pantomimes would no longer have clowns, harlequins and dancers from this country because all these performers acquired their skills before the age of 16. The result of the law would be children being taken abroad to train, returning as fully fledged performers at 16.

After the third reading of the Bill on 22 July – during which the Lords had much humour trying to exactly define an acrobat – the bill was thrown out. Professional performers breathed a sigh of relief, but it was far too soon to relax. Keep on reading!

1872_07_24 WASHINGTON, USA (Metropolitan Hall).   FATAL GUN ACCIDENT

The actor was Mr J Keegan, shot and killed through "the gross carelessness of the property man". This inept person used stout brown paper for the wadding covering the powder, and when the musket was discharged the wadding penetrated Keegan's skull "making an orifice through which the brains protruded". He died at home five days later.

1872_07_30 WIGAN (Theatre).   GUN ACCIDENT FROM FOOLING ABOUT

The Brighton Comedy Company was visiting the town and after playing *Trial of Friendship* – in which a pistol is fired – all ended as it should, after which Mr Weston the lessee of the theatre gave a speech. On hearing a pistol shot in the wings, he went to investigate. The pistol in the play had been used satisfactorily, but it was the practice to have a second loaded pistol on hand in case the first one misfired then the sound could be instantly heard by firing off the stand-by in the wings. It was this second pistol that had made the noise that interrupted Mr Weston and he found to his horror that one of the stagehands had been "larking about" and shot George Fry the property man full in the face, which was "besmeared with blood and black with powder", the wadding having entered one eye. Weston immediately asked if there was a doctor in the house. Three medical men responded and tended to Fry. It was feared that the sight in the afflicted eye would be lost.

1872_08_05 LONDON (Oxford).   ACCIDENT TO TRAPEZE ARTISTE

The performer was The Great Hawley on the flying trapeze. His major feat was to fly the length of the hall from one trapeze then catching another one that had been swung towards him. This was a copy of the original feat introduced to the world by Léotard, but whereas he flew over mattresses, Hawley was more up-to-date and had a large net beneath him. However, he fell into the net at the edge but the impetus of his swing bounced him out on to the stage where he landed heavily. Apart from a cut to his chin he was not injured, and the following night gave his usual performance.

1872_08_07 LONDON (Victoria).   DAGGER ACCIDENT

The play was *The Reign of Terror* in which the hero is stabbed in the back by an assassin. The actor playing the latter role misplaced his blow and instead of the dagger secretly passing between arm and side, it went in at the shoulder passing through clothing and inflicted a "severe wound" although the dagger was blunted. The man was taken to his dressing room and medically attended to before being sent home in a cab semi-conscious from loss of blood.

1872_09_07 LOWESTOFT (Theatre).   GUN ACCIDENT

The drama was *Cartouche*, the actor Mr S Geary. In the course of the play Geary had to fire a pistol, but on doing this it exploded in his hand causing "a fearful wound" in the palm. He was not expected to return to the stage for some time.

1872_11_27 BLYTH (Octogon).   GUN ACCIDENT TO MESSENGER BOY

A boy named Wilson, employed at the Octagon Theatre as a messenger was enjoying himself playing about with the swords and pistols that comprised weaponry stage props. A pistol went off injuring his hand and blowing off most of one finger. Silly boy.

1873_01_26c MILAN, Italy (Scala).   A NIGHT OF DISASTERS AT LA SCALA

This is a catalogue of woe that speaks for itself and none of the accidents is the slightest bit amusing, but put together as presented in the newspaper they do read like black humour:

"A Night of Disaster.—The Milan Correspondent of the *Swiss Times* writes: Last Sunday evening a series of distressing incidents occurred at the Scala. The clothes of a ballet-dancer caught fire, and but for the immediate aid of the scene-shifters she would have been burned alive; a modiste fell down the staircase leading to the wardrobe, breaking her leg; a stage assistant fell dead, stricken with apoplexy; and a musician in the orchestra went raving mad, and was forcibly conveyed to the hospital." *Thanet Advertiser* 1873_02_08.

1873_02_12 LIMERICK (Theatre).   OPERA SINGER FALLS THROUGH STAGE

Durand's Opera Company was presenting *La Sonnambula* when Frank Burgess, in the role of Allesio, suddenly found himself with both legs going down through a hole in the stage as the planks broke. Presumably the wood of the stage was rotten and anybody could have gone through at any time. (*see also* 1841_11_15/17) His legs were so injured that he was unable to appear for the last three nights of the Company's stay. The Durand Opera Company was led by baritone Charles Durand who assembled a troupe for an annual provincial tour. Durand even ventured to the USA with his troupe.

1873_02_15 NEW YORK, USA (Bowery).   CANNON ACCIDENT
The play was *Captain Kidd*, the actor seriously wounded playing a minor role was John Macintyre. One of the supers let off a cannon before he should have done and wounded Macintyre in the thigh. "The accident created great excitement for a time, but after the removal of the actor to hospital the piece was proceeded with." The show must go on!

1873_02_17 HANLEY (Theatre).   ACTRESS FALLS THROUGH TRAPDOOR
The play was the "intellectual drama" of *Mother Brownrigg* in which Mrs Julien was playing one of the villain's victims. Whilst ascending a shaft in the "burning house" of Mother Brownrigg, her support gave way and she fell through an open trapdoor into the cellar below, a distance of around 20ft. She remained unconscious for some time. Mr Burn the surgeon, who happened to be in the theatre, ministered to her until she came round when he diagnosed injuries to her head and arm. It was expected that she would be able to return to the stage within a few days.

1873_03_03 BLACKBURN (Theatre).   GUN ACCIDENT
The play was based on *Les Miserables* set in Paris; the hero Marius played by William Tallon, a great favourite with the local audience. In Act IV, a barricade scene, Tallon was poised centre stage brandishing a burning torch with which he was threatening to ignite a barrel marked 'powder'. Two supers dressed as soldiers were to fire guns at him. On stage, of course, guns without bullets or balls are used, but the gunpowder charge is kept in place by wadding which, as we have seen over and over, is a danger in itself, so the technique was to point the gun above the head of the supposed victim rather than at him. This, one of the supers William Ingram, failed to do and, from a distance of six feet, the charge struck Tallon over his right eye and he fell to the floor shrieking in pain. The charge was unnecessarily heavy and the paper wadding had made a hole in Tallon's face ¾inch in diameter and equally as deep. Mr Martland dressed the wound and Tallon was taken home.

1873_03_03c LONDON (Astley's).   ACCIDENT TO ACTRESS
This accident was certainly a very close brush with death, just a matter of a few inches. Marie Courtenay was playing a principal role in the pantomime and, at the end of the fairy scene, a 14ft length of heavy timber fell from the flies. It fell perpendicularly precisely on to Miss Courtenay's foot. "Her shrieks were fearful, and caused quite a consternation" understandably, as it was an immense roller for winding a stage curtain. Her boot was cut to pieces, her stocking torn as the end smashed her foot and cut the tendons. The blood flowed copiously. It takes no imagination to realise a very few inches further back and it would have been her head that was smashed and death instantaneous. As it was, she was confined to bed in a very weak state, facing many months before she would be able to leave her room, with the ever present fear of being lame for life when she could do so.

1873_03_13 PHILADELPHIA, USA (Fox's).   ACCIDENT TO HUMAN CANNONBALL
The venue was Fox's New American Theatre, the performer was Leo a boy gymnast. He was supposed to be fired from a 'cannon' – actually a metallic pneumatic tube – to be caught by Leopold on a trapeze 30ft above the stage. The signal was given too soon, Leopold was not ready, and the boy was shot a mere eight or nine feet before falling to the stage, breaking his leg.

1873_05_12 SPENNYMOOR (Cambridge).   GUN ACCIDENT

The play was a sensation drama *The Drunkard's Child*. In Act IV, in the struggle between hero and villain, by some accident a loaded pistol went off and the contents lodged in the face of Mr Dews the actor-manager. Though soon recovering, Dews was not able to perform for several days.

1873_06_14 BOSTON, USA (Theatre).   ACCIDENT TO MISS VICTORIA VOKES

[The Vokes family were a British institution. The five members of this family played pantomime at the Theatre Royal Drury Lane for ten consecutive years. There were three sisters Jessie, Rosina and Victoria and a brother Fred. The fifth member was an actor called Walter Fawdon who joined the family at a young age and stayed with them throughout, changing his name to Fawdon Vokes. They were as popular in the USA as they were at home.]

The play was *Black Eyed Susan* and here on a USA contract was Victoria with the rest of them. One Saturday night Victoria fell and broke her collarbone. Not knowing it was broken, she worked again on Monday. Having been informed of the damage, and suffering greatly, she still appeared on Tuesday and Wednesday when she fainted from the pain and was carried from the theatre. The other family members continued with tremendous success, and it was expected that Victoria would soon be back onstage.

64. *Victoria Vokes*

1873_07_19 CLAY CROSS (Alhambra).   GUN ACCIDENT

The play was *The Man with the Hand of Death*. Frank Danvers, playing the part of Hammonde Beefe, had to shoot a pistol in the course of the play. At this performance the pistol burst, blowing away a part of his thumb and breaking his fore-finger – not the *Hand of Death* but the *Hand of Injury*.

1873_07_20c ST ETIENNE, France (Circus Guillaume)   ACCIDENT TO TRAPEZE ARTISTE

We met Alvantee earlier (*see* 1869_04_20), now he was a performer with this touring show. Attempting a double somersault from one trapeze to another, it gave way as he clutched it, precipitating him head first into the ring. One of the Brothers Hadwin who was in the ring rushed forward and, at great risk to himself, broke the fall, Alvantee landing on his side. He was extremely shaken and suffered two broken ribs. I assume there was no safety net. The only visual evidence I have found for this performer is a coloured poster from some twenty years later when he is "King of the Slanting Wire" so perhaps he got fed up with falling from trapezes.

1873_08_10c PARIS, France (Franconi).   FATAL EQUESTRIAN ACCIDENT

Mr Lebman, a rider at Franconi's Circus, after throwing a somersault was intending to end on his horse, misjudged and, falling to the ground, broke his spine. I find the tenor of this report unpleasantly contemptuous – "Death was instantaneous. The corpse was carried out, and in came the clowns and restored the audience to good humour, the performances not being disturbed by this little *contretemps*." Talk about send in the clowns and death being a little *contretemps*. Nasty!

1873_09_06 BIRMINGHAM (Grand).   GUN ACCIDENT ON THE TIGHTROPE
    The venue was the Grand Concert Hall, the performer was Madame Laura who walked on a high wire and when reaching the middle discharged a six barrelled revolver. On this night, after discharging four of the barrels the revolver burst, sending bits of the weapon into Madame's face and breast. With remarkable equanimity she walked to the end of the wire, turned and walked back to the other end where she could descend. On reaching the ground she fainted. However, with the injuries proving none too serious, and Madame recovering well, a rapid return to work was anticipated.

1873_09_15 BIRMINGHAM.   ACCIDENT TO TIGHTROPE WALKER
    The venue is described as Birmingham Concert Hall; I do not know if this is the same place as the Grand Concert Hall (*see above*). If so, they do not have much luck with their wirewalkers. This chap, name of Wainratta, was walking on a sloping wire that, starting at the back of the stage, rose to around 20ft, where it was fastened in the Upper Hall. Wainratta was swinging about in the centre of the wire when he crashed to the floor. Obviously there was no net, but he escaped with a bruised shoulder that kept him off the wire for a day or two. (*see also* 1874_05_16 *and* 1886_04_24).

1873_10_02c HOBART, Australia.   TWO FALLS IN ONE COMPANY
    News from Australia took a long time to arrive in Victorian times so all we know is these two accidents happened whilst Miss Juno's company was in town. The first happened to Miss Juno herself who, after falling through a stage trap that had not been locked, was confined to her bed for several days. The second involved Mrs Alfred Phillips who, all dressed up and ready for the part of Lady Sowerby Creamly, on leaving the greenroom and going up steps to the stage, "fell forward striking the front of her head, and, in a most unaccountable manner, completely scalped herself, it being entirely removed from the forehead to the nape of the neck". Doctors were in immediate attendance and sewed her scalp back on, then she was taken home. It was feared the injury might prove fatal, but no the game gal was reported to be fully recovered and back onstage in mid-November.

1873_12_26 LONDON (Princess's).   ACCIDENT TO PANTOMIME CLOWN
    The pantomime was *Little Puss in Boots*. The Clown was Signor Delevanti, Pantaloon Harry Williams. I cannot find any mention of an accident to Delevanti in any of the papers, but he definitely suffered one that put him out of action for some time. We know this because in a letter to *The Era* it is stated "In your last issue you favourably criticised the performance of the Clown under the name of Signor Delevanti*. Permit me to state that Signor Delevanti unfortunately met with a severe accident on Boxing Night, and that he has not yet been able to resume his professional duties; in consequence of which the part of Clown was undertaken at a minute's notice, and has been played since without intermission, by yours faithfully, Harry Williams (Pantomimist)"
    The Era's review said "A better Clown than Signor Delevanti could scarcely be desired, Mr Frank Wright is an excellent Harlequin, Mr H. Williams a thoroughly efficient Pantaloon" It is no wonder the reviewers did not know, as press advertisements still proclaimed Delevanti as Clown and Mr H Williams as Pantaloon to the end of January. It was a common occurrence in the pages of *The Era* to have performers wailing that they had been mis-identified – and who can blame them when their livelihoods depended on their names.

1874_02_09 LONDON (Grecian Theatre).   TRAP ACCIDENT TO MISS PARKES

[The pantomimes at this theatre were known for the extensive trap work of its owner George Conquest. This prodigious performer specialised in bizarre roles and exhaustive gymnastic work involving many traps and flying wires. For the 1873/74 panto season not only was he the star of his own pantomime playing *The Wood Demon* at the Grecian every evening, in the afternoons he was at the Crystal Palace as the Ogre in *Dame Trot and her Cat* with son George as the Cat. In the 22 February 1874 edition of *Reynold's Newspaper*, George advertised that between the two venues he and his son had leapt, fallen and dived through 2,448 traps since Christmas Eve, and he had daily played twelve different characters – an Ogre, an Imp, an Astrologer, a Pear, a Dwarf, a Fish, Half a Giant, a Tree, Two Giants and Two Fiends. The Grecian pantomime ran the longest of all the theatres in London, usually running into April.]

One of the traps used by pantomimists was the vampire trap and at the Crystal Palace on this afternoon after George had gone through such a trap, the man under the stage forgot to replace the slider which held the stage boards solid when not in use. In the following scene Caroline Parkes, a popular favourite, stepped on this trap which gave way and she dropped down to her armpits. One of her legs was badly lacerated by the iron edge of the opening, and she was "much bruised and shaken". She gamely tried to carry on, but could not manage it. She was confined to her bed and it was expected to be a lengthy time before she fully recovered.

65. *Open trap accident*

1874_02_13 PHILADELPHIA, USA (Fox's).   ACCIDENT TO HEAD OF PRAEGER FAMILY

The Praeger family had been rehearsing during the morning at Fox's American Theatre, and just as they were about to leave Mr Praeger fell through an open trap on the stage, sustaining a dislocated shoulder and a broken arm.

The Era newspaper took the opportunity to berate irresponsible stagehands. When these men failed in their duty they incurred no penalty, unlike the signalman or pointsman on the railway, or the driver of the omnibus who is punished if he is responsible for causing an accident. *The Era* appealed to theatre managers to prosecute everyone who was the cause of an accident through his carelessness, stating it should be widely known that "severe punishment will surely follow guilt", and hoped that when one or two had been made an example, the rest would be roused to a better sense of their responsibility. I have found no report in the Victorian era of a pantomimist suing for injury.

66. *Another open trap accident*

1874_02_21 PAISLEY (Theatre Royal). FATAL ACCIDENT TO SUPER

The play was *Jack Robinson and his Monkey*. In the part of Captain was an amateur actor, Francis Sandford Keith Douglas, a student at Glasgow University. Among the supers was John Tibble, a corporal in the 21st Regiment of Foot who, often appearing as a super, was familiar backstage. It was quite customary for soldiers to act as supers, Henry Irving often employed them at 1/- a night. At the end of the play during a melee between the Captain and mutineers, Douglas fired his rifle at the head of Tibble from a distance no greater than 2ft. This resulted in Tibble's right eye being blown out and his left seriously injured. He was hospitalised in his barracks. In court, Douglas, charged with recklessly discharging firearms, was placed on bail for £15. On 15 March, after three weeks of agonising suffering, Tibble died. He had been in his regiment 14 years, six of which were spent in India. A post mortem was held and the case investigated by the Procurator-Fiscal. Douglas was exonerated from the charge of culpable recklessness in discharging firearms, and Crown counsel gave instructions that proceedings be dropped. A university student in those days was always "a young gentleman".

1874_03_05 BOLTON (Weston's). ACCIDENT TO TRAPEZE ARTISTES

It is the Culeen troupe again (*see* 1872_03_01). This time a man and boy were involved, both unnamed so we do not know if the man is Mr Culeen himself. The man was hanging from the trapeze by one leg, head downwards, while pulling the boy up with a rope. The end of the trapeze bar pulled out of its socket and both man and boy fell 20ft to the floor, the man on top of the boy who was "seriously hurt about the shoulders". Culeen clearly had not learned that a safety net was essential.

83

1874_03_19 NEW YORK, USA (34th Steet). FATAL ACCIDENT TO TRAPEZE ARTISTE

James Sylvester (20) and his partner Edward Baldwin were at the climax of their act – "the thrilling feat of throwing a somersault from the trapeze to a single rope." The trapeze apparatus was suspended across the auditorium, parallel to the front of the stage. Thus the rope – which was fastened to the ceiling – was hanging in front of one of the side boxes and firmly held in position by Baldwin. Sylvester had accomplished the somersault six times shortly before but, alas, not on this night as he miscalculated the distance, missed the rope, and was thrown with great force against the stage box. He fell to the stage, and was carried behind the scenes then, rapidly failing with a fractured skull, was whizzed off to Belle Vue Hospital where, unknown to the audience, he died within the hour.

1874_04_11 LIVERPOOL (Royal Alexandra). ACCIDENT TO ACTOR

The play was the new sensational drama *Genevieve; or the Missing Witness*. In the scene where he is thrown from the rocks into the roaring torrent below, Mr J F Stephenson, playing the hero Gustave, mistimed his leap, fell on to the stage and broke his leg.

All kinds of scenic effects were produced in these sensation melodramas of the period – dogs rescuing the heroine from the briny, railway engines thundering down on the heroine tied to the tracks, entire palaces collapsing etc. The scenic artists and stage managers would stop at nothing. With little in the way of machine energy available, stage managers headed a large force of labour that relied on muscle power to operate a wood and rope system akin to windmill and sailing ship mechanisms.

Many serious and fatal accidents occurred backstage which deserve a companion volume.

1874_04_13 HANLEY (People's).   ACCIDENT TO TRAPEZE ARTISTE

The performer, "Professor Johnson, a gymnast and a man of colour", felt one of the ropes holding his trapeze give way. He was performing above the pit and with "praiseworthy fortitude and admirable presence of mind" realised he would fall on to people in the pit, so with a mighty effort he made a terrific spring for the stage, on to which he fell with a sickening thud. The report says a distance of 20 yards which seems very far-fetched, probably more likely 20 feet. The professor's thigh was broken, and the auguries were that many months would pass before he could resume work.

1874_05_16 BIRMINGHAM (Day's).   ACCIDENT TO WAINRATTA THE WIRE KING

Ending his performance on the high wire, Wainratta was descending to the stage via a rope attached to a pulley in the ceiling, when within 12ft of the boards, the rope gave way and the Wire King fell with much force on to the footlights. As a result his head and face were badly cut, and he suffered a severe foot injury that was feared could be permanent. It was confirmed that Wainratta carried his own ropes and pulleys, and personally attended to their fixing. It would seem that Birmingham bore a jinx for the Wire King as he had suffered an accident in another hall in the town nine months previously. (*see 1873_09_15 and 1886_04_24*).

1874_08_30 DOUAI, France (Loyal's)   FATAL ACCIDENT TO TRAPEZE ARTISTE

84 "The death, at Douai, is announced of M Alexandra Loyal, an acrobat in the Circus bearing his name. In executing a flight along three trapezes he fell upon one of the edges of the bridge below and broke his vertebral column. He died on the spot." *The Era* 1874_08_30.

1874_09_23 KING'S LYNN (Theatre Royal).   ACCIDENT TO MISS BLACKWOOD

In *Little Nelly*, Virginia Blackwood playing the Marchioness was romping about when she fell heavily to the stage where she remained in an unconscious state for some time. The large audience, excited by this strange turn of events, as the supine lady was removed, surmised she had broken a leg. Whatever the cause, the performance was abandoned and the audience dispersed. The following day it was announced that she had displaced the cartilage in her knee and would be unable to appear. In fact, she would not be able to appear for several weeks as she only returned in mid-November at Ipswich.

1874_09_29 LIVERPOOL (Theatre Royal).   ACCIDENT TO ACTRESS

The actress was Ruth Edwin, the play a burletta of *Midas*. In the role of Apollo Miss Edwin was elevated on a platform controlled by a rope. When the platform was about six feet above the stage the rope snapped and the actress was plunged through a trap in the stage to the cellar below at "a considerable depth". While extremely shocked and bruised, fortunately she had not broken any bones, but remained out of action at Liverpool for a short time.

1874_10_08 LONDON (Philharmonic).   ACCIDENT TO TWO OPERA SINGERS

After the opera *Giroflé-Girofla*, the artistes Mr E Garden, and Walter Fisher a new tenor, were crossing the stage to their dressing rooms when both fell down an open trap into a cellar 15ft below. Fisher sustained wounds to his cheek and neck requiring stitches, Garden was injured in his back. Both were out of action for five days.

1874_11_18 WOLVERHAMPTON (Prince of Wales).   ACCIDENT IN *MAZEPPA*

The play was that old war-horse (ho! ho! ho!) *Mazeppa*; the hero who is bound to the back of the fiery steed was Bessie Reid. As the horse made its zig-zag way through the scenery it stumbled and fell, though only from a height of six feet. Although bruising and lacerating her left arm, fortunately Miss Reid was able to release herself, but the accident meant she was off the stage for several days. A horse cannot be blamed for stumbling when it has to clamber up sloping ramps sandwiched between bits of scenery with a non-horseman tied on its back. It's not surprising that an accident occurred; the wonder is that it did not happen more often. In fact it did happen an awful lot, but as the play was incredibly popular the risk was acceptable.

image© The British Library Board   67

1874_12_12 LONDON (Standard).   ACTOR SUES FOR DAMAGES   85

This accident actually happened in March when Mr Shore was acting the hero in a play *Peep O' Day*. In the quarry scene he had to leap for a tree to rescue the heroine. He missed the tree, caught his leg on a protruding piece of wood and fell 13ft on to the stage, damaging his head and receiving other injuries which prevented him from pursuing his profession. Nine months later he sued for damages against the lessees of the Standard Theatre where the accident happened. Their defence was that Mr Shore did not perform the business as was usual in the role in that scene. Shore stated that prior to the scene he had seen the projecting piece of wood and called the stage manager's attention to it. The jury found for the plaintiff, awarding £100 damages.

1874_12_23 LEEDS (Theatre Royal).   ACCIDENT TO PANTOMIME CLOWN

The pantomime was to have featured James De Green in the role of Clown, but rather drastically at the dress rehearsal he had broken his kneecap and was languishing in Leeds Infirmary instead of provoking festive laughter and earning a wage, whilst his wife and three children were thrown into a state of destitution. Johnny Matthewson of the rival Amphitheatre organised a whip-round and collected contributions ranging from a guinea from actor-manager Wilson Barrett down to several at 1/-. Further contributions were solicited via *The Era*.

On the 19 January 1875, De Green was able to write to *The Era* thanking his manager John Coleman for sending £2 each week to his wife, and for the organisation of a forthcoming benefit with all the company offering their services. He was also able to list the amounts gained by whip-rounds at some two dozen theatres throughout the country. Well done everybody!

1874_12_24 LONDON (Surrey).   ACCIDENT TO HARLEQUIN

The pantomime was *The Forty Thieves* and the Harlequin was Talleen Walsh, but only on the first night because during the course of the evening the poor fellow broke his leg, and since then had been confined to St Thomas's Hospital. The stage manager Walter Stacey organised a whip-round of the company, most of whom managed 5/- or 2/6d.

1875_04_12 WEDNESBURY (Theatre).   GUN ACCIDENT

John Dutton, a well-known local actor, in the course of the play had to draw out a pistol from his belt. In the process the gun exploded and blew away the middle of his hand. As the accident was at the close of a scene, the play carried on with another actor replacing the wounded Dutton who was likely to be out of action for many weeks to come. Gun accidents continue to be a regular hazard, and never seem to be a warning that more care should be taken.

1875_05_20 BEDFORD (Ginnett's).   FATAL ACCIDENT TO GYMNAST

Walter D'Altroy was performing in Ginnett's Circus on the horizontal bar when he fell and dislocated his neck; taken to the Infirmary, he expired within 24 hours.

1875_05_27 CASTLEFORD (Theatre).   GUN ACCIDENT

Thomas Lacey, performing under the stage name of Joseph Oliphant, was the unfortunate victim of a self-inflicted accident. He had to draw two pistols from his belt and in "a moment of excitement" grasping one by the muzzle, discharged both with the resultant loss of the thumb and first finger of his right hand which were blown off. He was detained in Leeds General Infirmary, and Mr Gaston Murray, interesting himself in garnering subscriptions, started by collecting a guinea each from E A Sothern, J B Buckstone, S French and S Kydd.

1875_06_10 PARIS, France (Ambigu).   DANGER FROM COLLAPSING SCENERY

The theatre was packing them in with a spectacular melodrama involving what appears to have been a realistic railway engine that was open for inspection after the show. In *L'Affaire Coverley*, actor Libert – playing the hero Ned Gordon – falls between the two rails as the train emerges from a tunnel. On this night, as the train appeared, a loud cracking sound was heard as though something had broken. This was followed by further sounds, and the engine was seen to lean alarmingly towards the public because, as all were then able to see, a front wheel had broken. Sensing the danger, Libert screamed out, and Madame Duguerret and Madame Pazza, standing alongside the lines, "appealed loudly for help to the audience". The engine driver, on hearing the first sound, slammed on the brake bringing the engine to a stop before it could topple over on to the actors and then fall into the orchestra pit. The curtain was hastily lowered.

Women in the audience fainted or screamed, and excitement reigned. The two actresses were so agitated by the affair that some time elapsed before they could resume their parts, and Libert had to come before the curtain to assure the audience that nobody had been hurt, and that all was under control. "The cause of the accident was not vouchsafed but the privilege that had been granted to visit the engine backstage was withdrawn".

1875_06_22 GLASGOW (Britannia).   FATAL ACCIDENT TO PANTOMIME CLOWN
     Charles Henry Goldsmith (31), professionally known as Charlie Bailey of Charles and Amy Bailey, sensational duettists, suffered a serious accident on this night which caused internal injuries. No details of the accident appear to have been given. He had taken to his bed and, after lying unconscious for 16 hours, he died on 30 June leaving his father, mother, wife and child.

1875_07_12 DUBLIN (Lloyd's).   ACCIDENT TO INFANT ACROBAT
     The reader may recall the rather sad accident to Mrs Trevanion which resulted in her death in premature labour (*see* 1871_06_08). The widower carried on as a gymnast, training very young children to be trapeze artistes. Mr Trevanion had a duo of infants called Sillo and Vertie at this venue who had been "creating quite a sensation". One afternoon Sillo fell from the gridiron into the paint room, a distance of some 20ft. He escaped serious injury, but suffered from the shaking he received. One has to wonder what the boy was doing up in the gridiron? Apparently, he ventured into the flies where he had no right to be, and the fall was nothing to do with his extraordinary theatrical performances.

68. *Tell & Tell*

     [The story of Trevanion and his various child trapeze duos is quite complex. At various times he had little trapeze artistes under the names Elspa, Lillo, Vertie, Echo, Sillo, Venus, Tell & Tell, and possibly more. It is very confusing to differentiate the boys and girls as reviews often muddled them. Lillo and Sillo seem to have been the same little girl whose name fluctuated, though the Sillo here was a boy. We will meet Elspa & Lillo in a future accident (*see* 1876_12_21). It was thought that for some reason Trevanion changed the name Sillo & Vertie to Tell & Tell but the latter pair appear to have been a new duo who became quite well-known on the halls for a couple of years.]

1875_07_16 TOLONA, USA (Cirquezoolodon).   ACCIDENT TO EQUESTRIAN
     Mrs Charles King, known professionally as Miss Bertie King met with an accident whilst riding in Warren, Henderson and Springer's show. During her act she was standing on her galloping horse about to jump through a paper hoop. The horse slipped, throwing her to the ground injuring her spine to such an extent that her physician "advised her to discontinue riding during the remainder of the present season."

1875_11_18 PHILADELPHIA, USA (Walnut St).   ACCIDENT TO MR FECHTER
     The eminent tragedian, acting in the play *No Thoroughfare*, fell from a 15ft high platform on to the stage below. It will be recalled that the poor chap had a previous long lay-off due to a fall on the ice less than a year before (*see* 1874_12_28c). Once again the same leg was in imminent danger from a wound that was not improving, plus an injury to his spine. He had to withdraw from his season in New York. Once again the theatre world was agog with rumours of amputation but these, fortunately, turned out to be false, though he did have to have several shards of bones removed from his leg. Once again he bounced back and was at Philadelphia on 28 February 1876 playing the Count of Monte Cristo.

1875_11_21 PARIS, France (Circus).   ACCIDENT TO HUMAN CANNONBALL

The feat of aerialist Mayol was to be fired like a projectile from a huge mortar to a trapeze bar 45ft away which he intended to grasp. He reached the bar but, his grasp being too slight, the impetus threw him beyond the safety net that was prudently arranged. Falling on to the balustrade, he lay apparently lifeless. Taken backstage, the circus doctor attended to the contusion of the head which appeared to be the sole injury, and within ten minutes Mayol had regained consciousness.

1875_11_24 CLEVELAND, USA (Theatre Comique).   ACCIDENT TO YOUNG TRAPEZIST

The performer was a boy called Master Lazelle. He ended his act by somersaulting from the trapeze to a carpet held under to catch him. One of the men holding the carpet let it slip from his grasp, and the boy hit the floor with a sickening crash. He was insensible with a fractured skull when carried from the theatre. Although this accident was in the USA, it added to the growing list of mishaps to juvenile gymnasts that concerned the UK authorities.

1876_01_25 LONDON (Lyceum).   SWORD ACCIDENT TO HENRY IRVING

[Henry Irving (1838–1905), was born John Henry Brodribb into a strong Methodist working-class family with no theatrical connections whatever. His childhood was spent in Cornwall but he went to the City Commercial School in London to train in office work. He joined a law firm at the age of 13 but all his spare time was devoted to a 'spouting club' and dreaming of becoming an actor. He was inspired by seeing Samuel Phelps the leading Shakespearean actor of the day whose ambition was to stage all 37 of Shakespeare's plays. He sought an introduction with Phelps who offered him a job which Henry refused. He knew he had a lot to learn and thought he would be better off making his mistakes in the provinces.

69. *Henry Irving*

Obtaining his first professional job in 1856 at Sunderland he adopted the name Henry Irving embarking on a long apprenticeship where he seemed to be getting nowhere. He eventually made his London debut in 1866 and began making an impression which led to him being taken on as leading man at the Lyceum at £17 a week. In 1871, he appeared in *The Bells* and became an 'overnight sensation.' He was soon accepted as the head of his profession and with Ellen Terry as his professional partner the pair became the first superstars. In 1895 Irving became the first actor to be knighted.]

During *Hamlet* Act V in the bout betwixt Hamlet and Laertes, Irving's foil rebounded upwards, the pommel striking the actor's cheek just below the eye. A medical friend of Irving was in the audience and did all that was necessary to reduce the damage. The great man was off the stage for a couple of nights when a substitute play was performed.

1876_02_05 NORTH SHIELDS (Theatre Royal). GUN ACCIDENT

Mr Clynds, the manager and tragedian, narrowly escaped being killed by a misdirected pistol shot. In the last act of the play *Cartouche*, his eponymous character is fired upon and on this night the wadding from the pistol penetrated his leather belt and entered his side causing a severe wound 1½" in diameter and an 1" deep. A doctor was soon in attendance and the actor was taken home. Subsequent performances had to be altered because of the lack of the leading actor. So far I have made entries for 44 gun accidents and there are 24 more years to go! The Victorian showbusiness world seems markedly dense about learning that guns are dangerous props.

1876_03_04 BIRMINGHAM (Prince of Wales). ACCIDENT TO PANTOMIME CLOWN

The Brothers Stevens were a featured attraction in the pantomime *Gulliver's Travels* and, being expert pantomimists, their work was gymnastic and physical. During the many dives and leaps Sydney Stevens damaged his kneecap. Nevertheless he changed into his clown motley for the harlequinade but after the transformation scene his leg would not support him and he had to retreat to the greenroom. The doctor was sent for and he pronounced it a severe strain on the principal cartilage of the knee which would require several days rest. The harlequinade carried on minus the clown, the pantaloon having to provide all the comic business on his own.

1876_03_27 LONDON (Adelphi). ACCIDENT TO MRS MANDERS

[Mrs Manders started her theatrical career at Exeter in 1825 and later married Thomas Manders "an admirable comedian". During her career she suffered several accidents including a fall from the flies at Sadler's Wells injuring her kneecap and collar bone, and in 1845 a fall in the street on her way to a rehearsal damaged her spine. Her husband died in 1859, and her brother-in-law – who was in the diplomatic service as an attaché for 60 years – also died. The death of both these men left Mrs Manders without any help and she had been a stalwart at the Adelphi for three years when she suffered another accident.]

Mrs Manders, the popular veteran actress was appearing in the hit play *Peep O' Day* when on this night she fell down the steps leading to the stage and broke her left arm. She survived by precarious isolated engagements but, with advancing age and restricted ability, these were hard to come by and not providing sufficient for her immediate needs, much less enabling her to avoid penury.

Facing destitution in her 77th year, in 1879 an appeal in *The Era* briefly recounting her career, laying stress on her "admirable conduct in private life", and "a career without blemish" as well as her "true talent allied with genuine worth". Contributions made to the fund included two guineas each from D'Oyly Carte, Toole, Charles Wyndham and Henry Betty and five contributions of £5 including those of Henry Irving and the Bancrofts. Clearly, Mrs Manders was a greatly respected veteran, and one hopes she garnered sufficient to keep her in tolerable comfort to eke out her remaining days.

1876_04_20c WARRINGTON (Prince of Wales). GUN ACCIDENT

This example is of particular interest as it discloses the kind of permanent penury in which the run-of-the-mill actor subsisted. The actor was J W Moreton and after the accident he was treated by Dr Fox who charged £1.15.0d for his services. Moreton refused to pay Dr Fox, stating that Brinsley Sheridan the lessee of the theatre was liable for the doctor's fee, as it was through the negligence of his servants that the accident occurred. Moreton sued Sheridan who paid that amount into court, prior to the case being heard.

Dr Fox sued Moreton for his fee, so all the parties were summoned to the County Court, Dr Fox being the plaintiff, Moreton the defendant. The judge ruled that any action against Sheridan would not relieve Moreton's liability to Dr Fox, therefore he gave judgment for the plaintiff, with costs. But, as Sheridan had admitted his liability by paying the money into the court, he ordered it to be given to the plaintiff at once. Moreton, asking if he could be given the money to pay his expenses to a new engagement, offered to pay the doctor's bill by instalments. The judge declined to entertain such a proposal. The equivalent of the fee in today's money is about £162.

1876_05_27 USA (Howes and Cushing).   ACCIDENT TO TRAPEZE ARTISTE

The circus was in a big top, the town not stated, the artiste was Mrs Leraux who often performed under the professional name of Mdlle Emoclew. The climax of the lady's act was to sit on the trapeze bar, swinging higher and higher until her head touched the canvas roof, and then to throw herself backwards with a scream as though falling, but save herself by catching the suspending ropes with her feet. On this occasion one of the supporting ropes gave way mid-swing and Mrs Leraux was thrown 40ft to the ground. Four men were holding a net, but the force of her descent into it tore it from their grasp and she was taken out in an unconscious state. A physician said though no bones were broken she had internal injuries that "would preclude her performing again for some months." I am still intrigued how internal injuries were detected prior to the discovery of X-rays in 1895.

1876_08_07 DUBLIN (Hengler's).   ACCIDENT TO TRAPEZE STAR LULU

[Lulu (1855–1939) born Samuel Wasgatt and adopted by the Great Farini, began his showbusiness career at the age of nine under the guise of El Niño Farini in a father and son aerial act 'Signor Farini and son, the Flying Wonders'. (*see* 1864_08_08). They came to England in 1866 where they appeared at Cremorne Gardens followed by a 320-night run at the Alhambra in Leicester Square. The pair made a good living and was well-established but they decided the act would have more appeal with a female performer. Thus Sam at the age of 16 transformed himself into Mdlle Lulu, a glamorous female trapeze artiste. As the pair was well known in London, Sam made his debut in his new guise in Paris playing the role so effectively that he was shot into instant stardom and pursued by many hopeful swains.]

70. Lulu

On this night he/she was at Hengler's Circus being shot from a sprung platform to a trapeze suspended some 60ft away, which he intended to catch, but failing to do so fell, not into the net provided for such accidents, but against the gallery railings thence into the arena. Gossip all round circus and theatreland spoke of injury and possible imminent death. These reports were wildly exaggerated as Lulu, writing to the press in what can only be described as a cocksure manner, claimed that he/she did not miss the net but failed to grasp it and fell out. He was not alarmed at any stage, having fallen into the net many times at practice and performance. He said his father caught him on the rebound, and he was only momentarily stunned; Furthermore, he was not so foolish as to not be fully prepared with a safety net, and now, having realised that it did not fully cover a possible variance of trajectory, he would arrange that it was extended. Lulu blamed missing the bar on the fact that the springing platform's setting was slightly higher at the front than it should have been. He/she was reported to be "rusticating in Plymouth . . . under the skilful treatment of Dr Owen, Lulu is progressing with greater rapidity than could have been expected." So much so that in September, Lulu was starring in the show at the Folies Bergère in Paris. Although many had previously suspected Lulu was really male, after the accident there was no doubt.

1876_12_05 BROOKLYN, USA (Conway's).   MAJOR TRAGEDY WITH 278 FATALITIES

[Some accidents were so horrific in their own time that they live on in history. The Brooklyn Theatre fire was one such. This theatre with a seating capacity of about 1,600, opened on October 2, 1871. As the theatre was only five years old it had adequate exits, wide doorways and passages, and had been approved on the grounds that the entire place could be evacuated in 5 minutes.

Before the advent of electricity, stage lighting was by gas jets. These were placed in a row at the front of the stage (the footlights), on 'ladders' between wing pieces at each side of the stage, and on battens between cloth or canvas borders stretching the width of the stage in the flies above. These were in a particularly vulnerable spot with masking borders in danger of being dragged or blown on to a naked flame. Incredible as it seems today this was a recognised hazard as it happened more than occasionally – flymen had poles to fend borders clear as cloths were raised and lowered.]

71.

On this night the play was *The Two Orphans* a successful attraction, just ending its run. Which is why not only was scenery for the current play on stage, but stacked up in the wings were flats and hanging in the flies backcloths for the following productions.

The actors on stage were first to spot some flames when they looked up into the flies, but carried on playing while passing *sotto voce* messages between themselves, expecting the stage crew to deal with it without disturbing the play. A forlorn hope, as the fire spread so rapidly that it soon became visible to the audience. Still the actors, hoping to avoid panic, urged the audience to keep their seats, which is often a sound ploy if attendants can get doors open quickly allowing the audience to proceed to exits in an orderly fashion. But there was no gallantry; it was every man for himself, with women overwhelmed and trampled underfoot. The entire place was now an inferno and the gallery folk, making a mad rush for the sole exit, charged down the stairs only to find at the bottom many who, managing to get there first, had stumbled and fallen. With the recent arrivals falling on top of them, the bodies were piling up. There were people wedged and intertwined when the flames reached them.

Within a mere 30 minutes of the fire being first spotted the theatre was left to burn. It was not possible to get any further people out. Starting at 11.20pm, it burned uncontrolled until 1am. By 3am it was under control and officials could enter the ruins of the building. It took three days to recover all the human remains, the burnt bodies being in such a dismembered state it was difficult for the removers to know how many complete corpses they had. A memorial states the number as 278.

1876_12_12 LONDON (Drury Lane).

72. *Barry Sullivan as Richard III*

ACCIDENT TO BARRY SULLIVAN

As Richard III, he was acting for the 60th night of the run in the final fight with Mr Sinclair as Richmond. Within a few moments of the swordfight, Sullivan stopped as he had been slashed on the side of his face, his eye narrowly escaping injury. The curtain was instantly dropped and after some minutes the audience was informed of the accident. Dr Mills and Dr Canton were called in and they discovered that the eyelid had been cut through and the effect of the injury was to cause partial blindness. The audience waited an hour to hear this news and then departed.

Sullivan was billed to play Macbeth the following night, but had to withdraw as he was "totally incapable of appearing". The role was taken by James Bennett.

The end of this mishap was not concluded until six months later. Although Sullivan was very soon back at work, his eye was acutely irritable for months afterwards. Eventually he was advised to consult Dr Critchett an eminent oculist of Harley Street, who soon found out the trouble. The original cure had been botched in that an eyelash had become embedded in the healed up wound. The expert dealt with the problem quickly and efficiently.

1876_12_21 HARTLEPOOL (Theatre).   ACCIDENT TO JUVENILE TRAPEZE ARTISTE

The Victorians really loved watching child performers and in acrobatic troupes it was often the youngest who was the star performer. Travanion really capitalised on the trend by training duos. One of Trevanion's duos (*see* 1875_07_12), a boy (Elspa) and a girl (Lillo) about 10 years of age were performing on the flying trapeze. Elspa was hanging by his feet from a bar above the stage, and Lillo leapt from a swinging trapeze at the other end of the theatre. Failing to grasp her catcher she fell and, glancing off the safety net, landed on the stage. She was carried off but returned to show she was only slightly injured. Another one to note for the attackers of juvenile acrobats.

1876_12_30c DUNFERMLINE.   FATAL SWORD ACCIDENT

"Henry Dillon, a young actor, has died at Kirkcaldy from a sword cut, received while acting at Dunfermline some days ago. Lockjaw caused death." *Huddersfield Chronicle* 1877_01_08.

1877_01_30 BATH (Ginnett's Circus).   ACCIDENT TO TRAPEZE ARTISTES

The Brothers Alveno were presenting a daring trapeze act whereby the bearer, hanging upside down from his trapeze, held in his mouth a leather strap to which was attached a swivel hook enabling the supported brother to spin rapidly around. At this show the swivel came adrift from the strap, and the now unsupported brother fell into the arena. He fell on his stomach but took some of the force on his hands which broke his fall to some extent as he rose from the ground and walked away without assistance. He returned to bow to the audience's applause. It should be noted that the danger in using one's hands to break a fall often ends in two broken wrists.

1877_02_26 WISHAW (Theatre).   GUN ACCIDENT

In the play *The Shaughraun*, actor Gardner Coyne received a strike in the face from wadding when a gun was fired at too short a distance. He was hit just below the eye and, though the wound was still bleeding two hours later, the eye remained unimpaired, and Coyne was able to play the same part again the following night.

1877_03_06 MANCHESTER (Alexandra).   ACCIDENT TO TRAPEZE ARTISTES 93

Jennie and Albert Lamont "American Gymnasts" were the unhappy sufferers. Their trapeze was situated in front of the stage about 30ft from the ground. One of the duo's feats entailed them sitting face to face on the bar, then suddenly throwing themselves backwards so they both ended head downwards with their feet interlocked above the bar. On this night, their feet failed to be intertwined and both fell to the floor, Albert landing on a violinist in the orchestra. He got up, staggered about a moment before dropping down unconscious. Jennie had fallen with her back across a rail surrounding the orchestra. Both artistes were carried out unconscious and taken to the Royal Infirmary where it was found that neither had any broken bones, the main injury being shock to the system, the lady particularly suffering.

The manager tried to carry on with the show, but indignant cries wanted to know how the trapeze artistes, especially the lady, were faring. On learning they were much less injured than had been supposed, the applauding audience allowed the show to continue.

1877_09_03 LONDON (Marylebone).   GUN ACCIDENT

Actors on stage in the drama *Bertha Grey* were Walter Grisdale, Mr Beckman and Mr Wieland. Threatened by Grisdale with a knife, Breckman retaliated with a pistol, Wieland getting the charge in the face. A piece of paper an inch long was extracted from the wound but in spite of looking a bit of a mess, it did not stop the actor appearing in his future scheduled work. When one realises how many plays of the time involved guns and daggers, and how often accidents with them occurred, it is astonishing that they were used in such a cavalier manner.

The name Wieland crops up from time to time in this book but they are all different people. The Wielands were a large theatrical family that figured throughout several generations.

1877_09_20c BOSTON, USA (Globe).   GUN ACCIDENT TO SHARPSHOOTERS

Frank Frayne and his wife Clara Butler were top sharpshooters, renowned for their accuracy and skill. During their act Frayne was holding an apple in his hand while his wife shot at it. She took off the ends of the first two fingers of his left hand. Unperturbed the act continued, with the audience unaware of the accident. Later in the day, after losing a great deal of blood, Frayne had the fingers amputated at the middle joint. In the future, Frayne was to be involved in a more dramatic and fatal accident (*see* 1882_11_30).

1877_11_03c MARKET HARBOROUGH.   HANGING ACCIDENT TO ACTOR

The venue was a travelling theatre, the play *The Wainwright Tragedy*, the actor unnamed. In the play – based on a recent case of a man murdering his wife and cutting her up – the actor playing the villain Wainwright ends by hanging in jail, as the husband did in real life. When the actor was pinioned and the rope placed around his neck, the stool he was standing on slipped over, leaving the poor chap in a situation of reality. He was cut down gasping, struggling and black in the face.

1878_02_10c VIENNA, Austria (Chantant Tauber).   FATAL ACCIDENT TO TRAPEZE ARTISTE

"A trapeze performer named Belmas has met with his death through a fall while performing at the Cafe Chantant Tauber, without using the precautionary safeguard of a net." *The Era* 1878_02_24.

1878_03_21 ST HELEN'S (Theatre Royal).   ACCIDENT TO MRS ELLIS

The play was *Macbeth*, with Mrs H Ellis playing the part of Hecate. In those days the play had become more like a musical with singing and dancing witches, Hecate being a sort of chief witch. Mrs Ellis had to be hauled up on a rope, but during her ascent it gave way and she fell around 15ft on to the stage. Although not too badly hurt, she had to be off work for a couple of weeks.

1878_03_23 LONDON (Queen's).   SWORD ACCIDENT TO HUNGARIAN TRAGEDIAN

Herr Neville Moritz was a newcomer to London, arriving with the plaudits of continental critics resounding through his biography. Alas, he failed to capture the London critics who, while conceding that it was difficult for a foreigner to act in English before an English audience brought up with Shakespeare on stage from the cradle, said that – ignoring his accent and delivery – he was just not up to the job and no better than an aspiring amateur.

On this night, while acting Othello, he trod on a sword that was lying on the stage. The edge was far too sharp for theatrical use and he cut his foot on the keen blade. In spite of the wound he acted the next night, but then had to concede the night after. Mr E H Brooke who was playing Cassio took over the part of the Moor and gave a very impressive performance which charmed the critics. Moritz, soon back, played until the end of April, then returned to Hungary before departing to the USA where he changed his name to Maurice Neville and caused great mirth with the professional performers there.

1878_05_06 DUBLIN (Exhibition Palace).   ACCIDENT TO GILFORT THE WIRE-WALKER

Gilfort, an American high wire-walker of 20 years experience – including a claim of traversing Niagara Falls though not mentioned on www.niagarafrontier.com – and reckoned by many to be the

94

equal of Blondin, was performing the highlight of his act which was to lie down, balancing across the wire with outstretched limbs. At this point on this night, a ring holding a guy rope flattened out, thereby slackening the wire and precipitating the bold gymnast groundwards. He tried to save himself by grabbing his wire but failed, and dropping 40ft smashed his ribs on both sides, receiving internal injuries that were predicted to prove fatal.

They were not fatal, as on 10 May the physicians said the bleeding from the lungs had almost stopped, and all immediate danger was past. Gilfort "revived considerably when he was told the performances next Wednesday night are to be for his benefit".

1878_05_13 NEWPORT (Victoria Hall).   ACCIDENT TO TRAPEZE ARTISTES
The artistes were The Great De Volas. At the end of the act the younger of the two performers climbed to the very girders of the building and threw himself forward into the safety net below. It has to be said that this is the way that every modern flying trapeze act concludes, providing a quicker and more exciting conclusion than sliding down a rope, or even worse tediously climbing down the rope ladder by which they all ascended. However, modern safety nets are exactly that – safe to dive into.

Young Mr De Volas threw himself into the net, but there was a loud crash when he hit it. The gymnast, staggering to his feet on the net, clambered down on to the stage, his leg bleeding profusely under his hand. He bowed and limped offstage. The accident was caused by the force of his fall into the net causing one of the supports to give way, and he had landed on chairs beneath. The backs were broken and the gymnast had impaled his leg on one of the bare uprights.

95

1878_05_18 ROTHERHAM (Theatre Royal).   ACCIDENT TO GYMNAST
"Accident to an Acrobat: At the Theatre Royal, Rotherham, one of the junior members of the Arlotti troupe broke his wrist. He is progressing favourably." *The Era* 1875_05_26.

1878_08_16c PARIS, France (Hippodrome).   ACCIDENT TO MARQUEZ DE GONZA
The famed trapeze artiste Marquez de Gonza had been packing them in for several months. On this night prior to the doors opening, the aerialist climbed up a rope to attend to his trapeze as he was wont to do. At a height of 40ft the rope broke and Gonza fell to the arena with a sickening thud. Miraculously, no bones were broken, only "a severe contusion of the right foot". (*See* 1885_05_08 for further information on this performer.)

1878_08_19 BIRMINGHAM (Concert Hall).   ACCIDENT TO TRAPEZE ARTISTE
This accident happened to Mdlle Florence Harvey, who performed with two male partners. On this night, in the part of the act where she wore a belt attached to a short rope held by her husband who twirled her round at speed the belt broke, and Mdlle Florence was thrown into the safety net. On landing, and failing to grip the netting, she was bounced out of the net landing with violence on the floor. She was borne away greatly shocked, but with no discernible broken bones.

One has to wonder at the inability of these safety nets to do the job intended. Performers falling into them either bounced out, or a support collapsed and they ended up crashing to the floor. A lot of problems arose from venues where the performance had to be over the heads of the stalls audience, so placing a fully tethered net with sufficient 'give' clearance underneath was very awkward.

1878_09_06 COLCHESTER (Theatre Royal.   GUN ACCIDENT

It was the first night of the season, the play *Poor Jo*, the unfortunate actor Fred Marshall. His character was due to be shot by Hortense played by Alice Willson who, unaccustomed to handling a pistol, was having trouble finding the trigger. Marshall, waiting to be shot, was in a ludicrous position and the audience's sniggering added to his discomfiture. Thinking to save the scene, he went towards Miss Willson to take the pistol when she succeeded in finding the trigger and pulled it within three inches of the poor chap's face. The wadding struck him between the eyes. He was taken home and attended by Dr Symmons, under whose care his sight started returning. A benefit performance was held for Marshall on the 25 September.

1878_09_21 KILDYSART (Circus).   ACCIDENT TO TRAPEZE ARTISTES

Ruth and Lefonze were trapeze artistes in Powell and Clarke's Circus and on this night their apparatus gave way, and both fell 25ft to the arena, Lefonze getting a blow on the head from the trapeze. He was rushed to hospital with his condition described as "precarious".

1879_02_13 DETROIT, USA.   ACCIDENT TO TRAPEZE ARTISTE

Three days previously, Marie Azurine had fallen but been caught unharmed in the safety net. However, she fell again on this night, apparently from some dizziness which, causing her to lose her hold on the trapeze bar, resulting in her falling headfirst on to the parquet seats (UK pit). She was carried on to the stage where physicians found her collar bone broken, in addition to severe internal injuries. She was completely unconscious for 36 hours, which "caused dread", but once she regained consciousness improvements in her condition were manifest, and it was expected to be only a matter of weeks before she was back at work.

1879_04_01 BIRMINGHAM (Concert Hall).   ACCIDENT TO HUMAN CANNON BALL

[The Human Cannonball Act was invented by Farini the wirewalker and adoptive father of Lulu. An early version was a method of spring propulsion which he patented in May 1870. Using the same technique he adapted it in December 1877 and obtained a new patent for shooting a person out of a tube. Whether the Brothers Auber were using Farini's apparatus I know not.]

This accident took place at a venue where we have already seen more than one aerialist come to grief. The act was the Brothers Auber from the Cirque Madrid. After a series of leaps, dives and somersaults from the three youths, the climax was the firing of the youngest boy named Alfred Bishop (12) from "a contrivance fixed at a considerable height" into a net some distance away. Assuming this "contrivance" was a form of cannon in which the propulsion is nothing to do with the explosive feature, it is particularly galling to learn that the material exploded too soon – "a sheet of fire" causing a severe laceration on the boy's thigh. He landed in the net, but had to be lifted out and taken to the General Hospital where he was detained as an in-patient.

Questions were raised in Parliament about this accident, whether such performances should be prohibited by law. The Birmingham Watch Committee received a letter from Mr Secretary Cross asking them to inquire via the police into the circumstances of the accident. The police report stated the injury was not a burn to the thigh, but damage to the lad's kneecap which he caught up in a rope while he was in the apparatus. So you cannot believe everything you read!

1879_06_14 LEEDS (Grand). ACCIDENT TO JOHN COLEMAN

Wilson Barrett was the lessee of this venue, where the play was *Katherine Howard*. Actor John Coleman was mounting the steps for the execution scene in the final act, while a front cloth scene was being played. The audience heard a crash, and shortly after stage manager Henry Hastings came on to announce that due to an accident to Mr Coleman, the play would have to end at that point. Coleman had been mounting steps that slipped away from the rostrum, and he fell to the stage, only 7ft or so, but received bruises and spinal injuries. Although clearly in great pain, the actor insisted on walking home to show he was not seriously hurt.

73. *John Coleman*

1879_07_01 BRADFORD (Star). GUN ACCIDENT

The Marchant family was giving melodramatic sketches during which leading man William Marchant was supposed to shoot the villain of the piece with a gun that was on the floor of the stage. As he picked it up the gun went off, and he received the full charge near the left temple. He fell to the stage with blood pouring from the wound. He was taken to the Infirmary for treatment but it was thought his condition was not serious. Marchant had recovered before the end of the month and the lessee of the Star gave him two benefit performances.

1879_05_22 LONDON. THE ACROBATS BILL

It will be recalled that previous attempts had been made in Parliament to legislate against dangerous feats by acrobats. A serious accident invariably provoked an outcry from certain members of the public and concerned members of Parliament. Over 15 years previously, after the Aston Park accident when Miss Geneive was killed (*see* 1863_07_20) an attempt was made to have a bill proposed. Then in 1872 Lord Brockhurst and Lord Shaftesbury got their bill – that of banning children under 16 from taking part in gymnastic acts – to the second reading (*see* 1872_07_04). That foundered because of difficulties of defining such performances, and much merriment ensued as members asked if school gymnasiums were to be banned, if a sailor climbing rigging would be covered by the act, or a jockey in a race, or a yokel cutting turnips etc.

Inspired by the accident to 12-year-old Alfred Bishop (*see above*), the noble lords, led by Lord De Le Warr, were having another go at preventing youngsters becoming acrobats. This time they had the precedence of other countries who had legislated on the topic. Most recently France, in December 1874, had brought in a bill "relative to the protection of children employed in the strolling professions". This stated that penalties would be imposed on any person, other than the child's parents, who employed children under 16 for perilous feats of strength or exercises of dislocation. When the parents were professional acrobats they could employ their own children if above the age of 12.

This was countered with the fact that only France and Germany had brought in this act, the reason being in those countries there were many small circuses that toured fairs, and the children were not only ill-used but often had little to eat. That bill was only passed after opposition, not from the performers but from members of their parliaments.

The position was very different here, as the children were not ill-used, were well fed, humanely trained, and usually were educated enough to read and write and know what was going on around them. There may have been 'black sheep' in the profession who mistreated children but there were already sufficient laws under which those disreputable people could be charged. If some people were cruel, why were they not arrested and prosecuted?

As all the arguments proffered by professional acrobats in 1872 still held, they were urged to come forth again by their fellows and defeat this latest attempt to quash their livelihood. An obvious counter was made from acrobats who did not go aloft. Known as 'ground acrobats', they asked where were the future clowns and tumblers to come from, if youngsters could not be trained at an early age.

Established acrobats of many years experience wrote explaining that they trained their own children and pupils from the age of seven or eight, without torture or cruelty, and they, growing up into accomplished performers, would earn their own living, as opposed to the many ragamuffins who lived in the streets from an early age with barely clothes to their backs, and little in their bellies. The performers stated the noble lords should be legislating for those children, and not interfering with an established wholesome way of life conducted by loving families which, should it be stopped, would result in even more destitute children thrown into the streets.

More pointedly, boys paid good money to train in gymnasiums for their own pleasure and recreation, with no interference from the proposed bill. Schools where healthy exercise was actively encouraged, was that too to be stopped?

1879_07_21 LONDON.   PARLIAMENT DISCUSSES ACROBATS BILL

In May a new bill was proposed to curb the employment of acrobatic children (*see* 1879_05_22). The bill had progressed, it was now called the Children's Dangerous Performances Bill, and amendments were discussed and agreed before passing to the next stage. It has to be said that the outcry from professional acrobats was very muted in that only a handful saw the implications for their future livelihood. The next passage regarding this topic is at 1880_01_01.

1879_08_18 DUBLIN (Hengler's).   ACCIDENTS TO TRAPEZE ARTISTES

"Hengler's Cirque in Dublin has been doing good business, with the Gonza-Azella troupe of clever gymnasts. Last week Mdlle Azella, in performing a flying somersault, fell from a trapeze to the floor, striking on a staircase; and another of the company had a fall the same night." *Glasgow Evening Post* 1879_08_18.

It would appear that Mdlle Azella and the Marquez de Gonza had formed a professional alliance. It was quite common for artistes to ally themselves for a limited period to colleagues. Often this took place after an existing member of a troupe had an accident or simply left and a replacement was necessary.

Even today you might see a troupe one year and the next year there has been a change of personnel.

74. *Mdlle Azella*

1879_08_18 ALTORF, France (Theatre).   LIGHTNING ACCIDENT TO TENOR
    "A painful scene recently occurred at the Altorf Theatre. As *Lucie* was being performed, a violent thunderstorm burst over the house. The tenor was singing the air in the malediction scene, when Edgardo fell forward, struck down by lightning. He was immediately raised from the ground, and, though alive, was found to be paralysed in every limb. The performance, of course, was brought to an abrupt termination, the accident leaving a sad impression on the minds of the audience." *The Era* 1879_08_19.

1879_08_19 NORWICH (Green Hills Gardens).   FATAL ACCIDENT TO COMEDIAN
    Matthew Hughson (28) was engaged to perform black-face songs and dances. On this Monday night, he had been drinking, though not excessively as he seemed able to do his song-and-dance material without any noticeable difference. However, catching his foot on a fixed plank, he fell off the stage to the ground, a distance of around 6ft. When picked up and seen to be bleeding, Hughson made little of it, although he had fallen on his head.
    The following night as usual Hughson went through his normal performance. However, on Wednesday, alarming symptoms appeared and he was unable to consider performing, so a doctor was called to attend him. The medical man advised that he should be moved to hospital, which Hughson declined. The comedian died on Thursday 21 August and was buried three days later.

1879_09_04 LONDON (South London Palace).   ACCIDENT TO HIGH WIREWALKERS
    The troupe comprised Romah and his two sons. Their apparatus consisted of two parallel wires stretching from the gallery to the top of the stage. On this occasion, one of the wires broke as the two youths were walking across hand-in-hand, and they fell into the safety net 18ft below. Neither was hurt and returned to perform directly afterwards. Some newspapers tried to play this up as more drastic than it was, presumably to give colour to the Children's Dangerous Performances Bill passing through Parliament. But the troupe had a safety net 35ft x 15ft, that admirably served its purpose, and if any warning can be taken from the event it is that such a thing is essential, and cavalier aerialists who scorn such a measure are not only foolish, but a liability to others including the audience.

1879_12_15 CHATHAM (Circus).   ACCIDENT TO ZAZEL
    [Lulu's catapult act led his father Farini to conceive a cannon-based act utilising apparatus that he had patented several years previously. This was launched in 1877 at the Royal Aquarium. Born in 1863, Rossa Matilda Richter became Farini's first human cannonball at the age of 14. Using the stage name Zazel, she was launched by a spring-based cannon, travelling through the air and landing in a net. Farini stated Zazel had practised it for five years (!), that the charm of the performance was not danger but the grace and elegance of a young girl of 17 or 18 (!) flying through the air. He also said the flight was of 30ft horizontally and she would be only four or five feet above the net which was 40ft wide and stretched across the building. This sensational act was the catalyst for a movement for legal controls over dangerous acts that gathered pace over the following years.]
    Zazel was the girl who made her living being shot from a canon. But she did other things too, and on this night she came a cropper on the trapeze by missing her hold and falling. Unfortunately, the net was not as safe as all that, as she slipped from it "owing to the net being little or no protection at

the spot where she fell." She was carried out apparently insensible, but roused herself to exclaim "I am killed! I am killed!" as she went. On examination backstage her injuries were not deemed drastic enough to cancel the performance and the girl herself later re-emerged to go through her act with her hands bandaged up. She was "evidently nervous" – and who could blame her? She was rewarded with several rounds of hearty applause.

ZAZEL

SHOT FROM A CANNON.

ROYAL AQUARIUM, Commencing Easter Monday

Very dramatic, except according to a letter sent to *The Era* by Lulu it was not like that at all. According to him, while Zazel was walking the high wire, the catch that released it opened, and she fell into the net. She then retired for ten to 15 minutes to allow the wire to be fixed up again. That being done, she re-emerged and went through her act as usual. Lulu was, of course, another performer under the aegis of Farini, and it was in the nature of aerialists to play down their accidents, just as newspapers liked to sensationalise them. It was also commonplace for newspaper reporters not to know the difference between a high wire and a trapeze!

75. *Zazel poster*

100

1880_01_01 LONDON   CHILDREN'S DANGEROUS PERFORMANCES BILL

On the first day of the New Year the new Children's Dangerous Performances Bill came into operation. After much discussion it had resolved itself thus:

"Any person who shall cause a child under the age of fourteen to take part in any public performance whereby, in the opinion of a court of summary jurisdiction, the life or limb of such child shall be endangered, is to be deemed guilty of an offence, and liable to a penalty not exceeding £10. The provision extends to the parents and guardians. Where, in the course of a public exhibition or performance which in its nature is dangerous to the life or limbs of a child under fourteen taking part therein, any accident causing actual bodily harm occurs the employer is to be liable to be indicted for having committed an assault, and the Court before whom such employer is convicted on indictment to have the power to award compensation not exceeding £20; but he is not to be liable to be punished twice for the same offence."

There was not much opposition from the profession to this act, and it must be said that if any mistreatment of children should occur, or the placing of them in a dangerous situation, it would invariably be during training rather than in public performance. The greater danger to the profession had not gone away. During this year a new Dangerous Performances Bill was proposed in Parliament which was intended to prohibit adult performers from risking dangerous feats.

1880_01_20 BIRMINGHAM (Holte).   NEW METHOD OF FATAL ACCIDENT

The venue was the Holte Theatre at Aston. It seems there were two electric lights to illuminate the stage. The wires for these, when not required – or as the report phrased it "when the candles are not burning" – ended in brass connections that were hung up over the orchestra pit. On this night Augustus Bredermann, known as Bruno the euphonium player, took hold of the two brass connections, presumably in curiosity as, of course, the phenomenon was new and rare to most people. The man in charge called out to him regarding the danger, but he was too late and Bruno received the full shock of the electric charge generated by powerful batteries that were installed for the purpose. As "the candles not being then burning", Bruno was unable to leave go of the wires, and the shock rendered him insensible. Medical men soon attended, but could do nothing, and Bruno was dead within 40 minutes.

1880_01_31 LONDON (Westminster Aquarium).   ACCIDENT TO AERIALIST ZÆO

[Zæo was a young woman who burst on to the scene in 1878 at the Royal Aquarium. Both a high-wire-walker and a trapeze artiste, she was a protégé of the theatre and circus manager Henry William Wieland. Her origins are a little mysterious but it was stated that she came from a good family and that her father was a clergyman. Not yet 16, she captivated the public with her youth, skill and daring. In October 1879, she was practising a new stunt involving a "ballista" (a spring loaded catapult based on the old Roman weapon). This hurled the performer through the air to land in a safety net. Zæo came to grief in rehearsal and was out of action until December.]

76. *Zæo*

Zæo was "an elegant lady performer on both the trapeze and the high wire", or "a young woman in scant attire pitched out of a ballista for the morbid gratification of the brainless youth of the metropolis" depending on which newspaper you read. However, at the matinee on this day, when she had successfully accomplished her flight and landed in the net, it gave way and she fell to the ground. Zæo had to be carried out unconscious. A medical man issued a statement that she was suffering "a general shaking of the system", and she did not appear at the evening performance. She was back to normal the following day and resumed her daily performances but the incident gave rise to another burst of indignation calling for a ban on dangerous acts.

The talented young woman found herself in great demand and after the season at the Aquarium she went on to engagements in several countries and it was fully ten years before she returned to perform in the UK.

1880_02_13 LEEDS (Prince's).   ACCIDENT TO SPECTATOR BY CANNONBALL

Herr Holtum was a Strong Man whose act was to display feats of strength and stunts such as a tug-of-war with a horse. There were other strong men on the music halls, the doyen being Eugene Sandow whom we shall meet later. But there was only one Holtum, King of the Cannon Ball. What did this chap do? He caught a cannon ball fired from a cannon, issuing a £50 challenge to anybody who could equal his feat. On this night at the Prince's Palace Music Hall, Herr Holtum had three spectators willing to make the attempt. The first was a market porter called Elijah Fenton. He failed as the ball hit him on the head and he fell insensible and bleeding to the ground.

Hauled off the stage, a surgeon summoned, and quick departure to the Infirmary was his reward. The next man stepped forward to "attempt the foolish act" but the audience protested as they, not wishing to see a repeat of the accident, would not allow the performance to proceed.

At the Infirmary, Fenton was dying. Holtum was arrested and remanded for maliciously wounding him. It seems that other men had been hurt on previous occasions – in Manchester a bruised hand, in Bradford a wound, Hastings a broken shoulder, Grimsby and Hull men severely hurt. Holtum was to be tried at the assizes which were two months after the actual event, in the meantime he was free to continue his work. Obviously he had dropped the challenge.

The trial was one long discussion on points of law. If Fenton had died then the charge would have been manslaughter, but Fenton recovered so there were several variations of malicious wounding. Two things were in Holtum's favour – Fenton had tried the challenge a year previously so he fully knew what the conditions were; Holtum was against him trying again and it was only the insistence of the audience that made him concede. The other thing was Holtum had provided a marked spot for Fenton to stand, telling him not to deviate, and not to get his head in line of the trajectory. Fenton admitted he would not have been injured if he had not deviated from the mark indicated. The accusation was framed as "unlawfully and maliciously inflicted grievous bodily harm", but as the jury considered the fact that Fenton had volunteered, and it was the second time he had done so, then the verdict must be 'Not Guilty'. Even though it was a stupid challenge, it is nice to hear that Fenton had no grudge against Holtum – who had financially supported his treatment – and did not hold the performer responsible.

77. *Holtum poster*

1880_03_04 BILSTON (Theatre Royal).   GUN ACCIDENT

The play was *The White Chief*, with leading man Mr Stanton posed with his hand on the chest of Mr Cavendish when Mr Walton a third actor fired a gun in a horizontal position. The charge shattered Stanton's hand, thus Cavendish escaped receiving a wound in what could well have proved a vital part, or even fatal. But poor Stanton!

1880_04_28 BOLTON (Temple OH).   ACCIDENT TO TRAPEZE ARTISTES

The performers were the Brothers Nestor and Venoa, Continental aerialists. One trapeze was hanging about 20ft above the stage, the other hanging in front of the gallery. A safety net was erected above the audience. All went well until the brothers' big finish – Venoa hanging head downwards with his legs around the bar on the stage trapeze, Nestor swinging on the other trapeze building up momentum, to the instant he let go of his bar, turned a double somersault, and then grasped his brother by the hands. Alas, he misjudged the distance, fell, missing the net, and landing on the stage floor. Venoa, in an attempt to save his brother, moved his position, slipped from his bar and also fell on to the stage landing on his head. Both men were stunned and carried off to a dressing room where a doctor was summoned. It was established that no bones were broken and the pair were taken home.

Recovering during the following day, the performers were keen to disclaim the accident as reported, saying they had merely slipped from each other's hands, landed in the net, and bounced out on to the stage, a distance of 4ft. Thinking the accident provided a good enough climax, they did not attempt to repeat the trick, but deliberately drove round the town to show they were unharmed, and performed as usual the next evening.

1880_05_17 BRADFORD (Peel Park).   ACCIDENT TO BICYCLE PERFORMER

78. *Leonati*

The occasion was the Whit Charity Fêtes when many attractions were booked by the organisers, one being Leonati the Spiral Bicycle Ascensionist. The reader may recall the ascensionist who walked up a spiral track on a large ball (*see 1871_08_07*), this present chap had similar apparatus, but rode up it on a bicycle, which in those days meant a penny-farthing. At 4.30pm he started his ascent but about half-way up he slipped off his narrow track and only saved himself by clutching the track plank and stays, gripping the bike between his legs. He remained swinging in the air until helped down to the ground.

His second attempt was made at 8pm and this time he gained the summit. Turning round for the descent, at a height of around 16ft the bike swerved over the edge of the track and he was thrown from his seat. The bike fell, Leonati desperately grabbed for the apparatus but, unable to get a hold, fell to shrieks from the crowd. Dr Roberts examined the man and had him taken to the Infirmary. No bones were found to be broken, but he suffered a wound on the head, bruises down one side and an injury to the spine. Shortly after he recovered he went to fulfil a contract in America.

103

1880_06_25c HAMBURG, Germany.   AERIALIST LOSES HER FAMOUS TEETH

[Leona Dare – born Susan Adeline Stuart in 1854 – was an aerial gymnast famous for two things – hanging upside down from a trapeze with a rope in her mouth at the end of which was a rapidly spinning man; and being courted by a besotted young Austrian prince worth £95,000. At what appears to have been a louche party in a restaurant given in her honour, the prince and a count misbehaved in such a dissolute manner that the Crown Prince of Austria banished them both from his court.]   After that unsavoury publicity, she carried on her usual work until coming to grief in Hamburg where she was injured in the mouth losing her four front teeth. Reports on this varied, mostly following the idea she had been hit in the mouth by a swinging trapeze, while an alternative story attributed it to a fall while trying to lift up Dr Jope Hope by his waistband. Whatever the truth of the matter, she was "incapacitated from again appearing in her *tours de force*, all her teeth being injured." In September, she was reported

79. *Leona Dare*

to be in Chicago having her teeth mended, after which her intention was to return to Germany.

    In February 1881, Leona was in the news again as she had married her count (Ernest Grunebaum) in lieu of the prince. He was a poor second choice because he was bankrupt and they occupied their time fleeing from creditors. In May 1882, she was appearing in Paris so the "Queen of the Air" was back in business, presumably thanks to the ministrations of Chicagoan dentists. (*see also* 1884_11_24)

1880_08_03c NEW YORK, USA (Wallack's)   SERIOUS ACCIDENT TO GEORGE CONQUEST

[George Conquest (1837–1901) was educated in France. In 1851, his father Benjamin acquired the Grecian Theatre and Eagle Tavern at Hackney. It was a melodrama house where George wrote some 100 plays, often adapted from the French. George was mainly an acrobat and pantomimist, producing and starring in nearly 50 pantomimes. On Ben's death, George inherited his father's theatre and ran it efficiently and despotically. As we saw in entry 1874_02_09, he became London's panto supremo. The following accident was at the height of his acrobatic prowess.]

80. *George Conquest*

    In 1880, George, George Jr and other family members set out for America for what was intended to be a lengthy stay. On this night, the two Georges opened at Wallack's Theatre, New York with *Grim Goblin* which was greeted with delight by the USA audience. Alas, during the chase of the two Demons, the wire sustaining George at a height broke, and he plummeted some 20ft to the ground, falling heavily into the wings shattering his leg which put him out of action for some weeks. Immediately afterwards, George Jr too, suffering a broken wire, was dropped on to the stage, but managed to land on his feet.

    Performances were suspended for two days then resumed with George Jr playing his dad's role, and Mr Manley standing in for George Jr. Alas, at exactly the same point the wires broke, with George Jr falling into the wings, and Manley dropping to the stage. Fortunately both men, escaping injury, finished the show. George was convinced that sabotage was responsible as the wires appeared to have been severed at exactly the same place and time on both occasions. At a later performance, Ada Conquest – playing a fairy – fell to the stage, smashing her face and breaking her nose and some teeth. The English contingent left for home as soon as was practicable. USA had been a disaster.

1880_08_10 LEIGHTON BUZZARD.   SERIOUS ACCIDENT TO FIRE-EATER

    This accident is not in a theatre or circus, but is of interest as this sort of act played the music halls and circuses. The venue was a public market place, the unnamed man described as "a travelling Negro fire-eater" – in old terms a 'busker', in modern parlance a 'street entertainer'. The man may have been a stage performer who was temporarily out of work. He was on a small stand performing the usual tricks still done today – licking glowing irons, extinguishing flaming torches in his mouth and so on. The climax was to be, as it still is today, blowing flames from the mouth. Officially called 'fire-breathing', the process involves holding flammable liquid in the mouth and blowing it through the lips as a fine mist to be ignited by a blazing torch.

    Our subject here was using benzoline (modern performers use paraffin because of its high flash point) and either did not know the technique, or muffed it, as it caused a disaster. He put a lighted match to his lips and set his entire mouthful on fire with the flaming spirit dribbling out all over his face, neck and chest. In intense agony he rushed from his stand and ran madly about the crowd, tearing off his clothes and howling in excruciating pain. He had swallowed some of the flaming spirit in addition to burning the entire inside of his mouth. The performer was taken to a chemist where salves and oils were applied. At night he was in a lodging house where he suffered an agonising frenzy and fled his bed in a state of nudity. He was captured by the police and taken to the workhouse infirmary where he remained "in a dreadful condition".

1880_09_24 ACCRINGTON (Theatre Royal).   GUN ACCIDENT
The play was *Staff of Diamonds*. At the close of one of the acts the leading man and leading lady both enter with pistols, the man's being empty, the lady's loaded. The property man John Owen Carew, seeing the actors had actually got each other's gun, ran onstage to prevent an accident. He actually caused one to himself as he seized the loaded pistol which went off and the charge hit him in the face. He was taken to Blackburn Infirmary as it was highly probable he might lose an eye, but the injury turned out to be slighter than originally feared.

1880_10_10c MARSEILLES, France (Chave).   SWORD ACCIDENT
The play was *Dame de Montsoreau* with Danvray as Chicot the gallant noble-hearted Jester of Heni III, and Reynald as Liverol. The two characters indulge in a sword duel, and Danvray got so carried away with his role that he actually stabbed his opponent in the chest. Chicot was then to drag some papers from within Liverol's coat. When the actor placed his hand to get the papers he withdrew it full of blood, and Danvray realising what he had done, fainted away on the spot. Reynald was taken back to the dressing room where it was soon ascertained that the wound was not, in fact, serious, but both actors withdrew from the rest of the play, their parts being read by substitutes to the play's end.

105

In an interesting comment on this accident *The London Daily News* remarked "how very seldom such accidents take place" considering the conditions where they happen. Up to now, I have noted 13 accidents with swords, of which only one was fatal, so I suppose the comment is apt; certainly, when compared with gun accidents, which up to now have reached 48 including 4 fatalities. The actor Junius Brutus Booth, father of Edwin Booth, was always somewhat wild in his swordplay, and his opponents had to be fully on guard. Knowing his own flaw, Booth addressed a new actor playing Laertes to his Hamlet, warning him to be careful because he often wounded his opponent. Laertes kindly thanked him for the warning, replying that "he too was very excitable and whenever he felt himself wounded he always ran his opponent through the body. Booth contrived to keep his mind and his sword under control while fighting with that Laertes."

1880_10_18 LONDON (Princess's).   FATAL ACCIDENT TO CHARLES HARCOURT
The company was using the Haymarket Theatre for a rehearsal. All the cast were unfamiliar with the stage. About noon, Charles Harcourt (42), while awaiting to rehearse his role in *Hamlet*, walked to the wings where it was dark. A trap had been left open, and as a result Harcourt fell into it, dropping a distance of around 10ft sustaining injuries to head, face and arm. In hospital he was making good progress but as the actor was very popular a ban on visitors had to be imposed for the sake of the patient. Alas, the actor did not recover but died in hospital from erysipelas.

1880_11_21 POITIERS, France.

81. *A scene from the play*

FATAL GUN ACCIDENT

The play in progress was *Pirates de la Savane* in which Andres the tiger-slayer shoots at Ribeiro the pirate chief. "Owing to some mischance" one of the barrels in the double-barrelled gun was loaded with a ball cartridge. So when the ball hit M Martigues – playing Ribeiro – in the breast he was instantly killed on the spot. The curtain dropped and the performance came to an immediate conclusion. It was a mystery how the accident could have happened. Additionally it was by a lucky chance that the actor pulling the trigger had not killed his own daughter as he had two shots to fire; the one that tragically killed his fellow actor, and one that he fired at a serpent coiled round a child called Little Eva, played by his daughter. The only explanation that could be found for the live ammunition was that the theatre had borrowed several fowling pieces from local sportsmen. It was the practice of these men to put in a double shot separated with a wad, and it is thought that the man charged with emptying the barrels had encountered one of the barrels loaded in this fashion and, having extracted the first shot, left the wadding, not realising it concealed a second one.

A month later the director of the company M Duriez was brought before the Correctional Tribunal of the city on a charge of 'manslaughter by imprudence' and escaped lightly with a fine of 300 francs.

1880_11_22 LEEDS (Theatre Royal).

GUN ACCIDENT

The play was *Soldiers of Fortune*. A super named Henry Kirk was tasked with loading a pistol that had to be fired during the course of the play. He was holding the gun with his left hand over the muzzle when it went off prematurely, completely shattering Kirk's left hand. He was taken to the Infirmary and, as the accident was unknown to the audience, the show continued. Presumably another actor took over the part unless the character did not appear again.

1880_12_04 DUNDEE (Theatre Royal).

GUN ACCIDENT

The play was an English version of *Pirates de la Savane* (*Pirates of the Savannah*), the unfortunate actor Augustus Wheatman. When firing his pistol, "his arm was accidentally knocked up, causing the entire contents of the weapon to enter and completely shatter his hand". He was taken to Dr Moon in a cab to be tended, but it was feared recovery would be quite slow. Wheatman said he had had a presentiment of danger during the rehearsal that morning but that was presumably because the recent fatal accident at Poitiers would have been on everybody's mind. (*see* 1880_11_21).

1880_12_26c DUNDEE (Music Hall).   ACCIDENT TO TRAPEZE ARTISTE

Mr Testo was hanging by his feet from a trapeze set some 10ft above the stage. He slipped his hold, falling head first on to the stage, then rolled off into the orchestra. He was cut about the face and complained of pains to his back and right leg. "The poor fellow was at once conveyed to the infirmary."

1880_12_27 LEICESTER (Royal OH).   GUN ACCIDENT

The pantomime was *Dick Whittington*. Pantaloon was to fire a stage pistol but it failed to work, then when Ted Jarrett the Clown was passing, it suddenly went off, the charge hitting him in the face. He fell to the floor, and at first the audience thought that was a bit of comic business. Jarrett was able to appear the following night, but one eye was completely closed.

1880_12_28 CHELTENHAM (Theatre Royal).   GUN ACCIDENT

The panto was *Little Bo-Peep*, the unfortunate actor George Collier. At the matinee, he received a gun discharge in the face, so the curtain was dropped, and medical aid sought. Fortunately, injuries were slight and he was able to go on in the evening, though in great pain. He continued to play all performances thereafter.

1881_01_03 HULL (Mechanics Hall).   ACCIDENT TO TRAPEZE ARTISTE

The artistes were Onza and Erno. Two trapezes were set – one in the centre of the hall over the audience and one over the stage. Their act progressed normally until the grand finale which was – as most such acts finished – a flying 'leap for life', with the flyer swinging on his trapeze to gain momentum so that, on letting go of his bar, he soars through the air to be caught by his partner the catcher who, hanging from his trapeze head downwards, swings out to grasp the flyer. It is a matter of exact timing and distance in order that the hands grasp each other (actually they grasp each other by the wrist). On this night, Onza, missing his partner, fell with a fearful thud on to the stage beneath. He was carried off insensible and taken to the Infirmary where it was found that a leg had broken just above the ankle. It appears that not only was no safety net in place, but Onza had met with mishaps of a similar nature previously, breaking an arm in Aberdeen, and a leg in Hull some time before. Perhaps they were not very good trapeze artistes? Or simply could not afford a net? One probable explanation is that some theatre and music hall managers were prepared to pay more to an act who worked without a net. One imagines these must be low-class dives who thought the act more appealing to their customers if there was a chance of a fall. Respectable managers would not offer a booking unless a net were to be used.

1881_01_10 PARIS, France (Porte St Martin).   TRAP ACCIDENT TO MDLLE TASSILY

The play was *L'Arbre de Noel*, and actress Mdlle Tassily was reposing on a rock, designed to transform into a bed. Suddenly both actress and rock disappeared beneath the stage, and a loud shriek issued from the poor woman as she fell into the cellar. "Happily, the actress, who is very stout, escaped unhurt." The two stagehands under the stage engineering the transformation were not so lucky, both being injured, one having a broken leg. The lady, who had "naturally" gone into a swoon, on recovery went before the house to excessive applause, leaving the stagehands wishing she had gone on a diet.

1881_01_22 WEST BROMWICH (Theatre Royal).   ACCIDENT TO PANTO CHILDREN

[The show was the pantomime *Forty Thieves*. The main component of a pantomime was the transformation scene which relied on dancers and children as fairies posed at different levels on a metal framework that carried a scenic fairyland. This was known as 'the iron' – not to be confused with the safety curtain also known as the iron. It was raised in the air and often – for safety – it was necessary to have the individual tied into place.] Two unnamed children of ten and 12 were being raised on a portion of the tableau from a trap in the stage. At a height of 15ft one of the pair, losing balance, fell off her perch on to the stage below. The other, frightened by her companion's fall, lost her presence of mind and also fell off. Both were very badly hurt and in this case would have been better tied on.

1881_03_05 SUTTON (Theatre).   COLLAPSE OF TRANSFORMATION SCENE

The pantomime was *The Sleeping Beauty*, with the transformation scene underway, when the whole framework and scenery collapsed forwards, covering the stage, orchestra pit, and enveloping several people in the front rows. There were some not too serious injuries, but a panic arose which was partly quelled by the manageress turning off the stage lights and shouting that all danger was over.

1881_03_14 LONDON (Drury Lane).   FALL OF FRONT CLOTH

The play was *The World*. After Act I, as William Rignold was leading Fanny Josephs before the front cloth in response to the call of the audience, the canvas tore away at the top, and only by rushing forward did the pair avoid the mass falling on them. Many of the audience sprang to their feet, preparing to make a hasty exit, but Rignold motioned to all to keep their seats. Then with stage crew who came on stage, he lifted the canvas off the footlights that had been promptly turned off in order to prevent fire. The scene was rolled up (drop cloths have a wooden batten or roller along the bottom) and carried off. It was 40 years old and used several times a night. Stage manager Edward Stirling entered and merely announced that for the rest of the evening the act-drop would have to be dispensed with, and the front green baize curtain used instead.

82. *William Rignold*

1881_05_06 PARIS, France (Hippodrome).   FATAL EQUESTRIAN ACCIDENT

[At this period in Paris the stars of the entertainment world were not the chansonniers of the cabaret or the scandalous can-can dancers but the female equestrians in the circus. All the poets extolled them and all the artists adored them. Mdlle de Ghyka, was one of these elegant fashionable lady riders, and had performed since childhood under the name of Francesca until her marriage to a Serbian count. European aristocrats had a penchant for wooing the equestrian ladies. She soon left her husband as he did not approve of her showbusiness life. A great success in Russian and Austrian circuses, she was new to Paris.]

While performing, Mdlle de Ghyka, who like all fashionable riders rode side-saddle, lost control of her horse which, galloping round the ring, stumbled and fell. In its struggle to rise up, it fell again with its full weight on the rider who had not been able to get her foot out of the stirrup. She was taken to the Hospital Beaujon where she died three days later.

1881_05_12 PETERHEAD (Fairground Booth).   ACCIDENT TO MAGICIAN

This is an accident in a fairground booth but, as the trick that went amiss was a favourite of stage performers, it has a place here. Joseph McAndrew of Aberdeen made his living giving conjuring shows at fairs and markets under the name of Signor Andrea. On this day, he was showing his 'bullet catching' trick which did not go to plan, as when the gun was fired he was hit in the face with the ramrod. The explanation of the accident details how the trick should have been done. The secret lies in the powder being put into the ramrod tube, which communicates with the nipple, instead of into the muzzle. Four bullets are rammed home into the empty barrel, and the gun then given to a spectator who shoots at the magician from six yards away. The gun appears to fire, but the bullets remain in the barrel and the magician produces duplicates having 'caught' them in his hand or mouth.

The boy chosen to fire the gun left the ramrod in place in its tube, a circumstance unseen by the Signor. Struck just below the left eye, he fell, suffering a wound on the back of his head. The ramrod cut a deep gash, and glancing off the nasal bone went through the canvas wall of the tent and lodged in the next door show booth. McAndrew was taken under the care of Dr Anderson.

1881_07_22 MOSCOW, Russia (Hermitage).   ACCIDENT TO KATE RAMSDEN

Walter Taylor (33) and Kate Ramsden (30) suffered a dreadful "flying machine" accident at the Jardins Hermitage, Moscow. "The flying machine was used to introduce an aerial dance similar to what some time ago was seen at the Gaiety". Taylor, the head of the company, had engaged Miss Ramsden, a well-known actress in Australia, three months previously. In a rehearsal the machinery broke, and she fell 60 feet, splitting the wood on which she fell, fracturing her shoulder, and also the lower part of the spine. Taylor seems to have escaped lightly as, attending to all Miss Ramsden's wants, he visited her frequently. "The injured lady is expected to recover, but she will be unable to follow her calling."

1881_08_12 GT YARMOUTH (Theatre Royal).   SWORD ACCIDENT

The play was the ever-popular *The Corsican Brothers*. In the final fencing scene, William Palling as Chateau Renaud made a lunge at Duncan Campbell playing Fabien de Franchi, and the sword nearly entered the eyeball. Campbell, "though in intense pain, pluckily finished the performance".

1881_08_18 WIGAN (Alexandra).   ACCIDENT TO TRAPEZE ARTISTES

The two trapeze artistes were Robinson and Makin, both Wigan men. Once again it was while one man flew from his trapeze to catch the other's hands that, failing to meet, both ended up falling into the pit. Robinson received an injury to one ankle, Makin just a good shaking. They did not have a safety net in spite of Mr Johnson the owner of the hall desiring them to do so. The same old questions must be asked – why did he not insist? Did the artistes not possess one?

It was very awkward to arrange flying apparatus in a conventional theatre, much less safety provision, but for a decade or more safety nets had been expected to accompany flying trapeze acts, whilst tightrope walkers working at great heights continued, and still continue, without safety nets. Of course, nowadays, the circus and stadiums are the places for flying trapeze acts, not theatres.

1881_09_12 LONDON (Royal Aquarium).   ACCIDENT TO CHAIR GYMNAST

[The Royal Aquarium opened in 1876 with a dozen large tanks intended to house fishes and other sea creatures. There was a huge glass-roofed hall 340ft x 160ft with palm trees and fountains which was mainly used for aerial attractions like Zazel and Lulu, a theatre, skating rink, art gallery, refreshment rooms and cafés but no fish! It seems it was such a huge and expensive place to run that the high-flown ideas of symphony orchestra concerts and up-market entertainments were soon abandoned and our familiar friend the Great Farini was drafted in to popularise the programmes.

83.

Zaro, the Wonderful Chair Manipulator, was appearing for the first time at this venue. You may have seen this act as it is a standard one, especially with oriental acrobats. The performer starts on a rostrum and then adds chairs one above the other until he has a chair-tower on which he performs a handstand etc. Zaro seems to have done a similar act though, defying his bill matter, it appears instead of chairs he was stacking small pedestals.]

It is said that these were wobbly and he used pieces of cardboard to pack the joints between them. He ended up with a tower 30ft high with a chair on top on which he did a handstand. All was fine up to this point then the whole structure gave way and he dropped like a stone to the ground. The band stopped playing and silence pervaded the hall as the intrepid gymnast was scooped up insensible and carried away. He was taken to Westminster Hospital where it was half-an-hour before he recovered consciousness. He had suffered a "very severe shock to the system" and had his arm in a sling when he was allowed to leave the hospital where a group of anxious well-wishers were enquiring after him. He was taken home in a cab. In fact – as Zaro was keen to explain in a letter to the showbiz press – other than having been stunned and shaken, he was not injured, his props did not let him down, he simply "over-balanced himself", and was ready to resume work any time.

1881_11_12 EXETER (Theatre Royal).   ACCIDENT TO MISS KEMPSTER

The play was *The Octoroon*, the afterpiece *The Sailor of France*. It was in the gap between the first and second acts of the latter drama that an accident happened to Ely Kempster. She was sitting on stage "conning her part" when some scenery was lowered in, striking her on the arm. Although a painful blow she went through her role without her colleagues or the audience realising she had been injured, such was her spirit and her control of the agony she was in. At the end of the play a surgeon, going backstage, found her arm was fractured above the elbow. Brave girl – the show must go on!

1881_11_14 HANLEY.   ACCIDENT TO TIGHTROPE WALKER

A juvenile high-wire-walker Henry Julius Newbold known as Bon Bon had been giving open air performances. It is not clear whether these were formal shows at an open-air function or pleasure garden, or a type of open-air busking where the hat was passed round at the end. On this afternoon he was crossing his wire with a younger brother on his back à la Blondin. On reaching the centre, one of the supports of his apparatus gave way and he fell some 17ft to the ground. The young boy had no bodily injuries, but Bon Bon broke his thigh in two places.

1881_12_08 VIENNA, Austria (Ring).   MANY FATALITIES IN THEATRE HORROR FIRE

This is another of those horrendous accidents by fire that live on to this day in the memories of citizens. A crowded house of 1700 people was eagerly assembling to watch Offenbach's *Tales of Hoffman*. At 7pm an explosion backstage was heard. This was caused by gas; the auto system for lighting the stage lights failed to fire the gas at the first attempt, and as the second attempt did the job it also ignited gas that had escaped during the previous failure. There were some 200 people backstage including the cast of singers and dancers plus the crew and, as the explosion was immediately followed by the lights going out, there was a mass rush for the stage door with half-dressed girls screaming in the pitch black.

84.

The explosion included a sheet of flame which, igniting scenery on the stage, sped rapidly up into the flies. Soon all the stage house was on fire. The theatre was not an old decrepit affair, it was built in 1873 at a cost of £90,000 and fitted with all the latest ideas in modern theatre. It had an iron safety curtain which should have been immediately lowered thus isolating the stage from the auditorium; that is its purpose. If it can withhold the flames from spreading to the rest of the building for even a short period, during that time the audience can make a controlled exit without immediate danger. The safety curtain was not lowered.

There was no need to shout "Fire!" as the audience, seeing the stage blazing away, fled for the exits. In the rush for the doors many stumbled and were trampled over, the concrete stairs and passages were jammed with fainting, crying and shouting people. It was fully ten minutes before any assistance arrived outside the theatre. During that time the second life-cheating error became apparent – the exit doors opened inwards. The pressure of people against them, acting as a lock, kept all the exits closed. The poor people in the galleries suffered the most. In one gallery the only exit door was ablaze, and three rows of people were found sitting in their places suffocated. By 2am, 150 bodies in various levels of incineration had been removed. The fire was still smouldering at 11am next morning, and though the stone outer walls were still standing, within them was nothing but a heap of smoking ruins.

85

The official death toll was 384. There was not just a post mortem, but a full blown trial as eight separate persons were accused of various crimes of negligence – Julius Chevalier de Newald (former mayor of Vienna), Herr Jauner (manager of the Theatre), Antony Landsteiner (Chief of Police), Leonhard Herr (Head of the Fire Brigade) and four of the theatre employees. Many witnesses showed up the total incompetence of the police force and stated the police attitude was 'let them burn' – there was evidence that those words were actually used. When various police officers were questioned, the judges decided that as the responses showed despicable cowardice, it was pointless asking any more to testify. At the end of three weeks the judges gave their verdict: Herr Jauner, Geringer (theatre fireman), and Nitchsh (theatre gasman) were all found guilty of contributing to the catastrophe by negligence and imprisoned for four months. The other defendants were acquitted.

1881_12_31 LEEDS (Grand).   ACCIDENT TO BOY ACROBAT

I have found no report of this accident, my brief account is garnered from letters to the press from concerned theatregoers. The show was the pantomime Red Riding Hood, and the acrobats involved were the Zetina Troupe comprising Mr Zetina and two apprentice boys.

At the Saturday matinee, one of the boys, while turning a somersault, landed on his head and back on the stage floor. Or as a correspondent graphically described it "a brutal outrage committed when this unhappy little boy was dashed senseless on the stage and then swung off by his hands". He was carried out senseless but expected to recover in time for the evening performance. Having failed to do so, it was thus some hours later when he was taken to the Infirmary. There, lying with his head shaved, he was found to be suffering from concussion. The eight-year-old apprentice had a lunatic father "and probably a few more bangs on the head will make his son one." Two different readers wrote asking for a law to prevent children performing such dangers. As we have seen, there was such an act (see 1880_01_01) so the objectors could have pressed for a prosecution, but they did not.

As usual, a letter from the perpetrator came in response, downplaying the 'incident'. Zetina said that it was a "slight mishap" rather than a "brutal outrage" and his boys were well treated, well fed, educated, loved their work etc. He stated the accident happened because a flap on the boy's costume covered his eyes as he somersaulted, thus obscuring his landing place. He would not have been hurt if they had used their customary thick mattress, not used here because of the shortness of time they were permitted. Zetina stated he would never again perform without a mattress when there were boys in his troupe. At the Infirmary, he was told the boy was out of danger and had been so for the last few days. The original correspondent replied to ask, as do I, if "a mattress takes all danger out of the act", as Zetina claimed, why did he ever venture on stage without one?

1882_01_05 LONDON (Drury Lane).   ACCIDENT TO CHARLES LAURI JR
[Charles Lauri Jr (1860–1903), English pantomimist and animal impersonator, born into a showbiz family, from an early age specialised in 'skin' work ie costumed as an animal performing animal antics. In 1878/79 he played a poodle in the Covent Garden panto, the following year he was an ape. Switching to Drury Lane for 1880/81 he was a bear. Now an adult, he had been around from the age of six as "the little ball of quicksilver". He went on to be a regular in the Drury Lane panto and was happy to go on being so as he was on £50 a week. It seems he had an extraordinary youthful appearance – when interviewed at the age of 29, the reporter was astonished as he looked like a youth of 15. At the time of this accident he was playing Man Friday as a change from being an animal.]

The pantomime was *Robinson Crusoe*. "Charles Lauri who nimbly and amusingly plays the part of Friday" had an accident on this day when, in the plot of the panto, a rope he was climbing to escape pursuers broke, and he fell to the stage injuring his foot. That put him out of the show for three days. Two days back when he leapt on to the rope the whole apparatus came down, miraculously without injury to anybody. *The Era* newspaper asked darkly whether these were actually "accidents or to design". This semi-accusation brought an immediate response from James Skimmer the machinist at Drury Lane. He pointed out it was not the rope that broke, but an "india rubber spring" that gave way. These were the property of Mr Lauri Jr and several had broken during the course of the panto, the reason being that the rubber perished in the heat of the gas battens in the flies. "Mr Lauri has been advised by me to avoid the use of india rubber springs, but he declines."

86. *Charles Lauri Jr*

1882_01_06 DONCASTER (Theatre Royal).   SWORD ACCIDENT
The play was *Michael Strogoff*, the company that of Mr C Dornton. In one scene Michael is supposed to be blind, and to keep up the illusion walks on to the sword of the Tartar chief. William Brougham in the star role miscalculated the distance, and the sword penetrated his chest just above the heart. The Tartar played by E J Henley, holding the sword firmly against his hip and quickly realising the error, withdrew the sword. The result was a flesh wound rather than a more serious one and, in spite of the agony, once he was bandaged up Brougham managed to stagger on to the end of the piece.

1882_01_18 BRADFORD (Keith's Circus). EQUESTRIAN ACCIDENT

[At this period, travelling circuses had universally adopted the Big Top tent whereas, before that import from America, circus proprietors had erected custom designed buildings that they occupied for several weeks. Charlie Keith was both a throwback and a pioneer as he devised a portable pre-fabricated wooden building comprising sections of planking with a canvas roof. This looked just like a huge wooden warehouse when erected but he preferred that to a Big Top.]

Mrs Ann Dawson sued Charles Keith the circus owner for £7.10.0 after attending his show at Darley Street. The following are the facts of the case when it came to court on 9 May; the reader may well be surprised at the verdict. Mrs Dawson paid her money and was shown to a seat from which she watched the show. During it, one of the artistes turning somersaults, landed on Mrs Dawson instead of his horse's back. As a result she was injured, and suffering much pain, had been put to considerable expense for medical attention, and "assistance in discharging her household duties".

The judge asked her lawyer if it was alleged to be the fault of the performer, the reply being no, but he was a trained man who could do certain things. The judge said "He could not ensure success, could he?" Keith's lawyer maintained that there was always a certain amount of risk in a circus performance, and that people were attracted to the show by that risk. The judge then stated "In the performance there was danger, and it was the danger in which consisted the attraction. That was one of the marks of a degraded nation."

Mrs Dawson's man claimed that the performance of an equestrian was not one involving danger. The judge replied "What, not a man jumping and trying to do a somersault on a galloping horse?" At which point Keith's man brought up the fact that the accident may have been caused by the horse not being in the right place, and thus the equestrian was as much a victim as Mrs Dawson. The judge then examined Mrs Dawson, and at the conclusion of her evidence said there was no pretence for the action. "This was a dangerous exhibition, and Mrs Dawson voluntarily exposed herself to anything which might happen. The performer, it was admitted, had done his best, but, having exhausted himself, he failed. There would be a non-suit with costs."

Mrs Dawson's man then asked for permission to bring an appeal, which was denied. It seems a flawed argument to me – the possible danger in a circus performance is to the performer, there should be no danger to a person who has paid his money to watch.

1882_01_27 LIMERICK (Henry Street). FIRE ALARM AT THEATRE

The company was that of D'Oyly Carte, the play *The Pirates of Penzance*, and the theatre full to the brim with hundreds turned away. The gas pipe which fed the footlights fell into the orchestra pit, and with the front line of the stalls so near at hand the immediate fear was that the burning gas lights would ignite the woodwork and cushions. Some person up in the gallery shouted "Fire!" and a few in the stalls got up and left, a handful of women fainted, but as stage crew immediately appeared and lifted the footlights back into position without any problem, the disturbance calmed immediately and the show continued. The company had announced it would play an afterpiece in addition to *Pirates* but for some unknown reason they did not do so, thereby bringing displeasure from the 'gods' in the form of hissing, and the breaking of lamps lighting the dress circle.

1882_02_20 LONDON (Globe). ACCIDENT TO ACTORS

[Kyrle Bellew (1850–1911) was born Harold Kyrle Money Bellew in Lancashire. In the early 1860s, Kyrle ran away from home to start a life at sea. His clergyman father, agreeing to allow his son to have a naval career, sent him to train on HMS Conway. After two years, Kyrle abandoned this putative career to go on the stage. Known for his romantic profile and blond looks he was the perfect leading man for the times. He travelled widely in Australia and America where he was deemed to have star quality. He married French actress Eugénie Marie Seraphié Le Grande in Melbourne in 1873 but they separated shortly afterwards, though not formally divorcing until 1888. He had extensive property in the antipodes and split his latter years between there and the USA.]

In the play *Mankind* the actors Kyrle Bellew and Miss Litton had reached the scene where the hero comes to the rescue of the heroine in a boat. At this performance the boat fell with a crash, raising fears that Mr Bellew – inside the boat – and Miss Litton underneath must be injured. After a brief interval, Douglas Cox the acting-manager came forward to announce that Bellew was hurt and unable to reappear and that his part would be read

88. *Kyrle Bellew*

115

by Mr Raynham, and that Miss Litton was slightly injured but would carry on with her arm in a sling. Thus the play continued for a short while, then Bellew reappeared with a great plaster round and beneath his chin and took up his part again, both performers being heartily applauded for bravely struggling on. However, on the following nights substitute actors took over the roles.

1882_03_13 LONDON (Toole's). ONSTAGE FIRE DURING PLAY

The play was a new farce called *Auntie*. During Act II a part of the canvas set caught fire and one of the actors, Billington, plus the theatre fireman between them instantly took to beating out the flames and tearing away the smouldering part. This was all done in a few seconds while Toole, the star of show, assured the audience that there was no danger and the show continued. The cause was a leak of gas at a join which caught fire, sending a jet of flame beyond the wires protecting the back of the scene.

1882_03_18 GRIMSBY (Theatre Royal). ACCIDENT TO ACTRESS

"On the first night of *The Orange Girl* at the Theatre Royal, Grimsby, in the scene of the Frozen Tarn, Mrs Walter Searle, who represented Jane Fryer, in leaping into the pool fractured her ankle. The lady was carried off the stage, and attended to at once by Dr Newby." *The Era* 1882_03_18.

1882_03_21 DUBLIN (Star of Erin).   FATAL ACCIDENT TO NOTED TRAPEZE ARTISTE

John Lilley, under the name 'Artois, the Flying Wonder' was a well-known trapeze artiste of the time. His act comprised various flights over the audience, several considered so daring that some people shouted "Enough!" There was no safety net as Artois spurned the very idea, having performed the act for many years. The accident – as so often noted herein – occurred when leaping from the gallery trapeze to one hanging over the stage. He grasped the swinging bar and actually went with it a couple of times, but then lost his grip. Artois fell 16ft, turning round once, on to the bare boards of the stage. The curtain was immediately dropped, and Artois was found to be bleeding profusely from nose, ears, mouth and head. Breathing was barely perceptible and his arms were becoming rigid. Dan Lowrey the owner of the hall whisked him off to Mercer's Hospital where, shortly after admission, this magnificently built man of 5ft 8in, "graceful and wonderfully active" in the air, died from a broken skull.

At the inquest, one or two interesting things came to notice, casting a light on the life of a music hall performer of those days. Lilley was a married man of 33, with a wife who had borne six children, three of whom were still alive aged 11, 8 and 6. He had been in good circumstances, but having lost his costumes in a fire was now trying to claw back his previous position. He had used a net in the past, but had dispensed with it for the last 13 weeks. The coroner asked if it was true that an aerialist performing without a net could command more money, and Lowrey agreed. He also said the use of one was more to protect the audience when an aerialist flies over them, than the performer himself. Even had a net been arranged it would not have stretched to cover the stage. The height of the trapeze bar above the stage was accurately measured and it proved to be only 13ft 9in.

Mrs Lilley was, of course, distraught and said she had no more than £4.10.0 in the world. It was only the second night of his engagement, but Lowrey agreed to pay her husband's wage for the week. He also proposed to start a relief fund for Mrs Lilley. The coroner and a member of the jury immediately gave a guinea each. Lowrey called a Saturday meeting of all the pros in Dublin at which 16 said they would be leaving after that night to go to various engagements in England, so they would solicit contributions from wherever they next went. Lowrey also wrote to *The Era* saying a fund had been set up with the intention of acquiring a property in Dublin which Mrs Lilley could operate as theatrical digs, so providing an income for herself and her children. The theatrical profession was large but close-knit, and many a performer in work would contribute to these appeals, even if the unfortunate was unknown to them, and even if they could only afford 1/-.

1882_03_21 BOSTON, USA (Mechanics' Hall).   ONSTAGE FIRE DURING OPERA

The opera was *La Traviata* starring Madame Patti as Violetta. It was the first night of the season, and at the end of Act I the stage crew neglected to remove a candelabra, the curtain descending on it and promptly bursting into flames. The crew redeemed themselves by ripping down the blazing curtain on to the stage and throwing water over it soon dousing the flames. It was said the audience "behaved well" which we may take as meaning there was no panic and no injuries. "The result of the accident was ludicrous." Which seems a bit extreme as all that meant was when the opera recommenced, with no curtain to hide the scene changes, the audience had a wonderful view of backstage activity. I venture to suggest they would actually have found it of great interest.

1882_04_15 PARIS, France (Cirque d'Hiver).   FATAL ACCIDENT TO STAR EQUESTRIAN

[Elegant ladies in fashionable riding gear seated side-saddle were the epitome of sophistication in the circuses of Paris. They were idolised by the public, beloved of the fashionable and courted by nobility. They were all stars but Mdlle Émilie Loisset was the starriest. She was admired, nay worshipped, by the literary and artistic *habitués* of the Champs Elysees. Her sister Clotilde, also a star equestrian, married into German royalty. However, Emilie having spurned the addresses of the Crown Prince of Austria, had a hubristic slogan on her riding whip *Princess ne daigne, Reine ne plus, Loisset suis* which defies accurate translation but can be loosely rendered as 'I deign to be a princess, a queen even more so, I am Loisset'.]

89. *Émilie Loisset*

This most elegant of riders of *haute école* was thrown by a restive horse while at practice. Refusing a jump it fell back on her and the horn of the saddle pierced her side. Mdlle Loisset, recently returned from performing in Berlin, and due to resume her performances in Paris, instead, tragically died two days later. She was only 26 years of age. In spite of the slogan it appears she had been engaged to Le Prinz de Hatzfeld whose family bought the horse (apparently named *Pour-Toujours* 'Forever' or *J'y pense* which translates as 'I think about you' or 'I'm thinking about it' – reports differ) and had it shot. It has to be said that so many fables have been built up around this star that any or all of them (including this entry) may be specious.

117

1882_04_22 EDINBURGH (Theatre Royal).   ACCIDENT TO MR HALLATT

Taken from Life was a sensation melodrama and in Act IV Mr Hallatt as Walter Lee was making his escape from the police by climbing down a rope from a hay-loft. The rope broke and he fell to the stage, the curtain was then lowered. Dr Liddle and Dr Gibson were soon on the scene, detected a broken left arm above the elbow and set it. Hallatt was then taken home, the play continuing with Arthur Lester in the part. The rope was found to be old and rotten. The manager of the theatre wrote to *The Era* denying this and said it was a touring production by Holt & Wilmot, who had a carpenter and property man with them to oversee the stage management. These two selected the rope, examined it and pronounced it suitable, and it was in use for 11 nights. If it was defective in any way, they must be responsible for "allowing it to be used at the commencement of the engagement".

The property man was James French who had been taken on at Edinburgh on 3 March at a wage of 30/-. He proved to be unreliable on several occasions and was finally sacked for being drunk and unable to perform his duties adequately. Hallatt was able to resume his role – his arm still in a sling – on 29 May, and that seems to have been the end of the matter.

1882_06_12 SOUTH PUEBLO, USA.   FATAL ACCIDENT TO TRAPEZE ARTISTE

The Alfredo Family was performing with John Robinson's Circus in Colorado when this accident happened. The Alfredo Troupe comprising three people – William, Lewis and his wife Emma – presented an act combining high wire and trapeze. William rode a bicycle across the wire, while suspended from the bike were two trapezes on different levels, on which the other two performed. In the middle of the act the wire collapsed due to a stake pulling out of the ground newly softened by torrential rain. At that moment both trapezists were hanging by their insteps, straight down with folded arms. Lewis on the lower bar plunged down about 13ft landing on the back of his head, Emma managed to grab hold of the lower bar and supporting ropes as she fell.

Lewis was taken to the dressing room where physicians attended to him, announcing that his spine was injured. He was moved to a hotel where he died at 4pm the following day. Lewis Alfredo's real name was Max File, aged 28, of German extraction but born in Philadelphia where he married Emma when he was 21. They had children aged four and two.

1882_07_05 LONDON (Drury Lane).   SWORD ACCIDENT

We have previously encountered William Rignold of Drury Lane (*see* 1881_03_14) and here he is again. The final fight between Macbeth and Macduff is an open opportunity for a sword injury and we have seen several already in this book. Rignold was Macbeth, his opponent was J H Barnes who, instead of thrusting his sword to the side of Rignold's body, managed to stick it in his chest. As it is the end of the play for Macbeth in any case, the audience was not aware of the accident. Medical assistance was immediately obtained and the wound found to be "of such a character that Mr Rignold will be unable to appear at present". His role was taken over by Mr Swinburne.

1882_09_04 LONDON (Astley's).   ACCIDENT DURING *MAZEPPA*

Adah Isaacs Menken was the toast of the town as 'the naked Mazeppa' in 1865. Now 17 years on, Maude Forrester had arrived – again from the USA – with her own steed Lightning to try to emulate her predecessor's success. Although, from the pictures advertising her role, she was decently clad in some sort of baggy shorts combined with a loose blouson affair, fetchingly dragged off one shoulder.

On this night, when the fiery steed with Miss Forrester tied on its back clambered up the ramps in the scenery, it stumbled and fell. There was much concern for Miss F, but lessee Mr Cooper came on and assured one and all that Miss F was not at all hurt and the scene would start again. So on came the horse once more and made it to the top of the set impeccably. There was wild applause. One newspaper said: "I hope Miss Forrester was not much hurt, and that her plentiful supply of flesh saved her bones." *Bell's Life in London*

90. *Maude Forrester*

was even more forthright: "Miss Forrester is quite the 'daughter of the gods, Divinely tall, and most divinely fair.' Truth, however, compels me to add that the lady is Rubensesque in breadth of beam. In order not to deceive the reader, Miss Forrester must be frankly described as fat". Try writing that in the newspapers today, lads.

1882_09_24 STOCKHOLM, Sweden (Mosebacke's).   FATAL ACCIDENT TO WIRE-WALKER

Herr Ricardo, known as the Swedish Blondin, was performing in the open air at Mosebacke's establishment on Sunday. Having crossed on his rope from the end of the esplanade to the hotel, on his return to his perch, owing to the heavy dew he lost his balance, dropped his balance pole and grabbed the rope to prevent falling. He changed his everyday clothes into a performer's outfit, while smoking a cigar etc, all while balanced on the rope. He then asked for the guy ropes to be given to him to descend. I am not clear what this means as guy ropes are attached at fixed points along a high wire to help prevent sideways sway and up and down motion. Whatever they were, they broke and he fell to the ground a distance of 62ft. He was immediately taken to hospital but languished there until dying on the following Thursday. Ricardo was only 24 with a wife and two small children and was well liked and respected by his brother artistes. A subscription for the family's maintenance was started at Mosebacke's headed by the Crown Prince of Sweden.

1882_10_14 BIRMINGHAM (Theatre Royal).   ACCIDENT TO ANGELS IN OPERA

The Carl Rosa Opera Company was presenting Gounod's *Faust* and everything had gone smoothly up to the last act where, in the final scene, Marguerite ascends to heaven surrounded by accompanying angels. A lovely effect enhanced by clever use of limelight, with wires to raise the angels. At this performance something went badly wrong and all the angels crashed stagewards tangled up together, to land with bent and broken wings, lop-sided haloes and dropped trumpets. Fortunately no bones were broken, but some claimed they were hurt, and several screamed as they fell. The opera ended "in a scene of excitement".

119

1882_11_21 PARIS, France (Folies-Bergère).   ACCIDENT TO CHILD ACROBAT

The performer was one of a trio of Japanese child acrobats. While on a pole some 32ft above the stage he fell, landing on the head of a lady in the audience. Both child and adult were taken out in a semi-conscious condition. The child, unharmed, returned shortly, but the lady was more seriously injured. Newspapers asked where was the net that should be there for all acrobatic performances?

[Such comments only betray a lack of knowledge of the differences in the various forms of aerial acrobatics. For certain aerial acts such as pole, static trapeze etc it might be more feasible to have thick crash mats below rather than a net. But how would you arrange a net for crossing the high wire over Niagara? You cannot; but modern day funambulists usually have a ring that slides along the wire, this being attached by a loose link to a belt round the performer's waist. A nuisance when you get to one of the side tensioning stays. There are many acts today that can use a belt clipped to a safety wire that goes to an overhead pulley, a method now often used for such acts as the above. Similarly used by many East European acts who, knowing that they are safe in a fall, attempt dangerous feats that succeed perhaps only half the time. Safety nets are almost only used by flying trapeze acts and human cannon balls.]

1882_11_25c BERLIN, Germany (Renz).   FATAL EQUESTRIAN ACCIDENT

The venue was the Renz Circus, one of the main continental shows. Equestrian Miss Sephora was thrown from her horse while taking a jump; she suffered a double fracture to her skull and died shortly afterwards.

1882_11_30 CINCINNATI, USA (Coliseum). FATAL GUN ACCIDENT TO SHARPSHOOTERS

We met sharpshooter Frank I Frayne previously when his wife shot his finger tips off (*see* 1877_09_20c). Mrs Frayne died in 1880 and the widower had carried on with a new partner – the 25-year-old Annie Von Behren – to whom he had become engaged. The play *Si Slocum*, especially written by Clifton W. Tayleure, was always the same, employing shooting tricks at climactic moments. The final dramatic scene in the play featured Frayne's most daring stunt named 'the backward shot'. In this trick Frayne shot an apple off his wife's head while he was turned backwards, resting the rifle on his shoulder and focusing in a mirror. To the audiences of the time this was quite terrifying, and Frayne's advertisements assured prospective audiences that, although the backward shot looked dangerous, it was really quite safe because the actress wore a chain mail skullcap, the apple then resting some six inches above her head on a hat. His late wife had played the part for five years without any mishap.

However, on this day, the rifle broke open as Frayne was firing, the explosion burned Frayne's neck and face and deflected the barrel so that the bullet penetrated the forehead of his fiancée. Police arrested Frayne for manslaughter, but he was exonerated and resumed playing in 1883 four weeks after the trial, but now leaving out his most hazardous stunts. There appear to be several legends surrounding Frayne. His son claimed that his mother was shot dead by his father during the act, though she actually died at 41 from a throat disease. And it was rumoured that Frayne gave up performing after the death of his fiancée, committing suicide a year later. In fact, he removed the

91. *Frank I Frayne*

mirror shot and carried on working. He later married his long time housekeeper Margaret Reed – his first wife's niece, and herself an actress. She joined Frayne, and the couple were still touring when Frayne died in 1891.

1882_12_05 BRUSSELS, Belgium (Circus Carré). EQUESTRIAN ACCIDENT

The unfortunate artiste was Romeo Sebastian the principal rider of the establishment. After falling off his horse into the stalls, when picked up he was seen to be bleeding copiously and was obviously injured but, unbelievably, wanted to continue. The audience protested vociferously, so he was taken away to hospital where he remained delirious for several days, but eventually recovered and was allowed home. It seems quaint today when the audience protest at an artiste wanting to carry on, not because they are offended, but they fear for the person's welfare. Similarly, it must be very rare today for a manager to go onstage and ask the audience if they want the show to cease or carry on.

1882_12_05 LONDON (Britannia).   ACCIDENT TO MRS SARA LANE

The play was *The Devil to Pay*, the unfortunate actress Mrs Sara Lane the manager of the theatre. In the bedroom scene, Mrs Lane as Nell jumped on to the bed and her foot slipped, resulting in a sprained ankle. She heroically carried on, though under some difficulty. Unfortunately, she was unable to perform on 11 December at her own benefit and was still *hors de combat* when her pantomime opened. It seems something was amiss with the blood vessels of her instep. Whatever her trouble, it was very troublesome indeed, as she remained indisposed for some months. In April 1883, she was reported to be convalescing in Hastings but was shortly expected back at the Britannia. Alas, she was still recuperating in August, now in Boulogne. She hoped to reappear at the Britannia in October. Finally, I can give you some positive good news Sara Lane was back onstage for her annual benefit on 10 December 1883, exactly a year after her accident; so more than a mere twisted ankle.

92. Sara Lane

1882_12_10 WALLINGFORD (Corn Exchange).   FATAL ACCIDENT TO OPERA SINGER

[This is very sad, of course, but gives an interesting light on a very little known aspect of Victorian Entertainment. Pepper's Ghost is a magical illusion created by a simple optical principle. If you look out of a window in daylight you see through it, but on looking through the window when it is dark outside you see your reflection. Professor Pepper took the principle, and using large plate glass sheets, black velvet and clever lighting he came up with a practical method of producing and vanishing 'ghosts' among living actors. This burst on the world in 1862, much used in theatres, but soon becoming more of a fairground sideshow affair.

However, in the late 1860s there arose the bizarre idea of basing an opera company around the illusion. This was so successful that, until the end of the century, several of these companies flourished. Among those that lasted some years were Gompertz, Harry Pool, Fred Smith, and Strange & Wilson. These companies tended not to use conventional theatres, but hired public halls for a week and set up their equipment, offering a nightly change of programme.]

At Wallingford, Henry Dunthorne was a singer appearing with 'Gompertz Pepper's Ghost and Spectral Opera Company'. Falling from a ladder during the performance, he was taken to hospital where he remained until his death on 20 January. The report of the company at the Corn Exchange said "On Monday night the entertainment was poorly patronised, but those present appreciated the performance of *The Stormy Thoughts* (founded on Schiller's poem). There are some talented vocalists belonging to the company." By the time the review was printed one of them would sing no more.

1882_12_23c PLYMOUTH (Theatre Royal).   ACCIDENT TO REHEARSALS BY WATER

The pantomime rehearsals were taking place on the stage as the Borough Surveyor was inspecting the water services. Suddenly the stage was deluged with a flood of water from above, swamping the actors who fled in distress. This theatre had, as a fire prevention, the ingenious idea of a 'water curtain' rather than an iron safety curtain. On the release of a lever a barrier of water descended at the front of the stage. The inspection had revealed a faulty valve. Fortunately, the water being away from the scenery very little of that was damaged, and the actors were not in costume.

1882_12_26 BRADFORD (Theatre Royal). ACCIDENT TO PANTOMIME FAIRY

This was yet another example of a fairy falling from her position in the transformation scene. The fall was 12ft and she received serious injuries. "The pantomime was brought to an abrupt conclusion."

1883_01_08 WEST HARTLEPOOL (Gaiety). ACCIDENT IN *MAZEPPA* TO MISS FORRESTER

We have already met the plump Miss Forrester and an accident with her horse in *Mazeppa* (*see* 1882_09_04) at Astley's. Four month's later she was on a provincial tour, and not a particularly prestigious one judging by this venue. Traversing a gangway screened by a piece of scenery, it gave way, horse and rider falling on to the stage. Miss F injured her arm sufficiently to call in the local doctor who dressed the wound, enabling the courageous actress to complete the performance, roundly cheered by the audience. It is wonderful how a doctor was always immediately to hand in those days, and the audience prepared to wait while he ministered to the injured.

1883_01_20 NOTTINGHAM (Theatre Royal). ACCIDENT TO HARLEQUIN

This accident was described as "singular" but as my readers will know, and the reporter clearly did not, this type of accident had been recurring for over a century, though admittedly much less frequently as harlequinades were rapidly going out of fashion. Charles Romaine jumped through the scenery via the traditional flap and there were no men with a sling to catch him. He fell on his back and had to be taken home where, the following day, he was diagnosed with internal injuries and a broken rib.

1883_01_25 COATBRIDGE (Theatre Royal). GUN ACCIDENT

The play was *Hue and Cry; or Evictions in Ireland*. Two robbers outside a house were demanding entrance, the actress Annie Hastings, playing the housewife, was behind the scenic flat depicting the door. On the occupier's refusal to admit the robbers they were both supposed to fire their pistols at the roof. One did so, the other fired at the canvas door on the flat. Miss Hastings was shot in the lower abdomen. Dr Munro the local medico declared the injury would not be fatal and, as I have found nothing further about the incident, we must presume Annie lived on.

1883_02_16 ST HELEN'S (Theatre Royal). ACTOR FALLS THROUGH STAGE

The play was *The Danites*, the unlucky actor J P Moore. During the action of the play he was thrown through a centre doorway, and on landing the floor gave way beneath him. Fortunately, he only fell through to his waist, receiving some bruising. "The limbs and lives of artistes are occasionally endangered for want of a few inexpensive boards."

1883_05_16 NEWCASTLE (Tyne). GUN ACCIDENT

The show was a sensation play called *Youth*. A realistic *tableau* depicted *The Defence of Hawk's Point* where "guns and rifles were freely discharged". One of the discharges was lower than it should have been and William Mundy (21) a super was hit on the side of his face, a wound that necessitated dressing at the Infirmary.

1883_06_16 LONDON.   ACCIDENT TO SWORD-SWALLOWER

It is not clear where this accident took place. It looks as though the man was busking. Frederick Smith (19) who lived near Drury Lane gave performances as a sword-swallower. At this showing, he swallowed a sword (which was blunted along both sides) then to prove it was a genuine sword and not a trick one that collapsed into the handle, he gestured for somebody to step forward and pull the sword out. The volunteer, either accidentally or maliciously, pushed on the hilt and the point penetrated Smith's intestines. He collapsed, and it was with some difficulty that the sword could be extracted. He was taken to a local surgeon who had him moved to St Thomas's Hospital.

1883_07_09 MANCHESTER (Star).   ACCIDENT TO STRONG MAN

The unfortunate artiste was Mons Hercule. He was intending to respond to a challenge to pull two horses with his teeth, but this being Monday the arrangements were not complete. His substitute stunt had a pulley fixed to a beam over which passed a rope, and while he had one end of the rope between his teeth, the other was held by a group of volunteer spectators. They had to pull on the rope, thereby lifting the strong man towards the roof. When he was almost at the top, they jerked the rope so that Hercule's face bashed against the beam. He tried to grab the beam with his hands, missed, and fell to the ground where he was found to have broken an arm and a leg.

1883_07_20 NOTTINGHAM (Royal Alhambra).   GUN ACCIDENT

The accident happened during a series of tableaux illustrating the story of *Jack Long of Texas*. The final scene had the hero threatening to shoot each of the baddies in the eye. Harry Smith was the actor playing Jack Long, and one of the baddies was Arthur Bradbury. Smith was pointing his rifle at Bradbury when it "went off unexpectedly". The paper wadding of the charge, lodging in the left eye, destroyed the actor's sight. Smith must have been a good shot. Bradbury was hurried to the General Hospital where, in addition to the major calamity, he was found to have further wounds to cheek and eyebrow.

1883_08_20c PARIS, France (Chatelet).   ACCIDENT TO CHARLES LAURI JR

We met Charles Lauri a little while ago (*see* 1882_01_05). Having become a partner with his father in the family pantomime company, he was appearing in a fairy spectacle called *Peau D'Ane*. The show had been a total success, but Charles Jr damaged his knee and had to be off for a few days. He was playing an ape, a role in which he specialised, so his father replaced him in the skin, without the substitution being advertised. *The Era* correspondent thought this unfair to both public and Charles Jr, as the father lacked the talent of his incredible acrobatic son.

1883_09_10 NEW YORK, USA (Colville).   COLLAPSE OF SCENIC BRIDGE

Othello was in dress rehearsal with a bridge formed by elevating a section of the stage boarding to a height of 4ft. A large number of players were marching across the bridge in turn. Suddenly, dropping with a crash, twelve bodies were hurled into the cellar 16ft below. Two actresses were only scratched, two more seriously hurt were taken home, one with a broken rib. Actor Price suffered a dislocated bone in his foot, and bleeding from others falling on him. Actor Brawley had also damaged foot bones. The fall was inexplicable, as elephants had been over the same set-up in the past.

123

1883_10_01c Trieste, Italy (Polyteama).   ACCIDENT TO MISS ZÆO

"At a recent farewell performance of the Amato Circus Company, at the Polyteama Theatre in Trieste, one of the performers, a 'Miss Zæo,' who has been a great attraction at the circus both for her beauty and her sklll on the trapeze, fell while performing on a wire rope elevated at a considerable height above the floor of the theatre. A safety net was placed underneath the wire, but unfortunately Miss Zæo only struck on the edge of the netting, and thence fell to the floor. Had it not been for the netting, however, the performer must have been killed outright; as it was she sustained injuries which must effectually close her professional career, even if they do not terminate fatally. She seems to have fallen on her face, the nasal bone being completely smashed, while there are deep and serious wounds on the forehead. The excitement among the audience was very great, and although the manager offered to continue the programme the public refused to allow the performance to go on, and left the theatre." *Bicester Herald* 1883_10_12.

1883_10_31 NORTHAMPTON (Theatre Royal).   NEAR FATAL ACCIDENT TO ACTRESSES

During Act III of *La Dame Aux Camelias*, Miss Alleyn and Miss Aidè were no more than 2ft back from the footlights, when the rope of the act drop broke, allowing the roller to descend with an almighty crash. The roller brushed the front of their dresses before hitting the floor, and if the two women had been even six inches further forward they would both have been hit on the top of their heads with death being a strong possibility. As it was, within a few minutes a new rope was fitted, the act drop hauled up, and the play continued.

124

1883_11_28 COVENTRY (Theatre Royal).   GUN ACCIDENT

The play was *Youth*, the unlucky man Joseph Swift, enacting Frank Darlington. A rifle with a blank cartridge was fired in his face and he got the contents below his left eye. He was off work for several days.

1884_01_12 LONDON (International).   ACCIDENT POSTPONES HEBREW OPERA

The Russian Jewish Theatre company was hounded out of Russia by new strict laws against the Jewish people. Particularly applicable to them was a ban on theatrical performances in any other language but Russian.

The 16-strong company thus fled its home and wandered the land, stopping in likely places to perform before travelling on. As displaced persons from other countries have found, England was a welcoming haven. They came to London without knowing a word of English but, aware there was a Jewish Diaspora, and relying on the country's open arms, they ended up in Whitechapel. Having arrived during the pantomime season, there was a problem in finding a venue, but eventually they proposed performing the "Hebrew Opera of *The Sorceress*" at the International Theatre. Unfortunately, the leading actress Madame Gradner suffered an accident and the production was postponed. However, the company gave two concerts in an Institute in Finsbury which whetted the appetite for more major productions. It was mainly a jingoistic occasion with an occasional infelicity, as when one item on the programme had been translated as *The Stabbed Jew* when it should have been *The Point of the Jew,* a song about Jewish policy.

1884_03_12 BLACKBURN (Prince's).   ACCIDENT TO TRAPEZE ARTISTE
The artiste was George of the Lazello Troupe. One of the trio was swinging on a bar head downwards with a rope between his teeth. At the end of the rope was a hook which George attached to a belt round his waist. The hook slipped or became detached, and George fell. He only dropped about 4ft but landed on his back across the stage footlights. Although not badly hurt, some broken glass penetrated his back.

1884_05_30 SHEFFIELD (Alexandra).   ACCIDENT TO MISS KELSEY
Lizzie Kelsey had already coped with a costume fire in January and escaped unscathed. On this occasion, after executing a rapid costume change, as she left her dressing room she tripped over a crank handle in the passage way, falling full length damaging her ribs, hands and face. As a result she contracted pleurisy and was off work, but was expected to return when the show reached Astley's on 16 June.

1884_06_07 GT YARMOUTH (Theatre Royal).   SWORD ACCIDENT
Macbeth was Henry Loraine, Macduff was Graham Malvern. In the fight Malvern, struck across the hand, received injury to two fingers, as a result of which he has "been unable to attend to his professional duties since." Of course, as Macduff is the victor, should he get injured it makes finishing the play properly a bit awkward. No problem if the actor playing Macbeth gets injured – all he has to do is to drop down dead as he would do anyway.

125

1884_06_12 COVENTRY (Theatre).   ACCIDENT TO MISS FORRESTER
Here we go again! The pleasingly plump Miss Forrester and her blinking horse in another accident. As previously (*see* 1883_01_08) a section of the horse's journey path gave way. On this occasion, however, the horse became "extremely violent" and threw over "the illumination" which could easily have started a fire but did not. Miss F succeeded in getting free, pacifying the horse, and the play continued.

1884_07_14 WORKINGTON.   HIGH WIRE ACCIDENT
After a band contest, a female Blondin commenced her performance on a high wire some 50ft above the ground. The artiste, Miss Storey (12) daughter of Thomas Storey, ascended the ladder to her perch at the end of the wire, closely followed by her father. He steadied her prior to her starting her walk. She had gone but two steps when the rope gave way at its fixings and the girl fell to the ground. Simultaneously the perch collapsed, so the father fell too. Miss S was feared to have been killed but she revived and was taken to the committee tent where Dr Moore, who was on the field, attended to her wounded back. Mr S suffered a leg broken in two places, and was taken to the nearest surgery and thence to his lodgings. One can only wonder if the father was an experienced professional, as he seemingly proved incapable to rig a high wire bearing the weight of a 12-year-old.

1884_07_20 GLASGOW.   AN UNANSWERABLE QUESTION
"A theatre manager was asked why he employed such bad actors, and replied 'Would you have me let the poor wretches starve?'" *Glasgow Evening Citizen* 1884_07_20.

1884_07_26 LONDON (Lyceum). UNUSUAL ACCIDENT TO ELLEN TERRY

[Ellen Terry was the third of eleven children of theatrical parents. She made her first stage appearance in 1856 at the age of nine when she joined the Charles Kean company at the Princess's

Theatre, remaining until the Keans retired in 1859. She was in the shadow of her elder sister Marion, but progressed to ingénue parts until marriage at the age of 17 to the artist G F Watts. The marriage lasted under a year, and she became the lover of Edward William Godwin, an artist à la William Morris, bearing by him a daughter and son. She retired from acting for six years. The relationship cooled in 1874 and Terry returned to the stage. She made a number of acclaimed performances and rose to be the brightest star of the West End. In 1878, the 30-year-old Terry joined the Lyceum Theatre as leading lady to Henry Irving. The pair became theatre's golden couple and may be regarded as the country's first superstars.]

Ellen Terry had a vaccination on her left arm but "by some unhappy mischance" the virus from the vaccination found its way through a slight flesh wound in her right thumb. Inflammation resulted, and she

93. *Ellen Terry*

became quite ill. Struggling on as actors do, she performed with her arm in a sling but finally had to succumb, and the performance of *Twelfth Night* in which she played Viola had to be cancelled. A telegram was sent to her sister Marion – staying with friends at Ambleside in Cumberland – asking if she could take over the role. Marion played the part successfully for several days.

1884_08_22 GT YARMOUTH (Theatre Royal). ACCIDENT TO EDWARD TERRY

[Edward O'Connor Terry (1844 –1912) was no relation to the famous Terry showbusiness family. Allegedly the illegitimate son of Feargus O'Connor the Irish patriot, he made his stage debut in 1863. Following the usual beginnings he played small roles in small companies. Progressing, he gained a season at London's Surrey then on to the West End stage where he established himself as a star comedian and singer at the Gaiety Theatre remaining for eight years. In 1887, he went into management, opening Terry's Theatre on the Strand.]

On Friday night, Edward Terry was appearing in the old warhorse *Paul Pry*. A pistol he was about to use exploded in his hand, causing a serious injury. The performance was halted and a surgeon summoned who dressed the wound. Again, one gets the impression that in those days there were medical men lounging around all over the place just waiting to be sent for! Although no permanent injury was likely, it meant Terry was indisposed on Saturday. He was due at Norwich the following week, but his doctor Dr Mallam Vores said his patient would be off for "some time to come." He missed almost three weeks of his tour, actually returning to the stage at Newcastle on 12 September, with his arm still in a sling playing Chevalier Walkinshaw in *The Rocket*.

94. *Edward Terry*

1884_10_07 COOKSTOWN (Lloyd's Circus).   TWO ACCIDENTS AT CIRCUS

Lloyd's Grand Mexican Circus had set up the show on this day and the tent was packed. Unfortunately, two separate accidents occurred, the first to the audience, the second to a performer. A section of the raised 1/- seating collapsed, dumping people and tangled planks on to the ground and on to each other. Apart from a few cuts and bruises the customers seemed to have got off lightly and the show continued.

The artiste was attempting to catch a cannon ball fired from a cannon. The unnamed performer, was possibly Holtum whom we met a while back, (*see* 1880_02_13) as he claimed to be the only man doing that particular feat, or he may have been a totally different twerp. This chap failed three times and on the fourth the ball hit him in the face breaking his jaw and "other facial bones". And not surprisingly "knocked him to the ground." So it was obviously not Holtum carried out. A doctor was summoned to tend the injuries, which were not considered life threatening.

1884_10_24 BIRMINGHAM (Duncalf's Circus).   FATAL ACCIDENT TO GYMNAST

William Henry Norton (26), a gymnast performing under the name of William Selmore (Selmo) with Duncalf's Circus at Aston, was practicing a new feat. This was a double somersault at which he had failed twice, injuring himself the second time. Attempting the feat a third time, he fell on his head and was rushed to hospital where the surgeon said it was a hopeless case as he had injured his spinal column. Selmo died two days later.

1884_10_26 GATESHEAD (Hall of Varieties).   FATAL ACCIDENT TO GYMNAST

The artistes were four acrobats forming the Poole Troupe. John Wightman (24) was intending to throw a back somersault from the shoulders of Edward Poole, but had insufficient impetus, landing on his head instead of his feet. Believing he had dislocated his neck he called on Poole to "pull his neck" which his partner did, twice, without effect. Wightman then said: "It's a bad job, Ned; don't leave me." A doctor was called for, and he attended the man on the stage. Poole asked if he had been at fault, and Wightman said: "No, no, I lost all control of myself when in the air; I even kicked to turn myself, but couldn't." He was moved to the troupe's lodgings where he died at noon the following day. He was a married man, and the news was telegraphed to his wife in Birmingham. The two other members of the troupe were boys.

1884_11_18 VALENCIA, Spain (Theatre).   FATAL ACCIDENT TO TRAPEZE ARTISTE

Miss Leona Dare was the performer, assisted by "a fine-looking young fellow" called George. It will be recalled that the intrepid aerialist had her teeth knocked out in a previous accident (*see* 1880_06_25c). Clearly her dentistry was still holding up as Miss Dare was hanging upside down from the trapeze bar, with a second bar suspended on a cord from her mouth. On this lower bar the assistant was going through various gymnastic motions when alas Miss L's teeth "gave way" and the unfortunate fine-looking fellow fell head first from the top of the building on to the stage. "He was taken up in a dying condition." M George was later confirmed to be dead and Leona Dare who had taken to her bed with hysterical exhaustion was described as in a "precarious condition". So her repaired teeth had lasted four years before collapsing. The reports did not mention her impoverished husband the pursued count.

127

1884_12_22 LEAMINGTON SPA (Ginnett's Circus).   ACCIDENT TO TRAPEZE ARTISTE

Le Blond was swinging on a trapeze fixed to the very roof of the building. His swings were so extreme that "the hooks by which the trapeze was suspended were jerked out of the iron holdfast". He fell with great force to the arena below. Though unconscious when taken up, he did not break any bones and was thought to be fit within a day or two.

1885_01_05 BIRMINGHAM (Prince of Wales).   ACCIDENT TO PANTOMIME FAIRY

Pollie Pownall was engaged to play a fairy and 'as required' in the annual pantomime at 25/- a week. She had appeared for several years in this role at the same theatre. Part of her duties comprised posing on a small ledge on the iron framework during the transformation scene. The girls, taking up their poses, strapped themselves in position. Pollie Pownall, with a dislike of this part of her work, had made many protests, the manager's response being that if she did not do it she would lose her job, as she had been contracted to play 'as required' – a standard clause that may well still be in present day contracts, it certainly was when I was a pro.

After the girls had appeared, the iron was hauled up into the flies. There were three girls on separate ledges, all at different levels. The girls got on and off the iron from a cross bridge high in the flies. The procedure was for the girl to wait until she was level with the bridge, undo her belt and be helped off by a flyman. At the end of the scene, Pollie, being the highest on the frame, was the first able to step on to the bridge. On this night, shortly before Pollie was level with the bridge, the rope that lowered and raised the whole contraption broke, and there was a sudden drop which was checked abruptly at 16ft by a safety rope. However Pollie, having unfastened her belt in readiness of stepping on to the bridge, was jerked off her ledge down to the stage and beyond, into the cellar, a distance of around 40ft. The other two girls had not yet unfastened their straps, so were not shaken off the iron.

Pollie's injuries were serious and she was bed-ridden for some time. The management paid her wage until the end of the panto run on 28 February, and also paid Dr Grindling's fees up to the same time.

The following day the manager visited her to say he had "a little present" for her, the condition being that she waived any responsibility for the accident that may be attributed to the management. She refused to take the offering – the sum was not stated. After that, all assistance was withdrawn, but the doctor kindly consented to attend her without payment, which he did for a further nine weeks. Another doctor who was called in said she would have to wear a kneecap and give up all thoughts of a future stage career. Dr Grindling was more sanguine, and thought she would be able to return in a year's time.

In April 1886, Pollie took the Prince of Wales management to court to claim £300 damages for her loss of earnings. She claimed that she and her eldest daughter had been obliged to turn down engagements at £3.10.0 a week. It was a long drawn out affair with many stage staff examined, and discussion on the ropes and whether she should not have undone her belt, and so on. The lessee of the theatre said the girls had permanent instructions not to undo their belts themselves, but wait for a stagehand on the bridge to do it. Probyn, the man on the bridge said he could not unfasten the belt and lift the girl off at the same time. The lessee stated the girls clambered around the iron like cats, and half the time did not belt up at all. At the end, Pollie was granted damages of £150.

1885_01_05 LONDON (Astley's).   ACCIDENT TO HARLEQUIN

During the pantomime performance, Alfred Lauraine (42) playing Harlequin injured himself through misjudging a somersault. He damaged his leg muscle by banging it against a bar as he went into his spring, and was taken to St Thomas's Hospital.

1885_01_06 LONDON (Astley's).   ACCIDENT TO CLOWN

During the pantomime performance, Alexander Coleman (35) better known as the clown Little Sandy misjudged a somersault, rupturing his Achilles tendon, and was taken to St Thomas's Hospital to join his colleague (*see above*).

1885_02_13 GLASGOW (Gaiety).   ACCIDENT TO TRAPEZE ARTISTE

The trapeze artistes, apparently of Russian nationality, were The Great Ostaras, Continental Wonders. The female of the pair was on the top bar of a double trapeze, the male on the lower one. The trick was for her to drop, catching her arms on her partner's feet. Failing to achieve this, she fell with a thud to the stage, a distance of only 7ft. She was taken off insensible, and attended to by a doctor who found her injured on the thigh and face. The Ostaras were quick to write to *The Era* stating the lady was only slightly hurt, and they would soon be back at work.

1885_03_02 GRIMSBY (Theatre Royal).   GUN ACCIDENT

The play was *The Centenarian*. The unfortunate actor Algernon Syms had a scene where he was shot by a lady. The actress with the gun, pulling the trigger early because of the lightness of the pistol action, accidentally shot the poor chap in the face from a yard away. On rising to his feet, blood was pouring from his face but his eyes escaped damage. He was still suffering at the end of the week, but clearly on the mend.

1885_03_17 MANCHESTER (Theatre Royal).   SCENERY FALLS ON ACTOR

95.

[Leonard Boyne (1853–1920) born in Ireland began his acting career at Liverpool in 1870. His London debut was in 1874 at the St. James's Theatre. After a long career playing a multiplicity of roles he ended playing the lead in a dramatisation of E W Hornung's *Raffles*.]

The play was *Claudian*. In the earthquake scene which involved the popular concept of the scenery collapsing before your very eyes, the arch of Claudian's palace, instead of falling forwards as per plan, fell backwards on to Leonard Boyne who was compelled to bear the entire weight for fully two minutes until rescued by stagehands. After a 15 minute delay he was able to struggle through the last act, but still suffering from the shock the next day.

1885_04_20 NEWCASTLE (Holtum's Circus).   ACCIDENT TO 'CANNONBALL' HOLTUM

[Holtum, a 40-year-old Dane who first appeared in 1866, had caught his cannonball in many parts of the world.] Herr Holtum, (*see 1880_02_13*), now had his own circus, a special feature being a military spectacle *The War in the Sudan* into which Holtum had inserted his speciality act with the balls. On this night, he missed catching the ball and it appeared to whizz by his head and thud into the side scene. At this point in the continuance of the play the British army came rushing in to rout the Arabs. Holtum had dashed off, and once the Arabs were defeated there was an awkward lull while the British soldiers stood looking lost as to what to do next. Holtum then reappeared holding the side of his head with a bloodstained cloth where it appeared the cannonball had hit him. Holtum, in a rather lengthy address, claiming it was but a flesh wound, said he would be all right by the following night. He then called for the National Anthem to be played and the audience left the Big Top.

1885_05_08 LUTON.   **DEATH OF MARQUIS DE GONZA**

This is not an accident, unless the result of a series of such, but a salutary warning against a dissolute life. In his heyday, Gonza was a top star on the trapeze earning as much as £120 a week. He had a wife and two children, but parked them with his father in Luton while he gallivanted round the world, the cynosure of the public and a drinking pal to all. He suffered several accidents but always bounced back. Eventually, drink getting the better of him, he became afraid of falling. Work dwindled, but the drink did not. In desperation, because his health was failing, he returned penniless to Luton. His father – from whom he had been estranged for 14 years – refused to pay the outstanding fare from St Pancras and it was paid by a friend. The Marquis, real name George Edwin Algar, found a friendly innkeeper and his wife who took him in without payment, and arranged for a doctor who organized his transfer to the Workhouse Hospital. In a matter of days, before he could be moved, he died, aged 38, without a penny to his name.

1885_05_15 ST HELENS (Theatre).   **FIRE ONSTAGE DURING SHOW**

During the Act II climax – "a representation of the fall of Khartoum" – a gas jet shot into the scenery, which was ablaze in seconds. The lessee of the theatre asked the public to keep their seats while the fire was tackled. This they did, thus averting any horrific panics such as those previously described.

1885_06_01 LEAMINGTON SPA (Theatre Royal).   **SWORD ACCIDENT**

Not the usual *Macbeth* or *Hamlet* bout, the wounded recipient was in the audience. The opera was *Rip Van Winkle*. In the closing chorus of Act I where the bayonets of the soldiers are struck down by the captain's sword, the weapon broke and the blade shot out into the audience, hitting a lady in the orchestra stalls on the temple. This created a wound that was tended to by Surgeon-General Ranking who was amongst the audience. Medical men really loved the theatre! I wonder if he had his bag with him? I recall reading that in Victorian times doctors often carried stethoscopes under their top hats.

1885_10_20 DARLINGTON (Victoria).   **ACCIDENT TO TRAPEZE ARTISTE**

The venue was the Victoria Theatre of Varieties, the artistes Ellier and Alza 'flying comets'. Ellier, after doing his great flight and double mid-air somersault, failed to clasp his partner's wrists and fell some 25ft into the pit. There was no safety net. He was lucky to escape with a sprained wrist and a damaged nose, though several women fainted.

1885_11_24 MANCHESTER (Boswell's Circus).   ACCIDENT AT BOSWELL'S CIRCUS

The unfortunate artiste was Mons Ethardo, the 'spiral ascensionist' whom we met 27 years ago in a previous accident (*see* 1858_06_20). This man's act was to ascend a spiral track walking on a globe. The apparatus was like the bare bones of a helter-skelter. On turning round when reaching the top he descended again, still walking on his globe. On this night, he was on the descent, about 12ft from the bottom, when he slipped and fell off his track. He was carried out but in a short time he was able to walk about.

Not only did Ethardo have a very long professional career where work possibilities must have been limited by his complicated apparatus, but on retirement he taught his act to two females, and became a manager to a wirewalker called Oceana who was renowned for her stunning beauty and figure.

97. *Ethardo*

1885_12_30 MANCHESTER (Theatre Royal).   LIZZIE COOTE COMPELLED TO LEAVE

Lizzie Coote was one of the many vivacious female performers current in the late Victorian period. Going on the stage as a child, she had grown into a beautiful young woman. She was an ideal principal boy, and was appearing as Dick in *Dick Whittington*, gaining good reviews. Unfortunately, she had suffered a fall some weeks previously, hurting her spine and, though working since, clearly suffered some injury not detected at the time, as only a few days into the run, Lizzie had to leave the panto through paralysis. She died on 18 February 1886 aged only 24.

98. *Lizzie Coote*

131

1886_01_11 SCARBOROUGH (Theatre Royal).   ACCIDENT TO PANTOMIMIST

In the show *Robinson Crusoe*, Mr W H Thorne in his role as Man Friday somersaulted over a table, but misjudging his distance, fell over the wire guard rails that protected the footlights. He quickly managed to untangle himself, but the wires had severely cut his wrist, arms and ankles. Nevertheless, he carried on with the show amid the cheers of a large audience.

1886_01_18 BIRMINGHAM (Theatre Royal).   M TREWEY FALLS THROUGH STAGE

99.

[Félicien Trewey (1848–1920) from an early age practised conjuring and juggling. At the age of 15 he ran away from home to become a professional entertainer. He was very versatile, being a juggler, magician, mime, balancer, tightrope walker, dancer, plate spinner, and a card thrower able to scale cards great distances. He also gave musical entertainments with instruments of his own invention and possessed the uncommon art of immediately writing any words selected by his audience backwards. He was also an exceptional lightning sketch artist. The astonishing thing is that he was not renowned for any of these talents, but for two speciality acts – shadowgraphy (casting amusing shadows with his hands) and chapeaugraphy wherein Trewey would pull different faces of the various characters beneath the hats he twisted from a simple circle of felt. His performances were so successful throughout Europe and America that chapeaugraphy became known by the name of Treweyism. Oh, yes, he also performed in several early cinema films, and introduced the Lumiere brothers to England. There is a very brief snatch of Trewey on You Tube.] *Personal Note: my early public performances included chapeaugraphy – my chapeau and band parts are, 65 years later, still in a drawer alongside me as I type.*

M Trewey was appearing in the pantomime when suddenly he dropped through the floor up to his armpits. He managed to raise himself up and out, then walked offstage. Failing his return, the panto carried on. Evidently he had inadvertently stepped on one of the many trapdoors that peppered the Victorian stage. These work by being braced from underneath, then when they are to be used the supports are withdrawn so the section of stage can be moved aside. On this occasion the supports had been removed in readiness for the transformation scene that was due to follow Trewey. He should have been warned to avoid the spot. Trewey, shaken and alarmed, suffered no injury except bruises to face and back.

1886_02_06 CHATHAM (Theatre).   ACCIDENT TO FIGHTING ACTOR

Coventry Davis was an actor in a melodrama called *Justice at Last*. In the climactic scene Davis had to make to stab his opponent, whereupon the other actor had to grapple him, a fight ensuing. This all went according to plan, though perhaps a bit too realistically, as Davis went down with a broken leg. Fortunately it was very near the end of the play.

132

1886_02_23 LONDON (Lyceum).   ACCIDENT TO IRVING AND ALEXANDER

The play was *Faust* in which, at the end of the first scene, Henry Irving as Mephistopheles and George Alexander as Faust make their exits in a cloud of vapour. This was achieved by means of a slide, but on this night they both fell off it, Irving hitting his head on the table and cutting his face badly in three places, Alexander injuring only his leg. The plasters over Irving's cuts were covered liberally with make-up that needed frequent renewal. Later leeches were applied to reduce the swellings so that they were barely perceptible. The performance had not been interrupted by the misfortune.

1886_03_12 WESTBURY (Institute).   GUN ACCIDENT

The play was *The Flying Dutchman*, the injured actor Mr H E Gordon. He was "shot in the arm at very close quarters" by the actor playing Captain Vanhelm. Having had his arm bandaged, Gordon, though in some considerable pain, finished his part.

1886_03_25 DONCASTER (Theatre Royal).   ACTOR IN DOG BITING ACCIDENT

This accident is a superb example of how the actors' credo 'the show must go on' really plays out. The production was *Uncle Tom's Cabin* in which a bloodhound was featured. On this night it was brought on without a muzzle, and when guns were fired it broke free of the man holding it, to fly at Mr Percival. The dog seized the actor by the arm, biting him deeply to the bone. Percival kept his presence of mind, carrying on with his normal acting and lines without an apparent qualm. At the end of the act he took his call with the others, then ran off to a doctor where he got his wound cauterised, and was back to go on for next act which he played adequately, though suffering great pain. Had the bite been half an inch lower, Percival would have bled to death before help could have arrived.

1886_04_15c VALENCIA, Spain.   ACCIDENT TO TRAPEZE ARTISTE

The venue was the Plaza de Toros, the artiste George Leoni, for many years of the Flying Leonis, then becoming half of Leoni & Hanlon. I could glean no details of the accident, but it was a very severe injury as Leoni was in hospital in Valencia for two months, half of which time he was unconscious. He then was able to return to England where he was an out-patient at St Thomas's Hospital. In October, things took a turn for the worse and he was admitted to Caterham Asylum. At this point his old partner D Leoni wrote to *The Era* soliciting financial aid for George's wife and eight children, the oldest aged only 13.

1886_04_24 LONDON (Gatti's).   ACCIDENT TO WAINRATTA

Wainratta the wire king had suffered two previous accidents – that we know about (*see* 1873_09_15 and 1874_05_16). This time it was not in performance but on a Saturday morning when the well-known wire-walker fell while fixing up his apparatus, breaking his leg. An Englishman by the true name of Alfred Wainright, he was an international performer of repute. A poster for him at the Folies Bergere depicts a man on the tightrope in top hat and tails so I should imagine he made his entrance from the audience as a tipsy customer and got laughs as the character wobbled about precariously on the wire. He would then strip off his finery to disclose the true wire walking outfit of the period and demonstrate his true mastery of his art. He was *hors de combat* for a long time as his leg had to be set thrice, and he was unable to work again until October.

100. *Wainratta poster*

1886_05_31 BIRMINGHAM (Museum).   ACCIDENT TO GYMNAST

The venue was the Museum Concert Hall, the unfortunate artiste was John Wilson of Wilson and Alza. While turning a back somersault from a horizontal bar he broke his foot in two places. He was taken to Queen's Hospital.

1886_08_13 LEAMINGTON SPA (Theatre Royal).   SWORD ACCIDENT IN *OTHELLO*

During a performance by Mr Henry Irving's Lyceum Company, in the scene where Othello separates the combatants in the drunken brawl at Cyprus, Mr Hughes as Cassio was cut across the hand by Mr Harbury playing Othello. The weapon was a scimitar, and the wound bled profusely.

[Mr Harbury playing Othello? Where was Mr Irving? Ah, this was not the Lyceum company in which Henry Irving and Ellen Terry regularly toured the provinces, but a group of Lyceum players who were normally in small supporting parts. The Lyceum, like most London theatres at the time, closed over summer. The small part players asked permission of their chief if they could tour as players from the Lyceum, thus giving them opportunity to play larger roles than he was wont to cast them in. Irving not only gave them permission but allowed the use of some of his costumes and pieces of his scenery. From 1888 to 1894 this company, renamed as the Lyceum Vacation Company, was organised by John Martin Harvey who played the leading roles. After 14 years of idolising Irving but never promoted, Martin Harvey formed his own company and in 1920 became Sir John Martin-Harvey.

133

1886_08_26 SUNDERLAND (Star).   ACCIDENT TO BLACKFACE COMEDIAN

Mr Hey of double act Carlin and Hey, was standing on a chair in the wings wearing a pair of long foot boots ready to start what was commonly called 'a big boot dance'. Leaping off the chair on to the stage, and getting his legs twisted, he fell just in front of the footlights. The audience highly entertained by this, laughed and applauded, thinking it was part of the act. They stopped when Hey was carried off to the infirmary, where it was found he had broken his left leg. [The big boot dance was a speciality of Little Tich (Harry Relph 1867–1928), who wore boots with soles 28 inches long, as can be seen on You Tube.]

1886_08_30 DUNEDIN, New Zealand (Princess's).   ACTOR FALLS THROUGH TRAP

In the course of the action of the play My Partner, actor George Rignold was called upon to convey that he had descended into a valley. This effect was achieved by his going off behind a piece of scenery representing rocks at the back of which was a trap in the stage where he sat until the end of the scene. On the Saturday night the trap had creaked but caused no uneasiness. Arriving at the theatre on the Monday, Rignold recalled the trap and asked the stage manager if it was all right. Being assured it was, he stepped on the trap which gave way dropping him 18ft into the cellar. Picked up unconscious, but reviving on being carried to his hotel, he complained of back pains. Examination by two medicos assuaged all fears that he had broken anything. When the scene under the cellar was examined it was found to be pitch dark, with windlasses, beams, wooden projections abounding, leaving hardly any free space. By pure luck, Rignold had been thrown off the descending trap board and clear of the clutter, landing on the only possible flat space. It was hailed as "a marvellous escape from death" and, as Rignold was a star actor in the antipodes, congratulations on his escape poured in from all the towns where he had played for many years. The theatre, closed until the Friday, reopened with W B Maltby playing Rignold's role in Called Back. Maltby was a London actor who happened to be visiting Dunedin at the time. Rignold returned on the following night in the play he was due to perform in when his accident happened. He received a hero's welcome.

1886_10_04 HANLEY (Gaiety).   ACCIDENT TO TRAPEZE ARTISTE

The climax of Hala's act was to launch himself into space – as though flying – to reach another trapeze but, having secretly attached some folded ropes round his ankles, what appears to be a failure to reach the trapeze and thus falling, is a false ploy as the ropes stretch out, and he swings harmlessly upside down at the end of them. That was what normally happened. But on this night a rostrum was misplaced, so that instead of swinging freely over it, his head bashed into it. He was knocked unconscious and the curtain was dropped. He had a profusely bleeding wound at the front of his forehead, and appeared to be in a "very precarious position". He was reported to be recovering by the end of the month and thanked all who had helped him by contributing to an Era fund.

[This trick is still current today and remains a spectacular effect if done well. Usually, the second trapeze is arranged so the performer reaches it and grasps the bar which breaks so for that second the audience thinks it has really gone wrong and sees the unfortunate king of the air hurtling to his doom, then the tension is relaxed when everybody realises they have been conned. Oh, how we laugh! Although one unfortunate performer ending his act with this trick, also ended his life when he performed the trick after forgetting to first attach the ropes.]

1886_10_04 STOCKTON-ON –TEES (Theatre).   GUN ACCIDENT

The play on Monday night was *The Sword's Point* but the accident was with a pistol. The actor W T Thompson, in the action of firing the weapon, managed to blow flesh from finger and thumb "clean away". He laudably struggled through to the end of the play, then went to the local hospital where the doctor cheered him up by saying "he had narrowly escaped losing his hand". Thompson, although unable to use his hand for some weeks, presumably was back on stage within quite a short time. On Friday afternoon the entire company, musicians and stage staff went to the hospital, fitted up a temporary stage, and gave a full two hour performance to patients and staff. That's gratitude for you!

1886_10_06 BLACKBURN (Theatre Royal).   SCENERY FIRE DURING PLAY

The play was *Human Nature*. Prior to the last act, scenery caught fire and the crowded theatre rose to rush to the doors but "the coolness of a few prevented any mishap". A patent sprinkler system over the stage connected to the water main was soon in action dousing the fire in minutes. The play could not continue, but hurrah for the sprinkler system!

1886_11_22 NEWCASTLE (Theatre Royal).   ACCIDENT TO ACTOR

The *Alone in London* company having reached Newcastle after a railway accident in Wigan, on the opening night suffered another set-back. At the end of Act III Mr W H Brougham had to leap from a boat to save the heroine (it was a melodrama). As he stepped on the seat to do his leap, it gave way under him, throwing him forward on to the stage with his arms doubled under him. He suffered ugly cuts and wounds to his face as well as to his body. "Although suffering acutely" Brougham struggled through to the end. He was off for several days.

1886_12_11 LONDON (Her Majesty's).   SCENERY ACCIDENT IN FRENCH OPERA

The French company performing the opera *La Grand Duchess de Gerolstein* was led by Madame Mary-Albert in the title role. In Act III the principal players were at breakfast in camp, and raised above them was the roadway descending in a slope down to the stage. Down this road the Grand Duchess made her entrance preceded by page boys. As the boys walked down, the planks quivered under their slight weight, but no sooner did Madame step on them they tilted up, and she disappeared with a scream. Her colleagues ran to assist, but all was confusion, through which the small audience solemnly sat. The curtain was dropped, an actor came on, confirmed the lady was not hurt, and the performance would continue forthwith. The curtain rose, Madame made her entrance – slightly lame –

101. *Mdme Mary-Albert*

and before she could speak her lines, warm applause issued from all parts of the house.

1886_12_14 NORTHAMPTON (Opera House).   ACCIDENT TO CHILD IN OPERA

The opera was Balfe's *The Bohemian Girl*. The villain Devilshoof was played by Richard Lansmere. During the action while the Count and his family are dining, Devilshoof kidnaps their baby girl and makes off over a bridge across a chasm. The Count's men give chase so, Devilshoof having got across with the baby, demolishes the bridge with an axe. All very exciting. Normally the baby was represented by a dummy, but Lansmere, wanting to add verisimilitude to the piece, demanded a real baby to carry across. This was in direct disobedience to the theatre manager who had instructed the property man to make up a suitable dummy child. But Lansmere borrowed a small girl called Lottie Kightley from her father who lived locally in Cow Lane. The action all went according to plan up to the bridge sequence, Lansmere crossing it with the child in his arms. The stage bridge was mere planking painted scenically, stretched between two solid firm rostra. Instead of standing on the solid rostrum to hack with his axe, the stupid man stood on the plank bridge itself thus, when it collapsed, he and child were plunged into the 'chasm'. So suddenly was all that done that the audience, thinking it was all part of the play, burst into applause – verisimilitude indeed. Lansmere, trying to protect the child, hurt himself and was in agony for the rest of the night. It was thought little Lottie was uninjured, but soon fears arose and she was taken to the infirmary where it was discovered she had broken her thigh. Lansmere kept working to the end of the week in much pain. Serves him right, silly fool!

1886_12_30 SHEFFIELD (Alexandra).   ACCIDENT TO PANTOMIME BARON

H H Rignold – a cousin of the more famous George and William Rignold – was Baron Badlot and in some amusing boxing and scuffling with Johnny Green and Johnny Stout, Rignold was accustomed to crossing to the stage box and throwing himself over backwards into it, getting a big laugh, quickly followed by another, as he peered over before climbing out again. However, on this night, he did not reappear, so Mr Blight, playing Johnny Stout, went to investigate what had happened to him. Rignold was lying there in painful agony unable to rise. He was taken to the hospital where he was examined for broken limbs. At the end of January he was reported to be recovering well, but unlikely to be able to resume his part before the end of the run.

1887_01_03c CARDIFF (Tayleure's Circus).   GUN ACCIDENT

Capt T B Transfield, late circus proprietor at Middlesbrough, was appearing in Cardiff where his daughter was principal rider. On this evening, Capt Transfield was in the dressing room, as was one of the clowns loading a pistol for his performing pig. The pistol exploded and the captain got the full charge in his face, slightly injuring his left eye and tattooing the side of his face with gunpowder. He was back in business within a few days.

1887_01_04 BRIGHTON (Theatre Royal).   ACCIDENT TO PANTOMIME CLOWN

In 1865, Rowella the clown was instrumental in saving many people in a fire at the Surrey Theatre. An entry with illustraton of this is in the companion volume. Tuesday night at Brighton was an accident to Dolpho of the Rowella troupe. The mill scene in which the troupe presented their pantomimic gymnastics ended with Dolpho leaping out of the window on to a large spinning water wheel on which he descended to the stage where a bed awaited him at the end of the stunt. On this night, the bed had been set in the wrong place and, whizzing off the wheel, he crashed on to the stage floor on his head. Fortunately, the injury only kept him off for the rest of the week, and he returned on the following Monday. Being a pantomime clown in those days meant you had to be stunt man as well as being funny.

1887_02_04 LONDON (Olympia).   CHARIOT RACING ACCIDENT

The company from the Paris Hippodrome was presenting a programme which included Roman chariot racing with female drivers. So Parisienne! A race was three times round the ring; on the third circuit the leading chariot, driven by Mdlle Cousinard, overturned. Following closely behind, the second chariot – driven by Mdlle Delvoir at a fast and furious rate – crashed into the capsized one and both drivers were thrown from their seats. Fears of injury were rife but the pair emerged with nothing worse than "a severe shaking and a few contusions". Dr Towers Smith, engaged to be present at every performance, was able to give the intrepid horse-

102. *Charioteers from the Paris Hippodrome*

women immediate attention. He discovered one had broken her collar bone.

1887_02_09 BIRMINGHAM (Theatre Royal).   ACCIDENT TO COMIC ACROBAT

The performers were the Two Macs, a popular comedy double act on the time-honoured big and little principle. They were in the pantomime doing comic acrobatic business when the younger Mac slipped and damaged his knee in such a manner he was sped off to the Queen's Hospital.

1887_02_15 LONDON (Opera Comique).   ACCIDENT TO MISS KATE VAUGHAN

103. *Kate Vaughan*

[Kate Vaughan (1852–1903) was a dancer and actress. She was best known for developing the skirt dance and has been called the 'greatest dancer of her time'. The skirt dance, a demure version of the can-can, was genuine leg dancing, unlike the Serpentine dance and similar which depended on arm movements and flowing trains. Her full-length lace skirts were a novelty and she invented the steps herself. She was a predecessor of Loie Fuller and Isadora Duncan. She retired from dancing in 1885, reinventing herself as an actress in classic comedies becoming a sparkling star in the works of Sheridan and Goldsmith, and one of London's biggest draws.] Which is why the trivial accident described caused a rumpus. Unknown players suffering far more drastic accidents had to beg for shillings via *The Era*. Miss Vaughan made her entrance with others just as two of the characters were about to have a duel. Lionel Brough, playing Bob Acres, had a pistol in his hand which went off accidentally, the wadding hitting Miss Vaughan "on the face immediately beneath the under lip". The wound was bleeding but Miss Vaughan "retained her presence of mind" and "with great courage remained to the end of the play". After the play "It was thought desirable that she should be seen at once by a medical man" so was taken to Charing Cross Hospital where "her injury received every attention." I bet it did. She was not injured in any way, performing the following night.

1887_03_15c PHILADELPHIA, USA (Opera House).   FIRE SCARE DURING PLAY

The Wilson Barrett Company was playing *Clito*, an ancient Greece piece that was a Barrett speciality, with Mary Eastlake and the actor-manager in the leads. During a scene between the two of them a candle in a candelabra, after flickering some time, fell from its holder on to the floor remaining alight. It was ignored by the two players carrying on as though unaware, though seen by many of the audience especially those in the upper levels of the house. Suddenly a large man standing by the door called out "Fire!" pushed open the double doors and fled out to the street. This was a signal for many others to rise and rush out, with women screaming and strong men shouting. More sensible people were calling for others to keep their seats and not panic. If they had heeded the latter advice they would have seen Barrett walk over to the candle and stamp out the flame which was now about 1ft high. Other members of his company came on and assisted, while Miss Eastlake exhorted the audience to remain in their seats as there was no danger. Barrett then joined her after dousing the flame. The gallery, who had seen all the action most clearly, heartily applauded the pair, and their coolness and self-possession encouraged the return of the (hopefully shame-faced) fleeing patrons. The pair continued to the end of the

104. *Wilson Barrett*

act, and the curtain fell to hearty applause and calls for the two actors who stepped before the curtain. Barrett took the opportunity to remonstrate the behaviour of the audience. He told them he had been fully aware of the situation from the first guttering of the candle, his company and the theatre staff were fully conversant with fire drill, the theatre was fully supplied with fire fighting apparatus. Because one man foolishly shouted 'fire' and ran out, they all acted like a flock of sheep, not men and women. He ended by saying "Forgive me if I seem rude, but do be more sensible." He was applauded with unbounded enthusiasm.

1887_04_11 CORK (Lloyd's Circus).   ACCIDENT TO TRAPEZE ARTISTE

The accident happened on Monday afternoon when Lloyd's Mexican Circus was in town. Mdlle Ritz, the trapeze artiste, had only just started her act when she fell, landing on her head and right shoulder. She was carried out unconscious and attended to by Dr Coates, who happened to be present and rushed to offer his services. He saw she must be taken at once to the Infirmary. She had broken a collar bone, and possibly fractured her skull.

1887_10_24 SALFORD (Prince of Wales).   ACCIDENT TO ACTOR IN FALLING STAIRCASE

The play was *Humanity*, and the actor T G Warry. Playing the role of the Jew, he had an accident during the scene with a falling staircase, breaking his leg in two places. Bravely insisting on completing the scene, he was helped to the front by two colleagues who supported him until the curtain fell. He was then taken to Manchester Infirmary. The play *Humanity* will forever be associated with the actor-manager John Lawson (1865-1920) who once he had played in it never stopped. The play started as a full-length melodrama at the Standard Theatre, Pimlico and from there went on a perpetual never ending tour round the provinces. The main appeal was a sentimental song *Only a Jew* and a spectacular fight scene. The reader will find that this play was responsible for many accidents in future years (*see 1891_04_15, 1892_03_15, etc*).

1887_11_03 PARIS (Cirque d'Hiver).   EQUESTRIAN ACCIDENT

Marguerite Dudley, another of the elegant and fashionable equestriennes (*see* 1882_04_15), while practising during the day, found her horse suddenly becoming unmanageable and rearing furiously. It then staggered for a few minutes and finally dropped down dead in the ring. Only Mdlle Dudley's skill and presence of mind saved her from being crushed by the animal. Her left arm was injured but it was expected that she would be performing in the ring again within a couple of weeks.

1887_11_11 BUCHAREST, Romania.   ACCIDENT TO MADAME THAL

"Madame Suzanne Thal, formerly of the Variétés, has met with a serious accident by falling through a trap-door at Bucharest. Both legs were broken, but it is hoped amputation will not be necessary." *The Stage* 1887_11_11.

1888_01_09 OXFORD (New).   ACCIDENT WITH FALLING SCENERY

The artistes on stage were Maude Elliston and Flo Brandon. Two disused scenery battens fell with a crash, just missing the two performers. It seems that the grid in the flies was supporting not only all the cloths for the current pantomime, but also a collection of used scenes that in a well-conducted theatre should have been lowered, rolled and stored away, leaving the grid entirely free for the panto production.

1888_01_16 LONDON (Surrey).   ACCIDENT TO MR GEORGE CONQUEST

We first met George Conquest when he suffered a major accident in the USA (*see* 1880_08_03c). After that he curtailed his hectic acrobatic performances, taking over the management of the Surrey Theatre where he wrote and directed a pantomime every year for 20 years, only actually performing in one himself. This was the one – *Sinbad the Sailor* in which as the Little Old Man of the Sea he made his entrance from a giant jar which ascended through a trap. At a matinee on this day, the jar toppled and George fractured a shoulder blade. He struggled for the rest of the panto (the show must go on, he was the boss and the star) even managing to change into his other character of the Rock Fiend. George retired from the show to be replaced by Mr Cruickshanks.

1888_02_02 PARIS, France (Cirque d'Hiver)   ACCIDENT TO CIRCUS AUGUSTE

This was one of the most unfortunate of accidents as the artiste had finished his act and had, as pros say, 'stormed them'; running back on to take his due deserts, he threw a double somersault, sprained his leg and had to be carried off. The medico said he would be off for two months. It is particularly galling when one knows one is 'showing off' and then comes a cropper!

Personal Note: at the end of a pantomime all the cast in glamorous finale finery come on in turn to take their call processing down a flight of steps. This procedure was known as 'all down for who's best'. At one performance as we went down Brenda caught the heel of her shoe in the hem of her dress and fell flat on her bottom. No injury – just embarrassment. And once in forty years is not so bad. Here I might add a wicked little trick that was sometimes played. As the cast line up at the top of the steps out of view, you ask the guy in front of you 'Which foot do you lead off with?' just as it is his turn to go down. It doesn't sound much, but it does if you have never thought about it before, and are just about to launch yourself off the top step!

1888_02_08 MERTHYR TYDFIL (Theatre).   ACCIDENT TO MARIE LEVISON

On this night, Miss Levison was injured by a heavy iron bar descending from the flies, striking her head and leaving a severe wound. She had been under medical care since but was fit to resume at Pontypridd on 14 February.

1888_02_11 BURTON-ON-TRENT (Theatre).   GUN ACCIDENT

Harry Lorraine's son, working under the stage name of Ernest Bright, was playing William Corder in *Maria Martin*. During Act I there was a struggle between Corder and Maria Martin with Bright attempting to fire his gun. It misfired and when he tried again the charge exploded, shattering his hand and blowing his first finger across the stage. Several people fainted and the curtain was lowered. The accident caused such a sensation that it was impossible to go on with the performance. Bright was still under care of surgeons at Manchester Infirmary in April and it was feared that they would have to amputate but fortunately that course proved unnecessary.

1888_03_03 CHESTER (Royalty).   ACCIDENT TO ACTOR ON SCENIC BOAT

The play was *Alone in London*, the actor William Perrette. In the scene where the hero dives from a boat to save the heroine, the stagehand deputed to work the boat moved it just as Perrette was about to jump, pitching him forward heavily on to the stage, severely cutting his hands and face and dislocating his shoulder. However, he finished the part – he was company manager as well as leading actor – and afterwards had medical treatment.

140

1888_03_21 CARDIFF (Theatre Royal).   KNIFE ACCIDENT DURING STAGE FIGHT

Fred Sinclair (hero) and Arthur Harding (villain) were fighting during a scene in *Little 18-Carat*. Sinclair accidentally stabbed Harding in the right side. Fortunately, the knife striking a rib, did not penetrate very deeply. John Sheridan the company manager swiftly got medical help which enabled Harding to carry on with his part though "greatly weakened by severe loss of blood".

1888_06_02 LONDON.   ACCIDENT TO CHARLES HAWTREY

[Sir Charles Henry Hawtrey (1858–1923) was an English actor-manager, specialising in debonair and louche but amiable parts in popular comedies. Once established he rarely left the West End, over the years being manager of 18 different London theatres. In 1884, Hawtrey had a huge success with his own adaptation of a German farce, reworked as the very English *The Private Secretary*. After a slow start, business built, and the show eventually ran for 785 performances, Hawtrey making £123,000 from it. The play was revived in London eight times during his lifetime. His long career saw him creating original roles in the plays of both Wilde and Somerset Maugham. The *Carry On* film star of the same name was no relation being actually George Hartree.]

105. *Charles Hawtrey*

Hawtrey was breaking in a new play called *The Arabian Nights*; unfortunately on this Saturday night as he left the stage after Act I he fell and broke his collar-bone. He struggled on through the rest of the play, but on the Monday was obliged to give up his role.

1888_06_04 GT YARMOUTH (Aquarium).   KNIFE ACCIDENT TO ACTRESS

The play was *Mr Barnes of New York*, the actress Gertrude Norman. In the final act of the play Marita Paoli (Miss Norman) struggles to take a dagger from her servant. Instead of a stage prop dagger the actor playing servant Tomasso had been given a butcher's knife. Oblivious to this, Miss Norman launched into the usual struggle getting severely gashed on her hand "in a fearful manner". Although "very much terrified" she finished the performance.

1888_06_14 WEYMOUTH (Theatre Royal).   KNIFE ACCIDENT

The play was *Mr Barnes of New York* again, the tour presumably taking in holiday resorts. The poor player to get stabbed here was James Craig playing Count Danella. The unlucky actor was not even on the stage set, but standing offstage behind a curtain which was where the character Anstruther was supposed to be lurking, like Polonius behind the arras, and where the servant Tomasso – yes him again – plunges his knife through the curtain to kill him. Instead he succeeded in cutting one of the tendons in the back of Craig's hand who lost the use of one finger as a result.

1888_07_16 BLACKPOOL (Prince of Wales).   FATAL ACCIDENT TO TRAPEZE ARTISTE

A gymnastic duo comprising William Walker (23) and Edwin Bent, known professionally as Bravo & Voltyne had been performing twice daily since 19 May. On this day around 9am while they were rehearsing a new trick, Walker fell into the safety net. However, calling out he was hurt he remained there immobile until his partner got to him. Having fallen on his head, it was thought he had dislocated his neck. Bent, putting his feet against Walker's shoulders, pulled his head. A crack was heard, but producing no improvement, Dr Ruxton was summoned who deduced the spinal cord was damaged as Walker was paralysed from the sixth rib downwards at both sides of the body. His mother was sent for and she, arriving around 1pm, found him lying on his back in one of the rooms. He was quite lucid and able to speak, telling his mother not to fret, he had had an accident but he would be all right soon. Alas, he was not, as he died four days later. He had been a professional gymnast for six years.

1888_07_27 LONDON.   PROJECT CANCELLED THROUGH ACCIDENT

"Messrs Henry Wardroper and W. Meadow's production of their new musical comedy, *The Fancy Ball*, has had to be abandoned in consequence of Mr Wardroper having had the misfortune to fracture his right knee-cap." *The Stage* 1888_07_27.

"Though the accident to Mr Henry Wardroper's knee has now proved of no permanent harm, it is deemed advisable by the doctors that the limb should still have some weeks of rest. Messrs Wardroper and Meadows' *The Fancy Ball* tour will therefore not commence this year." *The Stage* 1888_10_12.

1888_09_22 BRADFORD (Prince's).   SCENERY FIRE DURING PLAY

The venue was the Prince's Theatre which was built on top of a subterranean music hall. During Act III of the play the scenery caught fire from a candle in a scenic street lamp. Women screamed and people rose to make for the exits, but actor Kendall Young, tearing the front scene down, trampled the burning section underfoot. Bravo!

141

1888_10_09 PARIS, France (Hippodrome).   ACCIDENT TO TRAPEZE ARTISTE

Odan, falling from his flying trapeze, missed the net in his fall, as it should have been 1ft wider. The drop was around 30ft and the "impressionable French public screamed with horror when they saw Odan stretched apparently lifeless in the ring." During the disturbance while he was carried out and taken to hospital most of the audience left the building. Very sensitive, the French.

1888_10_30 SHEFFIELD (Grand).   KNIFE ACCIDENT

A production by Pleon's Picnic Party company featured a sketch in which Pleon and Ernest Lester struggled for a knife. Lester fell on the long knife which penetrated his left eye. He was whizzed off to the infirmary.

1888_11_14 STOCKPORT (Circus of Varieties).   GUN ACCIDENT

The performers were Wood, West & Lamont known as the Three Comets. George Wood was holding a pistol which burst, destroying part of his hand. He was attended to at the Infirmary.

1888_11_15 VIENNA, Austria (Ronacher's).   ACCIDENT TO TIGHTROPE WALKER

The artiste was a Columbian gymnast called Caicedo. Letting his balancing-pole slip out of his hands, he fell heavily to the stage 20ft below, was picked up senseless and had to be carried to the hospital. The sensational rumour then arose that it was not an accident, but a deliberate suicide attempt. During that day he had had a quarrel with his wife who, being of a jealous disposition, had rushed at him with a knife intending to stab him for some fancied misdemeanour. Caicedo had been overheard to say he would not live to see another day, which he certainly did because on You Tube you can see a clip of him somersaulting in 1894.

1888_12_11 OFEN, Austria (Orpheum).   ACCIDENT TO TRAPEZE ARTISTE AND HER CHILD

This is a frightful example of the lengths people often needed to go to make a living in showbusiness. The artiste Mdlle Clairette was hanging upside down from the trapeze holding her little boy of five years with her teeth when a supporting rope gave way and mother and child fell to the ground. On picking up the pair, the child's injuries included the loss of an eye, the mother's concussion of the brain. On examination it was found that the hooks of the trapeze were badly fastened.

1889_01_02 CARDIFF (Grand).   ACCIDENT ESCAPE OF PANTOMIME ACTOR

The performer was E W Colman, playing Idle Jack in the pantomime, when on this night a flat suspended in the flies "broke away and came down with tremendous force" on to the very tub in which Colman had been standing only a second before. Phew!

Personal Note: We have experience of escaping by inches from a falling flat. We were standing side by side behind a screen over which we show our puppets set immediately behind the front runners waiting for them to open. The stage crew behind us was changing the scenery when a flat fell forward, edge on, and crashed between us – a matter of a very few inches either way would likely have split one of our skulls open. As it was, it smashed the top cross bar of our screen and as we had to start immediately a stagehand crouched between us holding up the middle of the broken bar. We had to go through our act dodging around this rather beefy fellow with his arm in the air.

1889_01_07 BIRMINGHAM (Gaiety).   ACCIDENT TO TRAPEZE ARTISTE

The unfortunate performer was one of the Flying Erards troupe. Having climbed up to his lofty perch in the very roof of the building, he launched into his act, the apparatus gave way, and he fell into the net below. This too gave way and the man rolled heavily to the floor. When assisted to his feet he was found to have suffered no injury.

1889_01_23 MANCHESTER (Prince's).   ACCIDENT TO PANTOMIME ARTISTE

Edward Lewis playing the hero was in the flies ready to descend on a parachute, wire in hand, awaiting his cue. For some unaccountable reason the wire was jerked from his grasp and failing to grab it back he fell to the stage 30ft below, landing on his feet. Dr Edwards was in the building and hastened to give his expertise. No bones were broken but Lewis was taken home. He was unable to reappear until 8 March, the penultimate night of the run.

1889_01_26 LEIGH (Theatre).   ACCIDENT DURING BACKSTAGE FIGHT

This is a bit of a rum accident which was recorded in a very flippant manner. Two stagehands were fighting in the wings while a Shakespeare play starring J Dewhurst the manager and licensee was taking place on stage. One of the combatants apparently started biting, compelling Dewhurst to leave the stage to stop the fray. On his return to the play the pair immediately started scrapping again, so attempting to break the fight up a second time, Dewhurst returned to the wings and promptly received a blow on his mouth which knocked two teeth out. He sent for the police and the miscreant was found guilty of assault and banged up in jail for three months. One wonders what the audience made of this disappearing actor-manager!

1889_01_30 WARRINGTON (Public Hall).   ACCIDENT TO PANTOMIME HERO

The panto was *Sinbad*, the performer Maggie Gardiner. One of the necessary features of *Sinbad the Sailor* as a pantomime is the scene where the hero is borne aloft by a giant bird. In this production, having strapped herself to the eagle, it then took off by being hauled up on ropes. As it rose, the ropes broke, depositing Miss Gardiner on to the stage still strapped to the stuffed bird. Fortunately no great height had yet been attained so the distance was not far to fall. "Had the property eagle attained any height the result must have been serious, for Miss Gardiner is no light weight." Clearly 'body shaming' was not an offence in those days!

1889_02_09 LONDON (Haymarket).   ONSTAGE BLAZE AT THE HAYMARKET

The play was *The Merry Wives of Windsor* with Herbert Beerbohm Tree. In the fairy scene where small children as fairies tie Falstaff to an oak tree with flowery garlands, Edward Righton, carrying a spirit torch filled with naphtha, carelessly allowed some to spill on to the stage, igniting some miniature shrubs. As there was immediate danger to the fairy children's flimsy dresses, as well as the prospect of the flames spreading, a prominent drama critic in the orchestra stalls was moved to shout "Put it out Righton, put it out!" The actor, leaping to obey, then took the flaming torch off, reappearing with a lantern.

106. *Edward Righton*

1889_02_11 BELFAST (Circus). FATAL ACCIDENT TO TRAPEZE ARTISTE

The unfortunate flyer, Clara Feeley of a well-known acrobatic family fell, severely injuring her spine. She survived until 10 June then died in the Royal Hospital, the spinal injury being so serious it defied all treatment.

1889_02_20c LONDON (Alhambra). ACCIDENT TO LEADING BALLET DANCER

The principal attraction comprised two ballets, one *Irene* considered the best ballet in London at that time. There were six principal ballerinas in the piece, one being Signora Cossio "quite the most handsome and one of the best dancers" at the theatre. Stepping out of a chariot, a slight movement of the vehicle caused her to stumble, rendering damage to her foot ligaments. Although having recovered from her accident by the end of October, it was considered doubtful that she would ever dance again,

1889_03_08 LIVERPOOL (Prince of Wales). ACCIDENT TO PANTOMIME DANCER

The show was *Jack and the Beanstalk*. As the dancers trooped off stage to return to their dressing room, Miss Turner, missing her footing, fell down the staircase striking her head and injuring her spine. She was taken to the Infirmary accompanied by Miss Fanny Joseph the manageress of the theatre.

1889_05_14 CORK (circus). FATAL SHOOTING ACCIDENT

Harry Lyons, a sharpshooter in Kelly & Patterson's Circus, was firing at a target and performing other stunts without mishap. But when the audience left, a youth named John Murray (18) was found sprawled on the floor. Thought to have fainted, he was carried out into the open air. However, it was soon realised that he had been shot in the heart. He was immediately taken to hospital, but was dead on arrival. Lyons was arrested. At the enquiry it was noted that Murray had been 15 yards from the target, and 7 or 8 yards to the right of the line of fire, and it was assumed that a bullet, ricocheting off the target, had struck the young man. Lyons was exonerated from all blame.

1889_06_11 LONDON (Empire). SCENERY FIRE DURING SHOW

[Ira Albert Paine (1837-1889) was born in Hebronville, Massachusetts. He possessed a fine tenor voice and was educated in music, becoming a professional singer. He participated in his club's pigeon shoots and was capturing so many prizes in competitive shooting meets that he decided to take his act public on the stage and in the ring. During the 1870s and 1880s, Paine appeared all over the United States and the world, performing amazing sharpshooting feats.. He was equally skilled with a shotgun, rifle, pistol, or revolver. His career was meteoric but short. He died in 1889 while in Paris on a European tour, thus this accident was in the final year of his life.]

107. *Ira A Paine*

The sharpshooter Chevalier Ira D Paine was in full flow showing his skill when a curtain catching fire quickly surrounded him in a ring of flames. People in the back of the pit fled for the exit, the stage crew dropped the curtain bodily, and the blaze was extinguished. The shouts of the remaining pittites brought the fleeing few back again, and the Chevalier who had never left the stage continued with his act. Mister Cool!

144

1889_06_22 BIRMINGHAM (Theatre Royal).   ACTRESS FALLS THROUGH TRAP

The play was *Randolph the Reckless*. On this night Fanny Piddock fell through a trap on the stage and sustained injuries to her shoulder.

1889_07_06 OLDHAM (People's).   FATAL ACCIDENT TO GYMNAST

The venue was the People's Concert Hall, the performer acrobat James Peter Wise. One of his stunts was to place one table atop another and a chair on that, stand on the chair, hands in pockets, and throw a double somersault to the stage. The chair gave way, Wise, falling forward head first, striking the lower table, before hitting the stage. He was picked up unconscious and taken to hospital where it was found his spine was injured and legs were paralysed. He died the following day.

1889_08_27 STALYBRIDGE (Victoria).   SCENERY DESCENT ON TO ACTORS

The company was that of Miss Heathcote. At the end of the play of *La Mascotte* with the full company on stage, the act drop, well – dropped. Unfortunately, slightly too early, and the weight of the roller knocked the actors down like ninepins, leaving two – Mr White and Veta Manvis – to be carried off the stage unconscious. The audience was greatly agitated and several women fainted. All the personnel were able to perform as usual on the following night.

1889_08_28 SHEFFIELD (Handsworth Gala).   ACCIDENT TO CARTOONIST

['Lightning cartoons' was a regular act on the music halls done by talented men who, with a few quick strokes, could draw instantly recognisable caricatures of famous people. They added elements of skill and amusement by drawing what did not look like anything then, turning the image the other way up, revealing a splendid picture.]   Walter Westwood was one such performer and had been booked for the week at the Gaiety Music Hall, plus an extra at the Handsworth Flower Show Gala where he was to give two performances on an open platform. The dressing room was under the platform, with access to the performing area up some steps and through a hole cut in the stage. Crucially there was no form of railing around the hole.

His big finish was to draw Gladstone which, with a few flourishes he transformed into Disraeli, bringing far more applause than he expected or normally received at open air shows. He made his exit backing off bowing over and over but in his elation he had forgotten the unusual means of leaving and fell through the open trap, dislocating his arm. The accident put him out of work for three weeks. Westwood sued for £6. 10s and it came to court in late November.   His solicitor asked the theatre manager if they were going to compensate his client. They offered him a benefit, ironically on a night he could not do through a prior engagement. The jury found in Westwood's favour though some points of law were debatable but, rather than prolong the affair, the case was settled out of court.

1889_09_11 CHATHAM (Barnard's).   NARROW ESCAPE OF FEMALE IMPERSONATOR

At Barnard's Palace, performer Carl Ostend during his song stepped forwards a split second before a deafening crash was heard behind him. A beautiful chandelier falling and shattering into a thousand pieces landed on the exact spot where Ostend had been standing only moments before. Extremely startled and shuddering visibly he, nevertheless, carried on with his song, surrounded by broken glass, receiving an ovation from the audience.

145

1889_09_30 LONDON (Morton's).   ACCIDENT TO LEADING ACTOR

In the play *Randolph the Reckless*, the company's leading man W G Walford was having a last minute rehearsal of the bit where he was lifted above the stage on a cable. The cable snapped and he was dropped on to the stage from a height of 12ft. A doctor, swiftly summoned, finding Walford's arm broken, set the bone. Morton went before the curtain and explained the situation which necessitated changing the running order of the show, the farce to be played first, and the burlesque after. The players also changed parts in the accustomed promotional order that was commonplace until modern times. Forde took Walford's part, Crellin took Forde's role, and Harry Malcolm stepped up to Crellin's. Nowadays, that does not often happen – there are either proper understudies knitting or reading while waiting in a dressing room or, much more likely, the show is cancelled.

1889_11_13 LONDON (Royal Aquarium).   ACCIDENT TO JAPANESE GYMNAST

From a single trapeze in the roof of the building, the Torikata troupe leader hung head downwards supporting a triangle of three swinging poles. Three troupe members ascended, each to a pole. No sooner were they in position when one of the fastenings gave way pitching pole and man into the stalls below. Fortunately, landing between rows, the pole just missed the drummer in the orchestra pit. The gymnast got away with nothing worse than two sprained ankles, bruised back and shoulders. Asked by Mr Torikata if it was the audience's wish that the act should continue, they cheered when he assented to their cries of 'No!' There was no safety net.

146

1889_11_15 LONDON (Canterbury).   ACCIDENT TO FEMALE ASCENSIONIST

The artiste was Mdlle Alphonsine the Spiral Ascensionist. We have previously met her male equivalent in Ethardo (*see* 1885_11_24). Both did the same act – walking up a spiral ramp on a large ball. As Ethardo taught his act to two young women, it is likely Mdlle Alphonsine was one of them though she claimed to be the only female performer of this feat. She seems to have been less adept than Ethardo as on a couple of occasions she failed to complete the trick of reaching the top. On Tuesday, she fell off her globe, only saving herself by clinging to the framework of her apparatus. On Friday, she fell off again, clinging on to the ironwork of her spiral but unable to hold on, fell into the stalls beneath. There was a rush to pick her up and she was carried behind the scenes. She was in hospital but a short time and her injuries were slight.

SERIOUS ACCIDENT at the CANTERBURY MUSIC-HALL

108. *Mdlle Alphonsine* 109.

1889_12_23 STOCKTON-ON-TEES (Theatre Royal). ELEPHANT FALLS THROUGH STAGE

The pantomime was *Blue Beard* and the performers were Professor Henry and his elephant Sheriff. The elephant had done its act though this had been curtailed by the Prof as both he and the elephant were apprehensive about the strength of the stage. The Prof had got Sheriff to the back of the stage and turned him ready to walk off when the boards gave way and the back legs and hind quarters disappeared into the hole. The curtain was lowered and the lessee Lloyd Clarence in his Blue Beard costume, coming before the curtain, asked the audience to be calm and not panic as all was under control. The elephant was soon freed unharmed, the curtain rising again to continue the panto.

1889_12_27 PARIS. ACCIDENT TO SARAH BERNHARDT

The Divine Sarah was rehearsing for her debut as Joan of Arc when the burning at the stake finale went amiss, clouds of smoke choking the actress who, once rescued, then "indulged in the feminine luxury of a 'faint'". Although notorious for whipping up publicity, Madame Bernhardt was hardly likely to risk setting herself on fire, or burning two stage crew. When the fuss of "two stage crew injured, one fatally", had died down, the true facts emerged. It was the duty of stagehand Saclier to place a quantity of lycopodium powder among the faggots to produce the flames. By some mischance he set fire to the entire bucketful which went off all at once severely burning his face and hands. He was taken to hospital but was in no danger of losing his life.

110. *Sarah Bernhardt*

147

1890_01_10 NEWCASTLE (Theatre Royal). ACCIDENT TO PANTOMIME ARTISTE

Miss Warden was playing Selim in *Blue Beard*. In the scene of the bombardment of the castle a piece of scenery fell, striking her on the temple. Dr Ridley, who was in the theatre, dealt with the wound which was not serious but Miss Warden's understudy Daisy Stanton went on the following night.

1890_02_08 NEW YORK, USA. ACCIDENT TO MADAME MODJESKA

111. *Modjeska*

[Helena Modjeska (1840–1909), a renowned Polish actress specialized in Shakespearean and tragic roles. After a decade as the leading tragedienne in her home country, she emigrated with her husband to the USA where despite her accent and imperfect command of English, she achieved great acclaim at her debut in San Francisco following this with a tour of the principal cities to constant success. During her career, she played nine Shakespearean roles though her repertoire embraced comedy and romantic characters as well as tragedy. She acted for several years in England but returned to the USA where she became a citizen.]

On this night the famous Polish actress fell, wrenching her leg badly. This was followed by a fit. She was due to appear with Edwin Booth, but instead was lying ill in bed at the Grand Hotel. I cannot find how long she was out of action before resuming her tour with Booth, visiting Chicago and several other cities.

1890_02_10 ROTHERHAM (Theatre Royal).   GUN ACCIDENT

In the play *True to the Last,* Walter Copley – playing the villain – while threatening the life of his accomplice, was holding a gun within 12 inches of actor John Humphries's face. Unfortunately, the trigger was touched and the full blast went into the eyes and face of Humphries. The victim dropped to the floor, Copley stood as if stunned and the curtain was lowered. The poor chap's face was tattooed with powder marks and his eyes streaming blood. Dr Baldwin attended and the actor elected to carry on and, with his eyes bandaged, continued to play nightly.

1890_02_15 WOLVERHAMPTON (Theatre Royal).   ACCIDENT TO PANTO COMEDIAN

The show was *Robinson Crusoe,* the performer Tom McNaughton of The Two McNaughtons. The duo was going through some knockabout business when Tom fell through a trap. His partner astutely made out it was part of the show and the panto carried on. The stage manager had given the cue for the trap to be ready to open as was usual at this point but Tom, who normally walked round it for his exit, stepped on it and it opened under him. Actors had to be aware of their position on the stage all the time especially in pantomime when traps were widely used.

1890_03_10 BIRMINGHAM (Queen's).   SERIOUS ACCIDENT TO ACTRESS

The company was that of Lionel Ellis with actress Agnes Birchenough – aka Agnes May – rehearsing for the opening night of *The Right Man.* The rostrum upon which she and several others were standing collapsed and Agnes fell to the stage, a distance of only 7ft, but enough to break her thigh. Mrs Charles Franklyn happened to be in the city and – at a few hours notice – took over the part which she had never played before.

148

1890_05_8c PARIS, France.   FATAL ACCIDENT TO STRONG MAN

Henri Toch, a champion wrestler known as the 'Rampart of the North' because of his great strength, regularly appeared at fairs throughout France and Belgium, throwing all comers. He also presented typical strong man feats such as firing a cannon which he carried on his shoulders. It was this feat that killed him, as the cannon exploded on firing and death was instantaneous.

1890_07_16c LONDON (Grand).   ACCIDENT TO ACTON BOND

Acton Bond (1861–1941) was a well known Victorian actor who founded an acting dynasty. The play was *Paul Kauvar* starring William Terriss. Acton Bond playing Colonel La Hogue dislocated his kneecap during the performance but struggled on to the end ("the show must go on!") exacerbating the injury in doing so and keeping him off the stage for some weeks. Ronald Bayne, normally playing a lesser role, was promoted to take over.

1890_08_20 HUDDERSFIELD (Theatre Royal).   GUN ACCIDENT

The play was *Flying from Justice* by Mark Melford's No 1 Company, the actor involved was Frank Worthing. The pistol Worthing brandished about in Act I, although not supposed to be loaded, by some mischance was and, on pulling the trigger he received the shot in the palm of his right hand. A surgeon, immediately called in, dressed the deep and severe wound. Worthing then bravely continued his role, his arm in a sling.

1890_08_23 NEW YORK, USA (Academy of Music). ACCIDENT TO THE HANLON BROTHERS

[Not surprisingly, as they were a top star act of the time, we have met the Hanlons several times before. However, the Hanlons in this combination were not Hanlons at all but three former apprentices named Robert (Little Bob), James and William, who in 1875 had teamed up with two Sharpe brothers aka Rafael and Edouin Volta. One of the original brothers George Hanlon spent his life advertising and offering proof that none of the Hanlon-Voltas were family members.]

This was the first performance of a new combination called Hanlon-Volta-Martinetti. The three Hanlon Brothers were reaching the climax of what was recognised to be one of the finest acts of its type, with William, the youngest of the gymnasts, on a cross bar at the highest point of the building some 65ft up, revolving his body at arms' length. A supporting wire gave way making the bar lurch sideways causing the gymnast to fall towards the net suspended about 10ft above the audience. Glancing off the net, he crashed into the chairs on the floor below. Women fainted, men shouted, some fled for the exit as though they themselves were in danger. William was conscious and could speak in spite of his scalp being ripped from eyebrows to back of crown, and his right foot badly wounded. Carried into the dressing room to await an ambulance, he asked if "the boys had carried on and was reassured when told they had". Then, hearing the manager announce to the audience that although he was badly hurt, he would not die – provoking a burst of cheering and applause – William smiled and said "I'm glad of that, the boys must have made a big hit."

It is ironic that the original Hanlons patented the safety net, yet it proved inadequate in this case. All aerial gymnasts were quick to claim that a fall was never due to a lack of skill, but rather faulty apparatus, and this instance was no different with William writing to the press giving the facts and stating it was his first accident in 20 years. He returned to work on 25 September.

1890_10_23 LONDON (Lyric).   ONSTAGE FIRE DURING PERFORMANCE

[Lionel Brough (1836–1909) started his career performing in Liverpool. Moving to London in 1867, he joined a newly formed company that also included Irving, Toole, Wyndham and Ellen Terry. He soon became known for his roles in Shakespeare, contemporary comedies and classics. He was especially noted for his performance as Tony Lumpkin in *She Stoops to Conquer* playing it 777 times throughout his career – a character that has always seemed tedious in the productions I've seen. In the 1870s and 1880s, Brough was one of the leading comic actors in London. Although untrained musically, he also appeared in several successful operettas in the 1880s and 1890s including the one in the incident below. He ended his career playing Shakespeare's comedy roles with Sir Herbert Beerbohm Tree's company.]

112. *Lionel Brough*   The operetta was *La Cigale*. In the scene of the ducal palace, a Christmas ball was presented in which festive trees were brought on. One of these caught fire, and the flames shot upwards putting the stage borders in jeopardy. The actors stood immobile while the theatre fireman rushed across the stage. Several members of the audience left their seats for the exits. Lionel Brough "sprang up and dashed the burning tree to the ground". At that the stage crew ran on and stamped the flames to oblivion. "Mr Brough cleverly used the incident to gag later on." At the end of the show Brough was called for to receive great applause for his bravery.

1890_10_28 MARSEILLES, France (Palais Cristal).   SUPERS SHOT ONSTAGE

"During the performance at the Palais Cristal here yesterday evening of *Formose*, a pantomime of a military character, four supernumeraries were seriously wounded by musket shot. It was thought that the guns contained blank charges, and an investigation into the matter has been opened." *Western Daily Press* 1890_10_30.

1890_11_07 LONDON (Princess's).   COLLAPSE OF STAGE UNDER SUPERS WEIGHT

The play was *Antony and Cleopatra*. It was a rehearsal and the grand banquet scene was in progress for which a large number of supers were employed. Too many it would seem, as the boards of the stage gave way and 58 supers slowly sank out of sight into the cellar below. As a result the scene, comprised of several pillars, waved about and collapsed on the fallen people. Nobody was injured.

1890_11_14 NOTTINGHAM (Grand).   ACCIDENT TO FANNY ROBINA

[Fanny Robina (1862–1927), specialised in playing boy parts including principal boys in pantomime. Her parents were a music hall duo who met in the gold fields of Australia. They later toured England, where Fanny was born, starting to perform with her parents before her third birthday. After the early death of her parents, Fanny continued to perform in England, both solo and with her older sister Florrie, who was born in Australia.]

150   The play was a burlesque version of *Little Jack Sheppard*. In the prison-breaking scene, Jack and his companion Bluey (J J Dallas) had to climb a high wall. This was a clever stage effect utilising a sloat in which the scenic wall slowly sank down through the stage while the actors, remaining on the stage performing appropriate actions, gave the effect of climbing it. Following on from the scene the sloat should have been securely closed, but was not so. Miss Robina, as Jack, running upstage trod on the insecure board which gave way and her legs scraped down as the quick thinking Mr Dallas grabbed her, thus preventing her from plunging into more serious injury. To cheers from the audience, the plucky performer carried on with scarce a moment's pause.

1890_11_15 ABERAVON (Theatre).   ACCIDENT FROM FALLING SCENERY

The stage crew was dismantling the scenery after the Knobel-Rousby Company's performance of *The Golden Ladder* when a flat fell over knocking actress Louise Strathmore off the stage on to some steps and a number of packing cases. She sustained several injuries including a fractured rib, and was unable to fulfil her professional duties for some time.

1890_11_17 BIRMINGHAM (Queen's).   ACCIDENT IN *THE SINS OF NEW YORK*

The company was that of J Bannister Howard, the play a lurid melodrama. In the wharf scene in Act II, Mr G Belmont was apparently thrown into the water some 10ft below where, in fact, he had a mattress prepared to fall on. At this performance, missing his mattress, he hit the hard boards of the stage seriously injuring his ankle (those ankles again!) but "after the doctor had attended to him he pluckily finished his part" by being carried on and off the stage. For the rest of the week Albert Robertson took on the role, and probably for some time after, as Belmont was expected to be out of action for a while.

1891_01_22 COLCHESTER (Theatre Royal).   ACCIDENT TO LEADING MAN
    The play to be given that night was *New Lamps for Old*, so leading actor Tom Cannam was rehearsing a hazardous scene above the stage. His supporting rope snapped and he was thrown 20ft down on to the stage. He severely sprained his ankle preventing him from performing that evening and for some time thereafter. There must have been nobody to take his place – a rare event in Victorian times – as the performance was cancelled and a replacement actor sent for who was expected to take over the following night.

1891_03_11 COLCHESTER (Theatre Royal).   ACCIDENT TO HERMANN VEZIN
    [Hermann Vezin (1829–1910) was an American actor born in Philadelphia. After graduating with a law degree in 1850, Vezin moved to the UK determined to work as an actor. He made his first appearance at York then played leading roles throughout the provinces. Making his London début in 1852, apart from a brief tour of the United States in 1857–58, the majority of Vezin's acting career took place on the English stage. His last proper stage role was Old Rowley in Tree's production of *The School for Scandal*. He was active on the British stage for nearly sixty years, and was probably one of the most intellectual actors of the time, though most of his declining years were spent giving lessons to aspiring thespians, appearances at recitals and play readings.]
    During a performance of *Hamlet*, Hermann Vezin was struck to the floor by some prematurely dropped scenery. After a short hiatus he continued the performance with a sprained wrist and a dislocated thumb, this making for an uncomfortable fight with Laertes but gaining Vezin tremendous applause for his professionalism. William Lockhart the stage manager, accused of giving the cue too early, stoutly defended himself in what appears a humorous situation. Knowing the scene well, having played in it himself 100 times, he would not have given the cue in the middle of it. Not always able to be in the prompt corner during a scene change as he was playing two roles himself, he deputed the flyman to take his cue from two hand claps. Alas, the flyman hearing some claps let in the cloth. Nobody knows who this was or why they were clapping – possibly trying to attract somebody's attention. Lockhart claimed the fault was neither with the theatre nor himself but probably he should not have arranged a signal that anybody might give without thinking.

113. *Hermann Vezin*

151

    Vezin, out of action for six months, in February 1892 sued the Colchester theatre for loss of earnings based on weekly profits from his company of £25 to £30 and his personal salary of ten guineas. £40 a week in round figures ie over £1000. Vezin's case being that the theatre's flyman was negligent by dropping the cloth in at the wrong time causing him injury and loss of earnings. The theatre's defence was that the negligence was on the part of Vezin's own stage manager for giving the cue at the wrong time. The jury awarded Vezin £100 damages, £16 for doctor's bills, and costs.

1891_03_13 MANCHESTER (Comedy).   SCENERY ACCIDENT TO ACTOR-AUTHOR

The drama was *Man to Man* with the author William Bourne playing the leading role. During the train collision and explosion scene the front cloth was designed to fall, dramatically exposing the chaos. On this night the heavy wooden batten hit Bourne on the head, catching him exactly in the middle of his temple. Doctors were swiftly in attendance but, with the man totally unable to carry on with his part, an understudy took over for the rest of the evening.

1891_03_31 MANCHESTER (Cathedral Schools).   FATAL DUEL OF AMATEUR ACTOR

The play was *Romeo and Juliet* given by amateurs. The actor playing Mercutio was a young man called Thomas Whalley, a compositor by trade. As is well known, in the play Mercutio dies in a duel with Tybalt which Romeo tries to break up. In this amateur production, fiction became fact. The actor playing Tybalt stabbed Whalley in realty, his sword plunging into the poor lad's body to a depth of seven inches. Whalley managed with great professionalism to utter his lines "I am hurt. A plague o' both your houses; I am sped." as he collapsed. The play was immediately halted and Whalley rapidly taken to hospital but was dead on arrival. From the various witness statements the coroner was not able to decide whether the fatal wound came from the sword of Tybalt (Mr E Thompson of Cheetham Hospital), Romeo (Mr W Bagnall), or Whalley himself. He warned of the folly of using real swords on the amateur stage and passed a verdict of Accidental Death. The compositor was only 19 years of age.

152

1891_04_15 DARWEN (Theatre Royal).   ACCIDENT IN *HUMANITY*

[John Lawson (1865–1920) was a hard working actor of no particular prominence until 1884 when he played a Jewish role. He followed this in 1886 with a play called *Humanity* – the author reworking the play to introduce the Jewish role of Jacob Silvani especially for Lawson. This was a sensational melodrama that played at the Standard Theatre in London for 150 nights. From then on Lawson performed little else, touring the country year after year with a full company of 16, a mechanical collapsing staircase, and "all the London effects". The main attraction was a terrific fight with crockery and furniture thrown about ("£20 of pots smashed at every performance") and the climax of the collapsing staircase. From 1904, when sketches in music halls were thriving, he cut the last act to 18 minutes featuring the fight, making a fortune. In 1913, he made a silent film version.]

In this play there is a scene where two characters fight on a staircase, the climax being the scenic structure giving way taking both actors Lawson and Oswald with it. On this night the latter, severely shocked, was seriously hurt with both elbow and knee dislocated while Lawson escaped unhurt, presumably because he had been acting this scene for several years. Well, perhaps not, as Roy Hudd has disclosed that a lady who worked in the sketch told him that Lawson employed an ex-boxer to stunt double for him in the fight while the man himself watched from the wings. This ploy was honoured by time, as back in Regency days it was commonplace for the pantomime people to double for stunts required by straight actors.

1891_05_16c LONGTON (Queen's). ACCIDENT TO DANCING COMEDIAN

Charles Cassie, touring with the *Romany Rye* company, injured his knee during his dance in the racecourse scene, preventing him from walking and putting him out of work for a considerable length of time. Writing in July to *The Stage* that he was only just recovering, he praised the fact that he was insured to a small extent by having his 'card' in the newspaper every week, a benefit of the subscription being a modest insurance against injury. He eventually returned to his role in September. I am not sure how he managed this because *The Stage* informed its advertisers that they were insured free of charge if they were injured on any railway in the UK or on the continent of Europe. Via The Railway Passengers Assurance Co they would receive £200 for death, £3 a week for Total Disablement, or 15/- a week for Partial Disablement. Cassie was injured onstage not travelling. Perhaps there was a similar scheme for onstage injury via another insurance company?

1891_06_16 MANCHESTER (Palace of Varieties). ACCIDENT TO TRAPEZE ARTISTE

The act on the flying trapeze was by Nestor and Aerian. The latter was the catcher, swinging head down from his trapeze while Nestor flew across and down some 20ft. Aerian, grasping Nestor by one hand only, could not hold him, the impetus of the swing of the two men combined meaning that Nestor was dropped, and missing the safety net, fell face downwards on the stage. The curtain was rung down and medical men appeared to diagnose a broken wrist and concussion. Nestor soon recovered, but could not remember what had happened.

1891_06_22 GUNNISLAKE (Bostock's Menagerie). LION TRAINER IN FATAL ATTACK

115. *Lion attacking trainer*

Thomas Bridgman, appearing under the professional name of Capt Cardono, was a lion trainer with "a world-wide reputation". He entered a cage of five lions as he had done for many years but, on this day, was attacked by his largest lion. He got up to beat the animal off but "when rescued he presented a pitiable spectacle". Seemingly the other four lions did not join in the attack, instead attacking the disobedient lion. It was conjectured whether they were protecting their master through affection, or feeling resentment towards their colleague wolfing down a meal to himself which by lion social principles should have been shared between the five. Cardono, immediately taken to the hospital at Plymouth, died there a week after suffering intense agonies.

1891_07_13 CLINTON, USA (Forepaugh's Circus). FATAL ACCIDENT TO 'WILLIAM HANLON'

It will be recalled that William Hanlon fell from the trapeze bar the previous August at the Academy of Music in New York (*see* 1890_08_23) He recovered, and with much Yankee cheek, blamed a prop breakage and claimed he had returned to work much earlier than he actually had. The

153

two Volta brothers had retired to become agents, but the "Hanlon Brothers" (William, John, Little Bob) carried on as soon as William returned, and were working with Adam Forepaugh's Circus. On this day, William fell again in a similar manner, with a failing supporting rope precipitating him down into the ring. This time luck was not on his side. He broke his neck, death being instantaneous.

The man known as William Hanlon was not, in fact, the famous aerialist of that name, one of six brothers who had been true kings of the air for decades, but a man named O'Mara, an ex-apprentice of the famous Hanlon brothers. At the time, the real William Hanlon was 52 and producing pantomimic plays and inventing theatrical apparatus. O'Mara was 31 and had been apprenticed to the Hanlon Brothers at the age of ten as had John and Little Bob who went their separate ways to form their own troupes.

1891_07_25 LONDON (Drury Lane). **SCENERY ACCIDENT TO CHARLES WARNER**

[Charles Warner (1846–1909) was born in Kensington. He first appeared onstage at the age of 15 in 1861 at a special performance of Richelieu before Queen Victoria. Excelling in melodrama, he had successes in impulsive and emotional characters. His masterpiece was Coupeau in Charles Reade's *Drink* (a dramatization of Zola's novel *L'Assommoi*) and was said to have surpassed Gil-Naza, who first created the part in Paris. This was the role he was playing at the time of this accident. Later in his life he returned to the part in a compressed version of Reade's drama. He died by hanging himself in his hotel room in New York at the age of 63.]

116.

Charles Warner was playing his most famous role when, in the middle of the performance, a section of scenery fell, knocking him down and seriously cutting the back of his head. The curtain was lowered and the manager announced a suspension of the performance while the wound was attended to in the dressing room by three doctors, two of whom had been in the audience. After a lengthy hiatus the play was resumed, with Warner in evident pain and at the conclusion "greatly prostrated".

1891_09_01 BOLTON (Victoria). **ACCIDENT TO TRAPEZE ARTISTE**

Aerialist Akros fell from the top of his apparatus into the safety net. The force of the fall from such a great height caused the net to break through, and Akros to land on the floor. Although severely shaken he escaped injury which was considered miraculous. Although now in common use during the latter 19th century, safety nets still seemed unreliable through being neither long nor wide enough, strong enough, or not fastened properly.

1891_09_11 GRIMSBY (Prince of Wales). **FATAL ACCIDENT TO CEILING WALKER**

Sydney Bird from Lowestoft aka Una the Human Fly, performed feats on the trapeze, but the climax of his act was to walk along a suspended lateral steel ladder, head downwards, placing the insteps of his feet on to the rungs. The ladder was 15ft above the stage, with no safety net, there being insufficient room to fix one as some 7ft of space is needed below to allow for 'bounce sag'. Una had been doing this stunt for five years but on this night, the poor lad missed his footing and crashed down head first to the floor. He was carried into the dressing room while medical help was summoned. There was a fracture at the base of his skull and he died within the hour. He was only 16 years of age. At the inquest it was suggested where a net was not possible a thick mattress should be placed on the stage.

1891_10_02 LONDON (Elephant & Castle).   BARITONE STABS HIMSELF

James Leverett playing the part of the Earl of Chestermere had to break a baton across his knee. On this night he was so enthusiastic in his action that he stabbed himself, one of the broken ends penetrating his abdomen causing a serious enough wound to take him to St Thomas's Hospital. He was able to resume his role on 12 October when the show opened at Walsall.

1891_10_24 BIRMINGHAM (Grand).   ACCIDENT TO PREMIERE DANCER

Jennie Holland was one of the four featured dancers in a *pas de quatre* in *Faust Up To Date*. On this night, tripping over some scenery after leaving the stage, she fell to the floor, unable to rise. Taken to her room she was seen by Dr Clay. It seemed to be the ubiquitous sprained ankle and she was unable to walk and Dr Clay feared it would be some weeks before she could resume dancing.

1891_11_02 STOURBRIDGE (Theatre).   GUN ACCIDENT

Performing in *Uncle Tom's Cabin*, actor-manager Charles Hermann was carrying a Remington rifle when the trigger, catching in his clothing, caused the gun to fire injuring the palm of his hand. A member of the audience proffered first aid and a doctor was summoned. The wound was dressed and Hermann was taken to his hotel. The performance continued "thus the audience was prevented from indulging in any excitement." Which reads oddly today, but we must remember the meaning of excitement in those days meant disturbance or agitation, rather than the present day meaning of a feeling of great enthusiasm and eagerness. At the beginning of December it was announced that Hermann would not be able to return to the stage for another three months. In the meantime *Uncle Tom's Cabin* would carry on the fourteenth year of its tour with a replacement actor, while Hermann organised a No 2 company to play other dates. He, himself, actually returned to the stage in his usual part sooner than forecast, on 11 January 1892 at Rotherham.

155

1891_12_23c SHEFFIELD (Sanger's Circus)   FATAL GUN ACCIDENT TO ELEPHANT TRAINER

Elephant trainer Frederick Charles Hartley (28) was preparing a gun with blank shot – to be fired in the act by an elephant – when the gun went off, the wadding going into his hand. He went to the hospital to have the wound dressed, and the accident seemed slight with no fear of serious complications. However, as days passed with the hand becoming worse, Hartley was admitted to hospital as an in-patient where, suffering lockjaw, he died on 30 December. At the inquest his mother said that the wadding was not extracted from his hand until eight days after the accident. The inquest was adjourned until this claim could be investigated. Wilkinson the house surgeon said when he first saw the wound it was impossible to tell whether there was any paper in without opening the palm of the hand. He waited until the 27th then, seeing some shreds, he extracted a piece of paper. He held he had acted quite properly, and "for lockjaw to supervene on such an injury was a remote contingency." There were 15,000 people including the entire Sanger staff at the funeral.

1892_01_23 MIDDLESBROUGH (Theatre Royal).   ACCIDENT TO PANTOMIME CLOWN

In the pantomime *Aladdin* Thomas McOllive with his partner Mr McKane, did "some smart trap and acrobatic business" before leaping over an 8ft long table, coming a cropper, splitting his kneecap on the table edge and suffering serious injury. He was taken to the North Riding Infirmary.

1892_03_15 RUNCORN (Theatre).   ACCIDENT TO FRANK OSWALD

Yes, it is *Humanity* again (*see* 1891_04_15). The same actor Frank Oswald, injured once more in the collapsing staircase scene, on this occasion damaging his back and ankle. John Lawson again escaped unscathed, which we now suspect is because he was never in that scene. Perhaps Frank Oswald was actually Lawson's stunt double?

1892_03_19 MANCHESTER (Comedy).   SERIOUS ACCIDENT TO FAIRY QUEEN

Lonie Cassati, playing Fairy Queen in the pantomime was standing in the wings when a clumsy limelight man slipped and fell on her, breaking her ankle. She was off work for some weeks.

1892_04_19 McKEE'S PORT, USA (World's).   GUN ACCIDENT TO SHARPSHOOTER

Frank Sergeant was an exponent of the 'William Tell Feat'. His brave target – with an apple on his head – was Frank Ferguson on whom Sergeant would turn his back and, by taking aim via a mirror, shoot over his shoulder at the apple. After performing the feat for some five years without mishap, on this particular night his luck ran out when to the horror of all beholders Ferguson fell to the ground with a neat bullet hole in the centre of his forehead. He was not killed but it was feared he would soon die. This was the same stunt that Frank Frayne came a cropper over (*see* 1882_11_30).

1892_10_14 LONDON (South London).   ACCIDENT TO GEORGE LUPINO JR

156

[The Luppino family originated in Italy and several generations graced the stages of the UK. However, George was not of this family and only adopted the name after working with some family members. After marrying Rosina Proctor, George Hook (1820–1902) was the patriarch of the modern Lupino thespians, ten of their 16 children being performers. George Hook's eldest son, George Jr (1853–1932) is the performer in the accident here. George Lupino's nephew married into the Sarah Lane family becoming the Lupino Lane (1892–1959) of Lambeth Walk fame. His son Lauri Lupino Lane (1921–1986) was widely known for a 'slosh' act with George Truzzi which can be seen in Charlie Chaplin's film *The King in New York*.]

George was doubling at two London theatres – after playing Leporello in *Don Juan* at the Alhambra he had to dash to the South London Theatre to appear in *The Monster of the Deep*. In this he was through vampire doors, up and down traps, in a hectic gymnastic pantomime. At the end of all that an explosion from an off-stage battery took place. On this night, through a timing fault on somebody's part, the contents of the battery were fired into George's leg. He fell senseless to the stage and was carried to his dressing room where two doctors were summoned. He was immediately despatched to Guy's Hospital. George's role at the Alhambra was taken over by Mr Almonti, and his part at the South London by Harry Le Fre. He left hospital at the end of the month but did not expect to work again until Christmas when he was due to play in *Man in the Moon* at the Britannia Theatre. He gave a present to each of the nurses who had ministered to him, and a donation of a guinea to the Metropolitan and National Nursing Association

George, returning to the ballet *Don Juan* at the Alhambra on 12 December, was the life and soul of the production; later opening in panto at the Britannia on Boxing Day. In April 1893, compensation had still not been settled, but a casual meeting between a Mr Law, and Wells the lessee of the South London led to Mr Law acting as a go-between the parties, and a settlement reached.

1892_11_03 MARSEILLES, France (Palais de Cristal).   ACCIDENT TO TIGHTROPE WALKER

Quegaro, walking across a tightrope from the stage to the centre of the hall, lost his balance and fell to the ground. The distance was only 12ft but he sustained serious injury.

1892_11_07 PARIS, France (Cirque Nouveau).   ACCIDENT TO NATHAN JACKLEY

[Nathan Jackley, an Austrian acrobat surnamed Hirsch, was one of 24 children – his father went through four wives – and made his debut at the age of four. As an adult he formed a troupe the Jackley Wonders, which performed in circuses throughout Europe and the United States. His son George Jackley (1884–1950) was a comic actor and singer with a loud voice. George's son was Nat Jackley (1909–1988) the English comic actor whose trademark rubber-neck antics, lanky frame and funny walks made him a star comedian in variety and films and a top pantomime dame. *Personal Note: We were in four pantomimes with Nat Jackley.*]

117. *The Jackley Wonders*

Nathan Jackley's speciality was to throw a backward somersault off a tower of eight chairs, an act originated by him which became known as the 'Jackley Drop' by subsequent emulators. On this night he broke his kneecap while performing "his miraculous somersaults from a pyramid of tables." He was still in hospital at the end of the month after a successful operation wherein his fractured kneecap was sewn together with silver wire. Fred Higham organised a benefit on 8 February in which "over 100 turns have promised to appear" while the bill-posting crew had distributed the publicity without charge. It was held on an afternoon so most entertainers in London were free to either appear or attend. It was a huge success.

It was announced in July 1894 that Jackley having recovered from his accident "some time ago in Paris" (20 months!) would soon resume his table somersaulting act. In December he was back on the boards and earning universal praise for being "better than ever".

1892_12_11 NIMES, France.   GUN ACCIDENT

In a duelling scene in the play *Les Pirates de la Savane*, an actor with a fowling-piece – a rifle that shoots scattered shot for killing birds – not thinking it was loaded, discharged it at his opponent M Labourel who received the contents in his shoulder. After falling to the floor bleeding profusely, he was stretchered away leaving a horrified audience.

1892_12_15 WOLVERHAMPTON (Star).   HATCHET ACCIDENT TO ACTRESS

The play was that old lurid melodrama *The Red Barn* in which Gussie Everett playing the heroine had to tussle on a bridge with another actor who was attempting to destroy it with a hatchet. Miss Everett slipped and the hatchet, falling on the back of her hand, inflicted an ugly gash "from which the blood spurted in an alarming manner". The curtain was dropped and the fainting actress removed to her dressing room while medical attention arrived. The wound was stopped up, but with Miss Everett unable to continue, an understudy stepped in.

157

1893_01_16 DERBY (Empire).   ACCIDENT TO AERIAL GYMNASTS

The performers were The Espaliers "novel entertainers on the flying rings and mid-air performers". A rope from the front of the gallery across the body of the house to the stage was the means by which an Espalier, hanging by his teeth from a loop, slid along the length from high end to low. At the middle of his traverse the rope broke and he crashed down on to the people below. Succeeding in landing on his feet, he suffered nothing worse than a shaking, though he hit a woman and tore her dress. There was no safety net.

1893_02_08 LEICESTER (Crouеste's Circus).   FATAL ACCIDENT TO TRAPEZE ARTISTE

A young French artiste Mdlle Blanchard (17), performing high in the roof of the circus, missed a hold in her very daring act and plunged screaming to the arena. Her fall was slightly broken by brushing the edge of the safety net but, landing on the back of her head, she was picked up unconscious. A doctor ordered her immediate transfer to Leicester Infirmary but she was dead on arrival. [It is astonishing that the so-called safety nets proved useless in so many cases; rarely appearing to be large enough to cover the putative 'falling area'. The same thought must have occurred to others, as a question in Parliament was asked of the Home Secretary whether legislation could not be introduced ensuring that so-called safety measures were effective, thus eliminating failure at the very moment of an accident they were intended to prevent. The Home Secretary replied he had no power to stop such performances and, having previously sent warnings to the police that the responsible persons for these kind of acts must take all possible precautions, could not undertake to legislate on the subject.]

1893_03_24 LONDON (Palace).   ACCIDENT TO EUGEN SANDOW

[Eugen Sandow (1867–1925) was born Friedrich Wilhelm Müller in Prussia to a German father and a Russian mother. He left Prussia in 1885 to avoid military service, becoming a circus athlete adopting Eugen Sandow as his stage name. In 1889, in London he took part in a competition for strong men, winning the top prize which launched him on his career as an athletic superstar. He opened the first of his Institutes of Physical Culture, where he taught methods of exercise, dietary habits and weight training. His ideas on physical fitness, novel at the time, had a tremendous impact. In 1898, he also founded a monthly periodical and published several books which introduced the term 'bodybuilding'. His strongman act was full of weightlifting gimmicks such as bearing the weight of a man playing the piano. The accident below concerns another.]

This feat involved Sandow lying with a plank on his chest on which crossed a guardsman mounted on a horse which became restive resulting in both horse and rider rolling over on to the stage. The curtain was lowered amongst "a perfect storm of hisses". Because of the noisy displeasure the manager had difficulty in getting a hearing but brought Sandow, guardsman and horse back on stage to show all were safe and well, but he had advised Mr Sandow not to attempt a repeat of the trick.

118. *Eugen Sandow*

1893_03_30 BURNLEY (Gaiety). ACCIDENT TO ACTRESS FROM SCENIC WINDOW

Miss McCulloch was playing in *Spellbound* where one scene called upon her to escape from a scenery window 10ft above the stage. On this night as she climbed through the window the top batten of the flat broke causing her to crash down on to the stage floor. She fell on her head with a splinter forced under her scalp. Colleague Mr Charlton broke her fall, saving her from worse injury.

1893_04_11 STOCKTON-ON-TEES (Theatre Royal). GUN ACCIDENT

Edgar Leyton playing the part of Barabas in *The Sea of Ice*, was hit in the face from the blank charge of a pistol, part of the discharge going into his left eye. He immediately returned to London as the local practitioner feared he would lose his sight unless seeing a specialist as soon as possible. *Personal Note: In the 1980s, a friend whose act was to play the xylophone while spinning round on roller skates, suffered from a detached retina and had to be urgently flown back from Malta where he was working, to Moorfields Eye Hospital in London.*

1893_04_19 LONDON (Alhambra). SCENERY ACCIDENT AMONGST BALLET DANCERS

During the ballet of *Aladdin* heavy lengths of woodwork, becoming detached from the scenery, fell amongst the onstage dancers. Several were knocked to the floor and one unfortunate was knocked into the orchestra pit. The curtain was lowered and a hiatus occurred while the suffering females were attended to. By good fortune none was injured and in a short time the piece recommenced.

1893_05_13 SALTAIRE (Victoria Hall). GUN ACCIDENT ACTOR SHOOTS HIMSELF

The Lowe & Castleton Company was presenting *Lord Anerley* in which the villain, played by Wilford Selwyn, shoots himself rather than be taken alive. Selwyn – too enthusiastically realistic – actually shot himself in the hand which was "dreadfully shattered". The curtain was lowered, the actors called for a doctor, manager Lowe fainted and was out for an hour. Selwyn's third finger had to be amputated and he was detained in the cottage hospital. *Personal Note: I was educated at Salt Grammar School and our speech day and other events took place in the Victoria Hall including my first ever public performance at the school's Coronation Party. These buildings were part of Sir Titus Salt's model workers' village which he named Saltaire and is now a World Heritage Site.*

1893_05_30 LONDON (Tivoli). ACCIDENT TO LOTTIE COLLINS

119.

[Lottie Collins (1865–1910) was a singer and dancer, most famous for introducing the song *Ta-ra-ra Boom-de-ay!* to England. She started out in music hall at the age of 12 in a skipping rope dance act with her younger sisters as The Three Sisters Collins. In 1886, Collins became a solo act in music hall. She first toured America in 1889 during which she married Samuel P. Cooney with whom she would have three children. While touring in the United States she heard the song *Ta-ra-ra Boom-de-ay!* After she sang it in London it became her signature piece. She would sing the first verse demurely and then launch into the chorus, performing an uninhibited and exhausting dance with high kicks exposing her stockings, sparkling garters, and bare thighs much in the manner of the can-can. At the height of her popularity she was performing it five times a night at five different venues. Her first child became the musical comedy star Josie Collins.]

In the middle of a new mad hectic dance, full of high kicks, Lottie Collins fell to the floor. Her foot, slipping in an over-large shoe, caused her ankle to give way bringing her crashing down, to lie inert until attendants carried her to the dressing room. There was a doctor in the house, all the way from New Zealand, and he diagnosed a severely sprained ankle which kept her off the stage until her return on 10 July. This seems more than a simple twist-back-in-a-week job, so I have included it.

1893_08_07 SHEFFIELD (Botanical Gardens).   ACCIDENT TO CHAMPION HIGH DIVER
[Tommy Burns (1867–1897) born in Liverpool, was an athlete, swimmer and high diver. By the age of 21 he had won 400 awards and saved 40 lives. He started his showbusiness career as a glorified busker. He would arrive in a town, distribute posters and leaflets, and collect among the crowds of many thousands who gathered to see him dive off bridges. Progressing to stunt work, he became a music hall gymnastic star renowned for his very high dives. The accident below indicates how even a famous variety artiste was treated.]

The star attraction at the Bank Holiday Gala was Tommy Burns the world's champion high diver who was to dive 70ft into a tank of water 8ft deep. A tower had been built with a small stage, Burns being hauled up by means of rope and pulley to reach it. When he arrived at the platform his shoulder caught on the edge and dislodged the wooden beam that supported the rope which plummeted to the ground together with poor Tommy. He was taken to hospital where it was found his chest bone was broken and he had slighter injuries to shoulder and mouth. His doctor was astonished he survived the fall and attributed it to his wonderful vitality, pluck and marvellous physical condition. He had recovered sufficiently to leave the hospital at the end of the month, though against his doctor's wishes. Burns was confident that the Gala Committee would organise a benefit for him. At a meeting of the committee a letter from Mr Mumford was considered, proposing a subscription fund for which he offered a five guinea start. The committee did not see their way to open such a subscription but, on being informed that Burns was totally destitute, instructed the treasurer to send £10. On 9 October, a charity benefit for Tommy Burns was organised by Mumford and local admirers at Sheffield, at which the performers gave their services. More tickets were sold than people who actually turned up, but the response was not of the most liberal kind. Tommy Burns appeared in person looking hale and hearty though crippled still.

The accident was not the end of his career. He dived again seven months later, and several times over the next four years, but he had fallen on hard times since this accident. (*See* 1897_07_06).

1893_08_24 LONDON (Paragon).   BLONDIN LETS CHAIR FALL ON WOMAN
Mr & Mrs Welsh went to see Blondin the famous high wire-walker, paying 2/- each for seats in the front stalls. Late in the evening Blondin appeared carrying his balance pole and a chair. He sat and stood on the chair as it was balanced on the rope then, for reasons that were never explained, Blondin let the chair drop from a height of around 40ft. It hit the seat in front of Mrs Welsh and bounced back on to her, striking her left leg near the knee. She fainted and was taken home and seen by a doctor. She remained in her bed for many weeks suffering from the injury which badly affected

her walking ability, as a result of which she took the theatre to court for damages. At the hearing on 10 May 1894, she claimed that there had been no net to protect the audience should there be a fall by, or from, the artiste, nor had she been warned to move by any attendant or any other employee of the theatre, but she had noticed that several people left their seats when Blondin appeared. The theatre said there was no case to answer, Mrs Welsh must have known it was a dangerous performance, herself taking the risk of attending it and sitting where she did.

There was no jury and the judge disagreed with the theatre's defence. He said Mr & Mrs Welsh had accepted the usual kind of invitation to attend the theatre by buying tickets and had no reason to know that the seats were less safe than a normal seat purchased at that fee. They were not told that they were in a dangerous position and he said there was no doubt the theatre was culpable. The only thing to settle was the amount of damages. Here came disputes between doctors for defence and plaintiff about the severity of the injury. The judge, passing a remark that was the legal equivalent of thinking they were 'trying it on a bit', awarded £100 in damages. At no time does Blondin himself appear to have been involved or questioned which seems rather odd in the circumstances.

120. *Blondin*

1893_09_19 LONDON (Olympic).　　　　　　　　ACCIDENT DURING *MAZEPPA*

[*Mazeppa* was a poem by Byron published in 1819 and was such an immediate success that painters took up their brushes and composers sat at the keyboard. In light of all that Andrew Ducrow of Astley's circus had to produce a dramatic version in 1838. Mr West Jr was the hero. In the many productions since, the role has mainly been played by a female presumably because the character is tied naked on a horse. The Victorians idea of public nudity is not today's!]　This is another in the series of accidents in this hazardous play. Again the horse stumbled when mounting the sloping ramps that served for the flight of the wild horse of Tartary into the scenic mountains. This time the hero was Jeanie Burgoyne strapped to its back and "utterly helpless". She was speedily rescued and came before the lowered curtain to show she was not injured, to be greeted with "a storm of cheering". Despite a cut on her leg and being considerably shaken, the game gal continued her performance.

1893_11_30c PARIS.　　　　　　　　　ACCIDENT TO ONE OF THE WEBSTER SISTERS

[The Tiny Websters, Lizzie and Louise (fl. 1892–1895), were music hall duettists and dancers, billed as 'Lilliputian Wonders' whose song *Smacky, Smacky, Smack* sounds a bit dubious but their one notable hit, *I Don't Want to Play in Your Yard*, was recorded with exquisite tenderness decades later, in 1957, by American vocalist Peggy Lee.]

After a successful engagement in Paris, on starting back to London one of the sisters broke her ankle and was ordered to keep to her bed for three weeks. In fact, Lizzie was out of action for many months, not returning to work until 6 August 1894.

121. *Webster Sisters*

1893_12_16c NEW YORK, USA (Americn).   CHAOS AT END OF STAGE HORSERACE

The play *The Prodigal Daughter* featured a horse race with eight live horses. First staged by Sir Augustus Harris at Drury Lane in 1892, this was an American production which opened the new American Theatre in May 1893. The *New York Times* hailed it as "A Theatre Fit for the Noblest Plays and the Best Audiences – *The Prodigal Daughter*, a Good Melodrama of the Modern London Kind, Received with a Mighty Demonstration of Public Favor – A Real Steeplechase on the Stage." (23 May 1893).

However, at a performance in December the horses had raced across the stage twice and, in the next passage across, the winner was supposed to be the horse ridden by the hero, played by Leonard Boyne. Alas, on this night Mr Boyne caught his boot in the scenery while galloping across bringing some of it down, causing horses to stumble and fall. As a horrific result, in the full public gaze eight horses and their jockeys were thrashing about in a tangled heap. A jockey called Gould was repeatedly kicked in the head. The curtain was lowered and the jockeys – all unconscious – taken to the dressing rooms. Gould, the most severely injured, required stitches in his head wound, and a youth of 19 had internal injuries. There was blood all over the stage but all was cleared up for the final act of the play. At the curtain call, Boyne – the only one to escape the melee – said he had never witnessed such a scene, even on a real race track, and it was a miracle nobody had been killed.

1893_12_07 LONDON (Drury Lane).   GUN ACCIDENT

The play *A Life of Pleasure* had a scene with a Gatling gun, which on this night felled two men, presumably supers, named Harley and Deane. The former had a wound to his cheek, the latter on his left eye. They were taken to King's College Hospital where both underwent operations.

1893_12_28 NEWPORT (Empire).   MAGICIAN FALLS FROM A GREAT HEIGHT

This is a rum accident with a bit of a comically odd twist. Allan McAskell, a magician who, during the day while appearing at the Empire, climbed up to the fly-floor some 30ft above the stage. There, for reasons known only to himself, he hung by his hands from a cross beam, then losing his hold fell to the floor, spraining both ankles. In the evening, though "suffering great pain" he was carried onstage and gave his show "kneeling across two chairs to the interest and satisfaction of the audience." Very odd.

1894_02_27 BRADFORD (Prince's).   ACCIDENT TO ACTOR IN STAGE FIGHT

Two actors were engaged in a scene which involved a struggle and a strangle. Watson Mill was so vigorous in his part that he slipped on a skin rug and fell, dragging his opponent on top of him. This seemed very realistic acting to the audience, but Mill had damaged his knee. Two doctors were summoned and while Mill was being attended to, another actor continued the part. However, when it was the scene of dénouement Watson Mill reappeared with the aid of a stick and a crutch, having dislocated his kneecap. *Personal Note: The Prince's Theatre was uniquely sited, being built on top of the Star Music Hall which was entirely subterranean. An iron, sawdust and concrete floor 4ft deep separated the two. A lot of my early theatre-going was done there to see Harry Hanson's Court Players in 'weekly rep'. The Star was renamed the Palace in 1894 and, as it did not close until 1938, in his younger days my father often attended shows there where he saw rats scampering through the stalls.*

162

1894_04_09 LONDON (Adelphi).   ACCIDENT TO MISS JANET ACHURCH

122. *Janet Achurch*

[Janet Achurch (1864–1916) born as Janet Sharp, became an actress in 1881 adopting the name of her maternal grandparents who were the lessees of the Theatre Royal in Manchester. She made her London debut in 1883 and played many Shakespearean roles, but became a champion of modern dramatists and was known as a leading pioneer of the new form of drama. She toured extensively both in the UK and overseas in Egypt, India and the antipodes. In 1889, she became the lessee of the Novelty Theatre and played her most notable role as Nora in the English premiere of Ibsen's *A Doll's House*, becoming the foremost interpreter of Ibsen. G B Shaw wrote *Candida* especially for her and would not permit the play to be performed without her. In the following accident she was eschewing the gloom of Ibsen for popular melodrama.]

The play was *The Cotton King* and Janet Achurch cut her hand badly when smashing a window in Act II. She was able to carry on without the audience realising she was wounded, but had to act with her arm in a sling for a couple of weeks. The press remarked that the actress had "amazing adaptability in the way in which she turned her hand to melodrama."

1894_05_20 PARIS, France (Moncey).   GUN ACCIDENT TO SEVERAL ACTORS

The play was a farcical gymnastic comedy called *Voyage en Suisse*. This show had been created by the famous Hanlon Brothers in 1879 when they ceased performing as a gymnastic act. It was premiered in Paris and the brothers toured the world with it until 1891 when they sold the British and Irish rights to Charles Lauri Jr and the French rights to the Renads family. I assume it was the latter troupe involved in this accident. One of the scenes included the explosion of the boiler of a railway engine, the visual effect being accompanied by several guns in the wings fired simultaneously. At this performance the guns, carelessly pointed towards the stage, resulted in

123.

several actors being shot. A comedian was wounded in the thigh, an actress was hurt in the shoulder and arm, while two other actors received injuries of a slighter nature. The curtain was lowered on the carnage, and it was an hour before the performance was resumed.

1894_05_22 LONDON.   ACCIDENT TO DIRECTOR BY POISON

F Wynne-Scarlett, preparing and rehearsing a tour for a play called *Ali Baba MP* and worn out with three exhausting weeks, sent to the chemist for a tonic. After taking the 'pick-me-up' he suffered violent convulsions followed by total fatigue. He was assisted by two doctors who surmised that an overdose of strychnine had been accidentally added to the mixture. For several days he remained in bed, before he was declared out of danger. George Vokes stepped in to carry on with rehearsals.

1894_05_26 LONDON (Canterbury).   SHARPSHOOTER ACCIDENT TO DAUGHTER

Mr Manard, head of the Manard troupe of rifle experts, accidentally shot Miss Manard through the neck. She was immediately seen by Dr Brookes then sent to St Thomas's Hospital where she stayed until recovered.

1894_08_06 LONDON (Paragon).   ACCIDENT TO CHARLES LAURI

Charles Lauri, one of the leading pantomimists of the age, injured himself going through a vampire trap and inflammation of the knee set in. He was unable to fulfil his roles properly – doubling at the Paragon playing in a sketch *Satan Junior* and, at the Canterbury, the part of the ape Chadi in his famous long-running play *The Sioux*.

1894_09_15 LONDON (Drury Lane).   ONSTAGE FIRE ACCIDENT

During the opening scene – an Earl's dining room – in *The Derby Winner*, as coffee was being served, by some accident a spirit lamp on the table was knocked over setting light to the table cloth. The actors carried on with their lines, and a stagehand coolly walking on in front of the actors, took off his coat which he used to smother the flames. Sir Augustus Harris, watching from his box, dashed round backstage and not only gave the man money for a new coat, but doubled his salary. Incidentally, at this period Drury Lane Theatre was the only London theatre that was not insured – the premium was unaffordable and the management had faith in their anti-fire precautions.

164

1894_09_21 CHERBOURG, France (Grand).   FATAL TRAP ACCIDENT TO DIRECTOR

M Aréme the director of the theatre, while walking across the stage, passed over a trapdoor which opened under him because some incompetent fool had forgotten to lock it closed. He fell 18ft on to the cellar floor and was killed instantly.

1894_10_06 DIPTON (Hall).   GUN ACCIDENT TO HENRY BERTRAM

Henry Bertram, an actor of 40 years experience, was accidentally shot near the elbow of his left arm while playing a scene in *Jack Long of Texas*. He was taken to Newcastle Infirmary where he was an in-patient for seven weeks. By December, although recovering well, he was still unable to use his arm, but advertised he was open to offers for the spring. *The Era* was the main place to tout for work and it is in those pages you will see "At liberty" (need work now) "Resting" (need work now), and "open for immediate offers" (need work now). "Free from . . ." (need to fix future work now).

1894_10_13 BILSTON (Theatre).   ANOTHER ACCIDENT IN *HUMANITY*

John Lawson the actor described as "the well-known Jew impersonator" who toured endlessly in the play *Humanity* in which accidents were almost inevitable in the fight involving a collapsing staircase (*see* 1891_04_15 & 1892_03_15) on this night was himself injured.

In the fight where a large amount of crockery is smashed ("£20 of pots smashed at every performance") Lawson was so badly lacerated with a broken dinner plate that medical aid had to be summoned. "His place in the last act was undertaken by another member of the company." One presumes this was the man who, it is rumoured, was the star's regular stand-in for the fight scene. Lawson was off three weeks before well enough to resume.

1894_10_17c BOSTON, USA (Park).   SCALDING ACCIDENT TO 'NUDE' MODEL

This rather horrible unusual accident occurred during a scene in a *tableau vivant* named *The Birth of the Pearl* featuring a fountain with two women at the front corners wearing mermaid tails, while at centre back clad only in a thin under-vest and fleshings (*cf* modern body stocking) was Miss Strathmore standing with her arms upstretched holding a shell. As the curtain opened on this artistic scene, the fountain played water over Miss Strathmore. She had been doing this routine for six weeks and to make the water drenching her from top to toe bearable, a feeder of hot water had been added to mix with the cold, so that the water was at least lukewarm rather than icy cold. On this night for some accidental reason the cold water feed had not been turned on, and only the hot water sprayed down on the water nymph. As the water became hotter and hotter, Miss Strathmore, trying to bear it with equanimity, was finally overcome and crying out fell into a dead faint. The curtain descended and it was discovered the girl had been severely scalded. The same report that she was in agony and dying followed from paper to paper until mid-November then ceased, and I have been unable to find if the woman survived or not.

1894_11_17 BLACKBURN (Prince's).   ANOTHER ACCIDENT IN *HUMANITY*

This time it was one of the ladies in the cast who suffered an accident. An 8ft high rostrum had been set onstage and during the course of the action Jeannie Burgoyne stepped on to it but the top, insecurely fastened, collapsed throwing her down on to the stage. She was injured and obliged to take to her bed under medical treatment. Her absence from the stage was not a prolonged one.

1894_11_28 LONDON (Aquarium).   FATAL ACCIDENT TO A GYMNAST

Arthur Barrett (24), a member of the Duo Vollars, was performing a double somersault on the horizontal bar when his foot accidentally caught a guide wire attached to the apparatus which pitched him forward on to his back. The curtain was swiftly lowered, and the audience was unaware that a serious accident had taken place. Barrett was taken to Westminster Hospital where everything possible was done by Dr Nowell but, being "beyond medical skill" poor Arthur died the following afternoon.

1894_12_17 EDINBURGH (Theatre Royal).   ACCIDENT TO PANTOMIME COMEDIAN

Frank and Arthur Haytor were the leading funsters of the pantomime *Babes in the Wood* being both acrobats and comedians with a fund of routines like comic boxing matches and swordfights. During the second night of the show Arthur Haytor suffered an injury which appeared to be the ubiquitous twisted ankle. However, it put him out of the production, his part taken over by another in the cast, with brother Frank having to work his socks off to make up the deficiency. Arthur was off for seven weeks returning to the fold on 4 February.

1895_02_19 BURNLEY (Gaiety).   ACTOR INJURED IN *HUMANITY*

Well here we go again! An actor injured during the sensational collapsing staircase fight scene. But not any actor – Frank Oswald the same man injured previously (*see* 1891_04_15 *and* 1892_03_15). On this occasion he "somehow received an injury to his back". I await with bated breath to see if poor Frank has any more ill luck before the end of the century and these tales of woe come to an end.

1895_02_22 LONDON (Canterbury).   SCENERY ACCIDENT TO ACTRESS

Katie Neville – in the role of a stowaway – was shot in the bosom and fell dying in the arms of Charles Lilley playing the Captain. He laid her out and draped a Union Jack over her, after which the front cloth was lowered on the moving tableau. On this night she fell in the place where the cloth itself would fall but, being a dedicated trouper she was not going to spoil the effect by getting up to die again a couple of yards away, so bravely awaited the descent of the roller. It hit her on the right arm, crushing it. She had to perform thereafter with her arm in a splint. She subsequently sued for negligence – from both Lilley for lying her out in the wrong place, and the Canterbury management for one of their servants, ie the stage manager, not realising the cloth would strike her if allowed to fall. On 24 May, a jury in Southwark Court awarded her £40 damages.

1895_03_25c LONDON (Olympia).   FATAL ACCIDENT TO YOUNG RUSSIAN GYMNAST

Prior to the performance of a production called *The Orient*, David Feldman – one of a troupe of Russian acrobats – was onstage practising a double somersault when he fell on his back. Dr Collier, the consulting medic at Olympia, was summoned and as Feldman was paralysed from his chest downwards he was taken to West London Hospital where it was found he had fractured his spinal column. He died there on 1 April. He was only 17 years old and had never before attempted a double somersault. The "usual mattress had been used, and no one was to blame."

1895_04_08 LONDON (Pavilion).   FATAL ACCIDENT TO HENRY HAMPTON

While rehearsing the bridge scene in *Saved from the Sea*, Henry Hampton (45) a star in the theatres of the East End fell in his jump, coming down on his left heel with considerable force, splintering a bone in his foot. In great agony he was taken to his rooms remaining there indisposed for several months, until returning on 8 July as Hawkshaw in *The Ticket-of-Leave Man* at the Standard Theatre. Alas, it was the last performance he gave as he was taken ill with what the doctor described as pneumonia and, for the four days prior to his death, "paralysis of the tonsils" which deprived him of his voice.

1895_05_23c NEW YORK, USA (American).   MRS BROWN-POTTER STABS MR BELLEW

I could not resist this report for the closing line! We met Mr Bellew in a previous accident (*see* 1882_02_20). It was the opening night of a season starring English actors Mrs Brown-Potter and Kyrle Bellew with a play about the French Revolution. Reaching the scene where Charlotte Corday stabs Marat in his bath, Mrs Brown-Potter, carried away with enthusiasm, stabbed Bellew in earnest, drawing blood which soaked into his fleshings. It did not interrupt the play, and in the interval a doctor stopped the flow of blood, after which the show carried on. "He really lost less blood than did Mrs Brown-Potter when the bat fastened on her arm whilst she was playing Lady Macbeth in Calcutta."

124. Cora Urquhart Brown-Potter

1895_06_04 READING (New Town Hall).   FATAL ACCIDENT TO OPERA TENOR

Cavalleria Rusticana was the attraction on the final night of the tour of William Hogarth's Opera Company, with the Australian tenor Charles Harding playing Turiddu. As he fell to the floor in his death scene, Harding ruptured a small artery in his thigh which caused him to spend a few days in bed. I note that he was engaged to double the Canterbury and Paragon for the week commencing 1 July, but was unable to fulfil the contract as on that very day he died at the age of 49.

1895_06_07 LONDON (Covent Garden).   FIRE ONSTAGE IN *FAUST*

[Pol Henri Plançon (1851–1914) was a French operatic bass hailed as one of the top singers at the end of the 19th century. He made his debut at Lyon in 1877, and from 1879 became a stalwart of the Paris Opera for some ten years. His reputation enabled him to become an international star throughout Europe. He was a regular visitor to Covent Garden, and in 1893 made his debut in America where much of the rest of his career took place. He retired to France aged 57, his latter years spent in teaching. He died in 1914 aged 63.]

125. *Pol Henri Plançon*

During the first act of Gounod's opera *Faust* M Plançon made his entrance as Mephistopheles, entering via a doorway from the wings, suitably accompanied by red fire which unfortunately ignited the scenery. Stage crew ran on, with Mephistopheles joining in to help subdue the flames. Nobody shouted 'Fire!' although a few made for the exits. A voice from the stage shouted there was no cause for alarm, and voices around the auditorium cried "Seats! Seats!" The curtain was lowered and then the star of the evening – no less a personage than Mdlle Melba – entering to great applause, progressed across the stage in a stately fashion. As she made her exit the curtain rose to disclose no sign of fire, the damaged portion of the scenery having been taken away. The opera then restarted from the entrance of Mephistopheles and progressed in the normal manner.

1895_07_01 RUNCORN (Royal).   ACCIDENT TO JAPANESE WIRE-WALKER

Tarossan was an artiste on the slack wire, performing with the Vaudeville Novelty Company. On the opening night of the week at Runcorn he fell backwards on to the stage injuring his back. He was taken to Northern Hospital in Liverpool where he was found to have a dislocated spine and paralysis of the legs. After eight weeks in hospital, with the decision nothing more could be done for him, his removal was ordered for a week's time. At this news, his agent Will Sley wrote to *The Era* to say the Japanese was destitute with a wife and family, and would not be able to work again. The letter was an appeal for contributions to a fund, and by November Sley had been able to hand £45 to Mrs Tarossan who had opened a lodging house for performers in Manchester. His hope was to raise a total of £100 and he was handing 15/- a week to Mrs Tarossan as long as the fund would last. There was a substantial number of donations including many of very modest amounts of 2/6d and 1/- from individuals, presumably colleagues in the business; a whip-round at venues brought larger amounts from theatres and companies while the Music Hall Benevolent Fund contributed £4. In December, Tarossan had an operation and, thanking friends and colleagues for their Christmas cards, said he hoped to be back on his feet soon.

1895_09_13 KIMBERLEY, S Africa (Fillis's Circus).   ACCIDENT TO POPULAR ACROBAT

On this Friday, it was publicised that Dan Feeley would perform the following sensational feat – he proposed jumping over 30 men armed with rifles and fixed bayonets while they were firing a volley. This was included in a benefit for his boss Frank Fillis. On the day, Feeley was feeling unwell and colleagues suggested he postpone his leap. Refusing to contemplate the suggestion because the show was for his boss, Dan went ahead with the leap as planned. Falling short, he dropped on the last bayonet which impaled his leg at the back of the knee passing upwards into the thigh muscles. He was taken to hospital where surgeons decided by Sunday that gangrene had set in and the leg must be amputated. Much sympathy from throughout the Diamond Fields had cheered him, but the circus had moved on and was at Worcester when Fillis heard the news. He immediately returned to his employee, paid for him to have a private room and stayed with him until he was certain of Dan's complete recovery.

1895_09_21 BLACKPOOL (New Grand).   IRON SAFETY CURTAIN FALLS ON ACTOR

The play was a comedy called *Dr Bill*, the company that of Otho Stuart, the actor Murray King. The iron safety curtain was being lowered while King was on the stage. Through some unexplained mishap, it landed with some force on his head, jamming his chin on some projecting woodwork. He had severe concussion, nasty facial cuts and a scalp wound. He was taken to his apartment but after being seen by his medic he was transferred to hospital where he was detained for a couple of weeks, rejoining the cast in early November.

168

1895_11_18 LOS ANGELES, USA (Orpheum).   SERIOUS ACCIDENT TO CHAMPION JUMPER

126. *Jack Higgins*

[Jack Higgins (1871c–1930c) born in Blackburn, became a professional jumper at the age of 18. He jumped over many things with his feet together, holding weights in his hands which he dropped at the height of his jump. He had extraordinary delicacy, putting out candles with his feet en route, dipping his toes in a bowl of water held on the head of an assistant etc. He not only jumped high but also over 45 chairs – in succession – placed ten feet apart in a row. He was by no means alone in carrying out these eccentric feats, but his only professional equal was Joseph Darby whom he defeated in a £100 challenge in July 1893. An illustrated article appeared in the *Strand Magazine* in 1897, and there is a 1927 clip of him in action at the age of 54 on You Tube.]

Jack Higgins, the champion jumper, was in the middle of a highly successful tour of America where his amazing prowess was widely acclaimed. On this performance he jumped over two horses but landed very forcibly on his left heel breaking the tibia bone. As it was near the close of his act and by hopping at his exit nobody in the audience realised he had suffered a major injury. Fortuitously, in the audience was Dr McLain who set the limb and took him to hospital. It was feared that the accident would end Higgins's burgeoning career, but happily this fear was ungrounded.

1895_12_30 PROVIDENCE, USA (Opera House).   SCENERY ACCIDENT

The play *Christopher, Junior* opened with a scene of an attic interior, with the stars – John Drew and Maude Adams – in front of it. During the duologue this scenery fell forward on to them, Drew throwing himself in front of Miss Adams protecting her, bearing the weight of collapse on himself, incurring severe cuts about hands and face in doing so. The curtain fell, as it was feared that Drew must be seriously injured, but after a half-hour wait it rose again and the play carried on as though nothing had happened. The audience, appreciating Drew's heroism, cheered him with enthusiasm.

1896_01_11 DEWSBURY (Theatre Royal).   ACCIDENT TO ACTOR-MANAGER

In the play *My Sweetheart*, Frank Hertie made his entrance crossing a bridge at the back of the stage with a child on his back. In spite of having played the role many times, on this night, while descending the steps from the bridge he stumbled and fell. The curtain was lowered and a doctor summoned who found a compound fracture of the left leg. Hertie was taken to the Infirmary, and after a short delay the play resumed with another member of the company taking the role. Three things have always amazed me when compiling these accidents – how swiftly medical attention arrives, how patiently the audience waits in the hiatus, and how there is always an actor on hand to take over the part. It was not customary to have designated understudies but the show always went on – unlike today when only the major companies have understudies. *Personal Note: Twice during the first year working on this project, I travelled from deepest Kent to see plays at Hampstead Theatre to find the performance cancelled because of sudden illness of an actor. No longer must the show always go on.*

169

1896_02_19c HANLEY (Theatre Royal).   DRASTIC ACCIDENT IN WILD WEST PLAY

Hardie & Van Leer's Company was touring two Wild West plays *The Bandit King* and *The Cattle King* starring the American actor James H Wallick who had been playing in them for 15 years. Sam Finney was a well established actor in the supporting casts who suffered an onstage accident where his legs were knocked from under him. His fall, causing concussion of the spine, which developing into *locomotor ataxia* completely paralysed his lower limbs. I can find no contemporary report of the accident, the details here coming from May 1897 by which time Finney had been completely crippled, out of work for 13 months, and his savings totally exhausted. He wrote to *The Stage* setting out his past credentials of an 18-year career including several comic operas and 12 important provincial pantomimes, and was appealing for "a little money to enable him to enter into some small business whereby he might earn a livelihood for himself and support his two children who are entirely dependent on his exertions." *The Stage* championed his cause and agreed to accept contributions on his behalf, regularly repeating the cause for the Fund, and setting out latest donations. The Fund closed in the issue of 15 July 1897 with a total of £117.7.9d (around £13,250 in today's money) and Sam Finney disappeared from theatrical history.

1896_03_09 WEST HARTLEPOOL (Theatre Royal).   ACCIDENT TO HARLEQUIN

Abe Holt had just joined the pantomime company playing *Little Red Riding Hood* and was burlesquing the role of Harlequin. On his knee he was supporting Ernest Wingfield when he slipped and fell with Wingfield on top of him. A doctor diagnosed Holt had broken his leg in three places.

1896_04_04 LOUTH (Prince of Wales).   ACTOR SHOT WITH LIVE BULLET

The venue was a temporary theatre erected in the Quarry Field by a sharing company. In the course of the play *The Slave Hunt*, James Holmes was shot by fellow actor Jesse Hodgson, and sued for £50 damages as he was wounded, in hospital for four weeks and unable to work for a period thereafter. The case was complicated, the gist of it being that the man sent to buy blank cartridges found the shop did not stock them, only live cartridges, but was told to saw the lead bullet off them as this had been done before and would suffice. As was customary, the gun in the play was not intended to be pointed at anyone, only at the floor or flies for actual discharge. However, on this occasion the gun was mistakenly aimed at the actor and the remaining portion of the bullet penetrated eight inches into Holmes's chest. The gunsmith said it would have been preferable and easier for him to pull the whole lead bullet out and replace with a wad of paper – now he tells us!

1896_04_08 LONDON (Gaiety).   ACCIDENT TO EDMUND PAYNE

[Edmund James Payne (1863–1914) was an actor, comedian and singer best known for creating comic roles in a series of extremely successful musical comedies at the Gaiety Theatre which he joined in 1892 after a decade of provincial touring. He was only 5ft 4ins and affected a lisp, becoming a lovable comedian playing roles in long-running shows *The Shop Girl*, *The Circus Girl*, and *A Runaway Girl* between 1894 and 1900. In these he partnered George Grossmith Jr and the pair went through further light-hearted pieces well into the 20th century.]

Edmund Payne was playing Mr Miggles in *The Shop Girl* when the play had opened a year previously. Shortly after the beginning of its run he was taken ill with typhoid fever. Severe complications developed and he was out of action for over a year. Having sufficiently recovered, he returned to the show which had entered the second year of its run. He was greeted with loud and long applause on his entrance, even his fellow actors joining in. However, before the end of Act I he fell and broke his ankle. Not actually an accident but the result of debility following his long illness and disobeying doctors' orders not to attempt dancing.

127. *Edmund Payne*

1896_05_07 SYDNEY, Australia (Circus).   HIGH DIVER PLUNGES TO HIS DEATH

[Charles Owen Peart (1872–1896) was born in London and since 1886 made his living as a sensational high diver. He was seen by Daniel Fitzgerald of Fitzgerald Brothers Circus in London and engaged to tour with that circus in the antipodes. While touring Tasmania he was reputed to have dived into a tank of water only 2ft deep.] Now read on . . .

This was the first night of a season at Sydney. The final item in the programme was the sensational high dive by Professor Peart. A tank 8ft x 6ft had been dug into the ground and filled with water. This was all carried out under Peart's supervision. At the performance he examined the tank and requested that more water be added bringing the depth to 4ft. Then hauled up to a platform high in the big top, he prepared himself for the dive. He stated that the tank looked very small, something he often said to stress the sensational aspect of his feat and considered to be of little significance. He was at full liberty to dive when he chose, without any signal or other pressure necessary. He dived but was off-centre, his body scraping the side as he entered the water. He was helped out and asked if he was hurt. Replying that he would soon be all right, he walked back to his dressing room with some assistance. As Professor Peart was the last act, the audience streamed out of the tent for home, not knowing that a man had just killed himself for their entertainment. A doctor was called, he had the diver taken to the hospital where he died shortly after admission. He was only 24 years old. His funeral was a grand affair attended by thousands, his coffin borne aloft by fellow artistes. It pains me to record that one of the pall bearers had his pocket picked of £5 while carrying the coffin.

1896_05_18 NEW YORK, USA (Olympia).   ACCIDENT DURING 'SLIDE FOR LIFE'
        [The dramatically called 'slide for life' is a high wire stunt which comprises a long sloping tight wire that the performer walks up and having reached the summit then slides back to the bottom. The set-up on this night was the usual one in the theatres of the period – to have the bottom anchored on the stage and the top attached to the gallery.]   The artiste was Ben Abdullah on his first performance since arriving from London. Reaching the top he commenced – with rigid legs – his backward slide to the bottom end where a large upright cushion acted as a brake to the descent. Falling off the wire a few yards short of his destination, the nearest he got to his cushion was glancing off it with his shoulder before crashing down on to the stage. The curtain was lowered, and Drs Jenkins and Murphy who had been enjoying the show in the audience went hastening round to provide professional attention. Abdullah was unconscious, with a deep and gaping wound on the back of his head. He was taken to the Roosevelt Hospital. Fortunately he was not too badly injured though it was the end of the month before he was able to leave hospital. It was suggested that Abdullah had "not lost his sea legs" after the long voyage, and that performers such as gymnasts should wait a period gaining their land legs before commencing work.

1896_06_01 WAKEFIELD (Opera House).   ACCIDENT TO ACTOR-MANAGER
        Charles McCarthy the head of McCarthy's American Company was acting in a play *One of the Bravest*. A highlight of the melodrama was a scene of a building on fire where McCarthy, having rescued a woman from an upper storey, was lowered on a rope. At this performance the rope broke and both actor and actress fell to the stage. McCarthy injured his head and back and was taken to Wakefield Hospital. Melodramas incorporating rescues from blazing buildings were manifold in the Victorian theatre.

1896_08_10 LONDON (Novelty).   FATAL DAGGER ACCIDENT
        The play was the first performance of *Sins of the Night* presented by Miss St Lawrence's Company. In one scene, Temple Crozier playing the role of Ramez the villain of the piece, had to be stabbed with a dagger wielded by Pablo, a Creole played by Wilfred Moritz Franks. Crozier was actually fatally stabbed in full view of the audience who thought his drop to the floor was a bit of good realistic mime. This was very near the end of the play at 00.15am and the curtain fell, another audience streaming out not realising that a man had been killed in front of them for their entertainment. The doctor arriving at 00.30am found Crozier "quite dead". At 1.30am the police arrived and charged Franks who, totally distraught, was charged with manslaughter.

171

After the post mortem enquiry it was clear that a real weapon had been used. The standard stage technique with a dagger was to stab with a sweeping gesture turning the wrist at the last moment so that the clenched fist is the part that touches the other actor. The blade is actually lying alongside the attacker's inner forearm.

It seems in this case, in spite of several weeks (!?) rehearsing, the timing was out and Crozier had stepped forward before the manoeuvre was complete. The magistrate said the circumstances were clear, and of such a matter that it was unnecessary to present it before a jury, and Franks was dismissed. Temple Crozier was a clergyman's son, and only 24 years of age.

128. *Fatal onstage stabbing*

image© The British Library Board

172

1896_08_19 CROYDON (Grand).   GUN ACCIDENT TO ACTRESS SETS DRESS ON FIRE

This was an unusual accident combination. During a scene in Act I of *Tommy Atkins* by Milton Bode's Company, the villain and his wife have a tussle culminating in the lady being shot by her husband. On this night the gun went off accidentally and far too near the leg of Frances Delaval playing the wife. The charge, setting fire to her dress, entered her thigh. Suffering pain and very lame she struggled to carry on the following night thence for a couple of weeks before a complete recovery.

1896_08_24 DOUGLAS (Grand).   LAURENCE IRVING IN ONSTAGE FIRE

The play was *Trilby,* a dramatisation of the novel by George du Maurier first published in 1894. Svengali is an Ashkenazic Jewish man who seduces, dominates and exploits Trilby, a young half-Irish girl, and makes her into a famous singer. Lizzie Ruggles had the title role, and Laurence Irving, son of Sir Henry, played Svengali. As Trilby was alone on the stage, an iron lamp standard fell over, the burning oil spilling out in danger of setting fire to the wings. The curtain was lowered and several people rose to flee to the exits, but the band played lively music and within a minute or two the curtain rose to disclose nothing untoward, and the play continued on its way.

129. *Laurence Irving*

1896_10_20 CHICAGO, USA (Coliseum).   ACCIDENT TO TRAPEZE ARTISTE

John Howard of the Wonderful Dunhams was attempting a triple somersault from the trapeze bar into the safety net below. He either turned half a somersault too short or too much, as he landed on his neck. In the hospital his legs, from the knees down, were found to be paralysed.

1896_11_05 PARIS, France (Olympia).   FATAL ACCIDENT TO TRAPEZE ARTISTE

I have noted previously how often accidents to aerialists occur through faulty equipment rather than lack of skill of the artiste. This is another such case. La Belle Maude (21) was at rehearsal on a single trapeze set about 20ft above the stage. Going through her routine, on reaching a part where she was hanging by her heels, one of the swivels at the end of the bar gave way, and she plunged downwards – head first – to hit the stage. Her manager father, overseeing the rehearsal, was the man who fixed her apparatus. He rushed forward and gathered her in his arms, but she was torn away from him to be despatched to the Hospital Lariboisière where she died on arrival.

1896_12_26 LONDON (Pavilion).   ACCIDENT TO EUGEN SANDOW

Sandow claimed this was the first accident he had suffered, but we know better (*see* 1893_03_24). It was, however, possibly the first to cause sufficient injury to stop his working for a few days. It seems to have been very similar to the previous mishap. The strong man was on all fours with a wooden platform across his back forming a bridge between two solid rostrums. Across these went a horse and chariot with four men inside. One of his arms gave way and the bridge dropped. There were supporting 'stoppers' to prevent the bridge from falling past these and crushing the athlete's ribs. Off work while his arm mended, he promised to return to the stage on 18 January 1897.

1897 LONDON   THE DANGEROUS PERFORMANCES BILL

The reader may recall that at the beginning of 1880 a decree named The Children's Dangerous Performances Act came into being. This was to protect children under the age of 14 from being exploited, by prohibiting them from undertaking risky stunts in public. This act appears to have been highly successful as in this year a more far-reaching proposal reared its head – The Dangerous Performances Bill which was intended to extend the previous bill to include people up to the age of 18.

On 21 April, a meeting of interested parties was convened at the Canterbury Music Hall to oppose this new bill, and many gymnastic troupes sent representatives. Professional gymnasts know their business better than MPs, and all present agreed that the proposed bill was unfeasible as the ages from 13 to 16 are the prime time for training acrobats; to start training at 18 was impossible.

Often the star performer in a family troupe was well under 18. Parliament was acting 'grandmotherly' in seeking to prevent children performing because they falsely suspected cruel methods were employed. Cruelty simply did not exist as most gymnastic troupes were family based, with children employed as apprentices treated as if they were the master's own. If any performer witnessed a child being mistreated the miscreant would be knocked down by any other member of the cast and his professional standing seriously in jeopardy.

On the point of danger, this was eliminated by professional training carried out on safe and scientific principles, and much safer than riding bicycles in crowded streets. Gymnastic children were stronger and healthier than all the shop boys and messenger boys who thronged the streets. Would the same restrictions apply to schools and gymnasia catering for the desire of youths, male and female, to exercise and improve their health and bodies? The meeting concluded with appointing a solicitor to represent the profession against the bill, and creating a fund to finance such opposition. See 1897_08_07 for the passing of the act.

173

1897_04_15 LONDON (Washington). ACCIDENT TO FRED KARNO

Fred Karno of the noted sketch troupe that bears his name was placed in a perilous position during his sketch *Hilarity* in the course of which he was hanging upside down from a scenic piece depicting a house. This was in the nature of a 'flat' held up by braces but these, starting to give way, would be unable to prevent it falling forward with Karno's head downwards. Seeing the braces failing, Mrs Karno rushed to hold on to them, and Marshall Rhodes the theatre's secretary, who happened to be backstage at the time, also rushed forward to hold the scene up. Karno was released, his rescuers suffering nothing worse than a bruise and a slightly sprained wrist. Famous in later life, both Stan Laurel and Charlie Chaplin learned their knockabout art as members of Fred Karno's sketch troupe.

1897_05_24 GREENWICH (Morton's). ACCIDENT DURING MARIONETTE DANCE

In Act II of *The Artist's Model* Greene Taylor, playing the role of Cripps, performed a "marionette dance" which, I presume, imitated a puppet on strings. He slipped and fell while performing this, breaking his kneecap. He was taken to the Seaman's Hospital in Greenwich and it was feared he would be out of action for some time. He was off work until returning as Sammy Carrot in *The World's Verdict* at Dudley on 23 August.

1897_07_06 RHYL (Pier Head). FATAL DIVE FROM PIER INTO SEA

Tommy Burns the high diver we met earlier (*see* 1893_08_07) was contracted to dive off Rhyl Pier several times throughout the summer season. With only 3d in his pocket, he had to ask for an advance to pay his fare to the resort. His first dive was his last: after "four gin and sodas" during the morning, he lost control during his dive and had to be fished out of the sea. He was dead. At only 30 years of age, he left a widow who, after a marriage of a mere nine months, was now destitute. One of Burns's would-be rescuers was Samuel Baume, another high diver whom we shall be seeing at 1899_03_25c.

174

1897_08_07 LONDON THE DANGEROUS PERFORMANCES ACT

In spite of protesting gymnasts the act was passed in Parliament although a concession was made in that the age limit for boys was reduced to 16 whilst that for girls remained at 18.

1.—The Children's Dangerous Performances Act, 1879, shall apply in the case of any male young person under the age of sixteen years and any female young person under the age of eighteen years in like manner as it applies in the case of a child under the age of fourteen years.

2.—(1) Except where an accident causing actual bodily harm occurs to any child or young person, no prosecution or other proceeding shall be instituted for an offence against the Children's Dangerous Performances Act, 1879, as amended by this Act, without the consent in writing of the chief officer of police of the police area in which the offence is committed.

1897_09_08 BIRMINGHAM (Theatre Royal). DAGGER ACCIDENT

[Olga Nethersole (1866-1951) made her debut at Brighton in 1887, making her mark in London the following year. Known for her emotional acting and inventing the 'soul kiss', she and her co-star in the play *Sapho* were arrested in America for "violating public decency".]

The company was that of Olga Nethersole, the play *Carmen*. "An accident happened which, though comparatively trivial in its results, might have been very serious." In the duel between Don José and Mendez, Mr Kingston playing José was struck on the arm by his opponent's dagger causing an injury. Taken to hospital as soon as the curtain fell he had the wound dressed, then returning, carried on with the performance, the audience, meanwhile, quite unaware that anything untoward had happened. I am baffled by this – how long was the audience kept waiting for his return? He must have been seen and treated immediately at the hospital, but even so, getting there and back, finding a cab or whatever, must have taken some time as well as the actual treatment. How long did the audience patiently wait while unaware of the reason?

1897_09_11 MACCLESFIELD (Theatre Royal). GUN ACCIDENT TO ACTOR-AUTHOR

The play *Vengeance* was a new musical comedy-drama by Arthur St John who was also playing the leading role. During a struggle in the last act St John was holding a gun by the barrel intending to use it as a club to strike his assailant. The gun unexpectedly went off, the charge entering St John's hand. The actor-author refusing to give way to an understudy, continued with blood flowing into hastily contrived bandages. By the time the wound was properly attended to, blood poisoning had set in putting his right hand out of action for many weeks.

1897_10_30 BELFAST (Empire). ACCIDENT TO GYMNAST

The two Brothers Almaio were performing at the Saturday matinee when one of them severed the back tendon of his right leg. His leg was put into plaster of Paris and he was expected to be out of action for some time. In his brother's absence the other one performed with success as a single turn. I do not know when the Brothers Almaio were back to full strength but they were on the Christmas bill at the Canterbury Music Hall. Their act was described as "neat and smart. Shapely fellows are they, nimble and sure in their balancing, and they present a pretty, clever and interesting act."

1897_11_01 CREWE (Lyceum). ACCIDENT TO LEAPING ACTRESS

The play was *Homeless*, the actress playing the heroine was Maud Camfield. In the scene of the burning building she jumped from the window as in the script but her supposed rescuer failed to catch her in his arms as planned. Falling to the stage, she landed heavily on her back, suffering an injury described as "very serious". There appeared to be a number of melodramas that featured burning buildings and heroines desperate to be rescued from upper windows in the scenery. It is no surprise that personal injury occurred and entire theatres caught fire, is it?

1898_01_10 NEWCASTLE (Empire). SCENERY FIRE DURING PLAY

The show was in full swing at 9.30pm the audience, seeing the stage manager run across the stage just as a lady artiste made her exit, realised the curtain was on fire. A fire hose was rolled out in double-quick time, rapidly a huge amount of water doused the flames, the drop scene was lowered and acting manager Mr Thornbarrow entered to announce there was no cause for alarm and, as all had witnessed, the theatre had ample fire-fighting means. However, even as he was speaking, clouds of smoke came billowing down over the top of the front cloth – the fire was not out, it had gained a greater hold than before. People started panicking, many making for the exits, causing damage to seating and windows, though the exodus did not get out of control. Thornbarrow, seizing the hose again, played huge amounts of water on the flames until the stage and everything was awash. At one juncture a stagehand fell over the active hose deflecting it towards the audience thus drenching the orchestra and the front rows of prime seats. The orchestral instruments were saturated as were the players, at that moment valiantly trying to wring the water from their sodden shirts. Also the stage was soaked so it would be impossible to perform further that night. Now that all was perceived to be safe the audience began singing *He's a jolly good fellow*. So what caused the fire? This theatre was one lit entirely by electricity, no limelight was in use. The lighting was provided by arc lamps, one of which shattered, throwing sparks on to the proscenium curtain. Electricity was clearly not yet totally safe.

1898_03_30 LEIPZIG Germany.　　　　　　　　WAGNERIAN TENOR WINS RECORD DAMAGES

This item contains the result of a prolonged court case. Max Alvary was a noted Wagnerian tenor who was celebrated throughout Europe and America. In March 1894, he had a fall during rehearsals on the stage at the Opera House in Mannheim. Claiming this accident was the fault of a careless stagehand, he sued for damages from the management of the Opera House. They declined all responsibility so Alvary took them to court. The result was in favour of the singer who was awarded £1200 (£130,000 today), at that time the largest sum ever recorded for a stage accident in Germany. He retired in 1897 having succumbed to cancer, and died in November 1898 aged 40.

176 1898_05_09 ST HELENS (Theatre Royal).　　　　　　　　　ACCIDENT TO ACTOR

The play was *Honour Bright*, the actor William Clayton. In the scene where the hero crosses a high rope in the roof garden, Clayton fell to the stage breaking an arm. It prevented his appearing for several weeks.

1898_05_31 SOUTHAMPTON (Palace).　　　　　　ACCIDENT TO LOTTIE HALLETT

Lottie Hallett, one of the most charming and talented of dancers, was dancing what was commonly called the 'twist' – and you thought it was invented in 1960 by Chubby Checker, didn't you? Clearly not the same, but a dance in *The Little Mascot* during which, injuring her knee, she fell to the stage. The curtain was lowered and Miss Hallett was taken to the Infirmary where it was ascertained that her kneecap was broken. She was detained in hospital for some weeks. I have not found anything about her return except a billing announcement for London Music Hall, Shoreditch in October 1898.

1898_08_30 EASTBOURNE (Royal).　　　　　　　　　　　　SWORD ACCIDENT

The play was *The Days of Cromwell* presented by G Howard Watson's Company. During Act I, Ironhand (Henry Balding) struck Mardyke's (Leslie Carter) sword from his hand with a stick. Through a flaw in the manner that Carter was holding the weapon, it flew from the stage towards the conductor in the orchestra pit, who nimbly dodged out of the way, which was fortunate because the sword went through the conductor's cane bottomed chair.

This is the twentieth sword accident I have recorded. Surprisingly far fewer than the accidents caused by guns which now number 78. And we have not quite finished yet . . .

1898_09_01 HASTINGS (Barnum & Bailey's Circus).   ACCIDENT TO BOB HANLON
[I have raised the issue of the Hanlon Troupes identities previously (*see* 1859_11_05) and included several entries regarding accidents to various Hanlons. This one is referred to as "popular little Bob Hanlon" – an aerialist since 1870 when, at the age of nine, he was the 'flyer' flung between the original William and Frederick Hanlon.]   While fitting up his apparatus in the big top he fell, splintering his hip and receiving a compound fracture of the thigh. As usual this was proclaimed to be "the first serious accident that the famous gymnast has met with during his long career."
On 15 October, *The Era* carried a major feature on the Barnum & Bailey Circus with a photo of the Bob Hanlon Troupe at that time comprising Robert (Little Bob) Hanlon, his sons Robert Jr and Julius, and Charles Chalon. The accompanying text implied Bob would soon be back after his recent accident.

1898_10_01 LONDON (Comedy).   FALL OF CHANDELIER DURING PLAY
In the play *The Topsy Turvy Hotel*, some comic business coming amiss caused a serious accident. An elaborate chandelier was an important feature in Acts II and III, and Albert Le Fre made comic mayhem by swinging on it like a trapeze artiste. On this night the chandelier gave way and crashed down with Le Fre. The stage was filled with performers and some were struck by the thing as it fell. Arthur Playfair received a cut at the back of his head; Maurice Farkoa got a cut on his forehead; Violet Lloyd suffered most as she was knocked out and had a cut above the eye. The two actors manfully carried on to the end of the play. Miss Lloyd was taken home where her wound was stitched, and while recovering over several days her role was taken by Alice Bitelle

1898_10_19 LIVERPOOL (Grand).   GUN ACCIDENT
The play was *Siberia*, the actress Mrs Ennis Lawson. In Act IV this unfortunate actress was shot in the face by a blank cartridge. Bleeding profusely from a wound over the eye, she carried on "with great pluck" until the curtain fell. A doctor attended, removing the wad and thereby assured the lady that the after effects were not serious.

1898_12_31 NEW YORK, USA (Broadway).   ACCIDENT TO LEW FIELDS
[Weber and Fields comprised Americans Joseph Weber (1867–1942) and Lewis Maurice Fields (1867–1941) who were known for their broad slapstick sketches. They first appeared together at the age of nine and steadily progressed to develop an enormously popular 'Dutch act' in which they portrayed German immigrants speaking in mangled English. They went on to produce their own revues, and leased theatres. It is said they were the inspiration for Neil Simon's *The Sunshine Boys*.]   While performing in a skit called *Cyranose*, Lew Fields, climbing up to a balcony and feeling a sudden faintness, released his grip and fell to the stage on his back. It was not a long drop but, in fact, Fields was suffering from flu but refused to stop working, and his fall was more serious than it first appeared.

130. *Joe Weber*

131. *Lew Fields*

177

1899_01_05 LIVERPOOL (Empire).   ACCIDENT TO EUGEN SANDOW

We have seen two previous accidents in the strong man's act (*see* 1893_03_24 *and* 1896_12_26) this is another one. A piano with a seat attached was placed on a platform. After playing a piece, the pianist started to sing a song to the apparent ire of Sandow who seized the piano and carried it and the pianist off the stage. To assist in the lifting of the piano there were two handles, one in the middle and the other at the bottom. On this night Sandow stumbled with his great load, the piano crashing to the stage and Harry Leigh, the pianist made up as Paderewski, falling on his face. Sandow escaped unharmed but Harry injured his head and face and was attended to by Dr Casey who was in the audience. It is not clear if Sandow procured a stand-in or cut the stunt. However, it is very clear what happened to poor old Harry.

In November 1899, Harry Leigh brought a case for damages. Sandow denied negligence. Harry had toured previously with Sandow in 1898 doing the same routine for many weeks without any problems. This new tour started on 2 January with Leigh paid £2 a week. While Sandow was performing stunts prior to the one in question Harry thought he was not at his usual ease or strength and asked if he was all right to do the piano stunt. Sandow's reply was a brusque affirmative. Then the accident happened as described. Sandow claimed there was a ruck in the carpet that he had tripped over, and that it was Leigh's job to make sure the carpet was flat. In court, further evidence was proffered which bordered on the bizarre. Witnesses – including two stagehands who affirmed the carpet was the property of the theatre and their responsibility – agreed that when laid down it was perfectly smooth and flat because of its own weight. William Davis, who worked for Sandow, confirmed the carpet had no creases but added his boss seemed to experience trouble with some earlier stunts and appeared exhausted prior to the piano trick.

Dr Ryan said he first attended Leigh on 31 January then on and off until August. His total bill was £8.7.0. He said he was surprised his patient had not remained at Liverpool for longer to recover, as it was unwise to travel so soon after the mishap. The singular explanation for this was that Dr Casey suggested he should be moved to an institution, and to Leigh's astonishment he had been taken to the local workhouse infirmary. There, his watch and money were taken from him, and he was made to dress in pauper's uniform. The judge was astounded at this statement but Leigh's advocate said that this was done at the behest of Sandow. After two weeks, Leigh was able to leave and return to London where he was under the care of Dr Ryan for several months. Dr Kempston, examining the plaintiff in August, declared he was suffering nervous debility – the after effects of shock and concussion of the brain – and would not be fully recovered for six to 12 months. The defendant's doctor said Leigh knew the risks he was taking as he had done the stunt many times previously, it was his job to check the state of the carpet. Leigh stated that though he often did see the carpet was straight it was not, in fact, part of his duty to do so. Leigh was awarded £125 damages with costs.

In March 1900, Sandow appealed, and the judge here agreed that "there was not a tittle of evidence that the accident was caused by any negligence on the part of Sandow". If Leigh could prove that Sandow had been physically unfit to carry out the stunt, and Leigh had been compelled to take part, then the claim would have succeeded, but there was no such proof and therefore the former judgment must be set aside and judgment entered for Sandow with costs. There were public comments that a jury's decision was pointless if law lords could subsequently turn it over, and there was general sympathy for poor old Harry who, receiving no compensation, also had to pay his opponent's costs.

1899_01_11 LONDON (Princess's). ACCIDENT TO 'STUNT' DANCERS

It was not generally known that often in stage dramas when a hazardous scene was necessary, instead of the star straight actors risking injury, stunt doubles – usually acrobatic pantomimists – were employed as stunt men just as in film work today. In the production of *The Crystal Globe*, the leading characters – stars Lena Ashwell and Oswald Yorke – had to jump out of a blazing building. The reader will have observed there was a predilection for plays with either train crashes or burning buildings, both types of accident that were rife in everyday life. To spare the actors, Lynn & Collingwood a married couple of eccentric dancers were employed simply for the leap. On this night, the mattress on to which they leapt had not been put in place. As the distance was some 20ft they were both injured, especially Mrs Lynn who, damaging her spine and still suffering the effects a year later, meant they could not present their dancing *Legmania* act as they were wont to do.

The couple sued the lessees of the theatre in January 1900. The lessees Arthur and Gilmer although not contesting liability, challenged the amount of damages demanded. They had already paid £200 into the court, but when the case was heard the couple were awarded £410. 5. 0.

1899_01_18 COLCHESTER (Royal). ACCIDENT DURING *WHEN LONDON SLEEPS*

As in the play in the previous entry, one of scenes in this melodrama featured a burning building from which the heroine (again played by a stunt double) escapes. This lady with a child on her back, after climbing out of a skylight, walks her way across 'telephone wires' to another house. When halfway across, the cable suddenly sagged, precipitating actress and child on to the stage some 10ft below, bringing down a portion of scenery with them. Both were hurt and the curtain lowered. The floor where one of the cable ends was anchored was not strong enough to hold the fastening, probably through age or rot. A doctor attended, but the play was able to carry on because the injury was to the double, not the leading actress.

1899_02_07 BOSCOMBE (Grand). ACCIDENT TO H A SAINTSBURY

132. *H A Saintsbury*

[Harry Arthur Saintsbury (1869–1939) son of Frederic Saintsbury, an official at the Bank of England, began his working life as a clerk there. His stage debut was in 1887 as a super. His first leading part was Captain Temple on a tour of *Human Nature*. He was soon recognised as the perfect leading man in romantic costume dramas and was the author of several successful plays. However, he is chiefly remembered for the role of Sherlock Holmes which he first played in 1903, then 1400 times up to 1921. He is also known for casting the 14-year-old Charlie Chaplin in the role of Billy the pageboy.]

The well known actor was appearing in his own play *The Three Musketeers* in the role of D'Artagnan. On this night, dismounting from his horse, he stumbled and fell on his back on the stage. He made every effort to continue but, overcome with fainting, was led from the stage. He had sprained his shoulder and was obliged to wear his arm in a sling. When the accident happened Richard Hoodless, having already appeared in his role as Athos hurriedly changed, taking up Saintsbury's part until the end of the play. So presumably the audience was now watching *The Two Musketeers*.

1899_02_15 DERBY (Palace).   ACCIDENT TO PANTOMIME 'DONKEY'

The pantomime was *Aladdin* with Mr Stoneham in the role of the Wonderful Donkey. During the course of the action he collided with Mr Wilton playing the Emperor, as a result of which Stoneham, losing his balance, fell into the orchestra pit where he sprawled insensible. Evidently badly injured he was carried to his dressing room and medical assistance summoned. It is not clear if he was still in his donkey 'skin' when carried out.

1899_03_25c CHEMNITZ, Germany.   FATAL DIVE OF HIGH DIVER

[The venue was a circus building, the performer was Samuel Baume the son of W H Baume a well-known confectioner in Halifax. Baume, said to hail from Bradford, had been a swimming teacher at a public baths in London, then for three years appearing daily at Westminster Aquarium under the name of Professor Monte Cristo. It seems there were three high divers employed at the time, Baume, Ben Fuller and Annie Luker. From the very roof these three dived 90ft into a tank of water. Fuller's stunt was to drop feet first but suddenly became less of an attraction when another performer did the same thing diving head first. Determined to top the newcomer, Fuller unofficially ascended to the highest point of the new Tower Bridge and dived into the Thames. He never surfaced and the boatman waiting to haul him out suddenly disappeared. Fuller's body was fished from Limehouse Basin some months later. The manager of the Aquarium praised Miss Luker who had been at that venue for five years, while expressing doubt about some of the others because of the propensity of taking drink. He had never had an accident at his venue but had sometimes stopped a performer if he thought him 'unsteady'. Charles Peart was paid off after a week on those grounds and later met his death performing in Australia (*see* 1896_05_07). We have already noted Tommy Burns (*see* 1893_08_07 *and* 1897_07_06).]

So we return to Samuel Baume (37) who was presenting a dive he called the *Death Leap*. Dressed in gymnast tights, he donned some loose clothing then was hauled up to the diving platform 60ft above the water tank where an assistant awaited. Baume climbed into a sack which was then tied at the top. The stunt was to dive into the water, escape from the sack, divest himself of clothing and reappear in his tights. He duly rolled off, descending into the water "as straight as an arrow". Almost immediately the empty sack appeared, followed by the loose clothing which was fished out with boat hooks. The audience biting its collective nails, the atmosphere was tense. Like the famous escapologist Houdini, Baume liked to hold his breath as long as possible before reappearing which was, of course, a theatrical trick to build suspense. His head and upper body appeared then disappeared again. It was now four minutes since he entered the water in the sack . . . another minute passed . . . then another. The attendants with boat hooks reappeared and the inert body of Professor Monte Cristo was hauled out.

1899_04_17 CHESTER (Theatre).   SWORD ACCIDENT IN LADIES DUEL

The play was *A Life's Revenge* by Marie Dagmar's Company. Act II closed with a duel of buttonless foils between Princess Vanda (Dagmar) and Marcia Vittoria (Kathleen Eckart). Miss Eckart failed to parry a thrust and Miss Dagmar's foil penetrated her cheek striking her teeth. Blood spurted out covering Miss Eckart but she pluckily continued the "fight for over five minutes". She was attended by Dr Clarke and progress was favourable.

1899_05_03 LONDON (Alexandra Palace).   ACCIDENT TO THE 'AMERICAN BLONDIN'

[James Hardy, a Canadian high wire performer was, at 21 years of age, the youngest person to make several crossings of the Niagara Falls on a wire, his performances being the last tightrope walking displays permitted at the Falls until Nik Wallenda in 2012. Still only 25, Hardy had been working in the UK for some time after being brought to perform at New Brighton in 1897. Remarkable for his grace, ease and daring, he had emulated the late Blondin by crossing chasms, whilst on indoor performances such as Alexandra Palace, he worked at a height of 100ft without using a balancing pole.]   On this night he concluded his performance with a dive into the net below. However, the spring of the net bounced him up again to a great height, then falling down again he crashed into the orchestra stalls injuring his head, body and breaking a leg so seriously as to put him out of action for the foreseeable future. Hardy wrote to the press to contradict the above version of the accident, stating he did not 'rebound' but went clean through the net "as if it were but tissue paper". He was at a loss to explain why it gave way as it was "tested to stand a strain equal to that of an elephant falling into it". A benefit concert was arranged for 6 July. In fact, Hardy was out of action for a shorter time than feared returning to Alexandra Palace on 12 August.

1899_06_12 MANCHESTER (Metropole).   ACCIDENT TO ROY REDGRAVE

[Roy Redgrave (1873–1922), born George Ellsworthy Redgrave, was the founder of the famous Redgrave acting dynasty. In 1894, he married actress Judith Kyrle who is, presumably, the Mrs Redgrave at the time of the following accident. Redgrave spent most of his acting career in Australia. He also made ten silent films and had a complicated love life.]

181

The company was that of Mr & Mrs Roy Redgrave, the play *Robert Macaire* with Redgrave in the hero role. During Act I there was a duel scene with Prince Varsia (Walter Beaumont) in which the latter was supposed to be severely wounded. Instead Redgrave received a cut on the hand and the curtain was lowered. Medical attention, arriving forthwith, discovered Redgrave had an almost severed finger. Despite great pain Redgrave pluckily continued to play his role with his arm in a sling. Harry Glenney took over for the rest of the week.

133. *Roy Redgrave*

1899_08_07 CROYDON (New Theatre Royal).   SCENERY ACCIDENT

The company was that of Grahame & Battersby, the play *The Power & the Glory*. Act III featured a monument around which was a platform 18in wide with a railing 3ft high. During a struggle between hero (H C Ward) and heroine (Octavia Kenmore) the whole scenic edifice fell forward, pulling up the stage boards where it was braced. The two players were thrown down on to the stage, Ward chivalrously trying to protect Miss Kenmore. The latter, escaping with a few bruises, was able to carry on with her part, whereas Ward injured his nose and eyes as well as suffering severe shock. Ward was confined to his bed for the rest of the run and the cast rearranged to cover his absence.

134. *Octavia Kenmore*

1899_09_22 CHATTANOOGA, USA (Opera House).   DELIBERATE ONSTAGE MURDER

This entry is definitely not an accident, but probably the most sensational event in the book – an onstage murder in front of the entire audience. The play was called *Mr Plaster of Paris* given by a touring company that had only been on the road for three weeks. The manager and leading man of the company was Frank Leiden, the leading lady was Julia James whose husband Fred was also in the company. Mrs James acted under the name of Julia Morrison. During Act II Miss Morrison, drawing out a pistol, shot Leiden in the heart. Leiden immediately fell to the floor and Miss Morrison shot him again. She then put the barrel of the gun against his head and shot him a third time. The audience gaped but assumed this was all part of the action of the play until one of the actors came on and asked if there was a doctor in the house. A man on the front row asked if it was an accident to which the actor delivered what must have been the most thrilling line he said in his entire career – 'No, it is murder.'

135. *An onstage murder*

182

Panic followed, police arrived, Miss Morrison was arrested. At the coroner's inquest the accused claimed that Leiden had insulted her and made improper proposals to her. The company to a man (except Mr James) backed its chief, it was clear that Miss Morrison was not up to the job and Leiden had quarrelled with her extensively. The last straw seems to have been that Leiden was going to sack her when the show reached Atlanta and had told her so that day. This developed into a screaming bout with his leading lady slapping his face. Members of the company said Mr James should also be arrested, claiming that he put her up to the deed.

The murder trial caused a country-wide sensation with newspapers taking sides, many pushing the honour of Southern ladies, accusing Leiden of groping up the actress's dress. Miss Morrison's defence tried to make much from the fact that she had suffered a blow to her head in her youth and from time to time suffered blackouts. But she was acquitted mainly because it was beyond conceiving that a Southern lady could be anything other than innocent. She had been insulted by Leiden and was entitled to defend her honour.

However, after the trial Miss Morrison made a few unwise public remarks concerning letters written by Leiden's sister that were considered arrogant and not in keeping with the image of an 'innocent murderer'. She then embarked on a lecture tour called *The Other Side of Stage Life* warning young ladies of the perils of taking to the stage as a profession, and the danger of few women surviving with their morals untarnished. A year after the trial, Miss Morrison (ie Mrs James) filed for divorce from her husband, and after an incident with a married Professor Silver – who was probably a stage hypnotist – disappeared from theatrical history.

1899_10_04 LONDON (Empire).   FATAL ACCIDENT TO ACROBAT

Comedy acrobats the Kronemann Brothers, Kristian and Edward, performed a stunt where one held his arm outstretched and the other leapt up to land on it in a standing position. On this night, Kristian (36) the jumping brother stumbled from the arm and fell with his head against his brother's shoulder. There was so little to suggest it was anything other than a fluffed trick, and the curtain fell to great applause as though it was the normal end of the act. Backstage, however, it was apparent that Kristian had been injured in face, shoulder and side. He was taken to Charing Cross Hospital where he died four days later. The post mortem showed he had crushed his spine causing asphyxia. The deceased left a widow and two children.

1899_10_12 SUTTON-IN-ASHFIELD (Town Hall).   ACCIDENT TO ACTOR AND CHILD

The company was Gilbert's English Opera Company, the play was *The Bohemian Girl*. Mr K Campbell playing the character Devilshoof, was, with child in arms, supposedly destroying a bridge. In fact, the bridge supports collapsed, precipitating actor and child on to the stage below. There was some concern from the audience as the child (the daughter of Mr F S Gilbert) had blood streaming down her face. The rumour went round that she had been shot, but she had actually received a cut over her eye. Dr Nesbitt was summoned to stitch up the wound, and the show carried on.

1899_10_21 SYDNEY, Australia.   ACCIDENT TO GYMNAST ON ROMAN RINGS

Mamie Jordan of the Flying Jordans was performing a dislocation feat on the Roman Rings. In this stunt the artiste throws the body over while hanging from the rings, repeating it several times. Suddenly, letting go, she fell to the ring below having suffered a stabbing pain that caused her to lose her grip. Besides being very bruised and shaken she sustained a dislocated hip.

1899_11_25 NEW YORK, USA (Koster &Bial's).   ACCIDENT TO YOUNGEST CRAGG

136.

[The Cragg family of acrobats was one of the best and noted of the time. The father and founder of the troupe claimed to be the first to perform in evening wear rather than spangled tights, his new style then being widely copied. The troupe varied in personnel over time but at this period comprised father and sons, a photograph showing a group of seven when they were reputed to be on $3000 a week. The finale of their act had four members lying on their backs passing the youngest boy with their feet from one to another until he landed in the arms of a man in the wings. A similar family act called the Julians can be seen on You Yube.]

On this night, which was the last of their season, the lad slipped from the last man's grasp and fell to the floor of the stage breaking his arm just above the elbow. The family had engagements lined up to follow.

1900_01_10 SHEFFIELD (Alexandra). ACCIDENT TO PANTOMIME COMEDIAN

T B Fayme, appearing with much success as Soft Sammy in the pantomime *Babes in the Wood*, on this night slipped and fell mid-stage, breaking his right leg. He was taken to the Royal Hospital and detained as an inpatient. As it would be impossible for the man to return during the season, an immediate substitute was necessary. Nellie Coleman playing the role of Silly Sally in the show came to the rescue offering her 'resting' husband Arthur Vendome who took over the role of Soft Sammy "in capital style".

1900_01_31 LEEDS (Grand). ACCIDENT TO PANTOMIME PRINCIPAL BOY

[The Five Rudge Sisters were British actresses and dancers from Birmingham. None of them appeared to team up and all had individual careers by changing their names. Letitia became Letty Lind, Sarah became Millie Hylton, Elizabeth appeared as Adelaide Astor, Fanny Rudge took the name Fanny Dango, and Lydia chose to be Lydia Flopp. I think the last two would have been wiser to remain Rudges. It appears that Letty and Millie had the most successful careers, the first being a skilled skirt dancer and Millie a male impersonator. Two of the others married well and Lydia Flopp made it to 86 not dying until 1963.]

137. *Millie Hylton*

Pantomime time always threw up a spate of accidents, usually to comedians who indulged in knockabout business. This accident was caused by a comedian, the sufferer the principal boy – who in those days was always a long legged female – in this case Millie Hylton. The scene was a comic cricket match with Mr Thompson and others miming the action, Thompson wielding a large property mallet as a bat. Millie Hylton, although not participating in the match, was alongside ignoring it, preparing something for the following scene. Thompson, swinging his mallet to off-drive the imaginary ball, clouted Millie square on the head knocking her unconscious. She had to be carried off the stage while a "telephonic message" was sent to Mr Brown the surgeon who, arriving post haste found the lady had a "nasty cut down the right ear" and she was conveyed to her residence.

1900_02_19 SOUTH SHIELDS (Algie's Circus). FATAL ACCIDENT TO TRAPEZE ARTISTE

On Monday, flying trapeze artiste Elba fell while practising his act. Although working over and falling into a safety net, it was soon observed by onlookers that he appeared to be injured. The net was lowered and the poor fellow assisted to his feet. It appeared that Elba was suffering from no more than slight shock but it was thought prudent to have him taken to the Ingham Infirmary where he was detained, dying from unnamed injuries at 2am on Wednesday.

1900_04_02 EDINBURGH (Empire). ANOTHER ACCIDENT IN *HUMANITY*

The falling staircase may have been spectacular in this everlasting tour but it seems to have caused many injuries. This time to the star John Lawson who, as we have seen, may have usually kept clear and let a stunt man double for him. He was caught by one of the rails, cut his face, and a doctor was called in to stitch his wound.

1900_04_24 NEW YORK, USA (Dewey).   FATAL ACCIDENT TO ACROBAT

The Florence Troupe of ground acrobats included Frank Nicholi who wanted to achieve a triple somersault from the shoulders of a bearer, turning to land on his feet on the stage. His colleagues tried to prevent him from attempting the feat but he was adamant. For reasons that are not clear, at the time he was wearing the costume of a woman, perhaps like the famous Lulu he performed in drag? He sprang from the shoulders of Edward Florence, made two-and-a-half revolutions and landed on his head. He lay senseless as the curtain was dropped. He was rushed to Belle Vue Hospital where it was found the sixth vertebra was fractured and the fragments were pressing on the spinal cord causing paralysis. Frank recovered consciousness around midnight and sent a loving telegram to his mother. The surgeons also telegraphed for permission to perform a difficult and delicate operation, indicating that Frank was neither a Florence family member nor of adult age. Laughing and chatting prior to the operation, he refused the use of ether, so the surgeons "applied eucaine, a new preparation, to deaden the pain." The broken section of spine was removed and Frank's "neck and back were enclosed in plaster of Paris and he was placed in a swinging jacket." The doctors said he would recover but obviously would be confined to hospital for several weeks. The doctors were wrong, poor Frank died within days.

When the news of the accident first appeared it was thought to refer to the more illustrious Florenz troupe – a family affair which numbered six in 1898 and comprised 12 men and two women when working with Barnum & Bailey's Circus in 1904. The Florenz family in various computations featured for decades into the 20th century. However, it appears poor Frank Nicholi was a member of the confusingly named Florence Troupe about which I have been able to find nothing apart from them being in New York vaudeville at this time.

185

1900_05_01 LONDON (Daly's).   ACCIDENT TO TOPSY SINDEN

138. *Topsy Sinden*

[Topsy Sinden (1877–1950), born Harriet Augusta Sinden, was a widely admired English dancer, actress and singer. She was prominent in the West End during the 1890s and into the Edwardian era playing in many musical comedies at Daly's and the Gaiety. Her career foundered in 1914 when she suffered another accident. She retired from the stage except for a fruitless comeback in 1927. Topsy, a distant cousin of Sir Donald Sinden, never married and died in Bournemouth in 1950.]

This vivacious principal dancer in *San Toy* had the misfortune of her string of beads breaking mid-dance; slipping on a bead while dancing resulted in a fall. The damage must have been quite severe because *The Era* reported some ten weeks later that Topsy was making good progress and hoped to shortly be back onstage. This was optimistic, in fact making an enthusiastically received reappearance on 30 October.

1900_05_03 LONDON (Shaftesbury).   ACCIDENT TO COMEDIAN IN FAT SUIT

Richard Carle the leading comedian in *An American Beauty* came up with the idea of wearing an inflatable rubber suit so he could run into, then bounce off, the proscenium. This must have been an early use of a 'fat suit'. On this night, trying the gag for the first time on his exit, in spite of warnings not to attempt it, he bumped into the wall and was flung back several yards, landing with his head

striking the stage. The result was all he could have desired – as he lay on his back the audience, howling with laughter, shouted for him to do it again. Even when other members of the cast came to drag him off, it was considered to be all part of the show, and laughter came in gales, with cries of encore. Suffering from concussion, he had to be taken to Charing Cross Hospital still in his ludicrous outfit. He was off for two weeks, returning presumably without his fat suit.

139. *Richard Carle*

1900_07_20c PARIS, France (Folies Bergère).   ACCIDENT TO TRICK CYCLIST

Mrs Kilpatrick and Mr Barber, partners in a cycling act, had a trick where Mrs K somersaulted from Mr B's shoulders to land on the stage. On this night she slightly injured her foot on landing and was compelled to be off for two weeks. Mr Barber carried on alone as a solo turn. This would not have warranted my attention, having skipped many a similar item but I am including it because of *The Era's* comment which gives a perspective on music hall conditions. "A great compliment for kindness and consideration must be paid to Monsieur Marchand, who, contrary to the custom of many Continental managers, paid the full salary at the close of the contract, and did not make the slightest remark to Mr Barber. Such generous conduct really deserves to be brought to the notice of artistes, and the profession at large will certainly be gratified to Monsieur Marchand for such considerate treatment."

1900_08_28 WIGAN (Theatre Royal).   ACCIDENT TO ACTRESS

It seems remarkable how many different plays of the time depended on a dramatic rescue from a blazing house. This was another such, rejoicing in the title *The Black Vampire*. In the rescue scene the hero is hanging upside down from the telegraph wires and the heroine jumps from an upper room to be caught in his arms. "The lady failed in her leap and fell to the stage." Although not injured, the summoned doctor found her suffering from severe shock. As pointed out above (*see 1899_01_11*) stunt doubles were often brought in to execute these sensational scenes. It seems a bit much to expect actors to undertake such hazards themselves. No Equity or Health & Safety in those days.

1900_09_08 BUENOS AIRES (Argentina).   ACCIDENT TO SAMPSON THE STRONG MAN

140.

[Charles A Sampson (1859–19??) was a pioneer performing strong man who originally appeared in a double act with colleague Franz Bienkowski known as Cyclops. He was actually a charlatan in that his open challenges were fake. Nobody could lift the heavy weight because it was filled with lead shot when they tried but while Sampson pattered the concealed shot was allowed to run out through a hole so when he came to lift it he could do it most impressively.]

"Sampson has met with a serious accident at Buenos Ayres. He writes as follows – 'I am writing these lines with dislocated and partly split bones in the arm. I had an accident three weeks ago at the Victoria Theatre here. The arm was not set right, and must, therefore, be operated on under chloroform to-morrow. Should anything happen to me, I wish all friends goodbye.'" *The Era* 1900_09_08.

1900_09_18 LONDON (Hippodrome). ACCIDENT INVOLVING EUGEN SANDOW

Yet another accident involving this strong man, and again he escaped scot free. It happened in the stunt where he bears the weight of a bridge while soldiers including one riding a horse pass over it. The horse stumbled and fell with the rider underneath. He was extricated and rushed to Charing Cross Hospital where it was found he had dislocated his thigh. (*See also* 1893_03_24, 1896_12_26 *and* 1899_01_05).

1900_09_25 SWINDON (Queen's). FATAL ACCIDENT TO HARRY DAY

Harry Day (23), an acrobat for most of his life, had been a member of the Leopolds' *Frivolity* Company for two years. On this night, he was doing a double somersault on a specially constructed sprung table similar to a billiard table but, only achieving 1½ turns landed on the back of his neck. He fell off the table insensible, and was taken in that condition to Swindon Victoria Hospital where he was found to have broken his neck and was paralysed. There was little hope of his survival, and he died five days later leaving a widow Christina and two little children (18 months, and 3 weeks only). A subscription fund was set up by Edward Carpenter proprietor of the Queen's Theatre who started it off with £3, John Leopold following with a similar amount.

1900_10_17 PARIS, France (Grenelle). KNIFE ACCIDENT

Actor Huberville played a wine merchant getting murdered. Dulac, a young enthusiastic actor played the assassin with such realism and vigour Huberville was nightly apprehensive. On this night when Dulac stabbed his victim with the property knife the blade did not shoot up into the handle as it was supposed to do, and Huberville, stabbed in the head, fell to the ground with a cry, blood gushing from his temple. The audience was enthused by the realism of the scene while Dulac stood aghast thinking he had murdered his colleague in earnest. Fortunately, the wound while a severe cut, was not deep and not vital. Huberville was off for a few days and Dulac was excused as it was a pure accident.

187

1900_11_13 RUSHDEN (Theatre). FATAL GUN ACCIDENT ACTOR

The venue, a portable theatre erected in Duck Street, opened on Friday. Prior to the play called *Driven from Home* on Tuesday, the actors were gathered backstage to rehearse a poaching scene where a gun was used. The manager Harry Farriss was showing Wilfred Dewsnap – who had to fire the weapon – the correct way to hold it as the hammer would not cock without being held by the thumb. As he handled the gun it suddenly went off, and actor Frederick Barge, standing very near, was shot in the leg shattering the bone beneath the knee. The players were horrified as they had assumed the gun was not loaded. Howard was rushed to hospital where it was found necessary to amputate the injured leg. Later in the day it was reported that the man had died. He was a widower aged 53.

The inquest revealed that John Dench (18), the property master, had been despatched to buy cartridges for the gun in Rushden. He had not been able to purchase blanks, but the shop boy said he could draw the bullets, however, Dench said he would do it himself. He bought loaded ones intending to remove the bullets, something he had done on previous occasions. Unfortunately, on this day, forgetting to do this very necessary act, the gun was loaded with a live cartridge. Under examination Dench said he had loaded the gun with a live cartridge on a previous occasion at Skegness. The coroner, expressing surprise at that, asked if the bullet had not hit the scenery. Farriss explained the gun was aimed at the ground and even if a live shot was used it would disappear into the earth as they did not have a wooden stage. He also said that the gun was carried in Scene One by Dewsnap who always insisted it was unloaded, and Farriss himself loaded it before using it in Scene Two. In the light of this procedure it seems inexplicable why Dench should have loaded the gun at all whether blank or live. No doubt Dench was two sandwiches short of a picnic and the coroner had great difficulty in getting a coherent tale from him as he tried to explain culpable negligence and criminal responsibility. The jury was lenient and Dench was not charged, but reprimanded over his carelessness at loading the gun. Farriss was recommended to buy the cartridges himself and keep them in his possession in future, which he undertook so to do. Very sensible, but not much good to Mr Barge.

1900_11_20c NEW YORK, USA.   ACCIDENT TO E H SOTHERN

[Edward Hugh Sothern (1859–1933) always billed as E H Sothern, was an American actor who specialized in dashing, romantic leading roles and Shakespeare. His first appearance was in 1879 in the USA playing a supporting part to his father E A Sothern the English actor. Making his London debut in 1881, he toured with Charles Wyndham's Company before returning to the USA in 1883 to become the leading man at the Lyceum, New York for 12 years. Sothern dreamed of mounting a spectacular and precise production of *Hamlet*.]

188

141.

Sothern accomplished his long-held ambition to play Hamlet but in the first week during the fight with Laertes the latter's sword penetrated Sothern's big toe. It was a costly accident as blood poisoning and a broken bone caused the loss of over a month's work and $90,000 in receipts. He resumed his tour on Christmas Eve but it seems his production was blighted by ill fate as the sets and costumes were destroyed by a fire in January 1901. Although the theatre was full of people watching the production of *Hamlet*, Sothern, interrupting the second scene of the play, calmly requested the members of the audience to carefully make their way to the exits.

1900_12_01 LONDON (West London).   ACCIDENT TO GEORGE MONTFORD

"Mr Geo Montford, who has been playing Gordon Allington in *The Shadow of Night* for some time, met with an unfortunate accident on Saturday. He dislocated his knee in the situation where Gordon is escaping by means of a windmill in the second act. He will be unable to move for some time. Fortunately, Mr Frank E Petley (the original Gordon Allington) was able to take up the part, and play at the West London on Monday. He will play it all this week." *The Stage* 1900_12_06.

1900_12_27 LONDON (Camden).   ACCIDENT TO PANTOMIME 'HORSE'

One of the Val Brothers, playing a pony in a skin, was cavorting wildly about. As a result he tripped on the footlights wire, tumbling into the orchestra pit causing "confusion" amongst the musicians. He was gathered up and passed through the understage door to the dressing rooms. The report did not clarify whether he was still garbed as a pony.

Victorian pantomimes were full of actors in animal skins, the doyen being Charles Lauri Jr who ran a whole gamut of characters (*see* 1882_01_05). The familiar two-man panto horse was made popular by the acrobatic duo the Griffiths brothers who introduced it in 1885.

1900_11_03c PARIS, France (Hippodrome).

142

TRAINER ATTACKED BY LION

The lions were presented by George Marck and Madame d'Orsy. The climax of the act was for the lions in turn to leap through a blazing hoop. One beast was reluctant so Marck went to punish the lioness with his whip. Naturally not liking this she attacked the man, drawing blood, pinning him against the side of the cage and biting his arm. Spectators screamed, Madame d'Orsy shot off blanks from revolvers, and an attendant with a red hot pitchfork drove the animal back into her proper cage. Marck escaped lightly. A man who thinks he can tame a lion is very foolish.

*

[The crude exhibitions where the "brute tamer" went into the animals living cage to demonstrate his power over them was reliant on forcing the animals with flaming torches, iron bars, pitchforks and the lot. There was no logical attempt at training wild animals until Carl Hagenbeck (1844–1913) came along. An animal collector and dealer, he founded the first zoo without bars where animals could roam in large areas constrained only by moats. As far as circuses were concerned, he brought in training methods utilising the animals' natural movements, eschewing force, and giving rewards. In 1888, he introduced the circular cage to the circus ring thus creating a much larger area for the animals to work in. Many people today still think it is cruel to train animals to perform and that it cannot be done humanely and without cruelty. They do not seem to realise that a lion is far more formidable than a mere human being, and a lion's jaw and claw far more powerful than anything a trainer can wield. Should a lion be ill-used, it would not hesitate to take advantage of the trainer's vulnerability. Today, the trainer is showing his animals for your appreciation, he is not boasting of his power over them.]

FLAMING FROCKS

Of all ways of dying I think being burned to death must be the grimmest, and for it to happen in public view when you appear happy and smiling is particularly gruesome. Many years ago I learned of Postman's Park – a short distance north of St Paul's cathedral – which houses the Memorial to Heroic Self Sacrifice commemorating ordinary people who, dying while saving the lives of others, might otherwise be forgotten. One of the tablets reads as follows:

> SARAH SMITH, PANTOMIME ARTISTE. AT PRINCE'S THEATRE DIED OF TERRIBLE INJURIES RECEIVED WHEN ATTEMPTING IN HER INFLAMMABLE DRESS TO EXTINGUISH THE FLAMES WHICH HAD ENVELOPED HER COMPANION. JANUARY 24TH 1863.

It was not until I embarked on research for this current book that I came to realise that Sarah Smith was by no means unique, costumes of young women and children catching fire being almost commonplace. Stage gaslights with naked flames were the problem, especially those in the footlights. Thus most of these accidents are actually onstage in view of the public, though invariably it has to be somebody from the backstage crew who has to come to the rescue.

Herein you will find almost 150 examples including 46 fatalities (in **BOLD**).

1842_03_05c   Sheffield   James Dalton
In the play of *Le Perouse* there is a character of a chimpanzee. However, at Sheffield, either instead of or in addition to the chimpanzee, James Dalton was acting as a bear. On approaching a fire on the stage, the foot of his costume, made from canvas and hemp, caught fire and he was instantly in flames. Buckets of water were thrown all over the poor chap before they could wrench the costume from him. He was taken into the greenroom as if already dead. He was transferred to the Infirmary, where he was found to be alive but in a very dangerous state. He lingered in the direst agony and died on 18 March.

1842_04_15c	Liverpool	Unnamed child	severely injured
1842_07_20c	Frankfurt	Miss Dannecker	severely injured
1843_03_18	Lyons	unnamed dancer	severely injured
1844_08_28	Dereham	Mr Dillon	severely injured
1844_12_14	**London**	**Clara Webster**	

At Drury Lane Theatre, Clara Webster, one of the leading dancers, was appearing on Saturday night as Zulica the royal slave in a ballet called *Revolt of the Harem*. In the scene where the ladies of the harem are bathing, a portion of the stage was sunk where fountains and waves were placed. To illuminate these, gas jets were placed accordingly. The light drapery of Miss Webster's dress was caught by a flame from a gas jet instantly enveloping her entire person in flames. The reaction of the audience to this visual frightful accident was wholesale consternation, and screams from the ladies in the boxes, while the unfortunate young dancer herself, uttering heart-rending cries, dashed about the stage, in one instance clutching at a fellow dancer who luckily pushed her away as her dress momentarily caught fire too, but was instantly snuffed out. Miss Webster finally did what should have been the first thing to do, she rushed into the wings, was caught by Daniel Coyle a stage hand who throwing her to the ground, rolled himself over her. Another stage hand threw a coat over her. Coyle suffered burns to his hands and face.

Dr Marsden was in the audience and, rushing backstage, offered his expertise which appears to have been applications of spirits of wine, water, flour etc. Coyle was taken to King's College Hospital, Miss Webster was taken to her lodgings where the landlady looked after her.

143.

Miss Webster was much blistered round the face, eye-lashes and eye-brows burnt off, though the hair on her head was untouched. The worst damage was done to her lower extremities, hips and hands. Dr Liston ministered to her and visited throughout Sunday. On Monday, fearing a decline, as she appeared much worse than earlier in the day, he stayed with the girl from 10pm to midnight. He warned the Webster family and friends that nothing more could be done and there was no hope of saving the patient's life. He returned at 4am on Tuesday morning to find that Clara "had breathed her last a quarter of an hour previously".

This was by no means the first example of stage costumes catching fire – I have mentioned five previous ones already – but because it took place at the top theatre in the country, and involved a dancer expected to be a British international ballet star, the event caused more interest than before. The coroner had been introduced to a chemist who claimed he had a non-flammable solution that could be used to treat clothing. In court he demonstrated with a candle and a piece of treated cloth that not even a scorch mark appeared. People wrote to the newspapers:

"Accidents by Fire.—A correspondent of The Times newspaper, referring to the late melancholy accident which befell the unfortunate Clara Webster, says, The alarming frequency of such casualties, the more especially to young children, as well as adults, might be in some measure obviated by the simple means of dissolving an ounce or two of alum in the last water muslins, linens, etc, are rinsed in. This very simple method, if generally known and adopted, would render such light wares incombustible, or nearly so, and be the means of preventing numberless accidents we daily hear and read of." Bell's Life in London and Sporting Chronicle 1844_12_22.

"We have already called the attention of our readers to several preparations for rendering clothes anti-inflammable, and we now call their attention to an invention of Mr J Baker, who has prepared a solution which may either be mixed with starch, or supplied without starch to linen, lace, muslin, etc. It neither injures the texture nor the colours of the fabrics, and is so efficacious that things which have been wetted with it when dry will not flame even when submitted to the fiercest fire." Northampton Mercury 1845_01_11.

It is pleasing to see so much concern about these dreadful accidents caused to children and young dancers and that such simple remedies were available to prevent them in future. Reader, read on!

1845_02_09	Valenciennes	unnamed actress	unharmed
1845_10_25c	Madrid	Mdlle Steven	unharmed
1846_03_22c	Madrid	Madame Saqui	unharmed
1846_10_28	London	Madame Albertazzi	unharmed (153A.)
1847_03_18	London	unnamed child	unharmed
1848_03_18	London	Mdlle Julien	injured

144.

1849_02_25c	Paris	Mdlle Maria (above)	unharmed
1849_12_12	London	Susan Roberts	severely injured
1851_01_01C	**New York**	**Miss Leham**	

Actress Adele Lehman was mid-show at Niblo's Garden Theatre when her dress caught fire, and she was removed from the stage in a state of great suffering. She is said to have uttered these words on her death bed: "I feel that I am going: how lucky that my sister Mathilde was ill on that evening, and I played in her stead; she would have left a husband and children to mourn her loss; I, who am to die in her place. I am single!"

1852_10_12	St Louis	Madane Baron	severely injured
1853_02_23	Liverpool	Miss Appleby (a child)	severely injured
1853_06_20c	New York	unnamed dancer	severely injured
1854_06_20	Plymouth	Mrs Hudson Kirby	injured

1854_07_25	Belfast	Georgina Smithson	injured
1855_11_20	**Plymouth**	**Mdlle Julie**	

Mdlle Julie (18), was appearing at the Theatre Royal in the ballet *The Good Woman of the Wood* when her dress accidentally caught fire and the tarlatan material, being of a light combustible character, meant she was immediately enveloped in flames. In her panic she ran to the side of the stage where Hooper, a tall powerful man, seized hold of her. This was a correct thing to do but the girl in her frenzy pushed him away, and foolishly ran right across the stage again to the other side where Finch took hold of her, but again for some insane reason she pushed him away, and he, already badly burned trying to assist, was obliged to let her go. Mr Newcombe the manager, seeing the accident from front of house, ran round and finally managing to grab the girl, threw her to the ground so the flames were then able to be extinguished.

Two surgeons were sent for, arriving within minutes, and took her to her lodgings where every facility of medical aid was applied. The wounds were very serious and her life in jeopardy. She had played at Exeter, and after Plymouth was engaged for Dublin which now, of course, was impossible. She was the principal means of supporting a mother and a younger brother who were in anxious constant attendance. Although a surgeon proclaimed that the burns were not too serious, the unfortunate girl died five days later, the shock to her system being more than she could survive. A subscription list was opened for the support of her dependents.

It is unbelievable to learn that Morris, the landlord of the house where she lodged, would not let her have hot water, and she had to obtain it from a kind neighbour. Medicines brought to the house were not sent up, and anybody calling to enquire was simply told to go up and see, leaving them to grope their way upstairs in the dark. Mr Newcombe sent the landlord a sovereign for the rent but the rogue sent it back saying the rent had now gone up by 3/- a week and the patient would not be allowed to stay there if that was not paid.

On Julie's death, her mother wanted the body sent to London for burial, Mr Newcombe going to the station and undertakers to make all the arrangements. The night before, Newcombe went to Morris to square all the arrangements and left thinking all details were finalised.

When the undertaker's men arrived to collect the body, Morris would not allow them in the house unless a payment of 11 guineas was made. It was necessary to get the assistance of the Magisterial and Board of Health authorities before the unfeeling fellow would release the body. Totally unbelievable!

Following on from the well publicised death of Mdlle Julia at Plymouth, the public concern about the dangers of naked flames and flimsy dresses started growing. Up to this point, as we have seen, there had been many previous examples but this particular one caused more attention – perhaps because of the dastardly way Morris treated the poor victim.

Letters to the press deploring the situation of the poor ballet girls who were nightly placed in danger, came with various suggestions of dealing with the problem: 'Humanity' from Bristol said that there should be a penalty for managements who did not have a blanket suspended in the wings at both sides of the stage. Backstage there were few workers with coats on, and those that had needed to have quick wits to snatch them off to wrap around a fire-girt dancer. Blankets ready to hand would solve the problem. Better would be blankets soaked in water and having efficient guards over the footlights!

1856_01_10c   Toronto   Miss Cook, a child
Miss Cook, the youngest daughter of Mr T Cook, the musical director of the orchestra, was playing a fairy in *The Enchanted Isle*. Miss Cook, who was but a child – a comely little girl and quite a favourite – brushed against a stove set in the wings, the lightweight fabric of her skirt catching fire. She was quickly enveloped in flames and all attempts to save her life proved fruitless. She was taken to the ladies dressing room, and in great suffering lingered until morning when her young life became extinct.

1856_01_20   London   Mdlle Leinstiff
Mdlle Leinstiff was appearing in *Aladdin; or the Wonderful Lamp* at the Brunswick Theatre. As she moved forward from the wings to make her entrance, she came too near a light and her thin gauze dress caught fire. Instantly all aflame she panicked, running to and fro. There was nobody at one side of the stage so the flames had taken a good hold before anybody could rush to help at the other. Dreadfully burnt, she was taken to her own residence where medical aid awaited. All proved ineffectual and she died the following day. It was exactly two months after the furore of Mdlle Julie. It would appear nobody was taking much notice of the advice in the newspapers about fire-proofing solutions.

1856_02_04c	Paris	Mdlle Lefebre	unharmed
1856_04_10c	New York	Mdlle Genet	injured
1856_09_20c	Moscow	Mdlle Cerito	injured
1857_01_05	London	unnamed child	unharmed
1858_04_25	Leicester	Mr Tadman	severely injured

1858_11_06   Portsmouth   Emma Glover aka Childs
Emma Glover, aka Childs, was yet another actress who had not learned to keep clear of the footlights. Her dress caught fire causing severe burns. She was removed to hospital but died of her injuries three weeks later.

1858_12_27   London   Emily Ann Harlow, a child
Yet another case of a ballet dancer's costume catching fire, but this was more tragic than most as it happened in a Penny Theatre called the Britannia Music Hall at Shadwell and the victim was Emily Anne Harlow a little girl of nine years. It took many willing hands some time to extinguish the blaze because there was no fire-fighting equipment in this unlicensed venue. The charred and blackened child was taken to the London Hospital where she died.

1859_01_10	Birmingham	Miss Munro	unharmed

1859_01_12   London   Annie Fowler
Miss Fowler the popular Columbine at the Grecian Theatre was acting in the pantomime *Guy Fawkes* when her dress caught fire. She was rushed to hospital but she died there a few days later.

1859_01_26   Macon, USA   Little Mary Marsh

Mary Eliza Guerineau, a gifted child actress known professionally as Little Mary Marsh, was performing in the play *Naiad Queen*, when her costume caught fire from the footlights. She was soon engulfed in flames and a gentleman from the audience, rushing on to the stage, enveloped her in his cloak, but the flames were only extinguished after her entire body was badly burned. She was taken to her hotel and died a few hours into the next day.

145. *Little Mary Marsh*

image: Theatrical Portrait Prints (Visual Works) of Women (TCS 45). Harvard Theatre Collection, Houghton Library, Harvard University

1859_06_15c   Chard   Julia Newton   injured

1860_02_18c   New York   Miss Louisette

A native New Yorker, Mrs Josephine Herskell (22) under the stage name of Louisette was a novice tightrope walker performing at the Volks Theatre on the Bowery. Having successfully concluded her act, she jumped down on to the stage but her dress coming into contact with the footlights enveloped her in flames in an instant. Her German husband, a musician in the orchestra pit, and some others leapt to her aid but, in putting out the flames, were burned all over hands and arms – not very jolly for a musician especially. Attended by Dr Shepardson, Louisette was taken home, lingering in agony to 9am the next morning "when death relieved her suffering."

146.

1860_02_24   Berlin   Miss Holke

The ballet girl in this case was called Miss Holke and she was working at the Berlin Opera. Her dress caught fire in the manner to which we are now accustomed, and she was taken off to hospital "dreadfully burned". She lingered the best part of three weeks before giving up the ghost.

1860_03_06	London	Laura Ennis	unharmed
1860_03_20	Paris	Madame Penco	unharmed
1860_04_15c	New York	Mdlle Fabbri	unharmed (153B.)
1861_01_16	Huddersfield	Miss Wright	unharmed
1861_02_05c	Caen	Madame Ugalde	unharmed

1861_08_05c New York Madame Molney

"Canterbury Hall: A fatal accident occurred on Wednesday night to Madame Molney, a *danseuse* engaged at this establishment. Her dress caught fire from having incautiously approached the footlights, and before the flames could be extinguished, she was so severely burnt that she died the following day." *The Era* 1861_08_25.

An article in the *Morning Chronicle* of 5 August 1861 drew attention to two recent domestic deaths whereby women had been burned to death by steel hoop crinolines catching fire. It also recalled that the poet Longfellow's wife died in this way, and the Princess Royal was injured. Oscar Wilde lost two half-sisters when their crinoline dresses caught fire at a ball. The article pointed out the many stage deaths caused by flimsy-costumed dancers coming into contact with gas flames, and said that the manager of our largest ballet company had been instructed to fireproof his dancers costumes but the ladies themselves had resisted on the grounds that the muslin would lose some of its lightness and aerial effect. Expounding at length on how many ladies had been injured and killed even in their own homes, it pointed out that Queen Victoria herself had ordered investigations into fireproofing material, and the recommended solutions were tungstate of soda, and sulphate of soda.

I, like the newspaper, find it incredible that, in spite of almost daily reports of burning clothing, so little prevention was taken. One would think that women who followed even the daftest of fashions would ensure that they were not actually dangerous.

1861_08_14c	Milan (Italy)	Mdlle Karsch	severely injured

1861_09_02	Leicester	Master Stevens	severely injured

Another drastic costume accident took place at a Leicester circus when Master Stevens (8), enacting the part of a man-monkey, climbed a rope that was set too near the circus lighting which would have been a naked flame in those days. His padded costume caught fire and he dropped to the ring and, although rolled over and over by colleagues until the flames were extinguished, was badly injured. The circus was crowded with spectators, and "much excitement was manifested." Accidents to gymnastic children were the source of great concern, and added to the mounting pressure of legal sanctions against such entertainments

1861_09_03	Cambridge	Miss Haydon	unharmed

1861_09_14	**Philadelphia**	**Hannah Gale**	
		Ruth Gale	

Adeona Gale
Zelia Gale
Mary Herman,
Phoebe Norton,
Annie Phillips
Anna McBride.

Abbie Carr,	severely injured
Margaret Conaway,	severely injured
Kate Harrison,	severely injured
Thomas Bayard	severely injured
nameless young man	severely injured

This is the most awful example of a gas light setting fire to a costume and more horrific than anything that has gone before. The theatre had been newly refitted by a veteran actor-manager William Wheatley who arranged a lavish production of *The Tempest* with a dozen ballet dancers. Four of the dancers were the Gale sisters and while they were changing for the ballet in Act II, Zelia Gale stood on a chair to reach her dress and pass it down. Through this simple action devastation followed. The dress caught on the gas light and burst into flames, which immediately leapt to her underclothes. Her three

sisters rushed to Zelia's aid but, as we have learned by now, that was an unwise thing to do as the flames spread to the sisters' costumes. The four sisters were now screaming which brought colleagues from other dressing rooms who foolishly tried to put out the flames without any equipment or even attempting smothering in blankets, resulting in the entire ballet troupe in flames soaring up to the ceiling. Zelia Gale ran downstairs screaming for help and was met by Mr Bayard the stage manager who wrapped her up in a sheet of canvas. He got severely burned himself in doing this noble action, but in short order Zelia was despatched to hospital.

Meanwhile, up on the second floor several of the girls leapt through the windows into the street, adding folly to foolishness, but we can forgive a lack of sense in panicking young women turned into human torches. Hannah Gale was one of them and, already badly burnt, fell on the pavement bruising her head and back, adding to her injuries. Phoebe Norton inhaled the flames and was shockingly burned, Annie Nicholls was also badly burned but in her panic jumped from the flies on to the stage – a distance of 25ft – crashing through glass and mirrors laid to represent a lake. She was painfully lacerated by broken glass. Ruth and Adeona Gale were burned in the hands and breast. All the following were gravely injured by burns – Abbie Carr, Margaret Conaway, Kate Harrison, Thomas Bayard and a nameless young man who inhaled the fire and had bleeding lungs.

The confirmed dead from the tragedy were Mary Herman, Phoebe Norton, Annie Phillips, Anna McBride and the four Gale sisters – Hannah (22), Ruth, Adeona (19) and Zelia (17) who were four of the six children of Lieutenant Gale, an aeronaut who had died falling from a balloon many years before.

As had become usual after such a major tragedy, there were questions in the press why ballet costumes were not flame retardant. One such bluntly stated: "The mere saturation of the ballet dresses in a solution of tungstate of potassium is sufficient to render them as safe from the action of fire as though they were made of asbestos. Why were not these chemical precautions adopted in the case of the Continental Theatre at Philadelphia?" Why not indeed? I have asked myself that many times since recording the first example in 1837 and the fifty+ – yes, 57 – that have followed *up to now*. Alas, following this catastrophe which was reported worldwide, there are many examples still to come.

1861_11_10   London   Anna Leaver (domestic)

Mrs Anna Leaver (39) and her daughter, visitors from America, were staying at the Fulham home of Charles Mathews the popular comedian. The household was rent by screams from Mrs Leaver and she was found on the stairs with her dress ablaze. The fire was put out but not before the lady had suffered severe burns to lower parts of her body. A surgeon was called but she was past all human aid, dying a few hours later.

Draperies surrounding the mantelpiece of the fireplace were also on fire, and scorching evident on the stairs. It was deduced that Mrs Leaver had turned to look at herself in the mirror above the fireplace, not realising that the crinoline former of her dress was forcing it into the fire. As the flames flowed upwards they ignited the fireplace surround and she fled screaming down the stairs. Yet one more domestic death caused by crinoline. Mr and Mrs Mathews were away at the time and a telegraph sent to them.

1861_11_20c   Nice   Tristali Vetant   unharmed

During the opera starring Mdlle Tristali Vetant and Signor Ronconi, the diva was so near the footlights that her dress caught fire. Ronconi, singing alongside, actually swiftly crushed the flame between his hands without interrupting the aria. He was summoned three times before the curtain to receive the applause of the audience who had been astonished and delighted at his amazing self-possession. "A French chemist has discovered that the lightest lace or muslin may be made fireproof by a mixture of starch and carbonate of lime or Spanish chalk. It is strange that so simple a safeguard should be neglected."

1861_11_21   Bendigo   Miss Annette (a child)   unharmed

At the theatre in the Australian gold rush town of Bendigo, the last scene of the extravaganza *Fortunio* was under way when the gauze dress of little Miss Annette caught on a flame from coloured fire being burned at the wings. In an instant she was alight. Trotter, the property man, Mr Marsh and others in the wings rushed forward and threw her down and extinguished the flames. Miss Annette escaped all injury although uttering "Oh, Papa, save me." Unfortunately her rescuers were burnt about the hands. Mr Marsh came before the curtain with the rescued girl, who was but a child. It appears that Marsh, who was most likely in charge of the troupe of children, had lost a daughter in the same way some time previously, and after the rescue fainted from the shock.

1862_01_16   Liverpool   Fanny Julia Power

During a ballet scene at the Theatre Royal, a shriek was heard from the wings and a cry of "Fire!" Immediately a portion of the audience rose to head for the exits until stilled by the entrance of Mr Hart who assured them there was no danger and to keep their seats. The audience resettled, but backstage Fanny Julia Power (20) was fighting for her life. She had been standing in the wings stooping to look at her shoes, and the rear of her dress had caught fire from a sidelight in the wings. Swift action followed – the lights were extinguished, Fanny smothered in an overcoat, and her costume remnants removed. She was taken into the greenroom and attended by Dr Rogerson. She was burnt all over her upper body and taken home where she lingered some days before dying on the 30th of the month.

1862_03_10c   Florence   Miss Van Norden   unharmed

1862_11_15   Paris   Mdlle Livry

[Emma Livry, (1842–1863) born Jeanne Emma Emarot, was one of the last ballerinas of the Romantic era and a protégée of Marie Taglioni. She studied dancing under Madame Dominique and attended the Paris Opera School, making her debut at the age of sixteen. Her innate talent soon bringing her fame, she became a widely respected ballerina.]

At the Grand Opera House, during the rehearsals for *La Muette de Portici*, Mdlle Emma Livry who was to play the role of Fenella, raised her tutu to sit without crushing the fabric, her dress got too near a lamp at the side of the stage and caught fire. The blaze reached three times her height. In terror she ran across the stage where Muller the fireman was able to throw a cloak around her thus dousing the flames. Muller's hands were severely burnt, and Mdlle Livry was taken to her dressing room where two doctors dressed her burns which covered 40% of her body. Her stays were burned on to her though her face was unblemished. A decree in France issued in 1859 had stated all ballet dancers must wear skirts soused in a fireproofing solution. The manager of the Grand Opera House then revealed that he prevailed on his entire *corps de ballet* to wear fireproofed muslin and they all agreed except one – Mdlle Livry.

148.

At the end of February 1863, the artistes of Paris presented an address of congratulation to Mdlle Livry on her recovery from the effects of her terrible accident. But, alas, complications from her injuries proved fatal as she only survived eight months, dying on 26 July 1863 barely 21 years old. Some remaining scraps of her costume repose in the Opera Museum in Paris.

| 1862_12_07c | Bordeaux | Mdlle Lamoreaux | unharmed |
| 1862_12_27 | Brighton | unnamed dancer | unharmed |

| **1863_01_24** | **London** | **Sarah Smith** | |
| | | Anne Hunt | severely injured |

Sarah Smith (real name Gibson), barely 17 years old, was appearing as a ballet dancer in the pantomime *Riquet with the Tuft*. On Friday night, during one scene, the dancers were to twirl across the stage, which was illuminated by special-effect lighting, created by a mixture of chemicals in eight fire-pans placed on stands – four on either side of the stage. It was brushing against, or a spark from, one of these pans that ignited Miss Hunt's flimsy dress and immediately spread to Sarah Smith as she rushed to assist. It was a foolhardy gesture, the other girls more sensibly fleeing from the stage. As a result, two flaming girls were simultaneously running in panic around the stage.

Stage manager Robert Roxby seeing a person on fire run through the wings, seized hold of her clothes, tearing them all off, as much as he could, wrapping his Inverness cape round her, ultimately extinguishing the flames. This girl was Anne Hunt. Then, realising a second girl was ablaze, ran to her, taking off his under coat to extinguish the fire.

Both girls were immediately rushed to Middlesex Hospital where Miss Hunt, who was actually a 20-year-old married woman called Perkins, was found to be the lesser burned of the two. The injuries which Miss Smith had received being of a much more serious character, it was feared she would not survive the night. She lingered, "her appearance when lying at the hospital was most painful to behold, the features charred to positive blackness, being scarcely distinguishable", before expiring on Wednesday evening.

This is the event commemorated with a plaque at the Memorial to Heroic Self Sacrifice situated in Postman's Park in London (see opening remarks).

At the inquest, Mr Roxby, who appeared with his arm in a sling and burns over his arms and shoulders, said that the girls, ignoring shouts to get down on the floor, had dashed wildly about in a panic. He was asked what fire precautions there were, the coroner remarking that he understood that some theatres had wet blankets or rugs in both wings. Roxby agreed, adding: "I do think that it would be advisable to have damp cloths or rugs. In this case it would not have been of any avail. The difficulty I have always found is to catch the person who is on fire."

Since 1842 I have recorded 68 cases (including 24 deaths) of costumes catching fire, mainly from stage lighting, particularly footlights, ground rows and 'ladders' in the wings. These lights were naked gas jets. The only precautions to tackle future accidents were:

    Buckets of water in the wings at both sides of the stage

    Blankets (preferably soused in water) hanging in the wings

    Treating costumes with a non-flammable liquid to make them fireproof

The first two were seldom punctiliously observed and the third was unpopular with dancers themselves and rarely insisted on by managements.

There appears to have been little done in the way of having wire guards on the lights – which surely should have been mandatory on footlights. Such guards were in place over lights in the flies where there was a danger of backcloths and borders wafting into these, but not in the footlights. The unpopular Argand lamps in the footlights had glass chimneys but the light was not as bright.

From the above, it would seem that protecting scenery was considered more important than protecting people. True, opera singers and actresses occasionally suffered costume fires but mainly it happened to the dancers – usually called ballet dancers, danseuses or coryphées but in the 20th century were called chorus girls – often they were children who dressed as fairies for pantomimes.

It is a regrettable fact these girls were not only hard-working and vastly underpaid, but lower class and tainted by many people with a reputation of being glorified prostitutes. When such a fire occurred, the toffs in the audience were often more put out by the show being interrupted rather than a human being in danger of death.

Sympathy in such accidents was often aroused by informing the public the injured girl was supporting decrepit parents, or bed-ridden younger siblings rather than the individual herself was injured, and possibly dying. An excerpt from a letter to the press probably expresses the feelings of most good-hearted people of the time.

    TO THE EDITOR OF THE MORNING POST.

For the sake of the sufferers, who belong to a class which seldom finds one to speak for it, I beg the insertion of these few lines.

201

Besides our pain at the sad accident at the Princess's Theatre, great is the disgust of all who are acquainted with stage arrangements that, especially after the numerous victims of neglect, blankets and fire-buckets full of water were not constantly at hand on each side of the stage.

Madame Vestris, when manager of the Lyceum, insisted on this, and, I am happy to add, Mr. Mapleson had the blankets, if not the water, at the "first entrance" on each side of Her Majesty's Theatre.

Such neglect ought to be repaired at every theatre in the world; and the girls who suffered recently should be handsomely provided for. Both may very likely be worthy, but one, I am well informed, is highly respectable. Pray, sir, do not let this matter drop.—I remain, sir, your obedient servant,

AN OLD STAGER.
5, Pump-court, Temple, London E.C.

Should we assume that An Old Stager would not be interested in protecting girls who were not likely to be worthy, or highly respectable?

| 1863_02_09 | London | Miss Nielson | severely injured |
| 1863_05_16 | London | Mdlle Tietjens | unharmed |

1863_07_05 **Bromberg** **Fraulein Bergguth**

"The Berlin papers state that Fraulein Bergguth, a favourite vocalist of the Bromberg Theatre (Prussian Poland), was lately burned in so dreadful a manner on the stage, through approaching too near the footlights, that she shortly afterwards expired. Those journalists severely blame the Manager for not having prevented the accident by covering the lamps with a species of wire fence." *The Era* 1863_07_05.

The reader will have been appalled at the number of flaming frock incidents already listed, but this type of accident was not restricted to the stage. There were many domestic frock fire incidents reported in the newspapers and still there was no major outcry or public clamour. Showbusiness newspaper *The Era* tried to emphasise the solution by reporting on a domestic post mortem in its issue of 19 July 1863: "The melancholy death by fire of Miss Goff, of Cumberland Place, Hyde Park, led to a Coroner's inquest, and the verdict was 'That the deceased was burnt to death through the accidental spilling on her light muslin dress of ignited brandy, and that the said death arose through misfortune'. The Coroner said it was much to be regretted that the process for rendering the materials of ladies' dresses uninflammable was not generally understood and used by the public. Either of three substances – phosphate of ammonia, tungstate of soda, and sulphate of ammonia – could be mixed in the starch, and at the cost of a penny a dress, deaths from fire would be rendered in point of fact impossible. Articles of apparel subjected to the action of these agents would, if they burnt at all, only smoulder, and in no case could they blaze up in the sudden and terrible manner described in the present instance."

| 1863_08_20c | Bordeaux | Mdlle Dolores | unharmed |
| 1863_12_04 | Kidderminster | Mrs Davenport | injured |

1864_01_21   London   Madame Marie Charles

Mary Ann Thorn (32) known professionally as Madame Marie Charles though unmarried, was engaged in the pantomime at the Pavilion Theatre, Whitechapel, to play Columbine. It was the third year she had played the role at this theatre. She was also the principal dancer and in the ballet scene she was at the rear of the stage in a tableau where she was not dancing but posing.

It was the practice in theatres of the time to illuminate the backcloth scenery with a row of gas-jets similar to the ones providing the footlights. This row was masked from the audience by a ground row (ie a low piece of scenery painted to match the scene). In the ballet scene on this occasion there was a row of 24 burners 16" off the floor with no wire protection but a ground row in front. Four feet forward of that was another ground row of only 10" in height. The dancers were instructed not to go on the stage area between these two ground rows.

The full force of 30 dancers – including 16 children between the ages of six and 12 – was ranged in a tableau at the time. Madame, however, consistently took up a position behind the 10" board and several people called to warn her not to go there. She claimed that she could make better poses in that space. On this occasion, by mishap the back of her dress caught fire as she had got too near the backcloth lighting. Consternation followed as usual, and people rushed to help with coats, rugs and a blanket until the fire was quenched. Madame was taken to hospital where she was able to discuss her accident, but within a few days was dead. At the inquest it was stated yet again that all the dancers' costumes should be treated with a fireproofing solution, and all ground lights should be protected by wire frames. At Madame's funeral "there were not more than half a dozen persons present at the grave, and not a single member of the Pavilion company. Several provincial actors, however, were in the second mourning carriage".

The death of Madame Charles at the Pavilion Theatre finally got through to the rulers of the country that steps should be taken to prevent these accidents constantly happening. Up to now I have detailed 32 costume fires in this country of which ten were fatal. The Lord Chamberlain did not think an act of Parliament was appropriate, but summoned a deputation of managers of all the London theatres under his jurisdiction to meet with him to discuss ways of preventing ballet girls' costumes catching fire. Discussion threw up several points:

_Fireproofing only lasted a short time, two weeks being typical

_The girls themselves did not like treated costumes as they made them stiff and prevented them 'floating'

_The girls provided their own undergarments and these were the cause of fires because they comprised many layers of gauze material, so they were still in danger even if the top garment were to be fireproofed

_The girls disobey the sternest instructions. As in the latest case of Madame Marie Charles who, like all the others, had been several times told not to trespass on the area between two ground rows

_Ground lights were constantly moving position depending on the scenery. It was a standard instruction to girls to keep away from all ground lights

As a result of these discussions, it was decided that the Lord Chamberlain would write to every London theatre with recommendations. It was further suggested that the Lord Chamberlain's instructions should be issued on a card that could be displayed backstage at all theatres.

1864_02_01c   Dresden   Madame Ney-Burde   unharmed

1864_02_20 LONDON (Philharmonic Institution).   DEMONSTRATION OF FIREPROOF DRESS
Professor Pepper – he of 'Pepper's Ghost' fame – was giving a nightly lecture at the Royal Philharmonic Institution entitled *Burning to Death and Saving from Death*. In this he practically demonstrated how unnecessary it was that women should die from their clothes catching fire. A shop dummy was clad in an ordinary muslin frock and a naked flame held to it. Immediately the garment was ablaze, and in a short time it was obvious that, no matter how many wet blankets were to hand, a young woman would have little chance of escaping death. After the fire was extinguished, a live young woman wearing an identical dress came onstage. This dress had been dipped in 'Patent Incombustible Starch' which was readily obtainable at most chemists. When a light was applied to this dress, it did not burst into flames, it scorched and shrivelled but flame it did not. What further proof did the public need?

image© The British Library Board

1864_09_09c   Marseilles   Mdlle Pancardi   injured
1864_10_08   Ulm   unnamed audience member
                           19 audience members   injured
The lamps in the chandelier at the Ulm theatre were fuelled by petroleum oil. In mid-performance twenty-four lamps in the chandelier suspended from the roof burst in succession like falling dominoes, and "burning oil fell like a shower of fire" upon a number of ladies seated below. The dresses of twenty of them were in flames resulting in serious burns. One of the women was so badly injured that she died within a few hours.

1865_01_06   London   Ellen Geary   severely injured
Mrs Ellen Geary was a regular dancer in the pantomime at the Britannia Theatre and in the transformation scene the *corps de ballet* were posed in a tableau, Ellen's elevated position being by the wings. To reach her place she had the use of a ladder, and a stage hand was stationed at the bottom to give help as required to the dancers using it. On this night, Ellen was late getting to the ladder from the

dressing room, and the man was no longer at his post, having left to attend to another duty. Ellen climbed the ladder to reach her position and while doing so her skirt, catching an adjacent light, burst into flames. Realising what had happened Ellen flung herself on the floor face downwards and a wet blanket was thrown over her, as well as a bed from one of the scenes. This at once extinguished the fire but Ellen, dreadfully burnt up to the shoulders, was taken to St Bartholomew's Hospital.

The Britannia management looked after Ellen very well, paying her salary of 9/- for 14 weeks and organising an appeal which totalled £2.4.0 by April when a benefit performance was held. She slowly recovered, regaining unrestricted movement and not suffering any disfigurement.

As a result of this costume fire, the Lord Chamberlain put pen to paper again and wrote to every theatre in the kingdom: "It is clear that the accident would have been prevented — 1st. If the clothing of the poor woman herself had been of uninflammable materials; 2nd. If the side lights had been screened by wire guards, so as to prevent her clothing from coming in contact with them, for it appears that glass shades are not sufficient for this purpose. The Lord Chamberlain begs therefore again to call the attention of managers to the advantage which would result from a use, by the ladies of their establishments, of uninflammable materials for dress; he is aware that there are difficulties with respect to it, but feels certain that these might be overcome. The Lord Chamberlain must also earnestly impress upon managers the immediate necessity of screening with wire guards every light within reach of any part of the theatre, and he would warn them most solemnly that they will be in future held responsible for any accidents which may occur from a neglect of this instruction. The Lord Chamberlain suggests that he may be favoured with an acknowledgment of this letter as soon as possible."

1865_07_03 Birmingham Mrs H Egerton
Fanny Hinton (aged 14)

The ballet was *The Feast of Roses* and featured Mary Ann Egerton leading a troupe of 36 child ballet dancers representing fairies. At the back of the stage was a scenery cave in front of which were some silver revolving cylinders to resemble running water. Alongside was a short run of unguarded gas jets no more than 2ft long. There was no requirement for any of the child dancers to go anywhere near them as they entered though some bowers of roses placed at the sides of the stage. Mrs Egerton made her entrance from the cave.

The children having done their dance were arranging themselves in a tableau when one child – Fanny Hinton – stumbled, falling into the only unguarded gas lights on the stage – the ones by the cave. Immediately the poor child's flimsy dress caught fire and she ran across the stage to the wings, followed by Mrs Egerton who sought to help the child. Having caught her, Mrs Egerton's dress also started to blaze. Other dancers, hurrying forward to assist, were fortunately thrust out of the way by stage crew, and Mr Hughes Jr a scene painter, grabbing a rough jacket, smothered the child in it, while another man threw Mrs Egerton down and rolled a bundle of rough clothes over her. All the other children who had been running about screaming and crying were herded off to their room.

Of course, the performance was suspended, and surgeons arrived to find the child was barely scorched, but Mrs Egerton rather more so. Manager Mr Soward and actor Mr Hicks calmed the audience, explained that all was well, that Miss Hinton had been taken home, the ballet had dispersed for the night, and the rest of the programme would now continue, which it duly did.

In fact Fanny was taken to the General Hospital where she subsequently died, and Mrs Egerton (29) the wife of the stage manager Henry Egerton was taken home. She seemed to be doing well until suddenly falling into despair and dying on 16 July.

1865_11_28c   St Petersburg   Mdlle Ehlers

Louise Ehlers described as "one of the prettiest ladies of the company" was dancing in a German opera. In the guise of a Mexican she was performing the popular dance the Cachuca, in which she came to the front of the stage, dropped to her knees and played the castanets. At that moment her gauze petticoats caught fire from the footlights and she was enveloped in flames, upon which she rose and ran wildly about the stage thus fanning the flames in the manner we have already seen a number of times. Two fellow actors, Lobe and Zimmerman, who were onstage, threw themselves upon the wretched woman and hustled her into the wings. The other gauze-clad players fled for their lives, and who can blame them?

The curtain was lowered, but the audience declined to leave the theatre until they had news of Mdlle Ehlers. The news came some time later . . . she was dead.

1865_12_28   Sunderland   Louisa Ricardo (aged 12)

The pantomime *Robin Hood* at the Lyceum Theatre was drawing to a close as usual with the harlequinade. Clown was Mr Ricardo, Harlequin his eldest son, junior Columbine was his daughter Louisa (12), two other members of his family were also engaged. Behind a wing piece a gas pipe with multiple jets was connected with a flexible pipe to another gas pipe on the stage. Louisa, with some others, was waiting in the wings when the flexible tube made of *gutta-percha* came disconnected, the gas rushing out catching fire and exploding. The flames soared upwards in view of the audience causing them to rise and make for the exits. Simultaneously, Louisa finding her dress in flames, ran on to the stage where her father was in the midst of his clowning antics. The audience, stunned at the sight of the flaming girl, stopped laughing and several sprang on to the stage to assist Mr Ricardo and his colleagues trying to tear the flaming costume off his daughter. The stage was a mass of confusion until a stage hand threw her down, and Mr Bell the lessee, who had seen all from his box, sped down and threw his overcoat over the poor Columbine extinguishing the flames. Medical attention arrived and she was removed to her father's lodgings with severe burns to arms and chest – her face was spared. The pantomime continued to the end in her absence, Mr Ricardo, with severely burnt hands, doing his best to raise some laughs along with his Harlequin son.

The opinion of the medical men was that the injuries were superficial and on the following morning Louisa seemed much recovered. The medico thought that within a few days she would be able to resume her professional duties, but, alas, the shock to her system was too great and she died that afternoon.

In the aftermath, both the press and public condemned the theatre for continuing the pantomime after the deplorable incident. The stage manager William Champion gave his explanation pointing out that of the 2000 people in the house many were rushing to the doors. He had a man at each door, these being thrown open to permit egress. To prevent panic he set the show going again hoping to draw attention to the stage and thus avoid the danger of crushing in the stairs and corridors such as frequently happens in panics. The ploy worked, and anybody who wanted to leave could do so without the hazard of crowding and broken limbs. As doctors had declared that the child's injuries were superficial nobody, including her father, had anticipated they would prove fatal.

Walter Joyce of the St James's Theatre started a fund to defray the expenses of Louisa's funeral, and help Mr Ricardo who was unable to work because of his burns. This fund, publicised in *The Era* newspaper, drew a letter from "one of the company" who said that Mr Bell had defrayed all the expenses for the funeral, Ricardo was on £8 a week, had a good benefit and many presents from local people so couldn't be too badly off, and he was surprised that Mr Ricardo should use his daughter's death as a means of gain. This rather offensive missive drew an immediate response from Ricardo who wrote that his unsullied reputation of 29 years should surely quash any idea that he would choose to gain from such a domestic loss. He pointed out that if monetary gain was an object he could sue the management for neglecting to have wet blankets to hand in the wings – as he had requested several times from the very first rehearsal. He stated that had such been available his child would have been saved. Also, he knew nothing about Mr Joyce's fund until he read about it. Joyce had written to Champion the stage manager at the Lyceum stating his proposal. Ricardo had replied that he did not require assistance, he was back at work and earning and, politely thanking Joyce for his concern, requested he abandon his fund. Ricardo had not received any of the payments. He agreed that Mr Bell had paid for the funeral and doctors, and under the circumstances of the accident being through the carelessness of his servants at his theatre could Mr Bell do less? Ricardo had received unsolicited money from local friends amounting to £8.2.6d which he used to pay for a tombstone to Louisa's memory, small cards, advertisements etc. "I don't think I have had much gain from this." Yes, his benefit had been a good one, bringing in £43.17.10d, and his share by agreement was a third of the gross receipts which brought him £14.12.7¾d. But these arrangements were standard and would have taken place without the accident. From that sum he paid for his own printing, and black for his family, again not much gain from that. He suggested that "one of the company" must be activated by petty jealousy or some paltry spite, and deplored that this anonymous person opened a fresh wound which condolences of friends had partially allayed.

Ricardo was writing from the Whitebait Music Hall, Glasgow. As a result of this published letter, came one winging in from Mr Joyce saying he had raised £10.3.6d (as listed in *The Era*) and in return received a letter from Ricardo saying thank you for the money raised on my behalf and it "will be most thankfully received by me". Joyce, having read the letter from "one of the company", deciding to enquire further before raising any more contributions, wrote to several people in Sunderland "whose veracity could not be doubted" and concluded that Ricardo was not worthy of his assistance. This was strengthened by a report that at a meeting of the Lyceum company it was unanimously agreed to advise Joyce to return the money, or use it for a more worthier object.

Back came Ricardo refuting half of Joyce's statements and concluding that "his mind had been poisoned against me by some busy and insinuating individual." It does look as though at least one member of the *Robin Hood* company had a deep dislike of Ricardo and was engaged in a vendetta. This correspondence had dragged on into March before it petered out, without the whole truth of the matter becoming clearer. I find it incredible that so much mean spirit should have arisen that a grieving father should be so traduced.

1866_01_04   Taunton   Lavinia Warren   unharmed

1866_05_10c   Nancy, France   Mdlle Noelly

The play was *The Saltimbanques* and during the third act, Mdlle Noelly, having made her exit, thought she would stay in the wings and watch to the end of the act. She had the unfortunate idea of climbing a ladder in the wings to get a good view. Behind each side flat were three rows of gas jets and Mdlle Noelly, wearing a very short muslin dress, was no sooner up the ladder than her dress was in flames. Mdlle Noelly uttered a shriek as she fell to the floor trying to protect her face with her hands. She was immediately rolled on the ground and covered with a top coat, but being badly burned, especially on the chest, the coat stuck to her skin. She cried: "I am lost! Pray go and say so to my poor mother." Mdlle Noelly was described as "one of the youngest and prettiest of the troupe".

1866_09_17   London   Bolossy Kiralfy   unharmed

The ballet at the Royal Alhambra was *The Pearl of Tokay* starring Bolossy Kiralfy. During the action M Kiralfy was bound hand and foot with muslin streamers. In this helpless state he rolled down towards the footlights. Victorian stages were raked, ie sloped downwards from the back to the front, hence the terms 'upstage' and 'downstage'. Thus poor Mr Kiralfy rolled into the footlights where the muslin bindings promptly burst into flames and he, being bound, was in an impossible state to deal with the flames himself. The musical director managed to push him off the lights and then the ballet ladies – with a lack of commonsense regarding their own peril – immediately stamped out the flames. Kiralfy resumed to tremendous applause, which I hope the ballet girls shared. The Kiralfy brothers went on to become major impresarios.

1867_02_02c   Rio de Janeiro   Mdlle Leonie Chatenay

"A dancer, Mdlle Léonie Chatenay, was on the stage at Rio Janeiro when her gauze dress caught fire at the footlights, and, notwithstanding the efforts of her fellow performers to extinguish the flames, she was so dreadfully injured that she expired the following day." *Dublin Evening Post* 1867_02_02.

1867_02_06   Modena   La Barbizan   unharmed

1867_10_30   Adelaide   Maggie Lester

Maggie Lester (18), a dancer late for her cue, rushed on to the stage. As she passed a burning pan of red fire, her costume caught light and she ended up as a blazing torch. Never recovering from the accident, she lingered some weeks, dying on 13 January 1868.

1867_12_31   Sunderland   unnamed child   unharmed
1868_01_18   Marseilles   Madame Juteau   unharmed
1868_02_10c   Orleans   Madame Stefani   unharmed

1868_03_20   Birmingham   Fanny Smith (below)

Frances Ann Higginbottom (22), was a steel pen grinder, but for three years in the evenings she transformed herself into Fanny Smith dancer at the music hall. On Friday night, somehow Fanny's dress caught fire. Nobody seemed to know how it happened, but there were four naked spirit lamps on pedestals at each corner of the stage, and it was surmised that with her fairy wand she had knocked a lamp, and the wick had fallen on her dress.

image© The British Library Board

Fanny ran off into the wings but there were no people to assist, eight of the stage crew were at the back of the stage, having been told to leave the sides clear for the dancers' exit at the end of the scene. One of the gas men George Clive, on hearing the scream, ran forward in the wings only to see Fanny, in flames, running back onstage. Clive then rummaged about for the bucket of water that had green baize soaking in it. Although expressly there for this very purpose, it was trapped behind a piece of scenery. By the time he got the bucket out and ran onstage, already there was a man putting his coat around her. William Cox, an outfitter's assistant, had been on the ground floor of the hall at one side, only two yards from the footlights (which incidentally were guarded by seven wires). He leapt on to the stage, threw Fanny down and wrapped his coat around her, dousing the flames. She was taken in a cab to hospital where she was quite able to speak to her mother, saying she did not know how it had happened but did not blame anybody.

Fanny died on Monday morning. It seems the venue had hosepipes at both sides of the stage, and a bucket of water with a baize cloth soaking in it. Both sensible fire precautions at the time, but no designated person to use the bucket and cloth facility, or to make sure it was always accessible.

1868_05_06	York	Emily Johnson, (aged 6)	severely injured
1868_12_26	Toulouse	Mdlle Mathias	injured
1869_07_21	London	Mdlle Schneider	unharmed (153C.)

1869_09_10c Berlin Two unnamed dancers
"Two Ballet Girls Burned —A sad accident has just occurred at the Victoria Theatre in Berlin. Two of the ballet girls were dressing in their room, when one of them lighted an extra gas-burner Their dresses instantly caught fire, and although assistance was at once rendered, they were so badly burned that one of them died the same night, and the other the following morning." *Edinburgh Evening Courant*

1869_12_29	Croydon	Mdlle D'Arnauld	injured
1870_02_02c	Moscow	Adelina Patti	unharmed (153D.)
1870_04_21	Northampton	Lilly Davis	severely injured
1870_09_19	Manchester	Mdlle Grace Lucelle	injured

1871_01_10c   Brussels   Madame Emilie Dubois

Madame Emilie Dubois, a lady of the ballet, was burnt to death on the stage of the Theatre des Galeries. In December, her family sued for damages of 20,000f – about £800 – from M Delvil the manager. A tribunal was ordered to investigate whether there were sufficient precautions against fire to render the manager immune from responsibility.

1871_04_02	Philadelphia	Millie Fulmer	injured
1871_05_03	Brisbane	Eliza Wilson	injured
1871_08_28	Boston	Emily Smith	injured

1871_10_21c LICHTENSTEIN.   DEMONSTRATION OF FIRE-PROOFING SOLUTION

This is not an accident report but the very opposite. As the reader will know by now, the flimsy costumes of ballet girls were especially susceptible to catching fire, and in spite of various chemical formulas to render material fireproof which had been proposed over the years, the girls steadfastly refused to take advantage of them. Here to their rescue came the Prince of Lichtenstein who, a ballet lover, had become the patron of a Viennese chemist who had formulated a better concoction.

A numerous gathering witnessed the first demonstration of the solution. Two life size dolls dressed as ballet dancers were placed on the stage, each then set alight. The first one, flaring up immediately, was soon reduced to ashes. The other – "impregnated with the talismanic substance" – merely suffered a small hole burned in the frock. The Prince, pleased with this result, was reported as going further and proposed having a wooden theatre built at his expense with all the timber treated with the magic fireproof composition. Fires would then be lit at various parts of the building. If that proved the success expected, the anonymous inventor could expect a rich harvest of enquiries from theatres throughout Europe.

Perhaps after this I will not have any more flaming dancers to report to you?

210

1871_10_28	Paris	M Leduc	unharmed
1872_02_23	London	Annie Pitt	injured
1872_06_12	London	Milly Howard	unharmed
1872_11_09	Chicago	Miss Flora Newton	injured
1873_01_26c	Milan	unnamed ballet dancer	injured

1873_07_25   Liverpool   Josephine Fiddes   injured

The role was Lady Godiva. While on stage, standing near a table where a candle burned, Miss Fiddes's long wig caught fire. Fellow actors Arthur and Bromley immediately rushed to the rescue in the time honoured way of throwing her down and muffling the flames with a stout garment. She was burnt on her neck, face and upper arms but within a few days was well enough to resume her career.

1873_08_21   Vienna   Mdlle Anna Walter

"Mlle Anna Walter, a dancer at the Vienna Theatre, was burnt to death, on Thursday week, when preparing to enter on the stage. Going too close to a light, her dress caught fire, and, in her fright, she rushed along the corridor, enveloped in flames, so that when assistance was rendered she was found to be dreadfully injured. She expired the next day." *Illustrated London News* 1873_08_30.

1873_09_27   London   Ellen Pelly

Ellen Pelly (20) was a dancer in the Alhambra pantomime. In the transformation scene the dancers in their fairy costumes posed in a tableau, their places fixed on an iron frame which was hoisted aloft when all the girls were fastened in place. On this night, Ellen was late in taking up her position "to ascend in the irons" and while rushing from the wrong side of the stage her dress caught fire from a light. She screamed and made to run among her colleagues on the stage, which would have probably set the whole lot on fire. Fortunately, before that could happen a gasman grabbed her and, rolling his coat around her, successfully extinguished the flames. She was taken to hospital in great agony and died there a few days later.

   At the inquest, gasman William Rogers said that it was a rule that the girls should be in their places before the gas was lit, and if she had been on time and entered as she should, there would have been no light there to brush against. Two wet blankets were positioned at the side of the stage that night. The jury, returning a verdict of accidental death, made the recommendation that a greater number of blankets should be ready for use in such cases.

   So in spite of umpteen different chemical soaks recommended to render dresses fireproof, and wet blankets in the wings, young dancers were still being burnt to death. Juries feebly made recommendations which were either impractical or were ignored. When were laws going to be put in place? And obeyed? When was it going to be mandatory that all stage costumes should be of fireproof material? So far I have entered 111 costume fires in this catalogue of woe, 39 of which were fatal.

1874_01_19   Newcastle   Caroline Estelle
                Miss Estelle   injured

The time was 10pm when Caroline Estelle – one of four sisters employed in the annual pantomime – was changing her costume ready to play Columbine. Her dress caught fire from a gas stove in the dressing room. The clothes of one of her sisters who rushed to assist also ignited. The screams of the girls brought speedy assistance, but not soon enough as Caroline suffered severe burns to legs, body, arms and neck, while her sister's burns were restricted to her arms. The latter was taken home, while the former was taken to the infirmary where she subsequently died. It is noteworthy – but typical – that Caroline's three sisters were obliged and expected to continue performing in the pantomime, dressing in the same room and so on, as though nothing had happened.

1874_05_15   Tours   Mdlle Millie-Christine   unharmed

This was a costume fire to an unusual person. Millie-Christine "The Two-Headed Nightingale" was actually twins conjoined at the lower spine sharing a pelvis standing at an approximately 90° angle to each other. They were born to slave parents and sold off to a freak show owner. Passing through many hands until 1857 they were then taken up by Joseph Pearson Smith. On 1 January 1863, the

211

151.

Emancipation Proclamation ending their slave status, they were no longer anyone's property. Smith and his wife provided the twins with an education, teaching them to speak five languages, dance, play music, and sing. The twins enjoyed a successful career as "The Two-Headed Nightingale" touring all over the world, even meeting Queen Victoria during their time in Britain. In 1882, they commanded $700 a week. They retired when in their 30s to the farm where they had been born which was now their property. They died on 8 October 1912, at the age of 61 from tuberculosis, Christine dying 12 hours after her sister.

"Narrow Escape of the Two-Headed Nightingale. — Mdlle Millie-Christine, the 'Two-headed Nightingale,' has had a narrow escape of being burnt to death. She was performing at a circus at Tours, when her dress caught fire. Fortunately one of the company seized hold of her, threw her down, and put out the flames before they had done much harm. The courageous lady phenomenon insisted on finishing her performance, much to the admiration of the audience." *Edinburgh Evening News* 1874_05_15.

1874_06_12   Manchester   unnamed dancer   unharmed

1874_07_16   Manchester   Mrs Jones

On this night shortly before midnight, Mrs Jones the wife of a stagehand at the Casino Theatre was burning ink for a preparation to black the faces of minstrels. Her dress caught fire and she was burnt to death.

1875_12_28   Sheffield   Alma Oldale
Alice Gregory   unharmed

It was pantomime transformation time once again, the most dangerous period for young ladies of the chorus, these being the scenes where the girls were strapped on to iron frameworks and hauled up above the stage. Thus it was on this night, with men pulling on ropes, and gauzy scenes especially lit with extra gas lamps dissolving into each other in a series of magical transformations, that during the fourth change there was a flash as the festoon on stage left caught fire. The flames spread rapidly upwards igniting the flimsy fairy dresses of two girls above – Alice Gregory and Alma Oldale. There was a delay in getting them down as the structure was counterweighted deliberately to prevent the men accidentally letting go of the ropes and allowing the lot to crash down, hence they had to wind the ropes up and down by hand much as sailors weigh anchor. Seven men were involved, and they could only get one girl down at a time. Alice was lucky, she was the first.

By the time Alma was rescued she was severely burnt and lingered fully conscious until 10 January when she died. At the inquest several witnesses claimed to have been in the theatre business 20 years and had never heard of such a thing as a fireproof material. Similarly, there had never been an incident of this type in any of their careers. Both these statements are hard to accept in view of the large number of well publicised accidents and many deaths caused through blazing costumes, as well as advice on fireproofing dresses appearing often in the public press. So far in this text there are 130 such accidents taken from newspaper sources. Talk about the theatre industry being like a village living in its own world! Unbelievable!

| 1876_01_31 | Rochester | Betty Remmelaburg | unharmed |
| 1876_02_16 | Cincinnati | Miss Rosa Doyle | unharmed |

| 1876 04_17 | Kilkenny | Virginia Blackwood | unharmed |

We have previously noted an accident to Virginia Blackwood (*see* 1874_09_23) who ran her own comedy company. On that occasion she was off work for several weeks. However, the accident on this night was promptly dealt with. The company was playing W S Gilbert's *Sweethearts*. While enacting a scene with leading man Murray Wood, Miss Blackwood's dress caught fire from the footlights. Instead of screaming and rushing about as so many of the young dancers did, she stood stock still, and Mr Wood, gathering up her train where the blaze started and crushing it in his hands, extinguished it promptly. Loud applause came from the fashionable audience who had regarded the event in horror, and both performers, with coolness born of many years touring, immediately continued with the play.

| 1877_01_16 | London | Miss Cavendish | unharmed (153E.) |

1877_03_15c   Bremen   Mdlle Mila von Pachert

Mdlle Mila von Pachert, was playing at the Tivoli Theatre on the night of her benefit when her dress and a naked flame came together causing her to be severely burnt. She died in great agony three days later.

| 1877_04_09 | Paris | Two unnamed dancers | severely injured |

| 1877_11_08 | London | Jennie 'Topsy' Elliott | severely injured |

Jennie 'Topsy' Elliott, a young and vivacious dancer of "an amiable disposition and a private character beyond reproach", was the leader of the Sisters Elliott trio, probably the speediest in London. None of which had a bearing on the fact that she allowed her dress to catch fire. She was fortunate that at the South London Palace there were no fewer than six hydrants behind the stage, two tubs of water — one on each side of the stage — and 24 fire-pails full of water, plus two wet blankets, always ready for an emergency such as happened.

Thus she was singularly unfortunate that the fire started in her dressing room, forcing her to flee down the steps to the stage in her flaming dress. The stage crew were on the ball, and the fire extinguished with a hose pipe as speedily as could possibly be, although by then she had suffered bad burning.

As we have seen, costume fires were lamentably frequent, but a few seemed to make a larger impact than the others, and this is one of them. Topsy was a popular favourite both within the profession and the public, and as such commanded more attention and commiseration than lesser known girls. As a result of her misfortune, a subscription list was promptly set up. A benefit, held on 1 August 1878, drew a bumper attendance, the takings of which – added to all her other subscriptions – gave her an overall total of £500 (£46,700 in today's money). This sum enabled her to survive and recover comfortably for the two years she was absent from the stage, before finally returning on Christmas Eve 1879 as principal dancer in *Aladdin* at the Surrey Theatre.

1880_10_12 PARIS.   AWARD FOR NEW FIRE-PROOFING SOLUTION

This was a report from France announcing that the Socite d'Encouragement pour l'Industrial National had awarded the sum of 1000f to M Martin for a new fireproofing solution. This rendered materials and even the "superficial parts of wood uninflammable" for several months up to a temperature of 36°. The mixtures were not particularly novel, as they used known chemicals, but Martin specified formulae for four different uses, one of which was intended for "painted decor".

1882_02_07 ST PETERSBURG.   UNTREATED DRESSES BANNED

"The St Petersburg police have issued an order forbidding the appearance of any actors or dancers on the stage of the theatres of the capital whose dresses have not previously been rendered incombustible by means of chlorate of lime. The same rule has been in force in Berlin for five years." *Toronto Daily Mail* 1882_02_07. Not every performer obeyed the ruling as Mdlle Anderson in St Petersburg and Fraulein Sontag in Berlin will know. (*see* 1893_12_15 and 1889_06_22).

1882_10_30	Glasgow	Mrs Cannell	injured
1883_06_27	Paris	Mons Libert	severely injured
1883_12_26	London	Amy Lucille	unharmed
1884_01_22	Barrow in Furness	Lizzie Kelsey	unharmed

1884_05_03   Ayr   Miss Alice Galvin (amateur)

This latest costume blaze did not even happen to a professional, but the daughter of the manager of Dalmellington Iron Works. The young lady Alice Gavin venturing too near the footlights was so badly burnt before she was rescued that she died the following day.

     The first death from a costume blaze I noted in the Victorian period was in 1842 and here we are, over 40 years later, with the latest. Between then and now I have noted 44 deaths, plus many more costume fires where the victim survived. Why was nothing done about it? Why were fireproof dresses not compulsory by law? Until it became a legal requirement the slaughter remorselessly carried on.

1885_01_01	Liverpool	unnamed dancer	unharmed

1885_02_23   London   Annie Jones (domestic)

Throughout this special section I have noted many costume fires suffered by artistes on the stage. These have primarily been young dancers wearing flimsy lightweight dresses who have moved too near a gas flame of the stage lighting. As it has not been my remit, I have not addressed the matter of women in ordinary life who suffered injury and death from dresses catching fire in the home. Ladies of fashion were particularly vulnerable, as they adopted the crinoline. This was a fad for having very wide skirts, originally contrived by having many layers of underskirts of a stiff material made from horsehair (called crin) and cotton as a lining, hence crinoline. As the yen for these skirts to become wider and wider, the layers were replaced with a framework of cane or metal, so fashionable women went about looking as though they were protruding from the top of a bell tent. The circumferences of these dresses were incredible, measuring as much as six yards of material. It does not take much imagination to see how easily such a garment could get caught in fires, machinery, train and coach doors and so on. Thousands of women suffered injury and death through wearing this ridiculous vogue. The fashion eventually faded, to be replaced by another silly one designed to make the bottom protrude. Called 'the bustle', this started out as a padded cushion affair worn on the rump. Again women wanted this fashion to grow bigger and better so, taking up the cage idea again, the bustle was replaced with the 'dress improver' which was simply a metal frame that pushed out the rear of the dress which was made with a flat front but extra panels at the back. Again, an invitation for easy combustion.

Annie Jones (20), an actress (professional name Mabel McKenzie) was in her drawing room entertaining a gentleman named Mr Shepherd. Firstly she played the piano, then sat on the same chair as her guest, after which she rose and stood in front of the fire, with her back to it. She was wearing a dress made large at the rear by having a dress improver underneath. Her dress – of a light muslin material – caught fire and she was enveloped in flames. Shepherd immediately started pulling up the hearthrug but Annie ran from the room and down the stairs into the street. There some men took off their coats, smothered the flames, called a cab, and took her to hospital. On being asked by Dr Spicer how the accident happened she said the dress improver stuck out so far that it went too near the fire. The poor woman languished, gradually sinking, finally dying on 11 March.

1886_01_01   Paris   Nerida Sipière (child – domestic)

As this was an amateur production in a private house I was inclined not to include it but, as it casts a light on the life-style of a rich family, here it is. Mons and Madame Sipière owned a beautiful detached house and had recently added a little theatre. The children of the house, and their youthful cousins, had contrived the exciting and pleasant idea of presenting a specially written play in their new theatre. The parents had invited their friends to be the audience at this event. The play depicted the old year waning and the new one coming in. The eldest daughter Nerida, a charming girl of 14, was to be the Good Genius of 1886, dressed in a loose transparent robe. As the audience assembled, Nerida donned her costume and to admire her appearance went into her mother's bedroom where there was a long mirror. While gazing at herself, her loose sleeve brushed against a candle and flared up. She screamed for help and, not unreasonably, threw herself on the bed, rolling in the bed-clothes to extinguish the flames. Alas, the bed was covered with a lace coverlet and curtained with muslin as well as silk, so all she did was set the bed on fire, which then ignited the whole room. By the time help arrived Nerida was a mass of flaming cloth with every inch of her body severely burnt. She was beyond any hope but survived for many hours before her inevitable death. A fun event that ended in tragedy. Poor child.

1886_12_11   Toulon   Five unnamed mimes   severely injured

1887_12_26   Wolverhampton Miss Sappho   unharmed

This costume fire was self-inflicted. The performer was Miss Sappho playing Jack in the pantomime *The House That Jack Built*. It has to be said that the cause was very different from the usual accidental proximity to a gas jet that we have seen repeatedly in these contemporary reports. One can only think that the unfortunate girl brought it upon herself, but as it was a signature trick that she had done many times without distress, it must be classed as no more dangerous than a fire eater.

Miss Sappho's star turn was to soak a skipping rope with a flammable liquid and set light to it. When it was nicely flaming she skipped with it. Many in the audience shouted for her to desist. On this night, the flames caught her dress, but fortunately several colleagues in the cast rushing onstage quelled them before any injury was done. One would think Miss Sappho would at least have worn a dress treated with one of the many fire retardant solutions that people had been banging on about for years, and made sure water-soaked blankets were in the wings, but no!

1888_10_10c	Kimberley	Jessie Lynn (hotel)	injured
1889_06_15c	Berlin	unnamed dancer	unharmed
1889_06_22	Berlin	Fräulein Sontag	unharmed
1889_06_27	London	Angelina Spotti	unharmed

1891_01_02   Wiesbaden   Maria Lip
During the show at the Royal Theatre, the costume of dancer Maria Lip caught fire, with the flames immediately spreading to the scenery. The audience comprising some 3000 women and children panicked and rushed for the exits, many being seriously hurt. The fire was soon extinguished and the performance carried on without the poor girl who, severely burnt, shortly died.

216   1891_05_15c   New York   Mabel Fenton   severely injured

1891_06_20   London   Augustus Yorke (domestic)
Augustus Yorke (28), an amusing young actor appearing at Terry's Theatre, was badly injured at his rooms after the show on Saturday night around 2.30am. It was surmised that while in bed, after lighting a candle, he threw down the match which remained on the floor, still lit. Reaching with his slipper to slap it out, his nightshirt caught fire from the candle and instead of throwing off his garment or rolling himself in his bedclothes, quite losing his head he fled out into the street where he was grabbed by a more sensible fellow who, throwing him down, extinguished the flames. Yorke was taken to St George's Hospital where he remained until tragically dying ten days later.

1892_06_01   Providence, USA   Polly Macdonald (domestic)
Polly Macdonald was a soubrette working in a theatre, lodging in a hotel nearby. Lighting a match during the night to look at the time, somehow her nightdress caught fire. Unable to extinguish the flames she shrieked out for help, but her cries were heard too late as by the time the hotel staff had got to her she was horrifically burned and disastrously injured, dying within a few hours.

These two domestic examples show just how easy it was to start a clothing fire in the home. Although these victims were theatre performers they were the same as everybody else when in their domestic premises and should have known to be careful with lighted matches

1892_10_26	Bath	Miss Maude Murray	unharmed
1893_12_15	St Petersburg	Mdlle Anderson	severely injured

1894_09_18   Hanover   Nina Banciu (domestic)
This accident was not on the stage or even in a theatre. The Romanian actress Nina Banciu was at home trying to refill a burning lamp from a bottle of methylated spirits. The lamp fell on to her lap and her dressing gown caught fire.

| 1894_10_25 | Sunderland | unnamed actress | unharmed |
| 1896_08_19 | Croydon | Frances Delaval (below) | unharmed |

152.

| 1897_01_12 | Garston | Miss Morrison | injured |
| 1897_02_15c | Bantry | H Evan Gibbon | injured |

| 1897_05_28 | Norwich | Florence Hewitt | injured |

Florence Hewitt an "electrical dancer" had electric lights within her costume in an extension of the skirt dances of Loie Fuller (*see* 1895_06_15). On this night one of the wires in her frock shorted out causing a fire and turning Miss Hewitt into a human torch. Norman Mills the manager, rushing onstage, threw his coat around the lady and with some difficulty managed to extinguish the flames. The dancer Lizzie Villiers turned off the current in the wings, quick thinking which would have enabled water to be thrown on the blaze if such had been at hand. Miss Hewitt was severely burned about the arms, and was obliged to relinquish her engagement. She wrote to the press to assure people her apparatus was perfectly safe and could not set fire to her dress. The accident, she explained, was due to "an incompetent workman" who had to make "a small repair" just before she was due on stage but did the work incorrectly causing the wires to become greatly over-heated.

| 1898_01_03 | London | Fanny Eris | unharmed (153F.) |

| 1898_01_05c | New York | Vera De Noie | injured |

The play was the sensational melodrama *When London Sleeps*, with Vera De Noie playing the heroine.

In the final act the dastardly villain, played by W M Farnham, throws the heroine into a tank of kerosene then, seizing a burning torch, throws it into the tank. Of course, the tank is empty except for a row of gas jets to give the effect of burning oil. On this night, Miss De Noie's dress caught fire and the villain immediately became a hero by wrapping his coat around her, thus saving her life. The actress was severely shocked and her left arm burnt but incredibly escaped serious injury. The audience must have had some difficulty following the plot!

1898_01_13	London	unnamed dancer	unharmed
1898_02_07	London	Kate Levite	injured
1899_04_16	Swansea	Evans-Florador	unharmed
1899_07_26	Vienna	unknown dancer	unharmed
1899_09_30	Margate	Zeffie Tilbury (domestic)	injured (153G.)

1900_06_05   London   Lewis E B Stephen (domestic)

Lewis E B Stephens (36) was an established actor and playwright with experience gained in many touring companies. He and a party of chums were, on this night, celebrating the capture of Pretoria. Returning home around midnight in the best of health and spirits – possibly an excess of the latter – Stephens tottered down to his lavatory which, as customary until modern times, was situated at the bottom of the garden. He is presumed to have taken a spirit lamp with him to light his way. Mr Williamson a commercial traveller who lived next door, hearing shouts from his neighbour's garden, scaled the dividing wall to see flames issuing from the lavatory building. He found Stephens enveloped in fire, all his clothing ablaze. Dousing the flames, as other help arrived, a doctor was summoned and did what he could before despatching the poor chap to the Great Northern Hospital, where he died shortly after arrival.

Although I have recorded several costume-on-fire incidents since 1891, most have resulted in only slight or no injury which indicates that at long last theatre fire prevention was starting to be effective. The last four deaths of theatre folk by fire have all been domestic rather than onstage.

153.

A Emma Albertazzi   B Inez Fabbri   C Hortense Schneider

D Adelina Patti   E Ada Cavendish   F Fanny Erris   G Zeffie Tilbury

If you have kept up with me you will have noted 160 cases of onstage blazing costumes of which 45 were fatal.

AFTERWORD

While increased safety concerns in modern times have almost eliminated individual accidents to onstage actors and performers, they do seem to be inevitable occasionally because every eventuality cannot be provided for. An accident by its nature is unexpected and unforeseen.

Dancers can suffer injury – April 2004, Pauline O'Reilly (25) was injured performing in *Riverdance* in New Zealand and had to retire with damages of £22,000. Pantomime performers are still having accidents – December 2004, Janette Krankie fell off the panto beanstalk during a matinee at Glasgow, sustaining a fractured skull, broken rib and collarbone.

Incredibly, fatal accidents with weapons still happen. As I was writing this piece in October 2021, on a Hollywood film set actor Alec Baldwin shot dead the cinephotographer behind the camera.

And of course those brave souls the aerialists who aim to cheat death at every performance don't always succeed. By the nature of their work, aerial gymnasts, who strive for bigger and better feats, are the artistes who risk most and thus suffer more often from accidents. Even with modern safety nets, and the common use of safety wires, fatal accidents do still happen. For example:

2003_08_03	Eva Garcia (38) after falling 30ft at Gt Yarmouth Hippodrome circus.
2009_10_17	Oleksandr Zhuov (20s) fatally injured rehearsing with Cirque du Soleil.
2010_03_09	Tito Montoya after falling in a USA circus.
2013_06_30	Sarah Guillot-Guyard (31) after a fall in Cirque du Soleil, Las Vegas.
2017_03_17	Henri Beautour (18) as a result of a fall from on high.
2017_09_16	O Yun Hyok (21) after failing his attempt to achieve six somersaults.
2018_03_18	Yann Arnaud (38) after a fall in a double straps act at Cirque de Soleil.

While writing this, news came of a recent accident very reminiscent of the Victorian era where the falling gymnast often missed the safety net, which seems astonishing in this day and age. On 5 January 2020, Yulia Tikaeva (20) fell 40ft during a trapeze act at Gomel, Belarus but, clipping the edge of the safety net, crashed on to the hard ground below. Carried away by stretcher, she was in intensive care with "serious head injuries", but survived. As this accident was loaded on to You Tube, it was covered by newspapers throughout the world.

We do not permit wild animals in circuses any more in the UK because people who know nothing about the subject have shouted very loudly to a parliament that knows even less. However, there are still opportunities to see these splendid animals at their best on You Tube as other countries are less bigoted. Probably the finest modern lion trainer in the world is Martin Lacey Jr an Englishman who has been showing lions since he was 17 and is now the head of the German Circus Krone. Have a look at him on You Tube performing at the Monte Carlo Circus Festival in 2019. A man who was not kind to animals would not survive long surrounded by 20 of the beasts if they were yearning to get their own back!

To close this book of past accidents, here is a piece of news from the present century about a modern Lion Queen: In April 2003, a woman lion trainer (45) ran away from a circus in Germany with eight lions, two tigers – and the director's 20-year-old son!

SELECT BIBLIOGRAPHY

Performing the American Frontier, 1870-1906. Roger A Hall. Cambridge University Press 2006.
Man-Monkeys: From Regency Pantomime to King Kong Alan Stockwell. Vesper Hawk 2017
What's the Play and Where's the Stage? Alan Stockwell. Vesper Hawk 2015
British Theatrical Patents 1801-1900 Terence Rees & David Wilmore STR
The Hanlon Brothers: From Daredevil Acrobatics to Spectacle Pantomime, 1833-1931
Mark Cosdon. Southern Illinois University Press 2009
The Clown King: Popular Entertainment 1840-1860 Gareth H H Davies. CreateSpace 2015
Theatrical & Circus Life or The Secrets of the Stage John J Jennings. Sun Publishing 1882
Blondin: His Life and Performances George Linnæus Banks. Routledge, Warne, and Routledge 1862
Les Jeux du Cirque et la Vie Forains – Hughes le Roux. Paris 1889
The Great Farini: The High-Wire Life of William Hunt Shane Peacock Penguin 1996

SELECT INTERNET

British Newspaper Archive
Archive.org
Hathi Trust
Gallica.bnf.fr
Circopedia.org
Overthefootlights.co.uk
arthurlloyd.co.uk

theafricanblondin.com
oldtimestrongman.com
themarvellouscraggs.co.uk
africansinyorkshireproject.com
A Chronological Timeline of the Hanlon Brothers 1833 -1931 Mark Cosdon

YOU TUBE CLIPS

Julian Troupe (family acrobats)	www.youtube.com/watch?v=TLwY5HClc98
Jack Higgins (champion jumper)	www.youtube.com/watch?v=IVV_C2YuM-8
Caicedo (wire walker)	www.youtube.com/watch?v=XScNiMlKXlI
Felicien Trewey (hats)	www.youtube.com/watch?v=EcKDB4rTaa0
Felicien Trewey (plate spinning)	www.youtube.com/watch?v=hdv69qGmElQ
Little Titch (big boot dance)	www.youtube.com/watch?v=MFB4oHajwGw
Ally Ford (big boot dance)	www.youtube.com/watch?v=bUVsUMwahMw
Loie Fuller (skirt dance)	www.youtube.com/watch?v=Dda-BXNvVkQ
Martin Lacey Jr (top lion trainer)	www.youtube.com/watch?v=XwCR_SykvU4

ILLUSTRATIONS:

Perils of the Victorian Stage

The intention of this book was to focus on the many dangers that could be faced by actors and artistes while appearing before the public. However, there is more to a theatre than the visual stage and performers were not the only personnel at risk.

In Victorian times a large behind-the-scenes crew could easily number 100 people. Key workers were the men responsible for hauling the ropes to whisk backcloths up and down whose place of work was the narrow fly gallery high above stage level, and in the very act of changing scenery an astonishing number of men were injured and killed – falling from a great height being prevalent.

The dangerous nature of the "stage house" and the hazards lurking therein to ensnare the stagecrew were manifold. Below the stage was a deep cellar housing the mechanisms for the various trapdoors that were widely used in Victorian times. Trapdoors which punctured the stage were not always meticulously locked. Without health and safety regulations, the backstage of a theatre could be a death trap. (Ho! Ho! Ho!) Limelight which depended on mixing two gases led to a spate of explosions.

The main component of a theatre is the auditorium and many buildings used for professional entertainment in Victorian times were of some antiquity, often converted from non-theatrical premises. Some were entirely of wood, others were jerry-built. Even solidly built brick and stone walls housed flimsy interiors which were unable to bear the weights imposed by hundreds of tramping feet – stairs and balconies were particularly vulnerable to collapse. Until very late in the 19th century there were no official regulations imposed by law, and all theatres were hazardous by modern day standards. The Bowery Theatre in New York was burned down and rebuilt four times within ten years. It was estimated that the average life of a theatre in the 19th century was a mere 23 years!

Fortunately most theatre fires happened when the premises were empty but some did occur while the audience was enjoying the show. Fatal frenzies could arise much too often – sometimes from a single cry of "Fire!" when there was no such thing – resulting in tragic events with mass fatalities. There were many ways that an individual could suffer an accident while attending a show; an incredible number of people fell over the front of the gallery into the stalls below.

A companion volume to this present book is now available. In similar format, the new book, encompasses a miscellany of accidents BACKSTAGE and in the AUDITORIUM.

A companion volume
Jeopardy within the Victorian Theatre
ON SALE NOW

OTHER BOOKS OF THEATRICAL INTEREST BY ALAN AND BRENDA STOCKWELL:

What's the Play and Where's the Stage?

The lives of eminent London actors of the Regency period are more than amply recorded. This book ploughs a more unusual, rarer, furrow. It reveals the theatrical lives of a family of provincial players who tramped the highways and byways bringing the latest London hits and classic plays to unsophisticated audiences in tiny country theatres and large manufacturing towns. The author offers not a specialist tome for theatre historians - although they will find previously unknown material and new revelations here - but a beguiling story of a family of three thespian siblings, their spouses and their children. This is a Regency world far removed from the novels of Jane Austen. There are highs and lows, riches and poverty, twists and turns, and extraordinary events as in the script of any modern television saga. The marked difference being that - for the Jonas and Penley Company of Comedians - this was real life.

ISBN 978-0-9565013-6-3 *Hardback* 420 pages rrp £16.95

MAN-MONKEYS: From Regency Pantomime to King Kong

This is the first and only book about the man-monkey phenomenon and its major stars. From the first stage play to feature a chimpanzee as a character back in 1801 to the present-day popular film franchises of *'King Kong'* and *'The Planet of the Apes'*, many actors have played apes and gorillas – some rising to stardom earning top money, others coming to a sadder and more tragic end. Men-in-fur like the ill-fated Parsloe who fell from fame in London to suffer an early and lonely death in America, the irascible almost legless trouble-maker Hervio Nano, Teasdale who found God in prison after stabbing his wife, and the simpleton East End potboy who was transformed into Monsieur Gouffe attracting the *bon ton* of London and making a fortune. Within these pages you will find some of the oddest, most unfortunate, ill-requited, and doomed performers who ever chose to tread the boards – the artistes known as 'man-monkeys'.

ISBN 978-0-9565013-7-0 *Paperback* 234 pages rrp £8.99

VESPER HAWK

amazon

For further information visit www.vesperhawk.com

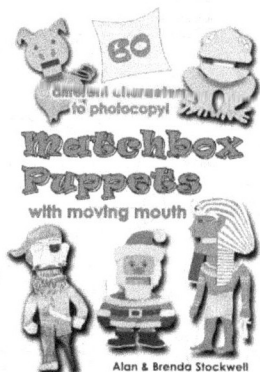

MATCHBOX PUPPETS

This delightful collection of easy-to-make puppets will be a boon to all parents, teachers and entertainers of children. The puppets are based on an ordinary household-size matchbox which enables them to have opening mouths. The pages are designed to photocopy on to A4 card, cut out and colour as fancy takes. With a choice of some sixty different characters there is something for all ages and abilities in these simple but clever constructions. The collection varies widely from a simple flower to the Minotaur, a whale to Henry VIII, octopus to Roman emperor, and a selection of characters which can be topical at different periods of the year - turnip lantern, Easter bunny, scarecrow, Father Christmas etc. The puppets have been designed by Alan and Brenda Stockwell who for over forty years toured primary schools throughout the UK and abroad with their educational puppet show conducting many puppet-making workshops for teachers. Now retired, they are placing their expertise in the hands of future generations. In 2000 Alan Stockwell was awarded an MBE for services to education, a rare honour for a professional puppeteer.

ISBN 978-0-9565013-3-2 A4 *paperback* 126 pages   rrp £9.95

MR DICKENS AND MASTER BETTY

Charles Dickens, the nascent novelist, is employed to write the life story of the former infant prodigy Master Betty known as Young Roscius. Dickens, a self-proclaimed "delver into the human soul", clashes with his employer's overweening arrogance and revenges himself by unearthing the hidden truths lurking in the older man's psyche. The story tells of two teenage boys, both with feckless spendthrift fathers. One scrapes a miserable existence in a boot-blacking factory for six shillings a week; the other earns fifty guineas a night idolised by the highest in the land. *"The sad decline - heart-breaking at times - of the infant prodigy compared with the upstart young genius. It makes an enthralling read. I couldn't put it down - it is a history of the time."* (Sir Donald Sinden - eminent actor and historian). This unusually-written short novel reeks of the atmosphere of the early 19th century; through its pages weave many historical personages in this true story imaginatively told.   *"Very fresh and vivid and illuminating of the young Charles Dickens."* (Simon Callow - noted actor and writer)

ISBN 978-0-9565013-2-5 *paperback*   190 pages   rrp £8.95

VESPER HAWK   **For further information visit www.vesperhawk.com**   amazon

www.ingramcontent.com/pod-product-compliance
Lightning Source LLC
Chambersburg PA
CBHW062059090426
42741CB00015B/3279